The Odd Couple
on Stage and Screen

ALSO BY BOB LESZCZAK

*Single Season Sitcoms, 1948–1979:
A Complete Guide* (McFarland, 2012)

The Odd Couple on Stage and Screen

A History with Cast and Crew Profiles and an Episode Guide

BOB LESZCZAK

Foreword by Mark Rothman

McFarland & Company, Inc., Publishers
Jefferson, North Carolina

LIBRARY OF CONGRESS CATALOGUING-IN-PUBLICATION DATA

Leszczak, Bob, 1959–
    The odd couple on stage and screen : a history with cast and crew profiles and an episode guide / Bob Leszczak ; foreword by Mark Rothman.
    p.   cm.
    Includes index.

    ISBN 978-0-7864-7790-6 (softcover : acid free paper) ∞
    ISBN 978-1-4766-1539-4 (ebook)

    1. Odd couple (Television program)   2. Simon, Neil. Odd couple—Stage history. I. Title.
PN1992.77.O333L47 214
791.45'72—dc23   2014027547

BRITISH LIBRARY CATALOGUING DATA ARE AVAILABLE

© 2014 Bob Leszczak. All rights reserved

No part of this book may be reproduced or transmitted in any form or by any means, electronic or mechanical, including photocopying or recording, or by any information storage and retrieval system, without permission in writing from the publisher.

On the cover: Tony Randall (as Felix Unger) and Jack Klugman (as Oscar Madison) in the *The Odd Couple*, 1970–1975 (ABC/Photofest)

Printed in the United States of America

McFarland & Company, Inc., Publishers
  Box 611, Jefferson, North Carolina 28640
    www.mcfarlandpub.com

This book is dedicated to the memory
of Jack Klugman, Tony Randall,
Jack Lemmon, and Walter Matthau—
with sincere thanks for all of the laughs, the smiles,
the fun, the memories, the honking, and the inspiration.

Acknowledgments

One needs to be more of a Felix than an Oscar to assemble a work such as this. The fine folks who helped to make this "Unger-taking" a true joy include (in alphabetical order) Nick Abdo, Bruce Bilson, John Byner, Jack Carter, Lou Cutell, Elinor Donahue, Peggy Elliott, John Femia, Ron Friedman, Lowell Ganz, Archie Hahn, Monty Hall, Ron Harper, Christopher Joy, Bo Kaprall, Carl Kleinschmitt, Buz Kohan, Michael Leeson, Chris Lemmon, Marlyn Mason, Charlie Matthau, Rick Mittleman, Jaye P. Morgan, John Rappaport, Mark Rothman, Jay Sandrich, Ed Scharlach, John Schuck, Charles Shyer, Joan Van Ark, Sherry Alberoni Van Meter, Dick Van Patten, Joyce Van Patten, William Woodson, and Joel Zwick. Thank you all for your time, your effort, your quotes, your knowledge, your photographs, and your friendship.

Amidst the unbridled giddy glee I experienced viewing these 114 classic episodes yet again, and again, and again, there were a few moments of pure melancholy as I reflected upon all of the talented cast and crew members who are no longer with us. They may be gone, but are certainly not forgotten.

Sincere thanks, also, to a few very helpful friends, Bill Feingold, Jack Kratoville, Richard Sackley and Joel Tator. I also can't forget my "go-to guys," Mark Rothman, David Schwartz, and Vincent Terrace. These three are my "Odd Squad," my guidance counselors, and my mentors—the "wind beneath my wings," if you will, who are always willing to help in any way they can. Having good friends such as these leaves me "Happy, and Peppy, and Bursting with Love."

Table of Contents

Acknowledgments vi

Foreword by Mark Rothman 1

Preface 3

ONE—The History of *The Odd Couple* 5

TWO—The Cast and Guest Stars 21

THREE—The Crew 133

FOUR—The Episode Guides 185

FIVE—*The Odd Couple* Extras, Flubs and Factoids 221

Epilogue 247

Index 249

Foreword
by Mark Rothman

Bob Leszczak is a fountain of information about TV sitcoms. I thought I was a fountain of information about TV sitcoms. Compared to him, I am but a mere dribble. When I worked on *The Odd Couple* and *Happy Days,* I often encountered Jerry Paris, who directed many episodes of both shows. Being much more of a fountain then than I am now, I would remind Jerry of things that happened on *The Dick Van Dyke Show*, incidents which he had completely forgotten. He was astounded—astounded that he had forgotten them, and astounded that anyone else would remember them. There is roughly the same ratio going on between Bob Leszczak and me. As my memory of *The Odd Couple* has somewhat diminished, the fountain that is Bob Leszczak has rekindled it, much to my astonishment. This book is designed for the *Odd Couple* devotee. It is everything *Odd Couple*. The play, the movie, the original TV series, *The New Odd Couple,* the female version of the play, the movie sequel, the later TV movie, the play revival.... Whatever you loyalists want, Bob is here to provide it. *The Odd Couple* was, and is, a classic, and I am very proud of my involvement with it. Bob Leszczak is a very thorough person, and he has tackled a subject that requires total thoroughness. You could not be in better hands.

Mark Rothman, born in the Bronx, is best known for having been involved in the creation and production of Laverne and Shirley. *He was also the head writer for numerous other Paramount Studio sitcoms including* Happy Days, *and the program on which he got his start,* The Odd Couple.

Preface

On November 13th, Felix Unger was asked to remove himself from his place of residence. (Unger's unseen wife slams the door, only to reopen it to sternly hand Felix his saucepan; only her outstretched arm is visible.) *That request came from his wife. Deep down, he knew she was right, but he also knew that someday, he would return to her. With nowhere else to go, he appeared at the home of his (childhood) friend, Oscar Madison. Several years (sometime) earlier, Madison's wife had thrown him out, requesting that he never return. Can two divorced men share an apartment without driving each other crazy?*

That immortal introduction (written by Tony Randall and Jack Klugman's agent, Abbey Greshler) was uttered by Shakespearean actor/voiceover announcer William Woodson in the opening credits for most episodes of the first three seasons of the TV version of Neil Simon's *The Odd Couple*. The word *childhood* was eliminated from that monologue beginning with the "Natural Childbirth" episode, which kicked off season two.

Simultaneously *sometime* was replaced with the more specific timeframe "several years" earlier. As Woodson, now a nonagenarian, recalled, "It's a wonderful monologue and whoever wrote it, I owe them a lot. I'm grateful to that person because it got me a lot of work elsewhere, just because of that one reading. It's a world beater, and I owe a great deal of gratitude." That monologue also set up the premise of all five seasons of the sitcom, and the hope (and eventual fulfillment) of the line "one day he would return to her" (that does indeed occur in the final episode, "Felix Remarries").

This book will take the reader through all 114 *Odd Couple* TV episodes with new eyes ("You're my eyes, Gloria"). The guest cast for each episode, as well as information about the directors, writers, producers and executive producers is included. A basic outline of the subject matter of each episode will, of course, be provided as well. When appropriate, comparisons will be made to the feature films which starred Walter Matthau and Jack Lemmon (with fond memories from Lemmon's actor son, Chris Lemmon, and Matthau's actor/director son, Charlie Matthau; actor Ron Harper, who portrayed Jack, and actor Lou Cutell, who played Abe in *The Odd Couple II* in 1998). The original Broadway production will also be addressed, and two related series will also be touched upon. There's *The New Odd Couple* with Ron Glass and Demond Wilson in the title roles, and supplying insight are director Joel Zwick, actors John Schuck and Christopher Joy, and Supervising Producer Mark Rothman. Even the animated version called *The Oddball Couple*, with voices provided by Paul Winchell and Frank Nelson, will be explored, as will the 1993 TV movie, *The Odd Couple: Together Again* (with the help of Dick Van Patten), which reunited Jack Klugman, Tony Randall, Penny Marshall and Garry Walberg. There were also many shows created with the same, or at least very similar *Odd Couple* premise, and those will not be overlooked.

This book is chock-full of fresh, new information. However, in a few instances (particularly with long-deceased members of the cast and crew), fresh factoids were few and far between. What will set this book apart from a mere "episode guide" are the interviews with remaining cast and crew, guest stars, writers, producers, and directors, to inform the reader about the goings-on each week on Paramount Stage 20 (on Melrose and Gower) during filmings, rehearsals, table readings, and rewrites. This work will even take you into the dressing rooms, behind-the-scenes for each legendary and memorable episode. Quotes, reflections and photographs have been provided by series regular Elinor Donahue (who portrayed "upstairs" Miriam Welby in 17 episodes), associate producer Nick Abdo, directors Bruce Bilson, Jay Sandrich, and Charles Shyer, writers Peggy Elliott, Ron Friedman, Lowell Ganz, Carl Kleinschmitt, Buz Kohan, Michael Leeson, John Rappaport, Mark Rothman, Ed Scharlach, and guest stars John Byner, Jack Carter, Archie Hahn, Monty Hall, Bo Kaprall, Marlyn Mason, Jaye P. Morgan, Joan Van Ark, Dick Van Patten and Joyce Van Patten. Some interesting "extras" at the end will supply the reader/aficionado with some fascinating *Odd Couple* factoids, and *Odd Couple* inconsistencies. Awards won by all incarnations of *The Odd Couple* will be noted, and words and phrases important to the true *Odd Couple* devotee will be listed in a special glossary. All of this (and some surprises) make for an "Oscar Oscar Oscar–worthy tribute" to *The Odd Couple* for a much better "Ungerstanding."

ONE
The History of *The Odd Couple*

The term *bromance*—a combination or portmanteau of the words *brother* and *romance*—came into use in the 21st century. Whereas very close, non-sexual male friendships are certainly not new, the moniker is. Actors such as Matt Damon and Ben Affleck, George Clooney and Brad Pitt, as well as the characters in the hit series *Entourage*, have come to epitomize and legitimize the new word in our vocabulary. Unquestionably, Felix Ungar and Oscar Madison were among the earliest and most popular of the bromances.

The entire premise of *The Odd Couple* was based upon actual events in the life of Neil Simon's older brother, Danny Simon (December 18, 1918–July 27, 2005). Like his younger sibling, Danny Simon was also a comedy writer. The Simon brothers worked together on Sid Caesar's TV programs, *Your Show of Shows* and *Caesar's Hour*. They also wrote for the early episodes of *The Jackie Gleason Show* and *The Red Buttons Show*. About the time they were both working on Buddy Hackett's live sitcom called *Stanley*, their lives suddenly took different directions. Neil opted to move on to writing for the theater, but Danny remained a TV writer, and penned scripts for countless sitcoms, such as *The Ann Sothern Show*, *Bachelor Father*, *The Danny Thomas Show*, *My Three Sons*, *The Joey Bishop Show*, *Petticoat Junction*, and *McHale's Navy*. While this was going on, Danny Simon's marriage to his wife of nine years, Arlene, was falling apart; they divorced in 1961. They had two children together, Michael and Valerie (and neither Danny nor Arlene ever remarried). At this juncture, Danny Simon, a very meticulous and tidy man, moved in with theatrical agent Roy Gerber, a slovenly divorced buddy, and, in short order, the two polar opposites drove each other crazy. *The Odd Couple* seed had been planted. Neil suggested to his brother that his current living conditions would make great fodder for a wonderful play. Danny loved the idea, but never really got the project off the ground. He had a severe case of "writer's block." When it became clear that Danny wasn't going to pursue this premise, Neil took over, wrote *The Odd Couple*, and the rest, as they say, is history. Many of the play's logistics, especially those concerning the "poker players," were worked out by Neil on a day at the beach (in real life, Neil loved playing poker for the camaraderie of it, but he wasn't particularly good at it). Paramount loved the original idea—the original concept—and because of Neil's prior proven success with *Come Blow Your Horn* and *Barefoot in the Park*, he was able to sell the motion picture rights before even one word of the original play had been written. Of course, Neil greatly exaggerated the idiosyncratic nature of both Felix (Danny) and Oscar (Roy) for the sake of the play (Danny Simon and Roy Gerber were never quite *that* eccentric). The play was produced by Arnold Saint-Subber, a theatrical producer who had won a Tony Award a couple of decades earlier for *Kiss Me, Kate*. Saint-Subber produced seven of Neil Simon's plays—*Barefoot in the Park, The Star-Spangled Girl, Last of the Red Hot Lovers, Plaza Suite, The Prisoner of Second Avenue, The Gingerbread Lady*, and *The Odd Couple*.

The play debuted on Broadway in the Plymouth Theater (later renamed the Gerald Schoenfeld Theater) at 236 West 45th Street in Manhattan, on March 10, 1965. Schoenfeld was chairman of the Shubert Organization (a theatrical producing organization and multiple theater owner started by the famous Shubert Brothers, Sam, Jacob and Lee).

To set the proper March 10, 1965, mood: Lyndon Baines Johnson was president; *Bonanza* was the top-rated TV program; gasoline was 31 cents a gallon; a loaf of bread was about a quarter; it cost five cents to mail a letter; about $2,300 would buy you a brand new car; and the Temptations had the number-one song in the U.S. with "My Girl," on Motown's Gordy Record label.

Now to set the scene—Oscar Madison is a divorced, untidy, disheveled sportswriter whose entire rumpled existence is in dire need of a good steam ironing. He is always in debt because of his gambling addiction and devil-may-care attitude. He enjoys poker and betting on horse races, cheap beer and greasy foods, loose women and manly sports. His cigar butt–laden pigpen of a bachelor pad on Riverside Drive, and his haphazard, disorderly lifestyle are turned topsy-turvy by the arrival of Felix Ungar, a recently separated old friend with nowhere else to go.

Unlike Oscar, Felix is an anal-retentive, overly tidy, sinus honking hypochondriacal buttinski who loathes dirt and disorder, and loves cleanliness, the use of coasters and the proper window treatment. Oscar and Felix couldn't coexist with their wives, and they certainly can't successfully cohabitate (and yet, in some weird, demented, inexplicable way, down deep they need, depend upon, and like one another). Despite their oil-and-water relationship, Felix is the yin to Oscar's yang.

Walter Matthau portrayed Oscar

Madison, and Art Carney was Felix Ungar in the original Broadway production. Carney had a considerable amount of experience playing off of Jackie Gleason's Ralph Kramden—a larger-than-life dreamer/schemer who bore some resemblance to Oscar Madison. Carney's Ed Norton and Kramden had a somewhat tumultuous friendship and more than their share of *Odd Couple* moments. For Carney, all of the conflict in Simon's play was familiar territory.

Directed by Mike Nichols, the play had "test runs" in big cities such as Boston, Wilmington, and Chicago before making its way to the Great White Way. There were problems with the third act, and a reviewer from Boston named Elliot Norton actually assisted in its revision (there were, in fact, numerous revisions before this revision). The first "preview" at the Plymouth Theater in Manhattan was March 8 (and there were two previews). Once the show officially opened in New York two days later, it caught fire. Tickets sold like hotcakes. Ticket scalpers were having a field day. Reviews, for the most part, were raves.

Matthau and Carney were a big hit (but Matthau received the lion's share of the favorable reviews). Broadway was abuzz with *The Odd Couple* and all things Neil Simon. By the end of 1966, Simon had four successful shows playing concurrently—*The Odd Couple, Barefoot in the Park, Sweet Charity,* and *Star-Spangled Girl.* A few months after it debuted, Art Carney took ill and was replaced by Eddie Bracken. A while later, Walter Matthau had to leave to fulfill a contractual obligation for a motion picture with Jack Lemmon for MGM titled *The Fortune Cookie.* Matthau suffered a heart attack at about the same time and was unable to return to the Broadway production when the film was completed. Filling the void, Jack Klugman assumed the role of Oscar Madison. Klugman knew immediately as he read the script for the first time that he would do the play—he thought it was the funniest thing he ever read (he even fell off the sofa from laughing so hard). Klugman received good reviews during his stay, but he eventually left the role for monetary reasons. He was earning $1,500 a week, but prior to that, Matthau was getting $5,800 a week. Klugman asked for, but couldn't get, $500 more a week, even though there was a savings of over $4,000 a week since Matthau left. Years later, Neil Simon came to rue the decision of not giving Klugman the raise he requested. Eddie Bracken remained as Felix for most of the rest of the run, but there were two other Oscars—first Pat Hingle, and then Mike Kellin. John Fiedler portrayed Vinnie in the play and the motion picture (he also guest starred in two episodes of the TV series as other characters); Nat Frey was Murray the cop; and Sidney Armus was Roy. The Pigeon Sisters were played by Carole Shelley and Monica Evans in the play, the movie, and in the first season of the original TV series. When auditioning actresses to portray the sisters, Neil Simon struck out in New York. He opted to then go to Great Britain to have actresses there read for the parts—and fi-

Jack Klugman (left) and Eddie Bracken (right) on an original Broadway program.

nally found his "Pigeons." The play moved to the Eugene O'Neill Theater (230 West 49th Street in Manhattan) on August 1, 1966, and continued until the show closed on July 2, 1967, after 964 performances and two previews. Neil Simon turned a tidy profit (on his original investment of just under $200,000). He shared some of the earnings with his brother, Danny, who had inspired the story.

After the original Broadway produc-

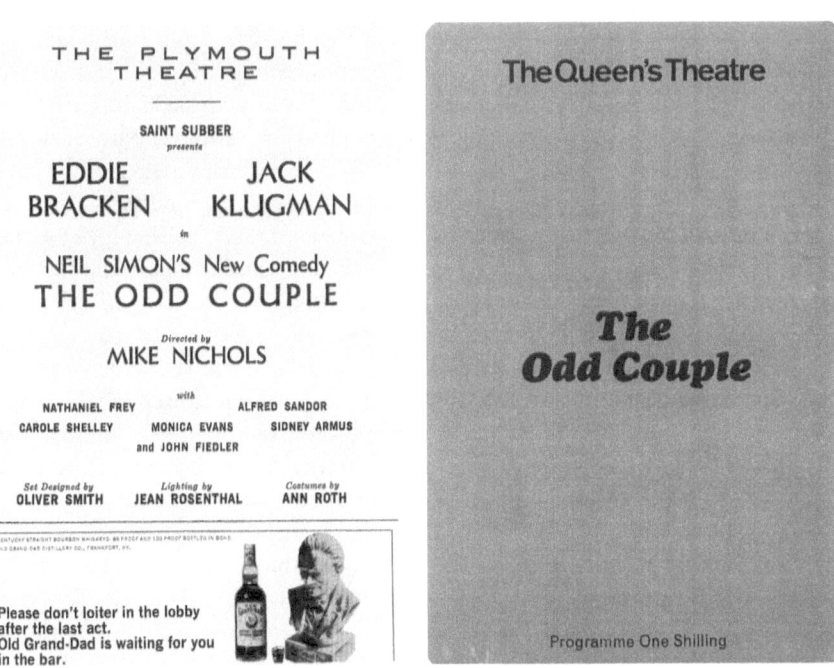

Left: The full 1966 Broadway cast list. *Right:* The cover of the program for the 1966 UK production of *The Odd Couple* at the Queens Theatre.

tion closed, many big names took on the roles of Oscar and Felix in road-show companies, among them Mickey Rooney and Tony Randall in Las Vegas. Jack Klugman portrayed Oscar again on the British stage and won a "Best Foreign Actor" award. His Felix in that version was Victor Spinetti.

The play has one set—Oscar's apartment—but, in 1968, when *The Odd Couple* became a Paramount motion picture, all of that changed. The film opens with Felix (Jack Lemmon) checking into a cheap hotel and requesting a room on an upper floor. He fully intends to jump out of the hotel room's window, but he can't get it open. This was not in the play, and neither was the scene in the coffee shop where we are introduced to Felix's histrionic honking. Neil Simon wrote the screenplay himself, and the scene with the burned meatloaf was based upon an actual event from his brother's life. Simon hoped to meet, or even surpass, the success of the 1967 motion picture version of his play *Barefoot in the Park* (which starred Robert Redford and Jane Fonda). *Barefoot in the Park* was directed by Gene Saks, and when it met with wild acclaim, Saks was brought in again to direct the big-screen version of *The Odd Couple* (Billy Wilder was the first choice, but the budget wouldn't allow it). The name of Hank Moonjean, the assistant director on the motion picture, can be heard being announced in the background as a newly traded baseball pro during a TV sports broadcast in Oscar's living room—a very inside joke. Paramount initially wanted Frank Sinatra as Felix and Jackie Gleason as Oscar, but that notion was quickly nixed. Matthau was back as Oscar Madison, paired this time with Jack Lemmon (they had previously been seen together in Billy Wilder's 1966 comedy, *The Fortune Cookie*). Matthau is alleged to have been paid $300,000 for his role, while Lemmon earned close to a million. About a week before the filming began, Matthau broke his left arm in a bicycle mishap and was in a cast. To accommodate him, the second act of the movie was filmed before the first act because Walter, as Oscar, had to use his arms less in the second act. Herb Edelman was Murray the Cop (a subdued portrayal), John Fiedler was Vinnie, David Sheiner was Roy, and Larry Haines was Speed. Up until the last minute, there was conjecture as to which of the two actors (David Sheiner and Larry Haines) would be Roy and which would be Speed. Because Oscar was a sportswriter, many name baseball players made brief cameo appearances in the film, such as Cleon Jones, Ed Kranepool, Maury Wills, and, at bat, second baseman Bill Mazeroski, who hits into a rare triple play. Mazeroski replaced Roberto Clemente, who, after numerous takes, grew weary and ran slower and slower (although some sources say Clemente just didn't wish to participate in the film, and Mazeroski was the second choice). Reviews for the movie were mostly favorable, and it became a whopping success and remained in theaters for a long, long time. It set records at Radio City Music Hall. This classic original film version is still available on DVD from Paramount Home Video, and there is also a newer Centennial Collection DVD with a lot of extras, interviews and commentary. On June 4, 2013, it was re-released on a Blue Ray/DVD set.

The Neal Hefti theme song and transitional music used in the motion picture also made the successful transition to the small screen. This theme song had lyrics (by Sammy Cahn), but they were never used. In fact, in a very memorable opening scene for the *Friends* episode titled "The One with the Dozen Lasagnas" (1995), the six regular cast members (Rachel, Monica, Phoebe, Joey, Chandler and Ross) hum *The Odd Couple* theme song in their usual hangout—The Central Perk. In the third episode of *Futurama*, titled "I, Roommate" (1999) Fry and Bender turn their apartment into a pig sty while *The Odd Couple* theme song plays in the background. A modernized/updated rendition of the song was also used in the 1982 remake sitcom, *The New Odd Couple*, but not in the 1975 animated DePatie/Freleng version titled *The Oddball Couple* (which featured a fussy cat as the Felix character and a sloppy dog as the Oscar character). An episode of *Batman* with Adam West which aired on December 21, 1967, was titled "The Ogg Couple," and featured Egghead and Olga (Vincent Price and Anne Baxter, respectively) stealing the Egg of Ogg from the Gotham City Museum.

In 1970, writer/producer Garry Marshall and TV comedy writer Jerry Belson had the idea of bringing *The Odd Couple* to the small screen as a situation comedy. ABC wanted Felix's ex-wife's name changed from Frances to Gloria, because it is the same pronunciation as Francis, a man's name, and they wanted to avoid any implication that the two main characters were gay. Many different performers were up for the roles of Felix and Oscar (Dean Martin as Felix, Jack Kruschen, Martin Balsam, Jack Carter and Mickey Rooney as Oscar, among others), but Garry Marshall knew exactly who he wanted. Both Tony Randall and Jack Klugman were reluctant at first, but eventually acquiesced. Klugman was actually asked by Garry Marshall's sister, Penny, to play the role while she and Klugman were guest starring in the same episode of *Then Came Bronson*, called "The Runner," in 1969. Klugman was not keen on the idea of another series, after his unsuccessful *Harris Against the World* in 1964. Randall really wanted Mickey Rooney to portray Oscar Madison (Randall and Rooney had performed the play together in Las Vegas), but didn't get his wish. Randall and Klugman had worked together in a live episode of *Appointment with Adventure* in 1955, but had not crossed paths since. Some tension between the two actors arose early in their *Odd Couple* experience when they were side-by-side in the same limo, even before they had filmed their first episode. Randall, an avid anti-smoker, was offended by Klugman's pungent cigars. Garry Marshall quickly remedied the situation by making sure, from that day on, that each of the stars had his own limo—one smoking, one non-smoking. From there it was pretty smooth sailing. At this juncture, Felix Ungar was changed to Felix Unger. It's interesting to note that Felix Ungar was also the name of a character in Neil Simon's *Come Blow Your Horn*. In that play, Ungar was an off-stage acting coach, and was never seen by the audience. Maybe Simon thought no one would notice if he used it again. We noticed.

The program's first few episodes were called *Neil Simon's The Odd Couple*, and the entire first season was filmed single-camera style (like a movie) with a laugh track. Oscar Madison's apartment greatly resembled the set from the 1968 motion picture (with the long hallway and the gates separating the living room from the bedrooms). *The Odd Couple* debuted on ABC on Thursday night, September 24, 1970, at 9:30. A lot of the rumpled clothes Klugman wore on the show were his own, brought from home. *The Odd Couple* immediately followed another Neil Simon Broadway play and movie-turned-sitcom, *Barefoot in the Park*, with an African American cast (Scoey Mitchell [sometimes spelled Mitchlll], Tracy Reed, and Nipsey Russell). *Barefoot in the Park* did not translate well to the television screen, and some internal issues (between Scoey Mitchell and executive vice president in charge of programming, Douglas S. Cramer) led to its being canceled after 13 weeks. *The Odd Couple*, on the other hand, was lauded by critics, but was not a Nielsen Family favorite. Even a move to Friday nights early in 1971 didn't help much. Along with the move to Fridays came the famous opening narration, by William Woodson, that begins: "On November 13, Felix Unger was asked to remove himself from his place of residence." That opening was used until the beginning of season four. I tried, in vain, to find out who hands Felix his saucepan from the other side of the door in that classic opening piece. I even sought the assistance of Garry Marshall's Henderson Productions. The wonderful Kimberly and the staff made a concerted effort to find out that particular piece of minutiae for me, for which I thank them dearly, but the body and person to whom that arm was attached remains a mystery. Incidentally, Jack Klugman was not a fan of that opening narration. Some say the spoken intro was included to make certain that the show's premise was thoroughly explained, but, more importantly, it was included to aver that Felix and Oscar were not a gay couple, but, rather, two divorced men attempting to make sense of their lives *sans* wives (however, in the 1993 TV reunion movie, Felix and Oscar dance together at Felix's daughter's wedding—something that would never have been allowed on the original series). Woodson's memorably dulcet tones were a step in the right direction, but the program hadn't yet hit its stride. Randall and Klugman were accustomed to working onstage with live audiences, and both yearned for *The Odd Couple* to be filmed that way. Randall even did guest spots on a couple of late-night talk shows, urging viewers to write in and ask that the laugh track be eliminated.

In season two, Randall and Klugman got their wish, and beginning with the episode titled "Natural Childbirth," all episodes were filmed in front of a studio audience. Of course, to accommodate the three-camera format and the studio audience, the layout of Oscar's apartment needed to change. As of season two, 1049 Park Avenue, Apartment 1102, looked very different. Gone were the elongated hallway and the gates. The kitchen was moved to the extreme left (stage right), and the windows were now on the opposite side of the living room (stage left). Beginning in season two, we saw much less of the remaining poker players (Roy was gone, and Vinnie and Speed sightings were few and far between). Much like Garry Marshall's hit sitcom *Happy Days*, when it made the transition from single-camera to multi-camera, *The Odd Couple* just seemed to come alive. In seasons two and three 23 episodes were filmed, and 22 episodes each in seasons four and five. Tony and Jack alternated each week saying, "*The Odd Couple* is filmed in front of a live audience." As in the motion picture, Felix often called Oscar "Osc," to which Oscar would invariably call Felix "Feel." All of the pieces seemed to be falling right into place—except for the ratings. The program had a very loyal fan base, and tickets to the live tapings were a very hard "get," but the show was never a hit and was technically canceled each year it was on. What saved it each season was the fact that the program rated higher during the summer months than during the rest of the year—more people were watching when the competition went into summer reruns, and avid TV viewers caught up on what they had missed on ABC. This brief surge each year saved the show from the chopping block. It was also an inexpensive show to produce—that helped, too (the budget and the purse strings were very tight). It was a rare show in that quality really mattered. ABC also loved that the program garnered Emmy nominations every season. However, *The Odd Couple* never finished among the Top 30 TV programs in any of its five seasons (the closest it ever came was number 36 for the year in season three). Its ratings and demographics also tended to skew to a more adult, mature audience than most other sitcoms. Even a barrage of guest stars failed to make the show a ratings winner, but did make for some very memorable and entertaining moments. Those celebrities who portrayed themselves in various episodes include Roone Arledge, Rona Barrett, Dick Cavett, Dick Clark, Richard Dawson, Monty Hall (twice), Hugh Hefner, Bob Hope, Deacon Jones, Billie Jean King, Allen Ludden, Jaye P. Morgan, Bobby Riggs, Rodney Allen Rippy, Neil Simon, Howard K. Smith, David Steinberg, Betty White, Paul Williams and Wolfman Jack. Three theater critics also guest-starred as themselves—John Barbour, Joan Crosby, and Dan Sullivan. Tony Randall wanted to add culture to the program, and after a good deal of begging, whining and arm twisting, got to invite Martina Arroyo, Richard Friedricks, Marilyn Horne and Edward Villella onto the program. Meanwhile, Klugman was allowed to invite a few sports figures of whom he was fond, such as KHJ Radio sportscaster Mal Alberts, ABC's Howard Cosell, and NFL stars Deacon Jones and Bubba Smith.

Inspired by a popular element of *The Dick Van Dyke Show* (on which Garry Marshall was a writer), *The Odd Couple* often featured flashback episodes. Among other themes they showed how Felix and Oscar met while they were both serving on the jury in the Leo Garvey trial; how Oscar's father almost killed Felix's dad; how Felix met Gloria; the birth of Felix's daughter; Felix's escapades during World War II; the time Gloria almost became a nude centerfold in *Playboy*; the vacation trip on which Felix and Gloria split up; Oscar and Blanche's army wedding; and why Oscar and Blanche eventually separated.

Many characters came and went over the program's five-year run. Murray the cop (Al Molinaro), Vinnie (Larry Gelman) and Speed (Garry Wahlberg) stayed (although only Murray was a regular). Vinnie and Speed sightings diminished after the first season and their appearances were erratic, at best. The Pigeon Sisters (Carole Shelley and Monica Evans), however, were gone after only a few episodes in season one (they just didn't click in the series). Roy (Ryan McDonald), one of the poker players, left after the first season. Miriam Welby (Elinor Donahue) entered the picture in season three and stayed until the end, but Dr. Nancy

Cunningham (Joan Hotchkis) only stayed around for eleven episodes, all of which aired in 1971 (some single-camera and some multi-camera). Garry Marshall loved the surname of Cunningham, and used it again in *Happy Days*. Myrna Turner (Penny Marshall) came aboard during season two and remained until the beginning of the fifth and final season. Ex-wives Gloria (Janis Hansen) and Blanche (Brett Somers, Jack Klugman's actual ex-wife) appeared in twelve and five episodes respectively.

Each year, the cast and crew spent a couple of weeks in New York City to film outdoor scenes pertinent to the topics of the shows for the upcoming season. However, on several occasions, outdoor scenes from previous seasons were reused (when needed). These include Oscar swinging a bat and hitting a rock on the streets of New York; Felix and Oscar jogging; the exterior of the court house; and Felix and Oscar seen from behind while walking and carrying on a conversation.

During the run of the show, Tony and Jack recorded an album (1973) for London Records titled *The Odd Couple Sings* (1973). Klugman openly admitted that he couldn't sing and was rather embarrassed about recording the album in front of the 85-piece London Festival Orchestra, led by Roland Shaw. Among the songs on the album: "Applause Applause," "You're So Vain," and even "The Odd Couple Opera," which takes up most of side two.

After 114 episodes, and six different time slots, *The Odd Couple* came to an end (in prime time) on the Fourth of July 1975. Like *The Fugitive*, *The Mary Tyler Moore Show*, *The Bob Newhart Show*, *Newhart*, and *M*A*S*H*, *The Odd Couple* had a final episode that provided the viewer with closure. Originally, ABC was dead set against the idea, thinking it might hurt the show in syndication, but after much badgering from the crew, ABC finally caved (but two different endings were filmed just in case the program was renewed for a sixth season). Jack Klugman won two Emmy Awards for portraying Oscar, and Tony Randall finally won one for portraying Felix after the show ended its run. Randall famously said that he was proud of and thankful for the Emmy, but wished he had a job. Klugman was earning five thousand dollars an episode and Randall was earning seven thousand. The total weekly budget was only about $125,000 per episode. Compare those salaries to those for the cast of *Friends* who, near the end of their run, each earned $1 million per episode, and Ray Romano's $2 million per episode for the final season of *Everybody Loves Raymond*.

After its prime-time run, the program really took off in syndication. The cast and crew knew they had made a good show, and the success it found in the popularity of the reruns finally confirmed this. At this point, especially in the New York market, *The Odd Couple* attained a cult status rivaled only by the unceasing showing of "the original 39 episodes" of *The Honeymooners* on WPIX Channel 11, and the phenomenon that is *Star Trek* (not a hit in prime time, but a blockbuster in syndication). As of this writing, *The Odd Couple* TV series was seen most recently on the Me TV cable channel. All five seasons and all 114 episodes (along with numerous extras, or Easter eggs, as they're called) are available on DVD from Paramount Home Entertainment. The only drawback of this wonderful DVD set (available as single-season sets, or all five-in-one) is that, because of music licensing issues, some parts of songs in some episodes are surgically removed or abruptly faded out early (two of the most blatant examples of this practice are "Strike Up the Band, or Else" and "Two on the Aisle" from season five). Only the season-one episodes contain commentary from Garry Marshall, Jerry Belson, Jack Klugman, and Carole Shelley. It's a shame that this insightful commentary wasn't utilized and continued for all five seasons on DVD. "Odd" aficionados would also like to have seen the "alternate ending" to the "Felix Remarries" episode included on the season-five DVD set, but, sadly, it was not to be.

When the sitcom came to an end in prime time during the summer of 1975, ABC was not yet done with the show's premise, and quickly turned to animation to continue the story. The two main animated characters in the cartoon version were freelance reporters—Fleabag was a slovenly dog (voice provided by Paul Winchell), and Spiffy was a tidy cat (voice provided by Frank Nelson), and even though they have similar jobs, they are vastly different characters. They live together, and they also work in the same office. Goldie Hound (voice provided by Joan Gerber) is their blonde secretary. Now called *The Oddball Couple*, the program ran from September 6, 1975, through September 3, 1977, Saturday mornings on ABC. Some 32 11-minute episodes were produced, and they are not currently available on DVD. These 32 animated episodes did not use the Neal Hefti theme, but rather music from Doug Goodwin, Eric Rogers, George Rock, and Joe Siracusa (the latter two had worked with Spike Jones). Instead of "Oscar, Oscar, Oscar," the pseudo–Felix character on *The Oddball Couple* (Spiffy) often expressed his disapproval and disgust with the phrase, "*Really*, Fleabag."

On Friday, October 29, 1982, *The New Odd Couple* debuted at 8:30 p.m. right after *Benson*. Not only was it "new," it was "different"—utilizing a mostly African American cast. The "new" spin on the old chestnut featured Ron Glass (formerly of *Barney Miller*) as Felix Unger, and Demond Wilson (formerly of *Sanford and Son*) as Oscar Madison. Oscar was still a sportswriter, and Felix was still a photographer. Oscar's ex-wife, Blanche, was never seen (only alluded to), and Felix's ex-wife was called Frances (Simon's original choice) and was portrayed by Telma Hopkins. *The New Odd Couple* also resurrected Roy (who hadn't been seen since season one of the original series), now portrayed by Bart Braverman. The Pigeon Sisters (who hadn't been seen since episode ten in season one of the original series) were now played by Sheila Anderson (Cicely) and Ronalda Douglas (Gwendolyn). John Schuck was Murray, the cop, and Christopher Joy was Speed.

Numerous scripts from the original series were reworked for the new black cast. *The New Odd Couple* was not a hit and was put on hiatus in February of 1983. Three more previously unaired episodes were shown in May and June of that year (a total of 18 were produced). Five episodes of this series were rerun by TV Land early in its history. As of this writing, *The New Odd Couple* is not available on DVD.

In the early 1990s CBS got Tony Randall and Jack Klugman back together for a two-hour reunion movie to be called *The Odd Couple: Together Again*. It was originally to be an NBC project, but the peacock network eventually passed, and CBS then ran with the ball. Also back for the event was Penny Marshall as Myrna, and Garry Walberg as Speed. Dick Van Patten stepped in as Roy, Jerry Adler was Murray, and Barbara Barrie was Gloria Unger. This made-for-TV movie was written and directed by Robert Klane and shot with one camera and no laugh track (it had the look and feel of every episode of season one of the original series and the original motion picture). In fact, the apartment was once again set up with the long hallway and the gates. This reunion movie had two different interwoven plot threads. Felix's daughter, Edna Frances Unger, was getting married. Felix was still married (for the second time) to Gloria, but his constant meddling prevented Gloria from getting her daughter's wedding plans sewn up. Getting the wedding on track could only be accomplished in a Felix-free environment, so he once again arrived at his friend Oscar's apartment, albeit for a shorter duration. The other subplot involved Oscar's voice. In real life, and in this movie, Oscar (Jack Klugman) beat cancer, but at a cost—his voice was little more than a hoarse whisper. Felix coaches him, his voice gets a little bit stronger, and he is then able to make a speech at Edna's wedding. Because of the cancer topic, several members of the original writing crew, and NBC backed out of the project. *The Odd Couple: Together Again* aired on September 24, 1993, on CBS, over 18 years after the final episode of the original series. At this same time, Klugman and Randall performed a series of TV commercials for Eagle Brand Snacks (potato chips and peanuts). Several years earlier, they had recorded commercials together for Nescafe instant coffee and also the Yahtzee Challenge game. After the TV movie, they reunited again, but as Anthony and Jack Swann (not Felix and Oscar) for the short-lived 1999 sitcom called *Brother's Keeper* in episode number 17, titled "An Odd Couple of Days," which aired on February 19, 1999. In the episode, Anthony and Jack are brothers-in-law who own a garage. Anthony is finicky, and Jack is carefree. Anthony's big gripe with Jack is that he continually splits infinitives in his sentences. There's even one scene in which Jack is watching an episode of *The Odd Couple* on the TV in the waiting room, and says, "Those two will never make it." Coincidentally, a regular character on *Brother's Keeper*, portrayed by eight-year-old Justin Cooper, is named Oscar (Justin Cooper works nowadays for the Fox Sports Network). Oscar is the son of the very neat, prim and proper Porter Waide (William Ragsdale), a widower who resides with his carefree, slovenly brother Bobby (Sean O'Bryan). This particular episode of *Brother's Keeper* is akin to an *Odd Couple* within an *Odd Couple*. This episode marks the final time Klugman and Randall appeared together on episodic television.

Coming full circle, Neil Simon wrote *The Odd Couple II*, a 1998 theatrical film directed by Howard Deutch. Lemmon and Matthau were in the leads, 30 years after the original *Odd Couple* motion picture made a "tidy" profit at the box office. Even though the material was not as sharp as in the original, Lemmon and Matthau were just ecstatic to get to work together again. (In all, they starred together in ten feature films.) At this juncture in their lives, Felix and Oscar had each been divorced three times, and Felix was eagerly seeking a fourth wife. Not unlike the 1993 TV reunion movie with Randall and Klugman, *The Odd Couple II* centered upon the upcoming nuptials of Felix's daughter (here known as Hannah, played by Lisa Waltz), but the twist was that her fiancé was Oscar's son, Brucey (played by Jonathan Silverman). Felix still lived in New York City, but Oscar now resided in Sarasota, Florida. They have a joyous reunion at LAX, the airport in Los Angeles, and take up again as if they had never parted. On the way to the ceremony, the two become hopelessly lost (along with Felix's luggage) and almost miss the big event. Along the way, they have major automotive issues and frequent brushes with the law (they even get kidnapped). There are fears they will miss the wedding, but they arrive just in the nick of time.

Even though there were no other movie or TV sequels to the original story, there have been frequent revivals of the original Broadway play throughout the U.S. and abroad. Among the most anticipated of those revivals came in 1996 with Tony Randall and Jack Klugman performing the original play (a three-month run) at the Theatre Royal in London, England, as a fundraiser for Tony's own National Actors Theater, founded in 1991. The actors had to use microphones so that Klugman could be adequately heard by the audience.

There were some similarities between Neil Simon's *The Odd Couple* and *The Sunshine Boys*, and Tony and Jack also performed as that "couple" (Al Lewis and Willie Clark) at the Lyceum Theatre for the National Actors Theatre revival. The play first opened on December 20, 1972, at the Broadhurst Theatre, and starred Sam Levene and Jack Albertson as a pair of vaudeville veterans who reunited for a TV program after a bitter break-up years earlier. Klugman recommended the play to Randall, and their chemistry and fondness for working together was immediately apparent to audiences.

A couple of "updated" versions of the original play were staged with a modicum of success. *The Female Odd Couple*, in 1985, starred Sally Struthers and Rita Moreno as Florence Ungar and Olive Madison, respectively (at the

The cover of the 1985 *Playbill* for *The Female Odd Couple* with Rita Moreno (left) and Sally Struthers (right).

Ahmanson Theatre in Los Angeles and the Broadhurst Theatre in Manhattan). Instead of poker, the game of choice in this version was Trivial Pursuit, and instead of the Pigeon Sisters, Florence and Olive had a date with the Costazuela Brothers (portrayed by Tony Shalhoub and Lewis J. Stadlen). Then came *Oscar and Felix: A New Look at the Odd Couple*, which was staged at Los Angeles's Geffen Theatre in 2002 (with updated dialogue and situations). Updated, in this case, did not necessarily equate with better.

Late in 2010, the musical group Weezer released a song called "The Odd Couple" on their *Death to False Metal* album. In this case, the subject was still a mismatched pair, but the Neal Hefti melody and the Sammy Cahn lyrics were nowhere to be found. The impact of the original Neil Simon play, however, was obvious.

La comedia e finite.

Two
The Cast and Guest Stars

WILLIE AAMES

Guest starred in "Win One for Felix" (as Leonard Unger). Albert William Upton was born July 15, 1960, in Los Angeles. He began acting before he was ten. He found work in episodic TV programs such as *The Courtship of Eddie's Father*, *Gunsmoke*, and *Adam-12*. On *The Odd Couple*, Aames portrayed Felix Unger's son, Leonard. In that episode, Felix takes over as the coach of Leonard's football team and changes all the plays (while Oscar calls plays from a secret location). Aames only appeared as Leonard this one time—future teen heartthrob Leif Garrett assumed the role for the rest of the program's run.

After portraying Fred in the short-lived *Swiss Family Robinson* TV series, Aames lucked out by landing the role of a lifetime as Tommy Bradford on *Eight Is Enough*, and had a five-season run. He would later land the role of Buddy in *Charles in Charge*. Aames experienced some well-publicized problems with substance abuse, and his recovery led him to become a minister in the 1990s. With his new calling, Aames took on the title role in the TV series called *Bibleman*. At last report, Aames, his wife, Maylo, and his daughter, Harleigh, reside in Kansas.

STANLEY ADAMS

Guest starred in "The Hustler" (as Sure Shot Wilson) and "The Big Broadcast" (as Ed). Stanley Adams was born April 7, 1915, in New York City. Never a big name nor a leading man, Adams racked up an impressive list of credits over a 25-year span, including small roles on the big screen in *Breakfast at Tiffany's*, *Lilies of the Field*, *The Gene Krupa Story*, *Critic's Choice*, and *Requiem for a Heavyweight*.

The stocky actor with the gravelly voice also made the rounds on television in *The Twilight Zone*, *Star Trek*, *Father Knows Best*, *The Lucy Show*, *The Dick Van Dyke Show* and *The Odd Couple*. In the latter, he twice portrayed a character who smoked heavily and had a hacking cough—first as an expert pool player named Sure Shot

Wilson in "The Hustler" (originally to be called "Sidepocket Saul," but the censors wanted it changed because it sounded "too Jewish"), and then as radio engineer Ed in "The Big Broadcast." Adams died of a self-inflicted gunshot wound on April 27, 1977. Adams had been in constant pain from a back injury and simply couldn't stand that pain any longer.

Jason Alexander

Portrayed Oscar Madison in Los Angeles' Wadsworth Theatre's (on Wilshire Boulevard) limited run *Odd Couple* production (2008). Jason Alexander was born Jay Scott Greenspan September 23, 1959, in Newark, New Jersey. He suffered from asthma as a child and, later, briefly attended Boston University until he found acting work in New York City. Little-known facts about Jason: he is an accomplished magician, a whiz at poker, and a *Star Trek* aficionado. He is best known for playing the hot-tempered, self-centered, woman-repelling George Costanza on the long-running NBC sitcom, *Seinfeld*. He has the dubious distinction of being the only one of the four main *Seinfeld* stars not to win an Emmy Award. His attempts at starring roles in sitcoms have thus far been ill-fated flops (*Bob Patterson* and *Listen Up*).

Jason won a Tony Award for his role in *Jerome Robbins' Broadway*, and performed in two Neil Simon plays—*Broadway Bound* and *The Odd Couple*. In the latter (a limited run at L.A.'s Wadsworth Theatre in 2008), Alexander played Oscar Madison to Martin Short's Felix Ungar. The two had previously worked together (much like Nathan Lane and Matthew Broderick) in a West Coast production of Mel Brooks's *The Producers*. These plays were part of the "Reprise! Series" for which Alexander is the artistic director. Coincidentally, Jason was also a member of his high school's production of *The Odd Couple* in the middle 1970s.

In 2010, Alexander became the new spokesperson for Jenny Craig weight-loss products. He has been married to Daena Alexander since 1982, and together they have two grown sons.

Tina Andrews

Guest starred in "The Big Broadcast" and "Old Flames Never Die" (as Tina). Tina Yvonne Andrews was born April 23, 1951, in Chicago, Illinois. She attended New York University, where she majored in theater. Her first acting credit was as Doreen on the famous Davy Jones episode of *The Brady Bunch*; this was followed by many more guest-shots on popular shows of the day, such as *Room 222*, *The Mod Squad*, *Marcus Welby, M.D.*, *Sanford and Son*, *Good Times*, and *The Odd Couple*. She was featured in two episodes of the latter ("The Big Broadcast" and "Old Flames Never Die") as Oscar's assistant, Tina (after Penny Marshall left the show).

After many more guest-starring roles throughout the 1970s, Andrews employed her writing talents for a TV-movie titled *Sally Hemings: An American Scandal* and the Warner Bros. motion picture *Why Do Fools Fall in Love?*, a 1998 biopic about doo-wop singer Frankie Lymon of the Teenagers.

Andrews is a multi-tasker—she hosts shows to display her paintings, continues to write and direct new projects, and accepts some two-dozen speaking engagements each year.

ALLAN ARBUS

Guest starred in "Cleanliness Is Next to Impossible" (as Ernie the hypnotist) and "The Hollywood Story" (as Oscar's director). Allan Franklin Arbus was born in New York City February 15, 1918. After attending City College, he and his wife Diane were intrigued by fashion photography. Arbus was a photographer in the Signal Corps, in Burma, during World War II. After being discharged, his interests grew to include acting; his best-known role was as army psychiatrist Major Sidney Freedman in numerous episodes of *M*A*S*H*.

Arbus's TV résumé boasted a rather impressive list of guest appearances on such popular shows as *The Mod Squad*, *Hawaii Five-O*, *The Rockford Files*, *Starsky and Hutch*, and *The Odd Couple*. Arbus portrayed two very different characters on the latter. As the hypnotist, he supplies Oscar with a post-hypnotic Shakespearean phrase which renders him tidy and finicky. As the director, he fires Oscar from a cameo role in a Hollywood movie.

Arbus later worked with Tony Randall again on his eponymously titled show in 1977, in an episode titled "Franklin vs. the Generation Gap."

Arbus's final TV guest shot was on a 2000 episode of Larry David's *Curb Your Enthusiasm*. Arbus died at the age of 95 on April 19, 2013. His love of photography was shared with his daughter, Amy.

ROONE ARLEDGE

Guest starred in "Your Mother Wears Army Boots" (as himself). Roone Arledge was born July 8, 1931, in Queens, New York. This broadcasting trailblazer was president of ABC sports from 1968 to 1986. He was responsible for starting not only *Monday Night Football* but also *20/20*, *Nightline*, and *ABC World News*. He was also president of ABC News for 20 years.

In 1975, he made his one-and-only appearance on *The Odd Couple*, as himself, in the episode titled "Your Mother Wears Army Boots," on which he appeared in the *Monday Night Football* broadcast booth alongside Howard Cosell.

Roone Arledge died of prostate cancer on December 5, 2002.

MARTINA ARROYO

Guest starred in "Your Mother Wears Army Boots" (as herself). Martina Arroyo was born on Groundhog Day, February 2, 1937, in Harlem, New York. Her older brother became a minister. Influenced by her mother's insistence that her children be cultured, Martina became infatuated with the theater. She studied romance languages at Hunter College and, as a hobby, studied opera. Although a natural talent, she needed proper training and quickly broke down many color barriers in opera for African Americans.

Arroyo does not have a long list of TV credits, but she did appear on a few episodes of *The Tonight Show Starring Johnny Carson* and one episode of *The Odd Couple*. Arroyo sings in this episode, and Felix arranges a meeting with her biggest fan, Howard Cosell. The original premise of the episode did not include Arroyo. She was included at the last minute at the urging of Tony Randall, and the script was completely overhauled to accommodate her.

Arroyo was the 2010 recipient of the Opera Honors Award from the National Endowment of the Arts, and was one of the Kennedy Center Honorees of 2013. She retired from singing in 1989, at which time she opted to teach and mentor promising young operatic talent.

John Astin

Guest starred in "Oscar's New Life" (as Buff Buffingham). John Allen Astin was born in Baltimore, Maryland, on March 30, 1930. Astin graduated from Johns Hopkins University, having studied mathematics. However, his heart was in the theater and that's what he pursued. His first big break in the business came with a small role in *West Side Story*, in 1961. The following year, Astin co-starred with Marty Ingels in the memorable physical ABC comedy series called *I'm Dickens, He's Fenster*. Just a couple of years later, he landed the role of Gomez Addams in *The Addams Family*, a TV series based on the popular cartoons in *The New Yorker* by Charles Addams.

It's interesting to note that Tony Randall discovered Astin's comic abilities in the early 1960s, and helped launch his television career. Years later, Astin guest starred in one episode of *The Odd Couple*—"Oscar's New Life"—in which he portrayed Buff Buffingham, the manager of a girly magazine called *Harem*, who hires Oscar for a high-paying job (after Oscar loses his job at the *Herald*).

Astin later co-starred in several other sitcoms: *Operation: Petticoat* (based on the 1959 film), *The Phyllis Diller Show*, *Night Court*, and *Mary* (Mary Tyler Moore's short-lived 1985 sitcom). He also supplied cartoon voices for characters in TV's *Duckman*, *Johnny Bravo*, and *Pinky and the Brain*. At last report, he was teaching method acting at his alma mater, Johns Hopkins University.

Christine Baranski

Co-starred in *The Odd Couple II* (as Thelma). Christine Baranski was born May 2, 1952, in Buffalo, New York. Her grandparents had been actors in Poland, and the acting bug skipped a generation. Christine studied at the famous Juilliard School in New York.

She began as an almost immediate success on Broadway in *The Real Thing*, for which she won a Tony Award in 1984. She won again, many years later, for the *Boeing Boeing* revival. Baranski is best known for her television work, especially her Emmy-winning role as Maryann Thorpe on the CBS sitcom *Cybill*.

After *Cybill* was canceled in 1998, Baranski earned a juicy role as one of the tough "dancing girls" who flirts with Oscar (Walter Matthau) in Neil Simon's *The Odd Couple II*. That innocent dance leads to a standoff with the girls' insanely jealous boyfriends. Baranski's most recent success story is her portrayal of Diane Lockhart on CBS's highly successful drama *The Good Wife*.

Leonard Barr

Guest starred in "Oscar's Ulcer" (as the boxer), "Lovers Don't Make House Calls" (as the panhandler), "To Bowl or Not to Bowl" (as Arnold), "Old Flames Never Die" (as Walter) and "The Hollywood Story" (as Stickman). Leonard Barr was born Leonard Barra on September 27, 1903, in West Virginia. Barr was Dean Martin's uncle on his mother's side. He was a stone-faced, one-liner comic in the tradition of Henny Youngman (we get to see a bit of his act in "Old Flames Never Die"), and a comic acrobatic dancer. Already nearing retirement age, Barr began making appearances on many TV talk shows during the 1960s. His first acting credits came about in the 1970s, in such films as *Diamonds Are Forever* and *The Sting*. He was active on television, too, on *Love, American Style*, *Little House on the Prairie*, *Szysznyk*, and yet another encounter with Tony on *The Tony Randall Show* ("His Honor vs. Her Honor"). Barr also made frequent visits to his nephew's NBC series, *The Dean Martin Show*.

Barr suffered a stroke and died a little over three weeks later, on November 22, 1980, in Burbank, California, at the age of 77.

Rona Barrett

Guest starred in "The Dog Story" (as herself). Rona Barrett was born October 8, 1936, in New York City, as Rona Burstein. She began as a gossip columnist locally in Los Angeles before becoming a national sensation, paving the way for countless other gossip venues, including TMZ. She wrote her autobiography, *Miss Rona*, in 1974, and joined the cast of *Good Morning, America* the following year. On one episode of *The Odd Couple*—"The Dog Story"—Rona reads a brief TV story about the dognapping of Silver, the Wonder Dog with the words "hot flash" emblazoned on the screen during her report. Rona always had the inside scoop, and, in her opinion, Silver had a "bone" to pick with his manager. She is also mentioned in "The Hollywood Story" episode.

Her charity, the Rona Barrett Foundation, helps aid senior citizens. In 2009, Barrett got her own star on the Palm Springs Walk of Stars.

Barbara Barrie

Co-starred in *The Odd Couple: Together Again* (as Gloria Unger). Barbara Barrie was born Barbara Ann Berman May 23, 1931, in Chicago, Illinois. She graduated from the University of Texas at Austin with a degree in fine arts. As of this writing, this enduring character actress has entered her seventh decade of guest appearances on episodic TV.

Barrie's first recurring role was that of Corporal Edna Martin on *The Phil Silvers Show*. Although Barrie is a fine dramatic actress, she is best known for her roles on TV sitcoms, such as Elizabeth Miller, Barney's wife, on *Barney Miller*, and as Susan's grandmother Helen on *Suddenly Susan*.

Barrie had two experiences with the works of Neil Simon. In 1981, she costarred as Mrs. Banks in the TV-movie version of *Barefoot in the Park*. A dozen years later, Barrie portrayed Felix's wife, Gloria, on the made-for-TV reunion movie.

Barrie was nominated for a Tony Award for *Company*, and an Oscar for *Breaking Away*. She made a full recovery from a 1994 bout with cancer, and remains very active.

Arthur Batanides

Guest starred in "Felix's First Commercial" (as the bartender), "Myrna's Debut" (as Nino Babaloni), and "One for the Bunny" (as the plaintiff lawyer). Character actor Arthur Batanides was born April 9, 1923, in Tacoma, Washington. While performing stand-up routines during World War II, he was bitten by the acting bug. His credits date back to television's infancy, in the early 1950s. He studied at the Actor's Lab in Los Angeles, and accrued an amazing list of TV and film credits, but never became a household name.

Among his TV highlights are guest shots on *Maverick*, *Colt 45*, *Peter Gunn*, *Johnny Midnight*, *Route 66*, *Bonanza*, *Rawhide*, *The Twilight Zone*, *Perry Mason*, *The Fugitive*, *The Outer Limits*, *The Dick Van Dyke Show*, *Gunsmoke*, *Get Smart*, *Lost in Space*, *The Green Hornet*, *Gomer Pyle, USMC*, *Mission: Impossible*, *Happy Days*, and *The Odd Couple*. All three of his guest shots on the latter were in the three-camera, live audience era.

Batanides' was probably best known for his recurring role as Mr. Kirkland in the *Police Academy* movies. After *Police Academy 6: City Under Siege*, he opted to retire. Batanides died on January 10, 2000, at the age of 77.

Richard Benjamin

Portrayed Felix Ungar onstage, in 1966, in Chicago. Richard Benjamin was born May 22, 1938, in New York City. He graduated from Northwestern University and studied extensively at their theater school. At about the same time he got his first TV credit on an episode of *Dr. Kildare*, he married actress Paula Prentiss. Truly one of Hollywood's most-enduring marriages, they have been together through thick and thin for over a half-century. They even worked well together in the hit film *Catch 22* and the highly touted but short-lived CBS sitcom, *He & She*. Benjamin also starred in the NBC cult space sitcom, *Quark*, in 1978.

Benjamin found even greater success behind the camera, directing such memorable films as *My Favorite Year*, *Mermaids*, and *The Money Pit*, and even two Neil Simon TV movies—*The Goodbye Girl* (in which he also produced and appeared) and *Laughter on the 23rd Floor*. He also played an agent in the motion picture version of Simon's *The Sunshine Boys*, alongside Walter Matthau and George Burns. Speaking of Neil Simon, Benjamin portrayed Felix to Dan Dailey's Oscar in the 1966 production of *The Odd Couple* at the Blackstone Theatre in Chicago. Benjamin was also part of the touring company of Simon's *Barefoot in the Park* with Joan Van Ark and Myrna Loy, as well as *Star-Spangled Girl* with Anthony Perkins. His most recent credit is for a guest starring role on the series *Pushing Daisies* in 2009. He and Paula have two grown children, Ross and Prentiss.

Eddie Bracken

Co-starred on Broadway (as Felix). Edward Vincent Bracken was born February 7, 1915, in Astoria Queens, New York. By the age of four, Bracken was singing and dancing and winning every talent contest he entered. After appearing in several locally produced silent films and the Our Gang comedies, Bracken hit it big in a string of musical comedies, beginning with *Too Many Girls*, in 1940. This led to a contract with Paramount Pictures. Over the next few years, he worked in films with Bob Hope, Betty Hutton, Bing Crosby, Judy Garland, Gene Kelly, and Marilyn Monroe.

With the advent of television, Bracken got a lot of work in live dramas, such as *Lux Video Theater*, *Gulf Playhouse*, *The Alcoa Hour*, and *Climax*. He also appeared as a regular panelist on the game show *Make the Connection* and was briefly the host of his own game show, *Masquerade Party*, in 1957.

Bracken first connected with Neil Simon in the touring company of *Come Blow Your Horn*.

When Art Carney, who portrayed the original Felix Ungar on Broadway at the Plymouth Theater, became ill, Eddie Bracken replaced him in the role. Bracken himself was replaced a while later by Paul Dooley.

Bracken remained very busy, appearing in such motion pictures as *National Lampoon's Vacation*, *Rookie of the Year*, *Home Alone 2: Lost in New York*, and *Baby's Day Out*. He also owned and/or operated several newspapers and radio stations over the years (the latter helped earn him a role of a radio broadcasting instructor on a 1977 episode of the CBS sitcom *Busting Loose*). Executive Producer Mark Rothman said, "I'd always been so impressed with Bracken's work in Preston Sturges's *Miracle of Morgan's Creek* and *Hail the Conquering Hero*, I just knew, without even having him read for the *Busting Loose* part. I was right—he was perfect in the role." Bracken died unexpectedly on November 14, 2002, following complications from neck surgery. At the time, he had designs on making more movies. He has two stars on the Hollywood Walk of Fame—one for radio and one for television.

Bart Braverman

Co-starred in numerous episodes of *The New Odd Couple* (as Roy). Bartley

Louis Braverman was born February 1, 1946, in Los Angeles, California, into a show business family; his father, Herb Braverman, was a producer. Bart, a child actor, guest-starred on a classic episode of *I Love Lucy*, as Giuseppe, in "Lucy Gets Homesick in Italy." At that time, he was billed as Bart Bradley, but began using his real surname a while later. Along with roles in episodic TV, Braverman also provided the voice for Puggsy on the cartoon series *Fangface*.

Braverman's best-known role was that of Bobby "Binzer" Borso in the Robert Urich crime-drama TV series *Vegas*, from 1978 to 1981. This role was followed almost immediately by his role in *The New Odd Couple*, starring Ron Glass and Demond Wilson. It's interesting to note that the character of Roy had not appeared since season one of the original *Odd Couple* TV series, when he was portrayed by Ryan McDonald. Roy was the only poker player on the original series who didn't remain for the run of the original show. Roy also magically reappeared in the TV reunion movie of 1993.

Braverman was also a frequent guest star in the upper-left chair (next to Brett Somers) on *The Match Game*, with host Gene Rayburn. Braverman has remained active in episodic television programs, such as *Castle* and *The Mentalist*.

Matthew Broderick

Portrayed Felix Ungar in the modern-day production of *The Odd Couple*. The son of actor James Broderick, Matthew was born March 21, 1962, in New York City. After a sports injury sidelined his physical activities, he followed in his father's footsteps and studied acting at New York's Walden School. Some of his early work was in Neil Simon vehicles—*Brighton Beach Memoirs*, *Max Dugan Returns*, and *Biloxi Blues* (for which he won a Tony Award). His biggest motion picture conquests were *WarGames* (1983), and one which hit a chord with everyone who has ever played hooky, *Ferris Bueller's Day Off* (1986). Broderick was the first choice to portray Alex P. Keaton on *Family Ties*, but he didn't wish to be tied down to a TV series at the time. Right after wrapping up the motion picture version of *Biloxi Blues* in August 1987, Broderick and his girlfriend, Jennifer Grey, were involved in a horrific automobile accident in Ireland that killed two passengers in the other car. Broderick suffered a broken leg.

Broderick, a Ping-Pong aficionado, began a long onstage association with Nathan Lane in Mel Brooks's *The Producers*. For the role, Broderick was nominated for a Tony, but lost to his co-star. Apparently there were no hard feelings because they both also enjoyed a successful stage run in *The Odd Couple*. Lane portrayed Oscar to Broderick's Felix at the Brooks Atkinson Theatre.

Broderick also supplied the voice for the adult Simba in Disney's *The Lion King* (1994). Broderick is married to actress Sarah Jessica Parker, and together they have twin daughters.

Albert Brooks

Guest starred in "Oscar the Model" and "Felix Is Missing" (as Rudy Mandel). Albert Brooks was born Albert Lawrence Einstein July 22, 1947, in Beverly Hills, California. Unlike the other Albert Einstein, this one became a *comic* genius. He attended Carnegie Tech in Pittsburgh, but dropped out to pursue stand-up comedy. After many years of nightclub work and two successful comedy albums (*Comedy Minus One* and the Grammy-nominated *A Star Is Bought*), he opted to try his hand at acting and filmmaking.

Brooks's early acting credits include an episode of another Paramount program, *Love, American Style*, and then two early episodes of *The Odd Couple*—both from the program's single-camera first season, on which he portrayed the head honcho for a men's cologne company called Mandar. Oscar Madison almost gets to be a spokesman for the company's new ad campaign.

Brooks really found his niche in filmmaking, with such triumphs as *Defending Your Life* (1991), *Lost in America* (1985), *Mother* (1996), and *The Muse* (1999). He has also provided voices for cartoon characters such as Marlin in *Finding Nemo* and Russ Cargill in *The Simpsons Movie*. Married since 1997, Brooks has two children, Jacob and Claire.

Bella Bruck

Guest starred in "Myrna's Debut" (as Aunt Lucille), "Take My Furniture Please" (as Woman number one), "The New Car" (as Pushover Page Livingston), and "The Moonlighter" (as the woman at the counter). Bella G. Solomon was born on December 11, 1911, in the Bronx, New York. This very funny, rather matronly physical comedienne was a late bloomer, and didn't get her first TV credits until the early 1960s. Her first recurring TV role was as Mrs. Spiegelman, the outspoken, pushy and very funny Jewish neighbor on the Desilu sitcom *Angel*, with Annie Fargé and Marshall Thompson. This led to guest appearances on other sitcoms, such as *Guestward Ho, The Munsters, Hennesey, F Troop, The Dick Van Dyke Show, The Addams Family, My Favorite Martian, Nanny and the Professor, Love, American Style, Rhoda*, and *The Odd Couple*. All of her *Odd Couple* appearances were the multi-camera, live-audience episodes. Her guest shot as Myrna's slow-typing replacement secretary (Aunt Lucille) in "Myrna's Debut" led to many hilarious outtakes. Bruck was so very funny in that episode Jack Klugman had difficulty getting through it with a straight face.

Bruck also appeared in numerous motion pictures, including *The Glass Bottom Boat* (1966), and two Neil Simon vehicles: *The Cheap Detective* (1978) and *Last of the Red Hot Lovers* (1972). Belle Bruck died on April 5, 1982, shortly after filming a sitcom pilot (unsold) with Al Molinaro, titled *The Ugily Family*, for Paramount.

Victor Buono

Guest starred in "The Exorcists" (as the shady Dr. Clove), and "The Rent

Strike" (as the evil, plant-loving Mr. Lovelace). Victor Charles Buono was born in San Diego, California, on February 3, 1938. Influenced by his vaudevillian grandmother, Victor was in many of his high school plays. He caught the acting bug, and abandoned his original plans for a career in medicine.

Even though his training was Shakespearean, Buono's bailiwick was portraying arrogant, unkind, larger-than-life comic figures. Maybe his biggest break came when he was cast as Edwin Flagg in Bette Davis's 1962 classic, *Whatever Happened to Baby Jane?* He continued to find work in such famous films as *Hush...Hush Sweet Charlotte* (1964), *The Greatest Story Ever Told* (1965), and *Robin and the 7 Hoods* (1964). He is likely best known for his recurring role as King Tut on ABC's popular *Batman* series. In later years, he played Jim Ignatowski's wealthy father on *Taxi*.

According to Elinor Donahue, who portrayed Miriam Welby on *The Odd Couple*, Tony Randall and Victor Buono did not get along very well. After the two episodes of *The Odd Couple*, executive producer Mark Rothman used Buono's talents again in 1978 in the role of Leo, the chef, on the unsold sitcom pilot, *The Rita Moreno Show*. In real life, Buono was a gourmet chef, and a favorite on daytime talk shows. He had a sense of humor about himself and his considerable girth, and even recorded a few comedy record albums which addressed his weight problem (and also made him appear older than he really was). Unfortunately, Buono suffered a massive heart attack at the young age of 43, and died on New Year's Day 1982, in Apple Valley, California.

JOHN BYNER

Guest starred in "The Bigger They Are" (as Lyle Hooper) and "The New Car" (as Bert, owner of the parking garage). John Thomas Biener was born June 28, 1937, in New York City, the fifth of six children. Early in life he discovered a gift for mimicking people and got his break on *The Ed Sullivan Show*, doing impressions of popular actors and singers. Among his first recurring roles was that of Dewey on the short-lived sitcom *Accidental Family* in

Funnyman John Byner guest starred in "The New Car" and "The Bigger They Are" (courtesy John Byner).

1967. He was also Gorshen on a memorable episode of *Get Smart* titled "The Hot Line." He found a lot of cartoon voice work, most notably as both *The Ant and the Aardvark* in the popular DePatie/Freleng Enterprises Saturday morning animation series (the ant's voice is an impression of Dean Martin and the aardvark is that of Jackie Mason). Byner became an immensely popular guest on talk shows, game and variety shows.

John guest starred in two episodes of *The Odd Couple* as two very different characters: Lyle Hooper in "The Bigger They Are," and Bert, the owner of a parking garage, in "The New Car." He recalled, "Tony and Jack were two guys who really appreciated life—they were regular people. I had a terrific time doing those shows and I'm proud to have worked with them. They were a lot like their characters. Tony was quite the stickler. For example, our dressing rooms were small cabins adjacent to the set, mine was about 20 feet from Tony's. I was in mine one day rehearsing my lines aloud in what I considered a normal, low volume voice when the stage manager knocked on my cabin door to ask me to 'please keep it down' (apparently, my voice carried over to Tony's and it was annoying him). There were lots of laughs doing the 'New Car' episode. In fact, there's an outtake from that show in the parking garage on YouTube, in which Jack loses his composure and begins laughing and Tony chastises him with, 'BAD boy! BAD, BAD, BAD BOY!'"

Did John Byner run into Randall and Klugman again in later years? Byner shared, "I recall standing backstage with Tony, talking and waiting for our intros on a variety show when a beautiful girl dancer passed by and Tony said softly to me, 'I'd like to do it with her ... and I'll tell you why.' As for Mr. Klugman, I was driving to work along the Pacific Coast Highway, when a limo began to pass me, then slowed alongside. The dark-tinted rear window slowly lowered and it was Jack. He leaned out the window and yelled out with a smile, 'I love you, John!' He was on his way to bet on the horses, just like his character."

Another guest star on "The New Car" episode was Dick Clark. John recalls, "Soon after being on the same episode of *The Odd Couple*, Dick and I were on the same flight to New York—he in first class and I in business with my four kids. My youngest daughter was having an ear problem and Dick came back to tell her that everything was going to be OK. As he walked away, she whispered to me, with wide eyes, 'Dad, do you know who that is? That's Clark Kent!'"

About Garry Marshall: "I worked with him several times over the years and each time we'd see each other at a party or other event away from the studios, he'd introduce himself as though I was meeting him for the first time. I later asked his sister, Penny Marshall, about that and she said, 'Oh, he does that with everybody.'"

John Byner is an ACE Award winner for his comedy work in *Bizarre* as well as *Comedy on the Road*. His recurring roles include Detective Donahue on *Soap*; Dr. Roland Caine on *The*

Practice; Johnny McNamara on *McNamara's Band*; and Cotton Dunn on *Silk Stalkings*. He was seen most recently on an episode of *The First Family*, as Malcolm MacDougal. Follow him on his website, www.JohnByner.com.

ART CARNEY

Co-starred in the original Broadway production of *The Odd Couple* (as Felix). Arthur William Matthew Carney was born into a large Irish Catholic family November 4, 1918, in Mount Vernon, New York. He was the youngest of six sons, and his father was a newspaperman. Young Art was injured in World War II, and the shrapnel left in his leg caused a very slight limp for the rest of his life.

On radio, Carney got his start as a singer, and as an impressive mimic. With the advent of television, Carney jumped in head first, working initially with Morey Amsterdam on his DuMont Network series, *The Morey Amsterdam Show*. On the live *Cavalcade of Stars*, also on the DuMont TV Network, Carney kicked off a long and fruitful relationship with "The Great One," Jackie Gleason. Carney portrayed many characters on the program, but none was more enduring or endearing than that of sewer worker Ed Norton, Ralph Kramden's best friend and neighbor. *The Honeymooners* sketches were initially live, erratically timed, kinescoped bits, which were part of the entire *Cavalcade of Stars* and then *The Jackie Gleason Show*. In 1955, 39 episodes were filmed as half-hour episodes of a CBS sitcom. Initially, Gleason signed on to do two seasons of the program, but decided after one year that it had run its course. He couldn't have been more wrong. One can see some similarities between the characters of Ralph and Ed, and Oscar and Felix—great friends who often get on each other's nerves.

In the 1960s, Carney hosted several of his own TV variety specials, guest starred in a memorable holiday episode of *The Twilight Zone* as Santa Claus ("The Night of the Meek"), and portrayed "The Archer" on ABC's *Batman* series. Carney garnered the role of the original Felix Ungar to Walter Matthau's Oscar Madison on Broadway. The rave reviews for Matthau dwarfed those for Carney. Nevertheless, Carney stayed with the play from March to October of 1965, and was then succeeded by Eddie Bracken. Carney was considered for the 1968 original motion picture version of *The Odd Couple*, but because Jack Lemmon was red hot at the time, the role went to him (even though Carney would have been a lot less expensive).

Carney then returned to *The Jackie Gleason Show* on CBS from 1966 to 1970, on which he reprised his role as Ed Norton on what are now known as "The Color Honeymooners." Sheila MacRae had replaced Audrey Meadows as Alice, and Jane Kean took the Trixie role originated by Joyce Randolph. These hour-long episodes came to resemble Broadway musical comedies, as there was now a goodly amount of singing and dancing in each show (they were actually restaged versions of

Lyn Duddy and Jerry Bresler episodes of the old black-and-white "Honeymooners" sketches).

Carney was seemingly never out of work, but likely the highlight of his life came in 1974 in his role as Harry Coombes in *Harry and Tonto*, from 20th Century–Fox, who takes a cross-country journey with his cat. Carney garnered a "Best Actor" Oscar for this role.

Carney has a star on the Hollywood Walk of Fame on Hollywood Boulevard. He died in his sleep just five days after his 85th birthday, on November 9, 2003.

JANICE CARROLL

Guest starred in "It's all over Now, Baby Bird" (as the woman), "The Hustler" (as Vivian), "Does Your Mother Know You're Out Rigoletto?" (as Agnes) and "The Big Brothers" (as Mrs. Grainger, with a young son played by Clint Howard). Janice Carroll was born February 19, 1932, in Hollywood, California. While in her twenties, she had small roles in some very big films, including *Shane* and *Stalag 17* (both 1953).

Most of her appearances on television were in sitcoms such as *The Many Loves of Dobie Gillis*, *Guestward Ho*, *Pete and Gladys*, *Gomer Pyle, USMC*, *McHale's Navy*, *Mister Ed*, *Hey, Landlord*, *The Bob Newhart Show*, and *The Odd Couple*. She guest starred in four episodes of the latter—each time as a different character. Carroll continued on episodic TV, and earned still more movie roles in *How to Succeed in Business Without Really Trying* (1967), *The April Fools* (1969, with Jack Lemmon) and *The End* (1978). On September 10, 1993, Carroll died in California's San Fernando Valley, at the age of 61.

JACK CARTER

Guest starred in "Your Mother Wears Army Boots" (as Joey Birney). Jack Carter was born as Jack Chakrin on June 24, 1923, in Brooklyn, New York. Truly one of television's comedy pioneers, he was one of the possible choices as host for *Texaco Star Theater* in 1948. The hosting duties eventually went to Milton Berle, and Carter moved on to the DuMont Network's *Cavalcade of Stars*. When Carter was then offered his own eponymously titled show, he left DuMont and recommended a young Jackie Gleason to take his place.

Carter's résumé in the theater and in television is unparalleled. In his 90s as of this writing, Carter still possesses that wonderful rapid-fire comic delivery for which he's famous. About *The Odd Couple*, Carter recalled, "I was originally up for the part of Oscar on the TV version. They gave the role to Jack Klugman, but I was up for it. That happened to me a lot during my life." Carter had previously performed in a production of *The Odd Couple* play (as Oscar) with co-star Dick Shawn (as Felix) at the Westbury Music Fair in Westbury, New York, in 1967. Carter shared, "Dick Shawn was a sweetheart, but in real life he was the sloppy one and I was the neat one. My dressing room was always very tidy and his was a complete disaster area. But what a sweet guy. It was a pleasure working with him." What's most interesting about this particular production is that it was directed by none other than Jack Klugman. As Carter recalled, "Klugman was a great actor, but wasn't great at directing." Carter added, "One night, in the opening scene in which I carry in the sandwiches for the poker players, one of the pickles from the sandwiches squirted out from between the slices of bread and lodged on one of the lights. The audience went wild, and the pickle stayed there for the rest of the act. Eventually, when I left the show, Lew Parker from *That Girl* and *The Bickersons* took my place."

Carter guest starred on *The Odd Couple* TV series in season five. In "Your Mother Wears Army Boots," Carter portrayed Oscar's hired joke writer, Joey Birney. Also in that episode was popular sportscaster Howard Cosell, about whom Carter said, "He was a brilliant man. What a sense of humor. Cosell was great."

Dick Cavett

Guest starred in "Two Men on a Hoarse" (as himself). Richard Alva Cavett was born November 19, 1936, in Gibbon, Nebraska. His mother and father were both teachers, and Richard attended Yale University. This erudite young man worked as a writer for Jack Paar on *The Tonight Show*, and eventually starred on his own talk show, which ran, on-and-off, from 1968 to 1987 on a myriad of networks.

While with ABC, Cavett did a guest spot on *The Odd Couple*. In the episode, "Two Men on a Hoarse," Oscar Madison loses his voice just before going on *The Dick Cavett Show* and Felix then steps in as his translator.

Dick Cavett has co-written two books: *Cavett* in 1974, and *Eye on Cavett* in 1983. He was married to actress Carrie Nye from 1964 until her death in 2006.

William Christopher

William Christopher was born October 30, 1932, in Winnetka, Illinois. He graduated from Wesleyan University in Connecticut and immediately sought work in the theater. After finding employment in several off-Broadway productions, Christopher moved to Hollywood, where he performed on episodic television programs such as *The Andy Griffith Show*, *That Girl*, *Death Valley Days*, and *The Patty Duke Show*. He also appeared in such motion pictures as *With Six You Get Egg Roll* (1968) and *The Fortune Cookie* (1966). The latter co-starred Walter Matthau and Jack Lemmon. Years later, Christopher portrayed finicky Felix Ungar to Jamie Farr's Oscar Madison as part of the Troupe American Tour's production. Christopher and Farr had previously worked together on the long-running CBS sitcom, *M*A*S*H*. Both actors also had bit parts in the 1958 Andy Griffith movie, *No Time for Sergeants*. Their paths have crossed many times.

William Christopher is alleged to be a descendant of Paul Revere, famous for his "midnight ride." Christopher and his wife, Barbara, have two sons, John and Ned.

DICK CLARK

Guest starred in "The New Car" (as himself). Richard Wagstaff Clark was born November 30, 1929, in Mount Vernon, New York. He got his start in radio in Syracuse, New York, as a newscaster. Eventually he landed in a suburb of Philadelphia and secured an on-air job at WFIL-AM. WFIL also had a TV station, and a program called *Bob Horn's Bandstand*. Horn stayed with the show for a number of years, but just before the popular program was to go national on ABC, the more youthful Clark was selected as host, and the rest is history. Hundreds of rock and roll stars lip-synced their latest hits on what was now called *American Bandstand*.

Clark parlayed that success into a series of other music shows (*Where the Action Is*, and *The Saturday Night Beechnut Show*), game shows (*The Object Is, Missing Links, Scattergories* and *The $10,000 Pyramid*), award shows (*The American Music Awards*), seasonal programming (*Dick Clark's New Year's Rockin' Eve*), and also the long-running *Bloopers* series of specials. Clark also appeared in a few motion pictures—*Because They're Young* (1960), *The Young Doctors* (1961), *The Killers Three* (1968) and *Spy Kids* (2001)— and on episodic TV shows such as *Batman, The Partridge Family*, and *The Odd Couple*. On the latter, Clark portrayed himself as a radio host in a short scene in "The New Car," in which Oscar wins an automobile in a radio contest on station WZAZ. The focus of the questions is opera (odd for a rock and roll radio station), and all of the answers are provided by Felix, which leads to some conjecture over ownership of the vehicle. Throughout his career, Clark did most of his TV work on the ABC Network, and *The Odd Couple* was no exception.

Clark suffered a serious stroke late in 2004, and he never fully recovered his speech. He greatly curtailed TV appearances at this time, but remained at least a part of the action on his New Year's Eve specials. He succumbed to a massive heart attack, which occurred after prostate surgery, on April 18, 2012. American's oldest teenager (as he was affectionately known) was 82.

ROY CLARK

Guest starred in "The Roy Clark Show" episode (as Wild Willie Boggs). Roy Linwood Clark was born April 15, 1933, in Meherrin, Virginia. The famous banjo picker was a frequent guest on both variety and talk shows such as *This Is Tom Jones, The Flip Wilson Show, The David Frost Show, The Joey Bishop Show*, and *The Tonight Show Starring Johnny Carson*. He also guest-hosted *The Tonight Show* and had more than a two-decade run on *Hee Haw*.

In 1975, he portrayed Oscar's long-time, very musical army friend Willie Boggs in *The Odd Couple* episode "The Roy Clark Show." In the episode, Clark sings his biggest hit, "Yesterday, When

I Was Young," and also shows off his classical music chops.

Clark has been a member of the Grand Ole Opry since 1987. Today, he lives in Oklahoma and pursues his passion for motorcycles and fishing.

BEATRICE COLEN

Guest starred in "Shuffling off to Buffalo" (as Floyd's secretary) and "To Bowl or Not to Bowl" (as the bride). Beatrice Colen was born January 10, 1948, in New York City. She was the granddaughter of Pulitzer Prize–winning author George S. Kaufman.

Colen had a recurring role as Corporal Etta Candy on *Wonder Woman*, but she is probably best known for portraying Marsha, the roller-skating carhop at Arnold's Drive-In on many early episodes of *Happy Days*. Another Garry Marshall show is among her earliest credits—two episodes of *The Odd Couple*. She portrayed Felix's brother Floyd's secretary, Ivy, at the Unger Gum factory in "Shuffling off to Buffalo," and she was the neglected bride (briefly abandoned by the groom, portrayed by Bo Kaprall) at the championship game in "To Bowl or Not to Bowl."

Sadly, Colen died November 18, 1999, of lung cancer, at the very young age of 51.

MICHAEL CONSTANTINE

Guest starred in "Engrave Trouble" (as Bill Green). Michael Constantine was born May 22, 1927, in Reading, Pennsylvania, as Constantine Ioannides. While still in his twenties, he made his Broadway debut in *Inherit the Wind* at the National Theatre. He also enjoyed a long run in *The Miracle Worker* before turning his attention to TV and movies. After years of guest-starring roles in episodic TV programs such as *The Defenders, Dr. Kildare, The Untouchables, The Twilight Zone,* and *Perry Mason*, Constantine garnered a co-starring role as Jack Ellerhorn on Garry Marshall's first sitcom, *Hey, Landlord*. In later years, Constantine admitted that the speech pattern of his character on that show was inspired by Marshall himself. Marshall later used Constantine in *The Odd Couple*, on which he portrayed a scary mob man with a soft spot for dogs in the episode "Engrave Trouble."

Comedy proved to be Constantine's forte, and he won an Emmy for portraying Principal Seymour Kaufman on ABC's long-running *Room 222*. Constantine also starred in the funny but short-lived *Sirota's Court* on NBC in 1976 (*The Odd Couple*'s Harvey Miller was the executive producer and frequent writer on that series).

A Greek-American, Constantine's most famous role was as Gus Portokalos, the man for whom Windex was a cure-all, in the surprise box-office smash, *My Big Fat Greek Wedding*. An attempt to bring the magic of that movie to the small screen as *My Big Fat Greek Life* (with Constantine reprising his role) was short-lived.

CURT CONWAY

Guest starred in "Maid for Each Other" (as Dr. Gordon), "Murray the

Fink," "One for the Bunny," and "My Strife in Court" (as a judge in the latter three). Curtis "Curt" Conway (sometimes Kurt Conway) was born in Boston, Massachusetts, May 4, 1915. After numerous small roles in motion pictures in the 1940s, Conway founded his own acting school in 1952—The Theater Studio, on West 48th Street in Manhattan. He also taught acting at the California Institute of Arts. Most of his TV credits came about in the 1960s and early 1970s, on programs such as *The Twilight Zone, The Outer Limits, The Fugitive, Dr. Kildare, Ben Casey, Peyton Place, Bonanza, Columbo,* and *Kojak*. Among his many movie credits are *Hud* (1963), *Gentleman's Agreement* (1947), *Singapore* (1947), and *The Naked City* (1948). He was married three times, most notably to actress Kim Stanley, with whom he had one child, a daughter.

Curt Conway died on April 10, 1974, a few weeks before his 59th birthday.

Alan Copeland

Guest starred in "A Different Drummer" (as Alan) and "Strike up the Band or Else" (as the piano player). He was born October 6, 1926, in Los Angeles, California, as Alan Weaver Copeland. He joined the smooth Modernaires vocal group shortly after completing high school. The group originally formed in 1935, but really hit its stride in the 1950s when they became regulars on Bing Crosby's brother's daily TV series, *The Bob Crosby Show*; they were later featured often on *The Red Skelton Show*. Alan Copeland was also a prolific songwriter, famous for his compositions, "Too Young to Know" and "Make Love to Me." He was also a frequent musical arranger for such legendary vocalists as Ella Fitzgerald, Sarah Vaughan, and Frank Sinatra.

Copeland also had roles in several motion pictures, such as *The Hunchback of Notre Dame* (1939), *Yankee Doodle Dandy* (1942), *The Glenn Miller Story* (1954), and *Thoroughly Modern Millie* (1967). On *The Odd Couple*, Copeland guest starred in episodes that featured Felix's band—"A Different Drummer" (with Monty Hall) and "Strike up the Band or Else" (with Pernell Roberts).

Copeland won a Grammy Award in 1969 for "Best Contemporary Pop Performance—Chorus" for the medley "Mission: Impossible/Norwegian Wood" (by the Alan Copeland Singers). Alan's autobiography, *Jukebox Saturday Nights*, was published by BearManor Media.

Ellen Corby

Guest starred in "Trapped" (as Florence). She was born as Ellen Hansen in Racine, Wisconsin, June 3, 1911. Ellen found supporting roles in motion pictures beginning in the early 1930s. She found small roles in famous films such as *It's a Wonderful Life* (1946), *I Remember Mama* (1948), and *Shane* (1953), before becoming a prolific guest star on dozens upon dozens of popular TV programs through the 1950s and 1960s.

In 1971, on the final episode of season one of *The Odd Couple*, "Trapped," Corby portrayed a neighbor of Oscar and Felix whose jealous husband thinks she is cheating on him with every man in the building. Only months after this episode aired, Corby landed the biggest role of her career—as Esther on CBS's *The Waltons*.

Corby died just shy of her 89th birthday, on April 14, 1999, in Woodland Hills, California.

HOWARD COSELL

Guest starred in "Big Mouth" and "Your Mother Wears Army Boots" (both as himself). Howard William Cohen was born March 25, 1918, in Winston-Salem, North Carolina, but was raised in Brooklyn, New York. He earned a degree in English from New York University, and a law degree from the New York University School of Law. He practiced law in New York, while also broadcasting Little League games on the radio. His love for broadcasting made him leave his law practice to pursue a job on a radio show on WABC in Manhattan. His association with ABC radio and TV (boxing and football broadcasting) lasted for decades.

Cosell guest starred as himself on *The Odd Couple* not once but twice: "Big Mouth" and "Your Mother Wears Army Boots." Each storyline related to the *Monday Night Football* broadcasts, and each episode involved an ongoing feud between Howard and Oscar. Among the highlights of "The Big Mouth" episode are Felix's attempts to correct Cosell's nasal-sounding voice.

After the death of his wife, Emmy, in 1990, and because of his own failing health, Cosell basically withdrew from the public eye until his death on April 23, 1995.

WALLY COX

Guest starred on "The Pen Is Mightier than the Pencil" (as Mr. Fegivny). Wallace Maynard Cox was born December 6, 1924, in Detroit, Michigan. His mother wrote mysteries, and upon divorcing Wally's father, she moved the family to Evansville, Illinois, and eventually New York. After serving in the army during World War II, Cox attended New York University. While Cox may have appeared slight and weak, he was actually quite the athlete.

A performance on *Arthur Godfrey's Talent Scouts* brought him a lot of attention, although he didn't win. Only a few years later, Cox earned the lead role in a new live NBC sitcom called *Mister Peepers*. The program was a big hit and ran for more than three years. The cast was chock-full of future stars—Marion Lorne, Jack Warden, and two people associated with *The Odd Couple*: Walter Matthau (in the pilot) and Tony Randall. Years later, Cox guest starred on an episode of *The Odd Couple* portraying Mr. Fegivny, a wannabe writer in Felix's journalism class; the title: "The Pen Is Mightier Than the Pencil." Randall is said to have treated his old friend like a king the entire week. At the time they worked together on *Mister Peepers*, Tony used to refer to himself as "the third best actor in the world." Cox jumped on the bandwagon, and used to introduce Tony in just that manner.

Cox had another short-lived sitcom, *The Adventures of Hiram Holliday*, on NBC in 1956, but is best known for two different achievements in the 1960s—earning a regular square (the upper left) on *The Hollywood Squares*, and providing the voice for unlikely superhero Underdog in the popular cartoon series ("There's no need to fear; *Underdog* is here!").

Wally Cox died at the age of 48 of a heart attack in his Hollywood home on February 15, 1973. It has long been rumored that Cox's ashes were given to his good friend, Marlon Brando, who kept them on his mantle.

Scatman Crothers

Guest starred in "The Subway Story" (as the blind man). Benjamin Sherman Crothers was born May 23, 1910, in Terre Haute, Indiana. The "Scatman" nickname was assigned to him as a more memorable, catchier name for his performances in the golden days of radio with Phil Harris and Arthur Godfrey. He was a talented musician, singer, actor, and performer.

Scatman was really on his way in 1953 when he landed a role in the motion picture, *Meet Me at the Fair*. It's interesting that this talented musician became even more famous on TV. He made frequent guest appearances on episodic TV programs such as *Dragnet, The Governor and J. J., Bewitched, Love, American Style, Ironside, Kojak,* and *The Odd Couple*. On the latter, he portrayed the bogus blind man selling chewed-up pencils on the stuck subway train on which Felix and Oscar were riding. The blind man's Seeing-Eye dog that is about to have a litter of puppies, brings everyone together as one in that episode, "The Subway Story."

His role as Louie, the garbage man on *Chico and the Man*, became his most famous, but he also had roles in popular films such as *One Flew Over the Cuckoo's Nest* (1975), *Silver Streak* (1976) and *The Shining* (1980). Crothers was also a talented voice actor, and lent his familiar tones to popular cartoon characters such as Hong Kong Phooey and Meadowlark Lemon of *The Harlem Globetrotters Show*.

Crothers, a chain smoker, developed lung cancer and died on November 22, 1986, only months after the cancellation of his final TV series, the short-lived *Morningstar Eveningstar*, on CBS.

Lou Cutell

Co-starred in *The Odd Couple II* (as Abe). Lou Cutell was born October 6, 1930, in New York City, but the family later moved to the Los Angeles area, where Cutell studied drama at UCLA. His list of TV credits over a very prolific career includes guest-starring roles on *The Dick Van Dyke Show, My Three Sons, The Wild Wild West, Room 222, The Mary Tyler Moore Show, Starsky and Hutch, The Bob Newhart Show, Newhart, Lou Grant, Kojak, Alice, The Golden Girls, The Bob Crane Show, Mad About You, Empty Nest,* and *Will and Grace*. He was also Dr. Cooperman in the famous "Fusilli Jerry"

Lou Cutell portrayed Abe in the movie sequel, *The Odd Couple II* (courtesy Lou Cutell).

episode of *Seinfeld*, and Leo Funkhouser in several episodes of *Curb Your Enthusiasm*.

Cutell also had roles in many famous films, such as *Young Frankenstein* (1974), *Frankenstein Meets the Space Monster* (1965), *Little Big Man* (1970), *Foul Play* (1978), *Pee-Wee's Big Adventure* (1985), *Honey, I Shrunk the Kids* (1989), and *Wedding Crashers* (2005). Cutell was also in *The Odd Couple II* in 1998. Cutell portrayed Abe, one of Oscar's card-playing friends. The action takes place both at Oscar Madison's home in Sarasota, Florida, and the Sarasota minor league baseball stadium, but as Cutell recalled, "None of our scenes were actually filmed in Sarasota. We filmed them in Long Beach, California. The baseball stadium is in Long Beach, and the place in which Oscar Madison lived was a real apartment we got to use for the movie. I had worked with Jack Lemmon almost 30 years earlier [in 1969] in a film called *The April Fools*. Lemmon was the quieter of *The Odd Couple* pairing. Matthau was extremely outgoing. He was a 'regular mensch.' He deserves every accolade one could say about such a giving, talented actor. He was a star but always retained an everyman quality about him. Some of the young stars today could have learned a lot from him, some coming out of no formal background at all. They lack respect, they lack decorum, and subscribe to the old studio pecking order. Not Walter. He, after all, started as a bit character actor, and although he became a leading man, he retained the common touch. Walter was different than any other star I had worked with. I was a supporting actor, and he knew what I was going through, and he made me feel at home. He would invite me to his trailer at lunch time to listen to Mozart (like me, he loved opera and classical music). He practiced his Italian on me, and loved that I was Italian. The opening scenes were shot on some of the hottest days in Long Beach, and between scenes sometimes there was no time to go to our air-conditioned trailers as they reset the cameras. One time, with umbrellas being held by assistants over our heads to protect us from the sun, Walter whispered to me, 'Lou, I think I feel faint, and I'm gonna die right here.' I took his hand, and began singing an aria from Mozart's *Don Giovanni*. 'La ci darem la mano, la me dirai di si' (We will hold our hands, you will, of course, say yes). He immediately began singing with me and doing that humming he is so well known for. I know I made him forget that he was not feeling well—I made him take his mind off that fear (according to rumor, he had some form of cancer). Working on that film was one of the major highlights of my life—it felt like no work at all and it was such fun. At the time, my 95-year-old alert mother was living with me. Instead of putting her in some assisted-living facility, I insisted she stay in my home. Well, wouldn't you know, my mother, seeing how happy I was working on the film and without me knowing, went into my phone book and got Walter's address, and she wrote a letter to him to tell him how happy I was working on the film with him, and how impressed I was with his kindness, generosity, and friendship. I only found out about the letter when Walter pulled me aside and asked, 'What, is your mother your agent?' I had no idea what he meant. 'She wrote me a letter and told me to make sure we use you in *Odd Couple III.*' Of course, my mother never said that, and she showed me a copy of what she wrote (she always wrote what she called a bad copy first and then corrected her mistakes). Walter was a joy. I'm not the kind of person to take pictures with celebrities or ask for autographs but, totally on his own volition, he sent me a marvelous autographed studio photo of the two of us signed by him and the words, 'Bravo, bravo, bravo!' I treasure it and guard it with my life. It is the only star's picture I have hanging in my house."

Was Neil Simon involved at all with the filming? Cutell said, "No, he was never on the set, but one knows going in that there is little or no experimentation in a Neil Simon work. He likes the script performed verbatim (usually the kiss of death, because actors most times help with lines, and in turn, the play). Even Walter never argued over lines. One time, Howard Deutch, the director, who was always great to me, asked Walter to change a line he thought was useless. Walter snapped back, and in a major basso-profundo Shakespearean voice said, 'What? And have to hear the screaming of the master in the screening room? Never!' However, he liked an ad lib of mine during the card game in which I say, 'Did we come here to talk or play?' That was left in. In fact, they called me back to rerecord the line so that it would be clearer and stand out. That was quite something. Imagine a character actor helping to write a Neil Simon script."

About the other co-stars, Cutell shared, "Alice Ghostley was a dear, dear fragile friend. And Estelle Harris, who flirts with Oscar in her convertible in the opening scene, and whom I had worked with in the 'Fusilli Jerry' episode of *Seinfeld.* Estelle Harris with her grating voice—she was a scream. I also enjoyed working with the young director Howard Deutch."

In recent years, Cutell has attained great success as a playwright. His *Sicilian Bachelor* ran for seven consecutive months at the Tiffany Theater, and was on tour for two years throughout the United States. His *Viagra Falls* had a five-year run throughout the U.S. and Canada, and finally was produced at a major off-Broadway house, the Little Schubert, by the iconic Nederlanders. He was most recently seen as one of the regular "pranksters" in the hit NBC series, *Betty White's Off Their Rockers*. As of this writing, he was a recurring character, Uncle Melvin, on *How I Met Your Mother*.

RICHARD DAWSON

Guest starred in "Laugh, Clown, Laugh" (as himself). Richard Dawson was born as Colin Lionel Emm in Gosport, Hampshire, England, November 20, 1932. His big break came when he was cast as Corporal Peter Newkirk on the CBS sitcom *Hogan's Heroes* in 1965, kicking off a six-year run. He remained very visible through the 1970s, on *Rowan and Martin's Laugh-In*, *The New Dick Van Dyke Show*, and *The Match Game* (lower row center), and also on game shows he hosted, such as *Masquerade Party* and the original *Family Feud*. Dawson also had a small role as an evil game show host in the motion picture *The Running Man* (1987).

In between all of that success, Dawson made a guest appearance as himself on *The Odd Couple* in the next-to-last episode of the series, "Laugh, Clown, Laugh," which featured Dawson and Jack Klugman co-hosting a talk show. Felix also had a connection with Dawson—they used to have an "act" while together in the army, and their split was less than amicable.

All of the kissing on *Family Feud* led to marriage for Dawson. He met his wife, Gretchen Johnson, when she was a contestant on the show in 1981. Dawson was also previously married (briefly) to British actress Diana Dors. Dawson died June 2, 2012, at the age of 79.

ELINOR DONAHUE

Guest starred as Miriam Welby in "Gloria Hallelujah," "The Pen Is Mightier than the Pencil," "Oscar's Birthday," "Password," "I Gotta Be Me," "My Strife in Court," "Let's Make a Deal," "Take My Furniture Please," "Last Tango in Newark," "The Songwriter," "The Pig Who Came to Dinner," "The Exorcists," "Cleanliness Is Next to Impossible," "New York's Oddest," "The Odd Candidate," "The Subway Story," and "The Rent Strike."

Elinor Donahue was born Mary Eleanor Donahue in Tacoma, Washington, April 19, 1937. She began studying dance at a very early age, and appeared in numerous films while still in elementary school. Her big break came when she earned the role of Betty "Princess" Anderson on the long-running and highly successful family sitcom *Father Knows Best*. She was, seemingly, never out of work—transitioning to *The Andy Griffith Show* and *Many Happy Returns* before joining *The Odd Couple* cast, beginning in season three. She had only performed on single-camera sitcoms previously, but when Donahue joined the cast of *The Odd Couple*, they were filming in front of a live audience. Donahue recalled, "It was strange for me at first. I was nervous, mostly because the studio audience was so far away from the action on stage. Had they been closer, I'd have been more at ease."

Fun between scenes with Elinor Donahue (left), Tony Randall (center), and Jack Klugman (right) (courtesy Elinor Donahue).

Her role on *The Odd Couple* was supposed to be a one-shot deal, and for Elinor Donahue, things did not begin very auspiciously, as she recalled, "I'm always very nervous at dress rehearsals. I'm fine when the cameras are rolling, but there's just something about dress rehearsals. Anyway, even though I had very few lines, I went totally blank and couldn't recall my lines. Well, Tony went absolutely crazy, pounding on a table shouting, 'Why can't you remember your lines?' After that, I didn't wish to go back the next day, but I did, and when I entered my dressing room, there were flowers everywhere and a sweet note of apology from Tony. From that moment on, everything went smoothly. Tony and I became buddies. In fact, he gave my character her last name. At the time, *Marcus Welby, M. D.* (with Donahue's former co-star, Robert Young) was also on ABC and very popular, so Tony turned the character of Miriam into Miriam Welby, and I appeared in 17 episodes of the show. Whenever we entered a room, Tony wanted us to enter laughing, so he would always do something to surprise me or make me laugh just as the cameras started rolling. He had a very bawdy sense of humor, which was especially prevalent the day we first rehearsed the 'Let's Make a Deal' episode. Felix was dressed in a chicken costume, which he absolutely loved by the way. Well, when my character, Miriam sees him in the apartment, she says, 'Hi, Felix,' to which Felix replies, 'How did you know it was me?' For fun, Tony egged me on to say, 'I recognized you by your cock.' Well, Garry Marshall was absolutely mortified, but the gang, crew, and young writers roared. Of course, that didn't end up in the show, but it really shows Tony's playful nature."

Miriam Welby was always impeccably dressed on the show, to which Donahue added, "Those were my clothes. I had a lot of nice clothes in those days, including a Chanel, a Givenchy, and a Halston suit. The show didn't have a big budget for costuming, so that came in very handy. My dressing room was down the hall from Tony's. We all kept our doors open most of the time, and I was a pacer. I would pace the hall before a filming, and Tony would often shout, 'Stop that pacing! You're driving me *meshugganah*' (a Yiddish word for 'crazy')."

In the episode titled "The Pen Is Mightier than the Pencil," Tony is reunited with his *Mister Peepers* co-star Wally Cox, and Donahue reflected, "Tony was extremely loyal to his old friend. Tony made sure that Wally was treated like royalty that week. Wally really needed the work, and Tony was especially kind to him."

About Garry Marshall, Donahue recalled, "He was constantly saying to us, 'I want perk and bubble, perk and bubble.' With his wonderful New York accent, it was more like 'poik and bubble,' to which his sister, Penny Marshall would always say, 'I don't do poik and bubble.' Donahue added, "Garry once told me, 'You couldn't deliver a punch line if I put it in a box with a ribbon on it.'"

There was one especially trying time for Elinor Donahue. It occurred in the episode titled "My Strife in Court." She recalled, "In one scene, I am supposed to sing a song from a musical I've just seen. Well, I got my start singing in radio and vaudeville as a child and I loved it. However, something that my mother did and said to me when I was 13 changed that. After that, I was terrified of singing in public. I had a phobia about that and I didn't want to do it. Director Jerry Paris was insistent that I do it, and the dress rehearsal went very badly. I was so upset, I pondered going home. I sat in my car for 45 minutes with the keys in the ignition during the dinner break, but eventually I went back inside to face my fears. I'm supposed to sing a few lines from the title song, 'Kiss My Face,' and at the end of it on a whim I stopped just short of singing 'Kiss My Ass.' I didn't say that word, stopping just short of it, but the audience got it and they roared, and my phobia suddenly turned into a triumph." Donahue also got to play the bass fiddle in one episode, and actually had someone come in to teach her the proper fingering so that it appeared authentic.

What was the weekly schedule like for the cast of *The Odd Couple*? "Mondays we had our table read," Donahue recalled. Tuesdays we had our first rehearsal. Wednesday and Thursday were for blocking and run-throughs. And Fridays we filmed the show. Garry did the audience warm-up from about 7 until 8 p.m. Then we did the filming, and the live audience was usually out by 10, followed by a few necessary 'pick-ups' after the audience had gone."

Regarding a few of the guest stars on the show, Donahue stated, "Without question, my favorite was ballet star Edward Villella in the 'Last Tango in Newark' episode. I had kind of a crush on him, and being a dancer, it was really a special episode for me." In "The Pig Who Came to Dinner," the guest star is Bobby Riggs, and Donahue recalled, "In that episode, things that Riggs says infuriate and offend my character Miriam, but in reality, he didn't offend me at all. He was actually very sweet, outgoing and funny."

There were a couple of guest stars whom Tony didn't particularly cotton to, as Donahue reflects, "Radio personality Wolfman Jack did a cameo in the episode called 'The Songwriter,' and Wolfman was a chain smoker. Tony had a thing about smoking—he really hated being around a smoker, and I recall Wolfman being 'jailed' in his dressing room. And then there was Victor Buono, who guest-starred on two episodes. There was something about him that really rubbed Tony the wrong way." There was also a nice surprise, as Donahue remembered, "John Lennon was a fan of our show. I don't recall which episode he came to see, but it was an honor to meet him, and I got an autograph for my son, which he still treasures today."

And, how do her children and grandchildren feel about her long career in television? Donahue shared, "I recently showed them an *Odd Couple* scene where the cast is marching around the living room, and I'm playing a fife, to which they responded, 'Stop, you're embarrassing us.'"

PAUL DOOLEY

Briefly co-starred in the original Broadway play as Speed, and also briefly as Felix. He was born Paul Dooley Brown in Parkersburg, West Virginia, February 22, 1928. He drew a comic strip for his local newspaper before joining the navy. Acting was kind of an afterthought in Dooley's life. Upon moving to New York, he supported himself as a stand-up comic, and as a clown for kids' parties.

Dooley eventually became a member of the Second City improvisational troupe. While with them, he was discovered by Mike Nichols, who cast Dooley as one of Oscar's poker-playing buddies, "Speed," in the Broadway production of *The Odd Couple*. When Art Carney left the show, the role of Felix Ungar briefly went to understudy Dooley. The Oscar Madison understudy was Louis Zorich, who later played Burt Buchman on *Mad About You*.

In television, Dooley has had recurring roles and has made guest appearances in numerous series, including *Coming of Age, Alf, Dream On, Grace Under Fire, Star Trek: Deep Space Nine, The Practice, Once and Again, ER, Curb Your Enthusiasm, Huge,* and *Desperate Housewives*. He was also the co-creator and writer for the popular children's program *The Electric Company.* Dooley has four children and three grandchildren, and continues to add to a long list of guest appearances on episodic TV.

Jane Dulo

Guest starred in "The Murray Who Came to Dinner" (as Murray's wife, Mimi) and "The Odd Couples" (as Oscar's mother). Actress Jane Dulo was born October 13, 1917, in Baltimore, Maryland. She began her acting career on Broadway in *On the Town* and *Are You with It?* Dulo then moved to the burgeoning new industry of television, and accumulated an enviable list of credits.

Dulo had recurring roles on such sitcoms as *Hey, Jeannie, The Phil Silvers Show, McHale's Navy, The Joey Bishop Show, Get Smart* (as 99's mother), and *Gimme a Break.* She made two guest appearances on *The Odd Couple* as two entirely different and age-divergent characters in the program's third season: Murray's wife, Mimi, in "The Murray Who Came to Dinner," and Oscar's mother in "The Odd Couples." The two episodes originally aired only a few months apart.

Dulo also had roles in several memorable movies—*Soylent Green* (1973), with Charlton Heston; *Beaches* (1988), with Bette Midler; and *Roustabout* (1964), with Elvis Presley.

One of Dulo's final guest shots was on *The Golden Girls* in 1992. She died on May 26, 1994, in Los Angeles, California, at the age of 76.

Liam Dunn

Guest starred in "This Is the Army, Mrs. Madison" (as Captain Wyatt). Liam Dunn was born in New Jersey November 12, 1916. Like the cantankerous character actor Charles Lane, Dunn always looked older than his years, and was cast accordingly. Most of his credits are from his TV work on such programs as *Captain Nice, Room 222, Mannix, Gunsmoke, All in the Family, The Partridge Family,* and *The Odd Couple.* On the latter, Dunn portrayed Captain Wyatt in the flashback episode "This Is the Army, Mrs. Madison," in which Oscar and Blanche were wed while Oscar was serving in the army (their honeymoon was in the barracks).

Beginning in the early 1970s, Dunn had roles in many famous films such as *What's Up Doc?* (1972), *Papillon* (1973), and numerous Mel Brooks vehicles, such as *Young Frankenstein* (1974), *Blazing Saddles* (1974) and *Silent Movie* (1976). Dunn died young—at the age of 59 on April 11, 1976, in California.

Herb Edelman

Co-starred in the original 1968 motion picture (as Murray the cop). Herbert Edelman was born November 5, 1933, in Brooklyn, New York, and later studied acting at Brooklyn College. The tall, balding actor was proficient at both dramatic and comic roles. In the 1960s, he was still being credited as Herbert Edelman on his many guest appearances on episodic TV and in motion pictures. That's how he is credited in *The Odd Couple* (1968) in which he played Murray the cop. Interestingly, no one who portrayed Murray—Herbert Edelman, Al Molinaro, John Schuck, or Jerry Adler ever reprised that role. Edelman also appeared in two other Neil Simon motion pictures: *Barefoot in the Park* and *California Suite*.

Edelman managed to secure numerous regular or semi-regular roles on a bevy of TV programs, including *The Good Guys*, *Big John Little John*, *Strike Force*, *Nine to Five*, *The Golden Girls* (for which he received an Emmy nomination), *St. Elsewhere*, *Knots Landing*, *Murder, She Wrote*, and *Ladies' Man*. Edelman had once been married to the star of *Ladies' Man*, Louise Sorel, but they had been divorced over a decade when they worked together on that series, obviously remaining on friendly terms.

Edelman was only 62 when he died of emphysema in Woodland Hills, California, on July 21, 1996.

Ann Elder

Guest starred in "Fight of the Felix" (as Irma). Ann Elder was born September 21, 1942, in Cleveland, Ohio. She is likely best known for her years on *Rowan and Martin's Laugh-In*, but she is also an Emmy Award–winning writer (often in collaboration with Larry Hovis). She started as a teenage model, and parlayed that into a successful and diverse career.

In 1970, she guest starred on the second episode of *The Odd Couple*, "Fight of the Felix," as the long-suffering girlfriend of jealous hockey pro Splint McCullough (played by Richard X. Slattery). Her sweet, kindly ways are mistaken as flirting by Splint, and Splint ends up giving Oscar Madison two black eyes. When Felix stands up for his friend, Splint challenges Felix to a boxing match.

Elder also appeared often as a celebrity panelist on the 1970s version of Gene Rayburn's *The Match Game*. Elder wrote for Mitzi Gaynor's stage show, numerous 1960s sitcoms, *The Hollywood Squares*, and the much-lauded Lily Tomlin TV specials. At last report, she was still actively writing and hosting a syndicated radio program.

Monica Evans

Co-starred as Cecily Pigeon in the Broadway play, the 1968 movie, and the original TV series in "The Laundry Orgy," "It's all over now Baby Bird," "The Jury Story," and "The Breakup."

Monica Evans was born in the UK in 1940. She studied at the Royal Academy of Dramatic Arts, and won a gold medal for best actress at London's Central School of Speech and Drama. Evans was the understudy for Joan Plowright in the play *Rhinoceros* (staged by Orson Welles). When Plowright took ill, Evans ably stepped in (as Sir Laurence Olivier's co-star). Evans then appeared in several British programs, including her recurring role in the long-running soap opera *Compact*.

In the U.S., Evans and Carole Shelley portrayed the Pigeon Sisters for the entire Broadway run of *The Odd Cou-*

ple. Neil Simon was unable to find the right girls for the roles in the U.S., so he auditioned actresses in the UK and found his Cecily and Gwendolyn there. For Evans, it was her Broadway debut. The same girls reprised the roles of Cecily and Gwendolyn Pigeon in the Jack Lemmon/Walter Matthau 1968 movie version. History was made when they took those same roles to television (for which they begrudgingly had to audition), and appeared in four early single-camera episodes of the Tony Randall/Jack Klugman version. These British lassies somehow got lost in the translation to the small screen, and quickly disappeared.

Evans also provided voices for two animated Disney films—*The Aristocats* (1970) and *Robin Hood* (1973).

When *The New Odd Couple* came to television in 1982, the roles of the Pigeon Sisters went to others for the first time—two African American actresses—Sheila Anderson (Cecily) and Ronalda Douglas (Gwendolyn).

Jamie Farr

Jamie Farr was born Jameel Joseph Farah July 1, 1934. He, and another famous actor/comedian of Lebanese descent, Danny Thomas, were raised in Toledo, Ohio. He was discovered at the Pasadena Playhouse and won a role in the motion picture *Blackboard Jungle* (1955) as a result. Much like his most famous role, Corporal Max Klinger on *M*A*S*H*, he served in the U.S. Army during the Korean War. The part of Klinger (a corporal who wears dresses in order to bring about his discharge) was supposed to be a one-shot deal, but the character proved so popular, he became a regular.

Farr and fellow *M*A*S*H* co-star William Christopher portrayed Oscar Madison and Felix Ungar (respectively) in a 1997 production staged by the Troupe American Tour (although, with his pronounced nose, Farr has said that besides Oscar, he would have also made a good Murray the Cop). Christopher and Farr also worked together decades earlier in the 1958 Andy Griffith film *No Time for Sergeants*.

Farr has been married to the same woman, Joanne, since 1963, and they have two children, Jonas and Yvonne (as well as one grandchild). Farr has a golf tournament named after him, but his playing has been curtailed a bit of late because of rheumatoid arthritis in his hands. At last report, Farr was hosting a regular syndicated radio travel program called *Traveling Farr*.

Herbie Faye

Herbie Faye guest starred in six episodes, "And Leave the Greyhound to Us" (as the racetrack official), and as the superintendent/electrician/handyman/maintenance man in "The Blackout," "Psychic Shmychic," "Felix's First Commercial," "The Rent Strike" and "The Exorcists."

Faye was born in New York City on Groundhog Day of 1899. Even though he was never the leading man or the star, his acting career encompassed four decades of TV credits, including regular appearances on *The Phil Silvers Show*, and *The New Phil Silvers Show* when he was already approaching the age of 60, as well as many guest shots on *The Dick Van Dyke Show, Here's Lucy, Petticoat Junction, Gomer Pyle, USMC, The Joey Bishop Show*, and *The Odd Couple*. On the latter, he appeared in six episodes, usually as the super or maintenance man but, inexplicably, he had different names—among them, Mr. Lambretti, Mr. Seltzer and Mr. Harvey Faffner. Coincidentally, Faye also worked with both Walter Matthau and Jack Lemmon in MGM's *The Fortune Cookie* in 1966.

Faye played a bartender twice for Rod Serling—once in *The Twilight Zone* episode titled "A Kind of a Stopwatch," and again in *Requiem for a Heavyweight*, which Serling wrote.

Faye died at the age of 81 on June 28, 1980.

Pamelyn Ferdin

Guest starred in three episodes, "Bunny Is Missing Down by the Lake" (as Cindy), and "Surprise Surprise" and "Good Bad Boy" (as Edna Unger).

Pamelyn Wanda Ferdin was born the day after "the day the music died" (the day after Buddy Holly, The Big Bopper, and Ritchie Valens died in a plane crash), February 4, 1959, in Los Angeles, California. Her distinctive voice garnered her a lot of acting and voice work in the 1960s and 1970s. She was the voice of Lucy Van Pelt in the *Peanuts* holiday specials. She was also a regular on two 1960s sitcoms—*The John Forsythe Show* (as Pamela), and *Blondie* (as Cookie Bumstead). In 1970, she played one of four campers who sought refuge at Felix and Oscar's cabin in the woods during a torrential downpour. In this episode, she portrayed Cindy, but the next time she guest starred on the show she assumed the role of Felix and Gloria's daughter, Edna Unger. That lasted only two episodes, however, as Ferdin was then signed to portray Paul Lynde's daughter, Sally Simms, in the 1972 ABC sitcom *The Paul Lynde Show*. At that point, the role of Edna was assumed by actress Doney Oatman.

Among Ferdin's career disappointments was losing the role of Regan MacNeil in the 1973 movie, *The Exorcist*, to Linda Blair. After a long hiatus from show business, Ferdin provided the voice for "Christmas the horse" for a TV movie titled *Eli Sparkle Meets Christmas the Horse* in 2009.

Ferdin continued to act on episodic television through the rest of the 1970s, before deciding to leave show business to become a registered nurse. At this time in her life she settled down and married a doctor named Jerry Vlasak (they have since divorced). She has, in recent years, become an outspoken activist for animal rights and against animal cruelty.

Craig Ferguson

Craig Ferguson was born May 17, 1962, in Glasgow, Scotland. He established himself as one of Great Britain's top comedians, and his connection to Neil Simon's *The Odd Couple* is his portrayal of Felix Ungar as part of the 1994 Scotland Tour, showing off the universal appeal of the play. This was just before he hit it big in the U.S. as Nigel Wick on the long-running sitcom *The Drew Carey Show*.

From there, he almost immediately stepped into a long-running late night CBS talk show called *The Late, Late Show with Craig Ferguson*, which opens each evening with the line, "It's a great day for America, everybody." Ferguson opted to discontinue the show in December 2014.

John Fiedler

Guest starred in "Security Arms" (as Mr. Duke) and "The Dog Story" (as Hugo). He was also Vinnie in the original Broadway production and the 1968 motion picture. John Donald Fiedler was born February 3, 1925, in Platteville, Wisconsin. After serving in the U.S. Navy during World War II, Fiedler kicked off a career as a character and voice actor which lasted over half a century. His face and his voice were familiar to millions, but he was never a household name. His first important role was as Juror number two in the much-lauded courtroom drama, *12 Angry Men* (with Jack Klugman). Countless roles in episodic television followed, including two episodes of *The Twilight Zone* ("Cavender Is Coming" and "The Night of the Meek"), and an episode of *Star Trek* ("Wolf in the Fold"). He also portrayed Mr. Penchill in the 1965 Elvis Presley motion picture, *Girl Happy*.

Fiedler's next big movie role came in 1968 when he played Vinnie in the original motion picture version of *The Odd Couple* (he also had originated that part on Broadway). Another diminutive, balding actor, Larry Gelman, portrayed Vinnie in the TV series version. Fiedler did make two appearances on the sitcom, and along with the Pigeon Sisters (Carole Shelley and Monica Evans), is the only other actor to appear in the Broadway production, and in both *The Odd Couple* movie and TV sitcom. Coincidentally, in each of the two TV episodes in which he guest stars, "Security Arms" (as Mr. Duke) and "The Dog Story" (as Hugo), Fiedler treats a pet dog rather poorly and sternly. Prior to playing Vinnie in *The Odd Couple*, Fiedler had Broadway roles in *Harold* and *A Raisin in the Sun*.

Fiedler is also well known as the meek, mousey, and high-voiced Mr. Peterson (with the domineering wife, Doris), a recurring role on *The Bob Newhart Show*. He was also Woody the director on *Buffalo Bill*, as well as the voice of Piglet in several Winnie-the-Pooh animated films. Coincidentally, Fiedler died of cancer at the age of 80 on June 25, 2005, in Englewood, New Jersey, one day after the death of Paul Winchell (the voice of Tigger in those same Winnie-the-Pooh films).

Filip Field

Guest starred in "Your Mother Wears Army Boots" (as the production manager), "Two Men on a Hoarse" (as a patient), "The Big Broadcast" and "The Odd Candidate" (the latter two as a director). Filip Field has TV credits on only two programs, but both of those programs prominently featured Jack Klugman.

Field followed Klugman over to

Quincy, M. E. and portrayed the lab technician in 46 episodes, between 1978 and 1983.

Phil Foster

Guest starred in "Two Men on a Hoarse" (as Dr. Krakauer). Phil Foster was born Michael Feldman March 29, 1914. His stage name came from Foster Avenue in his hometown of Brooklyn, New York. He began in show business by performing in talent competitions for monetary prizes. He became a stand-up comic in the 1930s, until joining the army during World War II.

Throughout the 1950s, Foster was a favorite on variety shows, and made dozens of short films, many of which were about Brooklyn. Foster's friend Garry Marshall urged him to come to Hollywood, and used him in an episode of *The Odd Couple* in the program's fifth and final season. Foster was familiar with the play—he had previously portrayed Oscar to George Gobel's Felix (in 1967 in Detroit, Washington, D.C., and Hartford, Connecticut).

Foster's impressive appearance on *The Odd Couple* led to his being cast as Frank DeFazio, owner of The Pizza Bowl on the long-running Garry Marshall show *Laverne and Shirley*. Foster died on July 8, 1985, in the Palm Springs area, only two short years after *Laverne and Shirley* ended its primetime run.

Mickey Fox

Guest starred in "The Flying Felix" (as a passenger), "Your Mother Wears Army Boots" (as an opera club member), "Oscar's Birthday" (as Judy Skelton), and "The Hollywood Story" (as Hannah).

Born Helen Fox on August 8, 1915, Mickey (her stage name) had a sense of humor about her considerable girth, and was already pushing 60 when she began getting her first motion picture and television credits (and there weren't very many of either). On the big screen, Fox had small roles in *Pete 'n' Tillie* (1972, with Walter Matthau), *Caged Heat* (1974), *California Split* (1974), *Eat My Dust!* (1976), *The Big Bus* (1976), and *Nice Dreams* (1981).

On television, Fox had guest starring roles on episodic shows such as *Love, American Style, Sirota's Court, Laverne and Shirley, Kojak,* and *The Odd Couple.*

After a brief show business career, Mickey Fox died on March 9, 1988, at the age of 72, in Los Angeles, California.

Richard Fredricks

Guest starred in "Does Your Mother Know You're out, Rigoletto?" (as himself). Richard Fredricks was born August 15, 1933, in Los Angeles. He is the former principal baritone of the Metropolitan Opera. Not only did he perform in the opera *Rigoletto*, he also guest starred as himself in an episode of *The Odd Couple* that focused upon it. In the episode, "Does Your Mother Know You're Out, Rigoletto?" Fredricks promises Felix Unger that he'll perform in his opera club presentation. However, when he breaks his leg playing softball with Oscar, Felix has to improvise.

Fredricks has held teaching positions at the Juilliard and Manhattan Schools of Music, and has worked in a tutorial capacity with Renatta Scotto and Giorgio Tozzi. Coincidentally, Tozzi also made a guest appearance on *The Odd Couple*, in the "Our Fathers" episode.

George Furth

Guest starred in "I Do, I Don't" and "The Flying Felix." George Schweinfurth was born December 14, 1932, in Chicago, Illinois. He graduated from Northwestern University, and then got his masters in fine arts at Columbia University. A few years later, he began to accrue TV credits, mostly on dramatic programs such as *The Defenders*, *The Alfred Hitchcock Hour*, *Run for Your Life*, *Adam-12*, *Ironside* and *Laredo*. He also squeezed in a few sitcoms, including *The Farmer's Daughter*, *McHale's Navy*, *Tammy*, *Broadside*, and *The Odd Couple*. On the latter, he guest starred years apart, first as a reluctant groom in "I Do, I Don't" in the single-camera first season, and then as Mr. Belkin of Belkin Airlines in "The Flying Felix" in season four.

Some of Furth's biggest successes were on Broadway. He won a Tony Award for writing *Company* in 1971, and a show on which he worked with Stephen Sondheim titled *Merrily We Roll Along* was named "Best New Musical" in 2001. Furth died at the age of 75 on August 11, 2008, from a lung infection.

Dee Gardner

Guest starred in "Oscar the Model" (as Tracy), "Oscar's New Life" (as a model), "Does Your Mother Know You're Out, Rigoletto?" (as Dee Dee), and "Psychic Shmychic" (as the lab girl). Dee Gardner's very first credit is for the 1969 Jack Lemmon film, *The April Fools*. Her small roles in each of the four *Odd Couple* TV episodes involved working with a famous guest star—"Oscar the Model" (with Albert Brooks), "Oscar's New Life" (with John Astin), "Does Your Mother Know You're Out, Rigoletto?" (with Richard Fredricks), and "Psychic Shmychic" (with Bernie Kopell).

During Gardner's short career, she also guest starred on *Love, American Style*, *Mission: Impossible*, *Banacek*, and *Search*.

Teri Garr

Teri Garr was born December 11, 1944, in Lakewood, Ohio. She came from a show business family—her father was a vaudevillian, and her mother was a Rockette. Teri was a background dancer in a lot of rock-and-roll movies, such as *Viva Las Vegas* (1964), *Fun in Acapulco* (1963), *Kissin' Cousins* (1964), *Pajama Party* (1964), and *Head* (1968). It wasn't until the 1970s that her career really began to blossom in such famous fare as *Close Encounters of the Third Kind* (1977), *Tootsie* (1982, for which she was nominated for an Oscar), and *Mr. Mom* (1983). About the same time she was seen in *Young Frankenstein* (1974), she guest starred in an episode of *The Odd Couple* titled "The Flying

Felix." Garr portrayed a frustrated airline insurance sales person—frustrated because Felix kept coming back to her counter to purchase more insurance before his flight. She later became a frequent and popular guest on *The Tonight Show Starring Johnny Carson* and especially *The Late Show with David Letterman*.

In 2002, Teri Garr confirmed that she had multiple sclerosis, and became an active advocate, raising awareness about the debilitating disease.

Brad Garrett

Co-starred in the Nathan Lane and Matthew Broderick stage version of the play (as Murray). Garrett was born as Brad Gerstenfeld in Woodland Hills, California, on April 14, 1960. Once an adult, he was standing six-feet-eight-inches tall, but instead of pursuing a career in basketball, he opted to try his hand at stand-up comedy. He had a real flair for his chosen profession, and was a big winner on *Star Search* in 1983. Before long, he was opening for some of the biggest names in Las Vegas.

His true break, however, was being cast as the brother that mother didn't love best, Robert Barone, on *Everybody Loves Raymond*. After the show's long run, he had the option to star in a spin-off, but instead took the lead role in a very different (yet successful) sitcom called *'Til Death*, which ran for four seasons.

As Robert Barone, Garrett played a cop. He got to play another cop—Murray the cop—in the 2005 production of *The Odd Couple*, alongside Matthew Broderick and Nathan Lane. This production enjoyed a run of 249 performances, with 28 previews.

Eddie Garrett

Guest starred in "This Is the Army Mrs. Madison" (as soldier number two), "A Different Drummer" (as Oscar's co-worker), "The Paul Williams Story" (as the bodyguard), "The Big Broadcast" (as an angry listener), "The Bigger They Are" (as Doyle), "Your Mother Wears Army Boots" (as the coach), and "Two Men on a Hoarse" (as the stage manager).

Eddie Garrett was born Edward Gehrt on November 19, 1927, in Milwaukee, Wisconsin. After performing an impression of Bing Crosby for his family and getting a lot of encouragement, Garrett eventually developed a repertoire of hundreds of voice impersonations and became a nightclub performer. Both of his parents died while he was young, and a move to Los Angeles in his teen years brought him closer to all the action in Hollywood. Garrett also developed a lifelong passion for taking pictures of celebrities—a hobby which began in the 1940s.

Garrett's first TV credit was for an appearance on *The Beverly Hillbillies*. Then came a series of dramatic shows, such as *Bonanza*, *Ironside*, *Mannix*, *The Fugitive*, *Batman*, *The Man from UNCLE*, and *Medical Center*.

Playing a myriad of different characters, Eddie Garrett guest starred on *The Odd Couple* seven times. He would later follow Jack Klugman to two other series—*Quincy M. E.*, and *You Again?*

Garrett died of a stroke on May 13, 2010, and his body was donated to Loma Linda University Hospital for research purposes.

LEIF GARRETT

Guest starred in "The Frog" and "Felix Remarries" (as Leonard Unger). Leif Garrett was born November 8, 1961, as Leif Per Nervik, in Hollywood, California. He is the older brother of actress Dawn Lyn, who portrayed Dodie on *My Three Sons*. Leif got his first taste of show business in the motion picture *Bob & Carol & Ted & Alice* (1969) at the age of seven. From there, he found a lot of work in episodic TV on shows, such as *Nanny and the Professor*, *Family Affair*, *Gunsmoke*, *Cannon*, and *The Odd Couple*. On the latter, he portrayed Felix's only son, Leonard Unger, in two episodes. Leonard, by the way, was Tony Randall's real first name. Garrett took over the role from Willie Aames.

In 1975, Garrett then co-starred in the short-lived MTM series, *Three for the Road*, as Endy Karras. Shortly after the cancellation of that 13-episode series, Leif had designs on becoming a recording artist. He was inspired by the teen idol success of Shaun Cassidy, and began recording hit singles in 1977, including "Surfin' USA," "Runaround Sue," and "I Was Made for Dancin'." In fact, both Cassidy and Garrett had the same producer, Michael Lloyd.

Garrett's musical career was short-lived, however, and his alcohol and drug abuse problems have been well documented. He portrayed himself in David Spade's *Dickie Roberts: Former Child Star* (2003), and his episode of *Behind the Music* on VH-1 received some of the series' highest ratings. In 2010, he took part in season four of *Celebrity Rehab with Dr. Drew*.

LARRY GELMAN

Guest starred in "The Laundry Orgy," "Felix Gets Sick," "The Breakup," "Oscar's Ulcer," "Felix Is Missing," "Scrooge Gets an Oscar," "The Blackout," "What Does a Naked Lady Say to You?," "Murray the Fink," "Where's Grandpa?," "Gloria Moves In," and "To Bowl or Not to Bowl" (as Vinnie Barella).

Lawrence Sheldon Gelman was born November 3, 1930, in Brooklyn, New York. His comedy mentor was Jack Benny, with whom he worked occasionally in nightclubs and on TV. Gelman had a very prolific career as a character actor, and guest starred in such films as *Old Dogs* (2009), *Mr. Saturday Night* (1992), *Rabbit Test* (1978), and *Funny Girl* (1968). His TV credits run a mile long, but the most remembered are his appearances as Dr. Binder on *Maude*, Dr. Bernie Tupperman (the urologist) on *The Bob Newhart Show*, and as the balding, bespectacled poker-playing Vinnie on *The Odd Couple*.

Gelman was nominated for a primetime Emmy Award for a guest appearance on *Barney Miller* in an episode titled "Goodbye, Mr. Fish, Part Two" in 1978, but he lost to Ricardo Montalban, who won for a guest appearance on *How the West Was Won*.

Joan Gerber

Voiced the character of Goldie Hound on the animated series, *The Oddball Couple*. Joanellen Gerber was born July 29, 1935, in Detroit, Michigan. Gerber was a famous voice actress who brought countless cartoon characters to life. Some of her earliest work was on *Matty's Funnies*, *Roger Ramjet*, and *The Bugs Bunny Show*. Her voice became a Sid and Marty Krofft Saturday morning staple on many popular programs, such as *H. R. Pufnstuf*, *Lancelot Link: Secret Chimp*, *The Bugaloos*, and *Lidsville*.

In the fall of 1975, immediately after the cancellation of *The Odd Couple*, that same network aired an animated David DePatie/Friz Freleng Saturday morning version called *The Oddball Couple*. The main characters were a dirty dog named Fleabag, and a tidy cat named Spiffy, who lived and worked together. They shared a secretary named Goldie Hound (a blonde, canine version of Goldie Hawn). A total of 32 11-minute episodes were produced, and aired for two seasons (with two episodes paired every week).

Gerber remained very active providing voice characterizations for programs such as *Ducktales* and *Duck Dodgers* into the 21st Century. Sadly, her many voices were silenced, on August 22, 2011. She was 76.

Lisa Gerritsen

Guest starred in "Bunny Is Missing, Down by the Lake" (as Bunny). Lisa Gerritsen was born December 21, 1957, as Lisa Orszag, in Los Angeles. Her great-grandparents had been actors, and, skipping a few generations, young Lisa followed in their footsteps, beginning at age eight. By the time she was ten, she had her first TV credits on programs such as *The Good Guys* and *Gunsmoke*. In 1969 she was brace-faced Lydia Monroe on the highly touted but low-rated *My World and Welcome to It*, which starred William Windom.

From there she immediately made the jump to the role of Bess Lindstrom, Phyllis's outspoken daughter on *The Mary Tyler Moore Show* (and the later spinoff, *Phyllis*). She also made a guest appearance on *The Odd Couple* in its first season, "Bunny Is Missing, Down by the Lake." As the title suggests, Bunny (played by Gerritsen) gets lost in the woods during a camping trip, necessitating a lengthy search. It is later discovered that Bunny had run away after becoming jealous of Felix's obvious feelings for her camp counselor, Julie.

Gerritsen had roles in *Airport* (1970), and *The War between Men and Women* (1972), with Jack Lemmon. After *Phyllis* was canceled in 1977, Lisa left acting. Today, she lives in Northern California, and has been married to a doctor since 2000. They have one son, and at last report, Gerritsen was working for a software company.

Alice Ghostley

Guest starred in "The Breakup" (as Mimi) and in the motion picture sequel, *The Odd Couple II* (as Esther, one of the card players). Alice Margaret Ghostley was born in Eve, Missouri, on August 14, 1924. She began performing at the age of five and never looked back. She briefly attended the University of Oklahoma, but dropped out to pursue acting. In this case, that proved to be a good choice.

Ghostley obtained roles in some very famous motion pictures, such as *To Kill a Mockingbird* (1962), *The Graduate* (1967), and *Grease* (1978). However, she is mostly remembered for an impressive array of television appearances, highlighted by regular roles as harried and hyper women on *Bewitched*, *Car 54, Where Are You?*, *The Ghost and Mrs. Muir*, *Captain Nice*, *The Tom Ewell Show*, *Mayberry RFD*, *The New Temperature's Rising*, *Evening Shade*, and *Designing Women*. She was truly one of the most prolific character actresses of all time.

Ghostley also has two connections to *The Odd Couple*. In an early episode of the original series, she portrayed Mimi Greshler, Murray the cop's wife (a role later taken over by actress Jane Dulo). In the Neil Simon motion picture sequel, *The Odd Couple II* from 1998, Ghostley portrayed the sight-impaired Esther, the whiner.

Ghostley was nominated for an Emmy (*Designing Women*) and two Tony Awards (*The Beauty Part* and *The Sign in Sidney Brustein's Window*); she won for the latter. Ghostley died on September 21, 2007, in Studio City, California, after a brave battle with colon cancer. She was one of the last surviving cast members from *Bewitched*.

Ron Glass

Co-starred as the fussbudget, Felix Unger in the 1982 remake sitcom, *The New Odd Couple*. Ronald Earle Glass was born July 10, 1945, in Evansville, Indiana. He studied drama and literature at the University of Evansville. After some school and local stage productions, Glass moved to Hollywood, where he made the rounds as a supporting actor on episodic TV sitcoms, such as *All in the Family*, *Maude*, *The Bob Newhart Show*, *When Things Were Rotten*, and *Sanford and Son*. Glass would again be teamed with one of the stars of *Sanford and Son* a few short years later.

In 1975, things really began to break for Glass when he was cast as Detective Ron Harris in the critically acclaimed sitcom *Barney Miller*. (A few of his scenes from the show are featured in the hit 2013 motion picture, *Lee Daniels' The Butler*.) *Barney Miller* had a seven-year run, and when it was cancelled in 1982, Glass stepped immediately into another series, co-starring Demond Wilson—Paramount's African American version of the original *Odd Couple*. It was difficult to step into the big shoes of those who had portrayed Felix and Oscar before, and after 18 episodes, *The New Odd Couple* was canceled.

Ron Glass continued to get consistent TV work through the 1980s and 1990s, acquiring numerous recurring roles in sitcoms, such as *Rhythm and Blues*, *Amen*, *227*, *Mr. Rhodes*, *Teen Angel*, and *All Grown Up*.

GEORGE GOBEL

Portrayed Felix Ungar onstage to Phil Foster's Oscar Madison. George Leslie Goebel was born May 20, 1919, in Chicago, Illinois. An only child, Gobel first sought work in country music. His music career was interrupted by World War II. By the time the war ended, his interests had turned to comedy.

In 1954, Gobel was awarded his own NBC comedy/variety show, produced by Hal Kanter. Gobel also had his own company—Gomalco—a combination of the name Gobel and his business manager, David P. O'Malley. Gomalco's greatest success was the sitcom *Leave It to Beaver*.

"Lonesome George" (as he was comically known) became a semi-regular on the original *Hollywood Squares* after the passing of Charley Weaver (who occupied the square on the lower left). In 1967, Gobel co-starred with Phil Foster in *The Odd Couple* onstage at the Fisher Theater in Detroit, and the National Theatre in Washington.

Shortly after heart surgery, George Gobel died on February 24, 1991; he was survived by his wife, "Spooky Old Alice" (about whom he often joked), and their three children.

LOUIS GUSS

Guest starred in "The Ides of April" (as the man in waiting), "The Hustler" (as Arnold), "Felix Directs" (as Ed), "Our Fathers" (as Moe), and "Two Men on a Hoarse" (as burglar number one). Louis Guss (sometimes credited as Louie Guss) was born on January 4, 1918, in New York City. He was a prolific character actor, and appeared most often in ethnic, blue-collar, tough-guy roles. His earliest TV roles date back to the 1950s in such dramas as *Decoy* and *Naked City*. He could also do comedy, and guest starred on programs such as *Maude, Rhoda, Phyllis, The Mary Tyler Moore Show, All in the Family, Taxi, One Day at a Time, Gimme a Break, Silver Spoons, The Nanny,* and *The Odd Couple*. He appeared in five episodes of the latter, never playing the same character twice (although they were all similar in nature). He was also in the pilot episode of Mark Rothman and Lowell Ganz's sitcom *Busting Loose* in 1977.

Guss's movie parts were also plentiful. He had roles in *The Godfather* (1972), *Moonstruck* (1987), *Harry and Tonto* (1974), *Fun with Dick and Jane* (1977), and *Girlfight* (2000). Guss died at the age of 90 on September 29, 2008, and had one son with his wife of over 40 years, Tsuneko.

ARCHIE HAHN

Guest starred in "Gloria Moves In" (as Roger, one of the poker players). Not to be confused with the Olympic sprinter of the same name, Archie Hahn III said, "I am the sprinter's grandson." He added, "My grandfather was winner of three gold medals for the 60-, 100- and 200-meter dashes in the 1904 St. Louis Games. He was known as the 'Milwaukee Meteor.' I inherited his speed—I can sort and fold laundry faster than anyone in our family."

Archie Hahn from *The Odd Couple* era (courtesy Archie Hahn).

Hahn is still amassing credits on his own amazing résumé. In motion pictures, he has appeared in *My Favorite Year* (1982), *This Is Spinal Tap* (1984), *Brewster's Millions* (1985), *Protocol* (1984), *Inner Space* (1987), *Gremlins 2: The New Batch* (1990), *Police Academy 5: Assignment Miami Beach* (1988), *The Brady Bunch Movie* (1995), and *The Sunshine Boys* (1975, with the original Oscar Madison, Walter Matthau). About the latter, Hahn reflected, "One clear memory working on *The Sunshine Boys*—the movie was directed by Herbert Ross (an imposing directorial force). I was cast as the 'assistant to the director' [Howard Hesseman], who was auditioning talent for the Frumpy's Potato Chip commercial. Willy Clark [Walter Matthau] was auditioning and was being difficult and cranky. I had a line commenting on Willy's ineptitude that I was to deliver to the director in reference to Willy, but as we got close to the line in the scene I thought of a funnier line which I improvised and indeed it was funny enough that the crew and several of the actors in the scene laughed out loud (a no no). Herbert Ross called, 'Cut' as the script supervisor advised him that my line wasn't in the script. He singled me out and said, 'Why didn't you say the line that was written?' I said 'I thought my line was funnier.' There was a brief but serious pause with everyone wide eyed ... then he said, 'Be that as it may Mr. Hahn we are filming Neil Simon's WORDS ... do you mind?' I sheepishly said 'No sir ... I'm sorry.' He said, 'Good,' then very generously said, 'Let's do it again ... *as written*. Back to one.' There was an audible sigh of relief from everyone. My line was funnier ... but I am forbidden to repeat it."

Hahn, the actor, was born in Morgantown, West Virginia, and spent his formative years in upstate New York; he later attended elementary and high school in Wilmington, Delaware. Hahn continued, "I graduated from Valley Forge Military Academy and studied pre-med at the University of Delaware, but decided not to go to medical school. I was drafted into the U.S. army, joined the National Guard, worked as a lab technician at the DuPont Company, and eventually saved up enough money to move to California to pursue my wish of becoming a comedy actor." Hahn recalled, "Two teachers were instrumental in planting and cultivating the acting seed in me. The first, Mrs. Tarkington, my seventh-grade English teacher (a cross between Jayne Mansfield and Mae West), cast me and Richard Kinsinger as 'End Men' (in blackface) in a school play she created based upon a River Boat Minstrel Show. Classically, End Men were the comedy relief between acts. We were a big hit and apparently very funny. That was when I knew what I wanted to be when I grew up—a black comedian. The second was Joe Simmons (my speech/drama teacher in ninth and tenth grade), who always, from day one, encouraged me to follow my dream. God bless both of them." Regular appearances on the improv show *Whose Line Is It, Anyway?* (the British version) really showcased Hahn's talents and put him on the map.

On television, Hahn's familiar face was seen on *The Bob Newhart Show*, *The Partridge Family*, *Maude*, *Three's Company*, *The Love Boat*, *Night Court*, *Eerie, Indiana*, and *The Odd Couple*. In the latter, Hahn, as Roger (from Oregon), is at the poker table, filling in for Felix, and he has a real lucky streak and keeps winning. About that role, Hahn recalled, "It was early in my career and was an important step along the way. I remember that everyone was very nice and treated me well. I played a rookie cop and was invited by Murray [Al Molinaro] to fill out the table at the weekly poker game. Al was such a nice, funny man and made sure I was included and comfortable. I was shy, and tried to stay out of the way. I was moved by his kindness. Speaking of being shy, that episode was directed by Garry Marshall, who is a big, friendly personality filled with humor—a major writer/producer (and a bit intimidating). He was always very busy with the show, or holding court, which made me even more reticent to get in his way or strike up a conversation. When the week was finished, I happened to overhear a comment he made regarding my week on the show. He said that I was very good but was 'not very friendly.' My heart sank when I realized I had left him with that impression. It was one of those things I wished I could undo ... for years. I wish I had been more confident and open. It was a minor role, but a major one for me. Working on a hit show was an important credential for a budding young actor, and I was grateful to be cast as 'Roger,' and privileged to work with the extraordinary producers, writers and actors—especially Garry Marshall. I really am very friendly when you get to know me."

Well, Hahn couldn't have left that bad an impression upon Garry Marshall, as he did get to guest star in two episodes of *Laverne and Shirley* ("Playing Hooky" and "The Defiant One"). He also reconnected with the former Felix Unger on an episode of *The Tony Randall Show* ("Case: The Lawndale Report").

Among Hahn's most recent achievements are roles in *John Tucker Must Die* (2006), *Mr. Woodcock* (2007), and *Alvin and the Chipmunks: The Squeakquel* (2009).

MONTY HALL

Guest starred in "A Different Drummer" and "Let's Make a Deal" (as himself). Monty Hall was born Monty

Halperin in Winnipeg, Canada, on August 25, 1921. He graduated from the University of Manitoba in 1945, and then served in the Canadian army before heading south to seek his fortune in the U.S. His diverse career in broadcasting encompasses sportscasting, producing, directing, acting, and singing. However, he is best known as the longtime host of the daytime game show *Let's Make a Deal*.

Prior to his two guest appearances on *The Odd Couple*, Hall portrayed Ann Marie's dentist, Dr. Pellman, in the *That Girl* episode "At the Drop of a Budget." In real life, Hall was a good friend of Jack Klugman. Their friendship was mirrored in his two guest shots on *The Odd Couple*. Hall recalled, "Jack, like his character of Oscar, was a big fan of horseracing. We went to the races together in real life, and we did an ABC special about gambling years later. On *The Odd Couple* show it was said that we attended college together. What an enjoyable experience it was being in those two episodes—among the most fun I've ever had. I got a call from Garry Marshall, who told me that he had an open and a close for the episode, but that I should write the middle part. It should be ad-libbed and creative, just like the real *Let's Make a Deal*. The cast was simply brilliant. Unlike other scripted shows on which I appeared, this one was not rigid by any stretch of the imagination. I was only casual friends with Tony Randall, but my daughter, Tony winner Joanna Gleason, knew him very well. Al Molinaro and I played poker together in real life. It was like

"The big deal of the day"—author Bob Leszczak interviews *Let's Make a Deal* legend Monty Hall.

working with family. We really did take Let's Make a Deal on the road a few times—to the Winter Carnival, to Norfolk, and even to Vegas, so it wasn't too much of a stretch for the plot of this episode that we were doing a few shows in Manhattan, where Odd Couple was set. One of my favorite parts of the show is when Oscar coaches Felix on how to be a contestant. Felix thought that Monty would select him if he just raised his little finger like a 'perfect gentleman,' but Oscar showed him the nuances and enthusiasm necessary to get picked to make a deal on the show."

About his second appearance on the show, Monty said, "In 'A Different Drummer,' I have my own talk show, and Oscar is scheduled to be a guest on the show to talk about sports. Well, Felix really wants to sing on the show, and Felix attempts to prove to me that Oscar is part of his band to sway me into letting the band perform. I promise to try to squeeze them in, but when Oscar's sports stories run long, they get bumped. There's so much ad-libbing and a wealth of creativity. It was a blast." Hall is also mentioned in the famous "Password" and "The Exorcists" episodes.

JANIS HANSEN

Guest starred in 12 episodes: "Felix's Wife's Boyfriend," "Hospital Mates," "Win One for Felix," "Security Arms," "Speak for Yourself," "Gloria Hallelujah," "The Odd Couples," "The First Baby," "Gloria Moves In," "The Odd Holiday," "One for the Bunny," and "Felix Remarries" (as Felix's ex-wife, Gloria Unger). Janis Hansen was born June 14, 1941, in Celoron, New York, near Jamestown (whence her inspiration, Lucille Ball, hailed). On Broadway, she worked in *Come Blow Your Horn* (a Neil Simon play) and *The Thurber Carnival*. She never had a series of her own, but she certainly did guest star in a lot of sitcoms. Her first credit was in *Car 54, Where Are You?* in 1962. Then came *Gidget, The Donna Reed Show, My Favorite Martian, The Rounders, The Good Guys, I Dream of Jeannie, Love, American Style*, and, of course, *The Odd Couple*. Hansen portrayed Felix Unger's harried ex-wife, Gloria. Felix is still madly in love with Gloria, and she still loves him but can't stand his fastidious and controlling ways. On the show, the estranged couple has two children, Leonard and Edna. In the episode titled "One for the Bunny," we find out that Gloria Unger had been a *Playboy* bunny in earlier years. That mirrored Hansen's real life: before breaking into acting in the early 1960s, she actually was a *Playboy* bunny.

Hansen also performed in several motion pictures, including *A Cannon for Cordoba* (1970) with George Peppard, and *Airport* (1970) with Burt Lancaster and Dean Martin. In her 40s, Hansen ceased performing in front of the camera, and instead started her own talent agency, Hansen Management.

RON HARPER

Co-starred in the 1998 movie sequel, *The Odd Couple II* (as Jack). Ron

Harper was born in Turtle Creek, Pennsylvania, on January 12, 1936. He was quite the scholar—valedictorian of his high school senior class, which earned him a scholarship to Princeton University. Eventually, he moved to New York and studied acting with the legendary Lee Strasberg. Harper recalled, "Right after a stint in the navy, about 1958, I was in my very first play called *A Palm Tree in a Rose Garden*. My co-star was Alice Ghostley, and how nice it was to connect with her again 40 years later when we both had roles in *The Odd Couple II*. I played a character named Jack, and she played Esther. The director, Howard Deutch, was just a wonderful director, and what a cast we had. It was nice because there was a lot of free time between takes. During that down time I got to connect with the cast. Jack Lemmon was rather quiet—a solitary guy, but there was a piano on the set for the wedding scene in the film, and I studied piano so I began playing to kill some time. That really made Jack Lemmon warm up to me. He started playing and was really good. I wasn't aware of how proficient a player he was. Walter Matthau was really great fun. He had a great sense of humor, and I especially remember a riddle of his; Walter asked me to figure out the riddle, which went like this—'There was a naked guy on a raft who had a pack of cigarettes but no matches, so how did he get to smoke his cigarette?' Well, I was stumped and Matthau's answer to the riddle was, 'The naked guy took one of the cigarettes out of the pack and threw it into the water, making the raft ... a cigarette lighter.' Well, he got me, and he was so proud that he was able to stump me. It was a wonderful experience from beginning to end."

This wasn't the only time Ron Harper co-starred with screen legends—he also worked on TV with George Burns and Connie Stevens on the sitcom *Wendy and Me*; with Jean Arthur in her eponymously titled show; with Robert Lansing and Norman Fell on *87th Precinct*; and on *The Planet of the Apes* TV show with Roddy McDowall. Harper was also a staple of daytime television in such soap operas as *Where the Heart Is*, *Love of Life*, *Another World*, *Capitol*, and *Generations*. Harper also understudied Paul Newman on Broadway in *Sweet Bird of Youth*, and co-starred with Warren Beatty in Elia Kazan's *Splendor in the Grass* (1961).

Today, Harper resides in Tarzana, California, and continues to act on episodic television and in films.

Estelle Harris

Co-starred in *The Odd Couple II* (as the "flirting woman in the convertible"). She was born Estelle Nussbaum, on April 4, 1928, in New York City. Estelle is the younger of two daughters born to Polish/Jewish immigrants who owned a candy store in Manhattan. She took on the stage name of Estelle Harris and got her first acting credits as she neared her 50s.

Harris guest starred on dozens of TV programs, such as *Married with Children*, *Mad About You*, *Night Court*, *Law and Order*, and *The Exes*. She has had recurring roles on *Good Advice*,

The Suite Life of Zack and Cody, and *Greetings from Home*, but is best known as George's opinionated mother, Estelle Costanza, on *Seinfeld*. Harris has also had a lucrative career in animation and, most notably, supplied the voice for Mrs. Potato Head in Pixar's *Toy Story 2* and *3* (1999, 2010, respectively).

In *The Odd Couple II*, Harris flirts with Oscar Madison (Walter Matthau) from her huge convertible in the opening scenes. Harris had previously worked with Matthau and Lemmon in the film *Out to Sea* (1997), in which she portrayed Bridget. She starred in the original Los Angeles production of *Odd Couple* head writer Mark Rothman's play, *The Wearing of the Greens*. Harris's newest project is a motion picture titled *CBGB* (2013).

Patricia Harty

Guest starred in "That Was No Lady" (as Melanie Metcalfe). She was born November 5, 1941, in Washington, D.C. She performed under two names—Patricia Harty and, later, Trisha Hart. She got her start on episodic TV programs, such as *Route 66* and a couple of soap operas—*The Doctors* and *Search for Tomorrow*.

In 1966, she and Michael Callan were cast as the leads in *Occasional Wife*, an NBC sitcom that lasted for a single season. They eventually fell in love in real life and were married. After that show failed, Harty was quickly cast as Blondie Bumstead in the 1968 sitcom version of the *Blondie* comic strip. Like its TV predecessor a decade earlier, this version of *Blondie* also bombed and was pulled from the CBS lineup after only 13 weeks. At this point, Harty returned to episodic TV, and played the opera-loving wife of a very jealous professional football-playing husband (played by Alex Karras) on *The Odd Couple*. Felix flirts with her, not knowing that she was married to the crazed Jake Metcalfe, and comedy ensues.

Few realized in 1975 that the formerly blonde Patricia Harty was now the brunette Trisha Hart. She was cast in the role of Ellie Wilcox, the wife on the short-lived *Bob Crane Show* on NBC. By this time, her marriage to Michael Callan had dissolved, and she married the associate producer of Crane's sitcom, Les Sheldon. There was then a long gap in her acting credits until she surfaced in yet another short-lived TV sitcom (if you're keeping track, there were four) called *Herbie, the Love Bug* (based upon the hit Disney film). Her most recent acting credit was in an episode of *The District*, with Craig T. Nelson.

Bob Hastings

Guest starred in "Myrna's Debut" (as talent scout Happy Greshler). Bob Hastings was born April 18, 1925, in Brooklyn, New York. He got his start in radio as Archie from the *Archie* comic-book series. The advent of television drew him to the new medium, and he quickly found work on *Captain Video and his Video Rangers* and *The Phil Silvers Show*. In the early 1960s, he was cast in a recurring role as Captain Binghamton's toady, Lieutenant

Elroy Carpenter, on yet another anti-militaristic show, *McHale's Navy*. Simultaneously, he supplied the voice for the raven on *The Munsters* (a little-known factoid). He has also voiced Commissioner Gordon in several *Batman* cartoon episodes.

Hastings was also, briefly, a game show host (*Dealer's Choice*), but most of his credits are in episodic TV programs. On *The Odd Couple*, Hastings portrayed Murray's theatrical agent cousin, Happy Greshler, who was not at all impressed with Myrna Turner's dancing audition (and causes a distraction to escape her horrid performance).

Hastings made frequent appearances at nostalgia and old-time radio exhibitions across the U.S. He passed away on June 30, 2014, at the age of 89.

Hugh Hefner

Guest starred in "One for the Bunny" (as himself). Hugh Marston Hefner was born April 9, 1926, in Chicago. In school, it was discovered that he had an IQ of 152. His work on his school newspaper pointed out the path his career would eventually take. He is the founder, publisher, and CCO of *Playboy* Enterprises. He started the magazine after a pay dispute at his job with *Esquire Magazine*.

Hefner made a cameo appearance as himself in a flashback episode of *The Odd Couple* in 1974. Felix was a photographer for *Playboy*, and when his ex-wife, Gloria, was one of the models, he attempted to keep Hefner from publishing her nude picture.

Hefner has a star on the Hollywood Walk of Fame, and was instrumental in raising funds for the restoration of the iconic Hollywood sign and also the restoration and preservation of films in the UCLA Film and TV archives. As of this writing, Hefner is married to Crystal Harris, who is 60 years his junior. "Hef" has a cameo in the 2013 motion picture about the Borscht Belt comedians who used to perform in the Catskill Mountains called *When Comedy Went to School*.

Sherman Hemsley

Portrayed Oscar Madison in a touring company production. Sherman Hemsley was born February 1, 1938, in South Philadelphia. His mother worked in a lamp factory, and Sherman did not get to meet his biological father until he was 14. Sherman served in the U.S. Air Force, and then took a job with the U.S. Postal service before becoming an actor.

His big break came when he was cast as Gitlow in the hit Broadway musical *Purlie* in the early 1970s. This led to his most famous role as George Jefferson, first on *All in the Family*, and then the decade-long spinoff, *The Jeffersons*, alongside his TV wife, the long-suffering Weezy (Isabel Sanford). His next venture, as Deacon Frye on the sitcom *Amen*, was also quite a success.

In 2003, Hemsley took on the role of Oscar Madison to Pat Morita's Felix Ungar in a touring show—among the oddest couplings of any two actors before or after.

Hemsley died, single and childless, on June 24, 2012, of cancer, at his home in El Paso, Texas. When his will was contested, Hemsley's burial was put on hold for a considerable amount of time. He was finally granted a military funeral on November 9, 2012, at Fort Bliss National Cemetery, in El Paso. He was inducted into the Television Academy Hall of Fame in that same year.

DARRYL HICKMAN

Portrayed Oscar Madison onstage in the early 1980s. Darryl Gerard Hickman was born July 28, 1931, in Hollywood, California. The elder of the Hickman Brothers (younger brother Dwayne had TV roles in *The Bob Cummings Show* and *The Many Loves of Dobie Gillis*), Darryl began racking up very impressive movie credits even before his teen years (*The Grapes of Wrath* [1940], *The Human Comedy* [1943]). Darryl guest starred on numerous episodes of his brother's sitcom, but for the most part, he found even greater success behind the camera as a programming executive and acting coach.

In the early 1960s, both Darryl Hickman and Charles Nelson Reilly appeared in the long-running Broadway production of *How to Succeed in Business Without Really Trying*. Hickman and Reilly were reunited in 1981 at the Burt Reynolds Dinner Theatre for a production of *The Odd Couple*. Reilly was Felix Ungar, and Hickman was Oscar Madison. In that same year, Reynolds and Hickman worked together in the motion picture *Sharky's Machine*. Hickman also guest starred as flamboyant Peter Grey in a memorable episode of *All in the Family* called "The Commercial."

PAT HINGLE

Co-starred in the original Broadway production (as Oscar Madison). Martin Patterson Hingle was born July 19, 1924, in Miami, Florida. He attended the University of Texas on a tuba scholarship, but left to join the navy during World War II. Upon returning to civilian life, Hingle was inspired by the work of actors Hume Cronyn and Walter Huston and, at that point, decided to become an actor. Hingle was never a household name, but his résumé is incredible and encompasses six decades' worth of film, television, and stage work. Early in 1966, Hingle replaced Klugman (who had replaced Walter Matthau) as Oscar Madison in the Mike Nichols–directed Broadway presentation of *The Odd Couple* at the Eugene O'Neill Theatre.

Hingle's motion picture credits include roles in *On the Waterfront* (1954), *Hang 'em High* (1968), and *Norma Rae* (1979). Hingle also portrayed Commissioner Gordon in four of the *Batman* movies.

After a long battle with a form of blood cancer, Hingle died on January 3, 2009, in Carolina Beach, North Carolina, at the age of 84.

PETER HOBBS

Guest starred in "Oscar's Promotion" (as Mr. Talbot), "The Odd Candidate" (as Simpson, the incumbent),

"The Bigger They Are" (as the emcee at the Dink Awards), and "The Rent Strike" (as Rodney Allen Rippy's lawyer). Peter Hobbs was born in France on January 19, 1918. He was raised in New York, and schooled in Pennsylvania. He fought in The Battle of the Bulge in World War II, and, upon returning to the States, he enjoyed a five-decade career on Broadway (*Teahouse of the August Moon* and *Billy Budd*) and in film: *Sleeper* (1973), *The Man with Two Brains* (1983), *The Andromeda Strain* (1971), *Any Which Way You Can* (1980), *Nine to Five* (1980), and *The Lady in Red* (1979).

His television credits are impressive, and include a long run as Peter Ames on *The Secret Storm*, as well as appearances on episodic programs, such as *The Farmer's Daughter*, *The Dick Van Dyke Show*, *The Bill Dana Show*, *Perry Mason*, *The Big Valley*, *Mannix*, *The Mary Tyler Moore Show*, *The FBI*, and *The Odd Couple*. He portrayed a different character in each of the four episodes of the latter, and is said to have been a very affable, easygoing professional. Hobbs remained extremely active well into the 1990s. After a brief illness, he died on January 2, 2011, in Santa Monica, California, just two weeks shy of his 93rd birthday, leaving behind three daughters, two stepsons, six grandchildren, and two great-grandchildren.

BOB HOPE

Guest starred in "The Hollywood Story" (as himself). Leslie Townes Hope was born May 29, 1903, in London—the son of a stone mason. Hope conquered all: vaudeville, Broadway, radio, movies, and television. He was nicknamed "Old Ski Nose" because the shape of his nose resembled a ski slope. He appeared in dozens upon dozens of motion pictures, including the popular "Road" films with Dorothy Lamour and Bing Crosby. He was passionate about golf, and owned a piece of the Cleveland Indians baseball team. He is most remembered for entertaining the troops from 1942 to 1988, and for his countless NBC TV specials.

Even with his busy schedule, Hope managed to find time to make a cameo appearance in one episode of *The Odd Couple*. Felix and Oscar encounter Hope putting out his trash while they were on a tour of celebrity homes. Felix gets a souvenir—an autograph on an orange peel from Hope's trash can. In real life, Hope's home was across the street from Garry Marshall's place in Toluca Lake, California.

Bob Hope lived to be 100, and passed away from pneumonia on July 27, 2003.

TELMA HOPKINS

Guest starred in "Frances Moves In" and "Oscar Dates Felix's Frances" (as Felix's ex-wife on *The New Odd Couple*). Telma Louise Hopkins was born October 28, 1948, in Louisville, Kentucky. Telma had two show-business careers. She began as a prolific background singer for many Detroit area hitmakers (many of whom recorded for Motown). She was then recruited to become, along with Joyce Vincent

Wilson, the vocal group Dawn to back up Tony Orlando. This led to numerous hit records and a hit variety show, but there was still so much more ahead for Telma. She seemed to hop from sitcom to sitcom, and was almost never out of work.

After the cancellation of the Tony Orlando variety show, she landed first in *A New Kind of Family* with Eileen Brennan, followed by *Bosom Buddies* with Tom Hanks. She then portrayed Felix's ex-wife, Frances, on *The New Odd Couple* in 1982. The character's name had been Gloria in the original series, but in this version she was Frances (as she had been in the original play and movie).

Other sitcoms on Telma's impressive résumé include *Gimme a Break*, *Family Matters*, *The Hughleys*, *Half-and-Half*, and a memorable co-starring role alongside Cindy Williams in *Getting By*.

Marilyn Horne

Guest starred in "Vocal Girl Makes Good" (as Jackie Hartman). Marilyn Horne was born January 16, 1934, in Bradford, Pennsylvania. She moved to Los Angeles with her family when she was 11, and before long she knew what she was meant to do—sing opera. She studied voice at the University of Southern California School of Music. One of her big breaks came when she was discovered by Igor Stravinsky, who invited her to sing in Europe.

Years later she became a regular at the Met, and *Carmen* made her famous. In fact, in *The Odd Couple* episode she portrays a shy opera singer named Jackie with a crush on Oscar Madison. With his encouragement, she is eventually coaxed into performing in Felix's opera group's production of *Carmen*.

Horne was wed to African American conductor Henry Jay Lewis from 1960 until 1979. At that time in history, interracial marriages raised many eyebrows. She was awarded the National Medal of Arts in 1999, and she performed at Tony Randall's funeral in 2004.

Joan Hotchkis

Guest starred as Dr. Nancy Cunningham in 11 episodes in 1971: "Lovers Don't Make House Calls," "You've Come a Long Way Baby," "What Makes Felix Run?," "Trapped," "Natural Childbirth," "Felix's Wife's Boyfriend," "Hospital Mates," "Sleepwalker," "A Grave for Felix," "Fat Farm," and "Felix the Calypso Singer." She was born September 21, 1927, in Los Angeles, to Preston and Katherine Hotchkis. Her mother came from a family of cattle ranchers. Joan began her acting career in the 1950s during which time she studied with the great Lee Strasberg. Her first regular series role came in 1969 in the much lauded, Emmy Award–winning (but low-rated) *My World and Welcome to It*. The NBC series, based upon the writings and drawings of James Thurber, starred William Windom.

A short time after the cancellation of *My World and Welcome to It*, Hotchkis appeared as Dr. Nancy Cunningham in an episode titled "Lovers Don't

Make House Calls," in which she makes a house call for a feverish Felix, but quickly becomes the romantic interest for Oscar Madison because of their shared passion for hockey and boxing.

At last report, Hotchkis was the CEO of Tearsheets Productions, Inc., in Santa Monica, California. She also has worked part-time as a paraprofessional in aggression training at the Institute of Group Psychotherapy in California. She has one child, a girl.

CLINT HOWARD

Guest starred in "The Big Brothers" (as Randy Grainger). Clinton Howard was born on April 20, 1959, into a show-business family, consisting of his father, actor Rance, mother Jean, and older brother, Ronny. Clint made a few appearances on *The Andy Griffith Show*, as Leon, but his first regular role came in the short-lived sitcom *The Baileys of Balboa*, in which he played Stanley. Then came the role of Balok on the original *Star Trek* (in the episode titled "The Corbomite Maneuver"), and subsequent roles in *Star Trek: Deep Space Nine* and *Star Trek: Enterprise*. He may be best known to many as Dennis Weaver's son, Mark Wedloe, on the popular *Gentle Ben* series.

On *The Odd Couple*, in an episode from the first season titled "The Big Brothers," Felix and Oscar become part-time big brothers to a fatherless young man named Randy Grainger, played by Clint. The idea of taking care of the boy was Felix's idea, but the young man greatly favors hanging out with Oscar (leading to some jealousy from Felix).

Clint Howard's credits run a mile long, with many small roles in his brother Ron's films, such as *Splash* (1984), *Cocoon* (1985), *Gung Ho* (1986), *Parenthood* (1989), *Backdraft* (1991), *Apollo 13* (1995), *How the Grinch Stole Christmas* (2000), and *Cinderella Man* (2005). Clint is an avid golfer, and has been married to his second wife, Melanie, since 1995.

BARNARD HUGHES

Co-starred in *The Odd Couple II* (as Beaumont). Barnard Hughes was born July 16, 1915, in Bedford Hills, New York. He began his acting career with the Shakespeare Fellowship Repertory Company in New York City, and appeared in their productions of *Hamlet* and *Much Ado About Nothing*. His biggest successes were on Broadway—*Prelude to a Kiss*, and especially *Da*.

Hughes found a lot of work in television, beginning with guest-starring roles on *The Phil Silvers Show*, *Car 54, Where Are You?*, *The Defenders*, *All in the Family*, and *The Bob Newhart Show*. Hughes also had several short-lived series of his own—*Doc*, *Mr. Merlin*, and *The Cavanaughs*.

His motion picture credits include *Midnight Cowboy* (1969, which really put him on the map), *Cold Turkey* (1971), *Oh God* (1977), *Doc Hollywood* (1991), *Sister Act 2: Back in the Habit* (1993), and *The Odd Couple II* (1998). In the latter, he portrayed a wealthy man named Beaumont, who just happened to be on his way to San Molina, California, where Felix and Oscar were headed—the site of their children's wedding. However, during the excruciatingly slow drive to their destination, Beaumont dies behind the wheel, leaving *The Odd Couple* stranded.

Barnard Hughes died on July 11, 2006, only a few days shy of his 91st birthday.

JILL JARESS

Guest starred in "My Strife in Court" on the original series (as Beth Olam), and in *The New Odd Couple* episode titled "The Hustler" (as Vivian). Actress Jill Jaress was born June 20, 1947. Jaress has an impressive résumé of guest appearances in TV sitcoms: *Love, American Style*, *The Bob Newhart Show*, *Rhoda*, *Benson*, and *Taxi* were among her early credits.

Jaress guest starred in both TV versions of *The Odd Couple* series. It's interesting that she didn't reprise her role as Beth in "My Strife in Court" on *The New Odd Couple*. Instead, she guest starred on another of the reworked episodes, "The Hustler." Currently, she writes, directs and produces her own family-friendly films for her own company, "Got a Laugh Entertainment." She also coaches and mentors young actors attempting to break into the business.

DEACON JONES

Guest starred in "Felix's First Commercial" (as himself). David D. "Deacon" Jones was born December 9, 1938, in Florida. He went on to play defense for the Rams, Chargers, and Redskins between 1961 and 1974. He gained NFL notoriety for his quarterback sacks and earned the nickname, "The Secretary of Defense." He parlayed his fame into numerous guest-starring roles on TV in such shows as *The Brady Bunch*, *Wonder Woman*, *Bewitched*, and *The Odd Couple*. On the latter he films a shaving commercial in Felix's studio. However, Felix has difficulty obtaining Deacon's cooperation without the assistance and presence of Deacon's good friend, Oscar Madison. Jones also earned a role in Warren Beatty's *Heaven Can Wait* (1978).

Jones was inducted into the Football Hall of Fame in 1980—his first year of eligibility. He reportedly made frequent visits to Iraq to meet with the troops. Jones died on June 3, 2013; he is survived by his wife, Elizabeth, and a stepson, Greg.

CHRISTOPHER JOY

Guest starred in numerous episodes, including "Frances Moves In," "Brother Can You Spare a Job?" and "The Night Stalker" (as Speed on *The New Odd Couple*). Joy later created and wrote an ABC pilot called *My Buddy* for Redd Foxx. He was also the creator of the Leslie Nielsen sitcom, *Shaping Up*. Christopher Joy began as a dancer and actor in Austin, Texas. His first credit was in a short-lived ABC series titled *The New People* from 1969 (a precursor to the wildly successful *Lost*). Joy was very active throughout the 1970s in episodic TV programs, such as *Police*

Christopher Joy, wearing his "Speed" necklace for *The New Odd Couple* (courtesy Christopher Joy).

Story, *The Rookies*, *Delvecchio*, and *Baretta*. He also co-starred in many motion pictures, including *Halls of Anger* (1970), *Hit Man* (1972), *Sheba, Baby* (1975), *Cleopatra Jones* (1973), and *Up in Smoke* (1978). Joy was the lead producer, co-writer and star of *Big Time*—a movie for which Smokey Robinson created the musical score, as well as financed and produced. It was Joy's role in *Up in Smoke*, however, which led to a co-starring role in *The New Odd Couple*. Joy recalls, "A top executive at ABC was watching the movie *Up in Smoke* on TV. I portrayed Curtis in the movie, and that ABC executive took a liking to my work and called casting director Jackie Brown to have me read for the part of Oscar Madison in 1982. I wanted to do the show, but physically I wasn't a big enough guy to play Oscar and I really didn't think I was right for the part. I did, however, get the role of one of the poker players, Speed."

About his co-stars, Joy said, "Ron Glass was cast first before they had an Oscar. Ron was very nice and very open to suggestions and ideas. When they cast Demond Wilson as Oscar, he and I really developed a bond and both of us entered the evangelistic ministry after leaving the entertainment industry."

Joy's take on why *The New Odd Couple* was not a success: "Had they not redone the scripts from the original series, I think we might have been more successful. We needed scripts that better highlighted our chemistry. The cast was frequently involved in changing some of the dialogue to better reflect how an African American male or female would express themselves in certain situations. I must add that Garry Marshall was a pleasure to work for—you'll never hear anything bad about Garry. He was great. Working on the program was great fun."

Evangelistic Dr. Christopher Joy currently lives in Rialto, California. He continues to follow his ministerial calling, traveling worldwide and preaching the good news of the gospel, writing and directing gospel plays, and doing signings for his book, *Rise Up and Step into Your Destiny*.

BO KAPRALL

Guest starred in "The Rain in Spain Falls Mainly in Vain" (as the guy at the bar) and "To Bowl or Not to Bowl" (as Klemble). Robert "Bo" Kaprall was born December 21, 1946, in Chicago, Illinois, and he guest starred on two consecutive episodes of *The Odd Couple* in the fifth and final season. Kaprall recalled, "I was friends with Penny Marshall, and I was called to play a guy who attempts to pick up Penny's Myrna character in the bar scene of an episode titled 'The Rain in Spain Falls Mainly in Vain.'" Harvey Miller directed that

Bo Kaprall guest starred in two episodes of *The Odd Couple* in season five, seen here (left) as Officer Norman Hughes on another Garry Marshall show, *Laverne and Shirley*. Also pictured—Penny Marshall (center top), Cindy Williams (right) and an unnamed stunt double (center bottom) (courtesy Bo Kaprall).

episode and, as Kaprall recalled, "Miller had a very dry sense of humor, and was a bit more elitist than the other directors. He was really good friends with Garry Marshall and Jerry Belson."

Kaprall got a call to come back to the show, and remembered, "They wanted to use me again the following week for an episode titled 'To Bowl or Not to Bowl.' I asked if they wanted the same character as the previous week, but they said I'd be playing a totally different one. In the episode, I'm on a bowling team called the King Pins, but I'm about to get married and will have to miss the big championship game. However, the guys talk me into bowling. Bowling was nothing new, I'd done it before. I wasn't very good, but that wasn't a prerequisite. This episode was directed by Jay Sandrich, and I was in awe of Jay. He was the Jim Burrows of the pre–Jim Burrows era. It was a lot of fun, and the rewrites went on constantly, even when we filmed the pick-ups after the studio audience had gone home. It kept you on your toes."

About Tony Randall, Kaprall remembered, "Tony and I got along very well. He was very nice to me. When I was writing for *The Carol Burnett Show*, Tony was a guest star and it was so great working with him again."

Regarding Garry Marshall, Kaprall said, "Once Garry liked you, he tended to use you over and over again. He was very loyal that way. Apparently he liked me, because I did those two back-to-back *Odd Couple* episodes, and then I later had a recurring role on *Laverne and Shirley* as Officer Norman Hughes."

At the time of the two appearances on *The Odd Couple*, Penny Marshall left the show. Kaprall explained, "She went over to MTM to do *Paul Sand in Friends and Lovers*, and played Paul's sister-in-law. I also worked on that show as the warm-up for the studio audience."

As of this writing, Bo Kaprall writes for *Saturday Night Live* and creates reality shows for such networks as the Discovery Channel and AMC.

Alex Karras

Guest starred in "That Was No Lady." Alexander George Karras was born July 15, 1935, in Gary, Indiana. He had two great careers—first, as a longtime defensive tackle for the Detroit Lions, wearing number 71 on his jersey, from 1958 to 1970. His second career, as an actor, surprised many. He portrayed Mongo in Mel Brooks's hilarious *Blazing Saddles* (1974), and had a long run as George Papadopolis on the sitcom *Webster*.

Karras guest starred in one episode of *The Odd Couple* and portrayed a short-tempered and overtly jealous football player named Jake Metcalfe. In the episode, Felix unknowingly asks Metcalfe's wife out on a date to the opera. In a different episode, "Your Mother Wears Army Boots," Karras is also mentioned, but not seen.

Karras died on October 10, 2012, of kidney failure. He was also suffering from dementia, due to repeated head trauma from his football days. He is survived by six children—five from his first marriage, and one from his second.

Mike Kellin

Co-starred in the original Broadway production (as Oscar Madison). Mike Kellin was born Myron Kellin April 26, 1922, in Hartford, Connecticut, and studied at Boston University and the Yale School of Drama. He became a commander in the navy in World War II, and, upon returning to civilian life, he became an actor. His start on Broadway was in a 1949 show called *At War with the Army*. About this same time, television was beginning to catch fire, and he guest starred on many live shows, such as *Philco Playhouse* and *Studio One*. He also found roles on TV sitcoms, such as the short-lived *Honestly, Celeste* with Celeste Holm, *Mister Peepers* with Wally Cox and Tony Randall, *Bonino* with Ezio Pinza, and *Stanley* with Buddy Hackett.

Kellin was usually cast as a street tough or mobster with a thick, wise-guy New York accent, or a military man, or a cop. He became quite a prolific character actor and found continuous work in episodic TV. He eventually landed a regular role on the TV version of the hit film, *The Wackiest Ship in the Army?* (1960), in which he portrayed CPO Willie Miller. In 1966, he was back on Broadway, replacing Pat Hingle as Oscar Madison.

In 1976, Kellin won an Obie Award for his role in *American Buffalo*. His film credits include *Hell Is for Heroes* (1962), *The Boston Strangler* (1968), *The Great Impostor* (1961), and *Midnight Express* (1978).

Kellin became a prisoners' rights advocate and was very involved in criminal justice throughout the 1970s. He continued to guest star on numerous drama and comedy shows until his passing at the age of 61, from lung cancer, on August 26, 1983, in Nyack, New York.

Dave Ketchum

Guest starred in "Trapped" (as the cop) and "The Fat Farm" (as Jock from the athletic department and food police). David Ketchum was born in Quincy, Illinois, February 4, 1928. A bit of a late bloomer, his first TV credits came in the early 1960s when he was already in his 30s. He starred as Spiffy in the single-season sitcom *Camp Runamuck*, and the majority of his credits (acting, writing, and directing) are for situation comedies. He was quite the multi-tasker. For Leonard Stern, he appeared regularly on *I'm Dickens He's Fenster* and *Get Smart*. On the latter, he portrayed Agent 13, who was usually stationed in the most unusual places, such as cigarette machines, phone booths, fire hydrants, lockers, bowling alley ball returns, and clothes dryers.

For Garry Marshall, Ketchum guest starred on *The Joey Bishop Show*, *Hey, Landlord*, *Mork and Mindy*, *Happy Days*, and *The Odd Couple*. On the latter, he guest starred in one single camera episode ("Trapped") and one very popular multi-camera episode ("The Fat Farm"). He also earned roles in two of Garry Marshall's motion pictures—*Young Doctors in Love* (1982) and, more recently, *The Other Sister* (1999).

Billie Jean King

Guest starred in "The Pig Who Came to Dinner" (as herself). Billie Jean King was born November 22, 1943, in Long Beach, California. She went on to win numerous singles, doubles and mixed-doubles championships. For a time, she was married to Larry King (no, not that one) and concealed her sexual preference for many years.

Among her most memorable matches was "The Battle of the Sexes" with the famous male chauvinist Bobby Riggs. King won that highly publicized match in 1973, and both King and Riggs appeared together as themselves in an episode of *The Odd Couple*. King's appearance was more of a cameo, while Riggs had lines in the entire episode. At the end of the episode, Riggs and King showed off their skills in a game of ping pong. She and Riggs are also mentioned in "The Rain in Spain Falls Mainly in Vain." In recent years, conjecture about Riggs throwing the match to pay off gambling debts have surfaced, but cannot be proven.

King was awarded the Presidential Medal of Freedom by President Barack Obama in 2009 for her work as an advocate for women, and the LGBT community. She was inducted into the Tennis Hall of Fame in 1987, and in 2006, the USTA National Tennis Center in New York was renamed the USTA Billie Jean King National Tennis Center.

Adam Klugman

Guest starred in "Our Fathers" and "Cleanliness Is Next to Impossible" (as Little Oscar). Adam Somers Klugman was born July 11, 1963, in West Linn, Oregon. He is the son of Jack Klugman and Brett Somers. Adam had a role, that of Lewis Madrone, in the popular Matt Dillon and Richard Crenna motion picture, *The Flamingo Kid* in 1984 (written and directed by Garry Marshall, by the way). In Adam's two episodes of *The Odd Couple*, he is seen in flashbacks to show how Felix and Oscar met as children, and to display the origins of Oscar's slovenliness. Adam worked with his dad again on the sitcom *You Again?*, as assistant to the producer, in 1986.

Today, Adam is very active in progressive causes, local elections, ballot measures, and even on the radio. He has a regular program, *Mad As Hell in America with Adam Klugman*, in Portland, Oregon. Speaking of "Mad As Hell," that describes Adam when the Emmy Awards failed to pay proper tribute to his dad in the 2013 Remembrance Segment.

Jack Klugman

Co-starred as Oscar Madison in the original Broadway production, the original TV series, and the 1993 TV reunion movie. Jack Klugman was born April 27, 1922, in Philadelphia, Pennsylvania, to Russian-Jewish immigrants. His boyhood nickname was "Jake." His mother was a milliner, and his father, a house painter. After a stint in the army, Jack studied drama at Carnegie Tech, and then pursued an acting career on stage, eventually working his way into television and movies. Not a matinee idol, his biggest asset was his everyman quality, and he was greatly inspired by the Jackie Cooper/ Wallace Beery film, *The Champ*, from 1931. Among his biggest breaks in film was landing the role of juror number five in Sidney Lumet's *12 Angry Men* in 1957, alongside Henry Fonda and Martin Balsam. In the early 1960s, Klugman guest starred in four memorable episodes of *The Twilight Zone*; he wrote and directed a few episodes of *Kraft Playhouse*; and he won his first Emmy Award, for portraying Joe Larch, on *The Defenders*, in an episode titled "Blacklist" (originally aired January 18, 1964). Klugman's first sitcom was called *Harris Against the World*, and it was part of a 90-minute sitcom block on NBC called *90 Bristol Court*. Coincidentally, Danny Simon (Neil's brother) was the script consultant for the program. Every week, Klugman as Alan Harris was pitted "against" something—his family, his secretary, his housekeeper, and so on. The other shows on the "block" were *Karen*, with Debbie Watson and Richard Denning, and *Tom, Dick and Mary*, with Joyce Bulifant and Don Galloway. All three shows were set in the same development and all three shared the same handyman. Only *Karen* survived beyond the original 13 weeks. At about this same time, Jack received great notices on Broadway for portraying the tough guy Cesario Grimaldi in *Tchin Tchin*, and as Ethel Merman's co-star in *Gypsy* (a role which garnered him a Tony Award). It was that role, incidentally, that first caught the attention of Garry Marshall. Ethel Merman was known to spit a lot when she sang, and Klugman never reacted, not even when standing face to face with his expectorating co-star. That was one of Marshall's gauges for great acting.

In 1965, Klugman replaced Walter Matthau as Oscar Madison on Broadway after Matthau left to film *The Fortune Cookie*. It should be noted that Jack Klugman also directed a 1967 production of *The Odd Couple* at New York's Westbury Music Fair (with Jack Carter as Oscar, and Dick Shawn as Felix). Jack Klugman was then considered for the TV series, but confusion with actor Jack Kruschen delayed the casting of Oscar Madison. Klugman and his new co-star, Tony Randall, had worked together once before, in 1955, on an episode of a summer-replacement show titled *Appointment with Adventure*. When *The Odd Couple* was cast in 1970, Klugman and Randall didn't hit it off very well—Klugman smoked, and Randall hated smoking, but they grew on each other and eventually became lifelong friends. Their friendship blossomed even stronger when the program was cancelled, and especially in their later years of failing health. During the course of the show, Jack and his real-life wife, Brett Somers (she played his ex-wife, Blanche, on the show), separated, but never divorced. Jack and Brett's son, Adam, appeared as "Little Oscar" in two episodes of the sitcom (proving that Oscar was every bit as unkempt and sloppy in his formative years).

Both Randall and Klugman found success beyond *The Odd Couple*— Tony Randall had *The Tony Randall Show* and *Love, Sidney*, and Jack Klugman had the title role on *Quincy, M. E.*, which ran for seven seasons. Klugman took Garry Walberg (Speed on *The Odd Couple*) with him over to the new show.

In 1986, Klugman again tried his luck at a sitcom. The result was a short-lived show titled *You Again?*, with co-star John Stamos. Jack fought a gallant fight with throat cancer in 1989, but lost part of one of his vocal cords in the operation. This left him with a soft, raspy, whispery voice. This was directly addressed in 1993 in a TV reunion movie *The Odd Couple: Together Again*. Felix's daughter, Edna, was getting married, and Oscar was present at the wedding. Also back for the reunion was Penny Marshall as Oscar's former secretary, Myrna Turner, and Garry Walberg as Speed. After this reunion, Randall and Klugman performed the original Neil Simon play on stage in a few very special performances.

Klugman often remarked that he absolutely loved playing Oscar Madison—he said that he could identify with the role. In 2005, Klugman released a tribute book about his friendship with the late Tony Randall, titled *Tony and Me: A Story of Friendship*, from Good Hill Press (with an attached DVD of hilarious *Odd Couple* outtakes). Klugman's final appearances were as Sam on a horror web series titled *Camera Obscura*.

Klugman and Brett Somers, although separated, never official divorced. He only remarried after Somers's death, in 2007. His second wife, Peggy (the former Peggy Crosby, who was married to Bing's son Phil), was at his side when he died on Christmas Eve, 2012, at the age of 90. He is survived by three children—Adam, David, and Leslie—from his marriage to Brett Somers.

Bernie Kopell

Guest starred in "Psychic Shmychic" (as Professor Faraday). Bernard Morton Kopell was born June 21, 1933, in Brooklyn, New York. He attended NYU and majored in dramatic arts. He served in the U.S. Navy, and then drove a taxi until things broke his way. His big break actually occurred in that taxicab. While transporting movie producer Dick Einfeld to his destination, Kopell convinced him that he was a really good actor who was simply between jobs. Einfeld gave him a break with a small role in *The Oregon Trail* in 1958, and he was on his way.

Kopell briefly had a role on a daytime soap opera titled *A Brighter Day*, but his biggest break was his funny recurring guest appearances on *The Steve Allen Show*. He became quite adept at accents, and was cast as Siegfried on *Get Smart*. He suddenly became a very busy performer, and could often be seen in recurring roles on *The Doris Day Show*, *That Girl*, and *Bewitched*. When those shows ended their respective runs, Kopell found steady work on two short-lived sitcoms—*Needles and Pins* and *When Things Were Rotten*. He also managed to squeeze in one guest appearance on *The Odd Couple* in 1972, employing his trademark German accent. In the episode, he attempts to debunk Felix's belief that he possesses psychic powers.

Kopell's biggest break came when he was cast as Doc Adam Bricker on the long-running *The Love Boat* on ABC with Gavin MacLeod. He reprised the role years later on *The Love Boat: The Next Wave* and on an episode of *Martin*. Kopell had a small role in the movie version of *Get Smart* in 2008, and still finds steady work in television, theater, and motion pictures.

CHARLES LANE

Charles Lane guest starred in "Take My Furniture, Please" (as Sid, the bargain hunter). He was born as Charles Levison January 26, 1905, in San Francisco. The bespectacled, unsmiling character actor always appeared much older than he actually was. His credits date back to the very early 1930s, and are ten miles long. He was usually typecast as a cranky boss, banker, judge, or politician. Those who worked with him say that his real-life demeanor was not much different.

Among his myriad film roles were parts in *Arsenic and Old Lace* (1944), *It's a Wonderful Life* (1946), *Mighty Joe Young* (1949), and hundreds more. He had regular, similar roles on TV sitcoms, such as *Dear Phoebe*, *Karen*, *Dennis the Menace*, *The Lucy Show*, and *The Phyllis Diller Show*. On *The Odd Couple* he portrayed Sid, the man who answered Felix and Oscar's ad placed to sell their old furniture in the very funny episode "Take My Furniture, Please."

Lane lived to be 102, dying on July 9, 2007, shortly after receiving a coveted TV Land Award tribute. Longevity ran in his family—his mother lived to be 100.

NATHAN LANE

Portrayed Oscar Madison in a Broadway revival of the original play.

Nathan Lane was born as Joseph Lane in Jersey City, New Jersey, February 3, 1956. He changed his name to Nathan, inspired by Nathan Detroit in *Guys and Dolls*. He caught the acting bug while in high school.

Lane attempted TV success numerous times (*Encore, Encore*, *One of the Boys*, *Charlie Lawrence*), but found his biggest successes both in motion pictures (*The Birdcage* [1996], *The Lion King* [1994]) and on Broadway in *Merlin*, *A Funny Thing Happened on the Way to the Forum*, *Guys and Dolls*, *The Producers*, and numerous Neil Simon vehicles—*Broadway Bound*, *Laughter on the 23rd Floor*, and the revival of *The Odd Couple*. In the latter, Lane was once again teamed with his *Producers* co-star, Matthew Broderick. Lane was Oscar to Broderick's Felix at the Brooks Atkinson Theatre, on West 47th Street in Manhattan, and they enjoyed 249 performances and 28 previews before closing. He has won numerous Tony and Emmy awards, he was inducted into the Theater Hall of Fame, and he has a star on the Hollywood Walk of Fame.

JOHN LARROQUETTE

Portrayed Oscar Madison in a West Coast production of the original play. John Larroquette was born in New Orleans on November 25, 1947. He moved to Hollywood in 1973, having developed a passion for theater. He got his first job a year later—as the narrator for *The Texas Chainsaw Massacre*. His first TV credits were on daytime soap operas. He is, however, best known for his role as Dan Fielding (for which he won four consecutive Emmy Awards) on the long-running NBC sitcom *Night Court*. He also starred in the eponymous and semi-autobiographical *John Larroquette Show*. His motion picture credits include roles in *Stripes* (1981), *Meatballs* (1979), and *Richie Rich* (1994).

In 2002, Larroquette assumed the role of the slovenly Oscar Madison to Joe Regalbuto's finicky Felix Ungar at the Geffen Playhouse in Los Angeles. John is an avid collector of rare books, and as of this writing, his most recent credit is for playing Senator Haverstock on the *Deception* series.

Phil Leeds

Guest starred in "And Leave the Greyhound to Us" (as Salty Pepper), "The Pen Is Mightier Than the Pencil" (as Mr. Katleman), and "The Moonlighter" (as the man at the counter). Character actor Phil Leeds was born April 6, 1916, in New York City. He attended City College of New York, and served in World War II. He began as a peanut vendor, and performed a stand-up comedy act in the Catskill Mountains (in what was known as "The Borscht Belt"). His career stalled when he was blacklisted during the McCarthy era, but eventually got back on track as he became one of the most prolific character actors on TV. His credits include *The Dick Van Dyke Show*, *The Patty Duke Show*, *The Monkees*, *Love, American Style*, and three episodes of *The Odd Couple*. On the latter program he played three different, yet very similar and very funny, characters. Despite his surname, Phil "Leeds" was never a "lead" performer.

Leeds died of pneumonia on August 16, 1998, remaining active and very busy until the end, with guest starring roles on *Maude*, *Barney Miller*, *All in the Family*, *Gimme a Break*, *Cagney and Lacey*, *Night Court*, *The Larry Sanders Show*, *Dave's World*, *Roseanne*, *Boy Meets World*, *Everybody Loves Raymond*, and *Ally McBeal*. He also had roles in several very popular films, such as *Rosemary's Baby* (1968), *Ghost* (1990), and *Beaches* (1988).

Leeds had a great sense of humor about himself, realizing that very few knew his name, but everyone knew his face. When a show or movie needed a funny old man, Leeds was "the go-to guy."

Chris Lemmon

(*Note:* Chris, not a cast member, shares memories of his famous father)

The son of Jack Lemmon and Cynthia Stone, Christopher Boyd Lemmon, was born June 22, 1954, in Los Angeles. It became apparent early on that talent was indeed hereditary. Chris was not only a musical prodigy, he also followed in his parents' footsteps with success in TV and motion pictures.

About his dad's take on playing Felix Ungar in the movies, Chris said, "Pop was Felix Ungar in that he was completely OCD, as am I. We used to go fishing together in Alaska. While everyone else was fishing, we spent all our time straightening up our tackle boxes. When we played golf together at Pebble Beach, he would spend hours laying out his golf outfits on his bed, then sleep on the couch so he didn't disturb them. That's a true story."

What did his dad think of Tony Randall's interpretation of Felix Unger? Chris said, "He loved Tony. We all did. An ultimate gentleman, a great actor, and he gave Felix a completely original spin, which was quite difficult to do after my father's rendition."

About Jack Klugman, Chris reflected, "Jack was a dear friend of mine. He was a fabulous Oscar Madison in the series for the same reasons I said that Tony was great as Felix. Both put such an original spin on their respective roles."

Chris shared a great anecdote from *The Odd Couple* movie, "My favorite *Odd Couple* quote came from Walter Matthau. He approached Neil "Doc" Simon wanting to move a question mark in the dialogue. "Doc" was a stickler for saying every word as written, and asked why. Matthau responded, 'That line is much funnier if you put the question mark in front of the word nuts instead of behind. That way, instead of, 'What are you, nuts? Hangin' out the window,' the line reads, 'What are you? Nuts hangin' out the window?' The joy of punctuation."

One of Chris's best buddies, Joel Zwick, directed most of *The New Odd Couple* episodes and had concerns that the 1982 African American cast would be perceived as a gay couple, to which Chris responded, "I have the utmost respect for Joel as an artist, a friend, and a person. Anyway, if anybody wants to read that into *The Odd Couple*, then let them, but there's plenty of other stuff to be worried about."

How did his dad feel about the movie sequel, 1998's *The Odd Couple II*? Chris replied, "He enjoyed it because he could be with his best buddy, Walter. In my opinion, the original *Odd Couple* could never have been made better, but when Hollywood has a chance to cash in on a franchise like that, it's very difficult to dissuade. Walter truly was my father's best friend. Right after Walter died, my dad took ill, too. He died almost exactly one year to the day after Walter, and I can't help but think part of that was from a broken heart. Honestly, I believe if Walter had ever learned to play golf, Pop would have married him."

Chris Lemmon writes about his dad and their relationship in *A Twist of Lemmon: A Tribute to My Father*, now in paperback from Parade Books.

Jack Lemmon

Co-star of the original 1968 movie, and the 1998 sequel, as Felix Ungar. John Uhler Lemmon, Jr., was born February 8, 1925, in Newton, Massachusetts, in an elevator. Lemmon was an only child—the son of the president of a doughnut company. Young Lemmon taught himself to play the piano by ear and for a while supported himself by playing in piano bars. He attended Harvard, where he was active in numerous drama clubs. After graduation, Lemmon joined the navy near the end of World War II and became an ensign. Coincidentally, Lemmon won his first Oscar playing Ensign Pulver in the 1955 motion picture, *Mister Roberts*.

Before his success in motion pictures, Lemmon and his wife, Cynthia Stone, dabbled in live television. They co-starred in *That Wonderful Guy* on ABC in 1949 (a live sitcom—no episodes have survived), *The Ad-Libbers* on CBS in 1951 (a game show hosted by Peter Donald), and *Heaven for Betsy* on CBS in 1952 (another sitcom). None of these shows were successful, but they were a great training ground for the enthusiastic young actor. He demonstrated his great skills of the acting craft in a long series of silver screen victories: *The Apartment* (1960), *Some like It Hot* (1959), *The Days of Wine and Roses* (1962), *The Wackiest Ship in the Army* (1960), *The Out-of-Towners* (1970), *Under the Yum Yum Tree* (1963), *The Front Page* (1974), *The China Syndrome* (1979), *JFK* (1991), *Glengarry Glen Ross* (1992), and *Grumpy Old Men* (1993). He won his second Oscar for his role in *Save the Tiger* (1973), and first collaborated with Walter Matthau in *The Fortune Cookie* (1966). Lemmon's next film with Matthau was *The Odd Couple* in 1968. Lemmon was nominated for a Golden Globe for his portrayal of Felix Ungar. Thirty years later, Lemmon's Felix and Matthau's Oscar were reunited in *The Odd Couple II*. Jack was approached to star as Felix in the TV version, but stated that he didn't wish to be tied down to a series at that time in his career. He did love the nuances both Randall and Klugman brought to their respective roles and was very impressed at how much they grew in those roles over five seasons.

Before filming any scene, right before the director yelled, "Action," Lemmon was said to always utter the phrase, "Magic time." Lemmon received the AFI Lifetime Achievement Award in 1988. His star on the Hollywood Walk of Fame can be found on Hollywood Boulevard. After a bout with cancer, Jack Lemmon died on June 27, 2001. He is survived by his second wife, Felicia Farr, a daughter, Courtney, and his son Chris.

Frank Loverde

Guest starred in "Felix the Horse Player" (as the hanger-on), "My Strife in Court" (as the policeman), "Surprise Surprise" (as Harry), and "Engrave Trouble" (as man number two). In 1972, Frank Loverde had small roles in a couple of motion pictures—*Evel Knievel* and *Last of the Red Hot Lovers*. Most of his work, however, was in episodic television on programs such as *Love, American Style, Search, The Streets of San Francisco, Fantasy Island, CHiPs, Bret Maverick, The Untouchables,* and *Missing Persons*.

Loverde had small roles in four episodes of *The Odd Couple* TV series, and can be seen in a 1995 short film titled *The White Gorilla*, on which he portrayed a character named Stan.

Allen Ludden

Guest starred in the beloved "Password" episode (as himself). Allen Ludden was born October 5, 1917, in Mineral Point, Wisconsin, as Allen Packard Ellsworth. His mother remarried after the death of his birth father, and he took on his stepfather's surname, Ludden. Allen studied English and theater at the University of Texas. His career in television mostly involved emceeing an array of game shows, such as *GE College Bowl, Stumpers, Liars' Club, Win with the Stars*, and the show for which he is best known, *Password* (in numerous different incarnations on all three networks, including *Password Plus* and *Super Password*). It was while on the original *Password* that Ludden met the actress who would become his second wife, Betty White. Both Ludden and White guest starred as themselves on the most popular episode of *The Odd Couple*.

In the episode, written by fellow game-show host Frank Buxton, Felix and Oscar become teammates on *Password* during a special charity week of shows. Felix's bizarre, obscure clues cause them to lose the game to Betty White and her partner (after which Felix is escorted from the set, kicking and complaining). The episode was rated number five on "*TV Guide's* 100 Greatest Episodes of All-Time," in 1997. Ludden died on June 9, 1981.

Janice Lynde

Guest starred in "Cleanliness Is Next to Impossible" and "Vocal Girl Makes Good" (as Phyllis). Janice Lynde was born March 28, 1948, in Houston, Texas. A very musical young lady, she began her show-business career by playing piano and singing solos for the Dallas Symphony. She studied music at both Indiana University and the University of Pennsylvania. After college, she moved to "the Big Apple," and pursued an acting career. Rather quickly, she was selected as one of the original cast members of *The Young and the Restless*, on CBS. A decade later, she had a nice run in *One Life to Live* as well.

Lynde also made numerous guest appearances on episodic TV shows, such as *Mannix, Medical Center, Barnaby Jones*, and *The Odd Couple*. On the latter, she was a romantic interest for Oscar Madison, although she opted not to let the relationship get too serious due to Oscar's sloppiness. A few years later, Lynde was again paired with Klugman in an episode of *Quincy, M. E.*, titled "Ashes to Ashes," in which she portrayed Tracy.

Lynde remains a busy working actress, and most recently had recurring roles on *Six Feet Under* and *Diary of a Single Mom*.

Guy Marks

Guest starred in "The Odd Candidate" (as Igor). Guy Marks was born Mario Scarpa October 31, 1923, in Philadelphia, the son of a classical clarinet player. Mario was the youngest of 11 children. After a stint in the army and the merchant marines, young Mario turned to performing and changed his name to Guy Marks. He had a natural gift for physical comedy and impressions, and soon became a popular guest on TV variety shows. He eventually landed some short-lived (but very funny) second-banana roles on TV sitcoms, such as *The Joey Bishop Show*, *The John Forsythe Show*, and *Rango* (starring Tim Conway). He even had a hit record called "Loving You Has Made Me Bananas" in 1968— it just missed the Top Fifty.

Marks also made the rounds as a guest star on *The Dean Martin Celebrity Roasts*, and numerous sitcoms such as *The Dick Van Dyke Show*, *The Ghost and Mrs. Muir*, and *The Odd Couple*. On the latter, he portrays Igor in a takeoff on a local east coast TV celebrity named John Zacherle, complete with ghoulish makeup and a coffin from which he emerges to address the TV audience. Coincidentally, Marks's final TV appearance came on another Jack Klugman sitcom, *You Again?*, on which he portrayed a poker player. Marks died on November 28, 1987, from cancer. He was 64.

Marjorie Marshall

Guest starred in "Oscar's Birthday" (as Mrs. Irene Langley) and "Old Flames Never Die" (as Mamie). Although Garry Marshall was not involved in the long-running TV sitcom called *Family Affair*, he turned his workplace into a "family affair." On *The Odd Couple*, Garry's sister Penny Marshall portrayed ditzy Myrna Turner; Garry's father, Tony Marshall, was named the program's producer; Garry's other sister, Ronny, made an uncredited cameo appearance in the episode titled "The Rain in Spain Falls Mainly in Vain"; Garry's brother-in-law Rob Reiner guest starred in that same episode; and Garry's daughter, Lori, played piano in "This Is the Army, Mrs. Madison." Garry's mother, Marjorie Marshall, portrayed Mamie and tap danced in one of the final episodes of *The Odd Couple*, titled "Old Flames Never Die." Marjorie's name at birth was Marjorie Irene Ward. She also portrayed Oscar's old dance teacher in "Oscar's Birthday."

Garry kept the "family affair" going, and brought them over to work on many of his other hit shows, such as *Happy Days* and *Laverne and Shirley*. Marjorie appeared in small roles on both shows.

Penny Marshall

Guest starred in "You Saved My Life," "Gloria Hallelujah," "Big Mouth," "The Odd Monks," "The First Baby," "Oscar's Birthday," "Password," "Sometimes a Great Ocean," "I Gotta Be Me," "Myrna's Debut," "Take My Furniture, Please," "That Was No Lady," "The New Car," "This Is the Army, Mrs. Madison," "Felix Directs," "The Pig Who Came to Dinner," "The Exorcists," "A Barnacle Adventure," "The Moonlighter," "Cleanliness Is Next to Impossible," "The Flying Felix," "Vocal Girl Makes Good," "A Different Drummer," "The Insomniacs," "One for the Bunny," "The Rain in Spain Falls Mainly in Vain," "Two on the Aisle," and the 1993 TV reunion movie, *The*

Odd Couple: Together Again (as Myrna Turner).

Carole Penny Marshall was born October 15, 1943, in the Bronx, New York—coincidentally on the same street Neil Simon was born. The Carole part was inspired by actress Carole Lombard, but she was never referred to as Carole, just Penny. Penny is the sister of Garry Marshall and Ronny Hallin. She attended the University of New Mexico and majored in psychology. Early in her career, Penny had a small role in a film directed by Jerry Paris, *How Sweet It Is!* (1968), and then in *The Grasshopper* (1970), which was written by Garry Marshall and Jerry Belson. She also worked with Jerry Davis on two episodes of *That Girl*, with Marlo Thomas. It was thought that she should become a stand-up comic, but being on the road alone was not her idea of fun. Then Penny was given a guest shot on an episode ("The Runner") of the Michael Parks series *Then Came Bronson*. Also guest starring on this episode was Jack Klugman. Garry had seen Klugman in *Gypsy*, and knew that he would be the ideal Oscar Madison. He told Penny to ask Jack if he'd like to play Oscar in the upcoming ABC TV version of *The Odd Couple*. Eventually, Penny would become a semi-regular on the show, playing Myrna Turner, the inept, slow-talking, nasal secretary with the most unique laugh, in 27 episodes. That laugh came about quite by accident. During a run-through, the script called for Myrna to laugh and Penny threw in a nasal 'heh, heh, heh,' and the die was cast. She hadn't worked on a three-camera show before, but Klugman (who recommended her for the role) took her under his wing and guided her through the new experience. Early on in her career, she steadied her nerves by stringing together and uttering a list of the dirtiest words she could think of before entering a scene. Penny stayed with the program until the first episode of season five, "The Rain in Spain Falls Mainly in Vain." In that episode, Penny marries her boyfriend Sheldn (they forgot the "O" on his birth certificate), portrayed by her real-life husband, Rob Reiner. Penny left *The Odd Couple* when she was refused a $100-a-week raise. She was quickly snatched up by Jim Brooks for a larger role in the MTM sitcom, *Paul Sand in Friends and Lovers*. Unfortunately, that program failed to catch on.

Penny briefly moved on to another MTM show, *The Mary Tyler Moore Show*, as Paula, the neighbor in Mary's new apartment building, but Penny had to leave that show when *Laverne and Shirley* came about. She couldn't possibly have known how big this new venture would be. After being introduced on *Happy Days*, *Laverne and Shirley* debuted at number one in the ratings and had a tumultuous seven-year run on ABC. It wasn't exactly the happiest set on the Paramount lot.

After hanging up Laverne DeFazio's "L" (which adorned seemingly every sweater she wore), Penny Marshall became a very successful director at the urging of her friend Whoopi Goldberg. Among the highlights of her directorial career are *Jumpin' Jack Flash*

(1986), *Awakenings* (1990), *A League of Their Own* (1992), and *Big* (1988).

In 1993, Penny reprised her role as Myrna Turner on the TV reunion movie titled *The Odd Couple: Together Again*, in which Myrna winds up getting her own advice column for Oscar's newspaper. Just like in the old days, Myrna still referred to Oscar as "Mr. M."

Penny's most recent credits as a director are for TV shows such as *According to Jim* and *The United States of Tara*, and as a producer for the motion pictures *Cinderella Man* (2005) and *Bewitched* (2005). Her company is called Parkway Productions, and her autobiography, *My Mother Was Nuts: A Memoir*, was published by Houghton Mifflin Harcourt. She has completely recovered from a 2009 cancer scare. She is an avid fan of the NBA and frequents both Los Angeles Lakers and Clippers games. She is the grandmother of three (her daughter Tracy's children), Bella, Spencer, and Viva.

BARNEY MARTIN

Guest starred in "The Jury Story" (as Mr. Moss) and "The Subway Story" (as man number three). Barney Martin was born March 3, 1923, in Queens, New York. After serving in the U.S. Air Force, Martin became a police officer. As a sideline, Martin wrote comedy for Steve Allen, and the original TV version of *Name That Tune*. He kicked off his onscreen career as a police officer in an episode of *The Phil Silvers Show*. He was also in the original 1975 production of *Chicago* as Amos Hart, and introduced the song, *Mr. Cellophane* (of which he was immensely proud).

Martin appeared in numerous TV commercials, and found many roles on episodic TV shows such as *Car 54, Where Are You?*, *The Patty Duke Show*, and *Jackie Gleason's American Scene Magazine*. In fact, because Gleason didn't like to rehearse, Barney Martin was his frequent stand-in so that Audrey Meadows, Art Carney, and Joyce Randolph could rehearse. In the late 1960s, Martin earned parts in some popular films, including Mel Brooks's *The Producers*, and Cliff Robertson's *Charly*.

Martin guest starred on two episodes of *The Odd Couple*. Coincidentally, he and Tony Randall co-starred in 44 episodes of *The Tony Randall Show*, from 1976 to 1978, and, like "The Jury Story" episode, it, too, took place in a courtroom.

Martin's most famous role was as Jerry Seinfeld's father on *Seinfeld*. Because of the role many people assumed Martin was Jewish, but he was Irish Catholic. Just days after his 82nd birthday, Barney Martin died of lung cancer in Studio City, California, on March 21, 2005.

MARLYN MASON

Guest starred in "They Use Horseradish Don't They?" (as Béarnaise Barbara), and "Don't Believe in Roomers" (as Lisa). Often mistakenly called "Marilyn," Marlyn Mason was born August 7, 1940, in California's San Fernando Valley. She made her first TV appearance at the age of nine, and throughout the 1960s she guest starred on dozens of popular TV programs, including *The Real McCoys*, *My Three Sons*, *Gomer Pyle, USMC*, and *Hogan's Heroes*.

She also guest starred in two episodes of *The Odd Couple*. About the experience, Mason said, "Garry Marshall was great fun to work with. He had a wonderful sense of humor and a calm demeanor. Many years later, I did a microscopic scene (four words) with Kate Hudson in *Raising Helen*, which Garry directed. I'm ninety-nine percent sure he didn't remember me."

About *The Odd Couple*'s lead actors, Mason recalled, "Jack Klugman was great to work with. A sweet man, utterly professional. Tony, on the other hand, was rude, insulting, and intimidating. On the 'They Use Horseradish, Don't They?' episode, at the table read, Tony turned to me and said, 'You don't speak properly.' I should have told him where to shove it, but I chose to ignore it. In the second episode, 'Don't Believe in Roomers,' the director changed the blocking and told me to move in another direction. Tony, unaware of it, yelled at me and stomped off in a rage. As I burst into tears, the head cameraman consoled me and said, 'Oh, Marlyn, he does that with all the women.' That helped, but not much."

"Don't Believe in Roomers" was a reworking of an episode of Garry Marshall's *Hey, Landlord* called "Same Time, Same Station, Same Girl" (on which Marlyn Mason also guest starred).

Mason calls working with Elvis Presley in *The Trouble with Girls* in 1969,

The lovely Marlyn Mason guest starred in two episodes of *The Odd Couple*—"They Use Horseradish, Don't They?" and "Don't Believe in Roomers" (courtesy Marlyn Mason).

"A career highlight—one hilarious ten-week ride. Elvis and I worked alike, and I loved him—everyone did." She still makes guest appearances at many Elvis fan club events and Elvis cruises, mostly in January (for his birthday) and August (for the anniversary of his passing).

Charlie Matthau

(Note: Charlie, not a cast member, shares memories of his famous father)

Walter Matthau's son, Charles Marcus Matthau, was born December 10, 1962, in New York City. He attended the University of Southern California and was named Charles after Charlie Chaplin—a friend of the family (and the young Matthau's godfather). Charles

Matthau began as a child actor, and got to work with his dad in great films such as *The Bad News Bears* (1976) and *House Calls* (1978). He worked with both his dad and Jack Lemmon in *The Grass Harp* (Charlie directed the film, and portrayed one of the barbershop regulars). Charlie said, "That was an amazing, unforgettable experience. It was so much fun, and I'll always treasure the experience."

In his pre–*Odd Couple* days, Walter met Neil Simon at a party, and as Charlie recalled, "Neil told my dad that he'd written a play for him called *The Odd Couple*, and he told my dad he wanted him to play Oscar Madison. So, Dad read the play and loved it, but told Simon that he wanted to play Felix instead, but Neil knew best." In many ways, Walter was like Oscar Madison, but as Charlie remembered, "He had a lot of Felix in him, too. He was a neatness and cleanliness freak. He wasn't a slob. He was always wiping down the telephone with rubbing alcohol before using it."

When the original Broadway production of *The Odd Couple* opened on March 10, 1965, Art Carney portrayed the fastidious Felix Ungar, and Charlie stated, "Carney was going through a kind of lost period in his life—he had a lot on his mind at that time. My dad got really good reviews as Oscar, and I think that may have caused a little bit of friction between them. However, they did get along just fine, and got to work together again a few years later in *House Calls*."

In the 1968 motion picture version of *The Odd Couple*, Walter was back as Oscar Madison and paired with his former *Fortune Cookie* co-star, Jack Lemmon. Walter received better notices than Jack (Oscar and Felix, respectively). Charlie said, "Even though Jack was a bigger star at this time, he generously said that it was about time my dad got recognition. They were such good friends, and every time they worked together it was like a party." It's fitting that Matthau mentions putting on a recording of Mozart in the film (right before the Pigeon Sisters enter), because, in real life, he was a huge Mozart fan.

About the TV adaptation of *The Odd Couple*, Charlie said, "Dad didn't really watch it much. He was so busy at that time. He never really said anything about it. That's one of the ways he was most like the Oscar character—he was very easygoing." Initially, Walter missed crossing paths with Tony Randall in the pilot episode of *Mister Peepers* in 1952 (Randall was added when it became a series, but Matthau was only in the pilot). But, as Charlie Matthau reflected, "They worked together in 1963 in the Warner Bros. comedy, *Island of Love*. Of course, neither had any idea that they would each play an important role in a legendary Neil Simon work a few years later."

About the 1998 movie sequel, *The Odd Couple II*, Charlie shared, "My father was diagnosed with colon cancer in December of 1995 and it spread to his liver. He wasn't given much of a chance for a full recovery, but he beat it. At the time the sequel was filmed, he had beaten the cancer and it was not recurring. The combination of that good news, and working again with his best friend, Jack Lemmon, made that a great time in his life."

Charlie Matthau is currently married to a dancer named Ashley, and his most recent project, a film titled *Freaky Deaky*, premiered at the Tribeca Film Festival, in 2012, to rave reviews. As far as words of wisdom imparted by his famous father, Charlie said, "When I was getting into the business, he told me that the definition of a director is a guy who's out of work. For that reason I tried to learn every aspect of the industry. Words of wisdom, indeed."

WALTER MATTHAU

Co-starred in the original Broadway production, the original motion picture, and the 1998 sequel (as Oscar Madison). Walter Matthau (nicknamed "Waltz") was born Walter Matthow October 1, 1920, in the Lower East Side of Manhattan. Unlike his frequent future co-star and friend, Jack Lemmon, who was born into a wealthy family, Matthau's family was not well-heeled. The name Matthow later sparked a rumor that his birth name was Matuschanskayasky, and he got a lot of mileage out of it. As Walter's son, Charlie, recalled, "That name came about when my father had a small role (the bar scene) in the movie, *Earthquake* [1974] and he was listed as Walter Matuschanskayasky. It's amazing how it took on a life of its own."

After serving in the U.S. Air Force during World War II, Matthau took acting classes at the famous Dramatic Workshop of the New School. Among his earliest credits is a one-shot guest appearance on the live sitcom, *Mister Peepers*, on NBC in 1952. Matthau portrayed the gym teacher, Coach Burr (credited as David Tyrell) in the pilot, which was simply called *Peepers*. Coincidentally, Tony Randall portrayed teacher Harvey Weskitt in the series. Matthau had a role in one of Elvis Presley's better films, *King Creole*, in 1958, and in that same year was nominated for a Tony Award for his role as Maxwell Archer in *Once More, with Feeling*. Matthau also began to solidify his star status with great performances in such films as *Lonely Are the Brave* (1962), *Charade* (1963), and *Mirage* (1965), in the early- to middle-1960s. In 1961, he was also the star of a short-lived syndicated crime show, *Tallahassee 7000*, as Lex Rogers.

His biggest break came in 1965 when he was cast as the original Oscar Madison in Neil Simon's *The Odd Couple* (directed by Mike Nichols). The play opened at the Plymouth Theater, with Art Carney as Felix Ungar. Matthau won a Tony for his portrayal of the lovable slob. The play moved to the Eugene O'Neill Theatre during its run, and, when Matthau suffered a heart attack, he was replaced by Jack Klugman. However, when it came time for the motion picture version, Matthau was back in the role he originated. Matthau would also earn roles in other Neil Simon motion pictures, including *Plaza Suite* (1971), *California Suite* (1978), *The Sunshine Boys* (1975), *I Ought to Be in Pictures* (1982), and *The Odd Couple II* (1998).

Some of Matthau's favorite roles

were those in which he got to perform with his best friend, Jack Lemmon. It has been said that the two gentlemen never had a cross word. They worked together in *Grumpy Old Men* (1993), *Grumpier Old Men* (1995), *Out to Sea* (1997), *Buddy Buddy* (1981), *The Front Page* (1975), *The Odd Couple* (1968), *The Odd Couple II* (1998), and *The Fortune Cookie* (1966). The latter garnered Matthau his only Oscar, but, strangely enough, he didn't win one for portraying Oscar. In *The Grass Harp* in 1995, Matthau and Lemmon were directed by Walter's son, Charles. Many credit Walter with opening the door in the industry for those who didn't possess traditional good looks.

Even though Walter Matthau made a life change after his first heart scare in 1966, he suffered another attack in 2000, in Santa Monica, California, and died on July 1, at the age of 79. Almost exactly a year later, his best friend, Jack Lemmon, passed away from cancer. Even though their wives didn't always see eye-to-eye, Jack and Waltz remained best buddies to the end. Their remains are buried in the same cemetery.

RYAN MCDONALD

Guest starred in "The Laundry Orgy," "Felix Gets Sick," "The Breakup," "Oscar's Ulcer," "Felix Is Missing," "Scrooge Gets an Oscar," and "The Blackout" (as Roy). Ryan McDonald was born September 4, 1930, in "The City of Brotherly Love," Philadelphia, Pennsylvania (also the home of Jack Klugman). Not to be confused with the young Canadian actor of the same name, nor the rugby player of that name, Ryan McDonald portrayed tall, bespectacled Roy, Oscar's accountant and one of the poker players in season one of *The Odd Couple*. After Roy left the show, he wasn't replaced (however, Vinnie, Speed and Murray remained).

Among his numerous other sitcom credits, McDonald appeared on *Empty Nest*, *The Facts of Life*, *Newhart*, *Carter Country*, *Here's Lucy*, *The Doris Day Show*, and *Nanny and the Professor*. He has also appeared on numerous soap operas, including *General Hospital* and *The Young and the Restless*, as well as the popular mini-series *Rich Man, Poor Man*. On Broadway, McDonald appeared in *Any Wednesday*, *Toys in the Attic*, and *Catch Me if You Can*.

DINA MERRILL

Guest starred in "Oscar in Love" (as Anita, the harpist). Dina Merrill was born Nedenia Marjorie Hutton December 9, 1925. She is the only child of the Post Cereal heiress, Marjorie Post, and the daughter of Wall Street broker E. F. Hutton. Much to her parents' dismay, she quit college because of the urge to perform. After some work on Broadway, she earned her first film role with Spencer Tracy and Katharine Hepburn in *Desk Set* (1957). Then came *Operation Petticoat* (1959), *The Courtship of Eddie's Father* (1963), and *BUtterfield 8* (1960).

Merrill's TV credits are plentiful, mostly on dramatic programs, such as *Dr. Kildare*, *12 O'Clock High*, *Bonanza*, *The FBI*, and *Marcus Welby, M. D.* She did, however, occasionally take a crack at comedy, as on *The Love Boat*, *Batman* (as Calamity Jan), and *The Odd Couple*. On an episode of the latter, Merrill appeared as Oscar's bride-to-be (with two young children who didn't immediately cotton to Oscar). She also did a guest shot on Klugman's next series, *Quincy, M. E.* (as Claire in the episode "Who's Who in Neverland").

Merrill's second of three marriages was to actor Cliff Robertson, who died on September 10, 2011. As of this writing, Dina Merrill is still married to Ted Hartley.

JAMES MILLHOLLIN

Guest starred in "It's all over now, Baby Bird" (as Mr. Humus), "The Princess" (as the barber), and "New York's Oddest" (as hiccup man). James Millhollin was born August 23, 1915, in Peoria, Illinois. He made his mark playing dour-faced, fidgety, nervous clerks or administrators. A late bloomer, Millhollin's first credits date back to 1954, when he was almost 40. His big break came in 1958 when he was selected to portray Royal B. Demming in the big-screen version of *No Time for Sergeants*, opposite Andy Griffith. He then began to make guest appearances on many TV sitcoms, including *The Many Loves of Dobie Gillis*, *My Favorite Martian*, *The Dick Van Dyke Show*, *Green Acres*, *Get Smart*, *That Girl*, *The Beverly Hillbillies*, *The Brady Bunch* and those three memorable episodes of *The Odd Couple*. He also had a regular role as employment agent Anson Foster on the Screen Gems single-season sitcom *Grindl*, starring Imogene Coca, in 1963.

Millhollin died on May 23, 1993, at the age of 77, in Biloxi, Mississippi.

SHIRLEY MITCHELL

Guest starred in "Cleanliness Is Next to Impossible" (as Alice, the receptionist). Mitchell was born November 4, 1919, in Toledo, Ohio. She attended the University of Toledo, and, later, the University of Michigan. After moving to Los Angeles, Mitchell got her start on the radio versions of *The Life of Riley*, *The Great Gildersleeve*, and *Fibber McGee and Molly*. She also scored roles in motion pictures, such as *Desk Set* (1957), *Because They're Young* (1960), and *The War of the Roses* (1989).

However, Mitchell is best known for her historic run on TV sitcoms—especially *I Love Lucy*, on which she portrayed Marion Strong. For a long time, she and Richard Keith (Little Ricky) were the only surviving cast members. Among the other highlights of her prolific TV career are *I Married Joan*, *The Real McCoys*, *Leave It to Beaver*, *Bachelor Father*, *The Adventures of Ozzie and Harriet*, *The Jack Benny Program*, *Make Room for Daddy*, *The Dick Van Dyke Show*, *Petticoat Junction*, *My Three Sons*, *Green Acres*, and *The Odd Couple*. On the latter she portrayed Alice, the receptionist for wacky Dr. Bates. When she and the doctor bicker and berate one another in the waiting room, Felix and Oscar decide to exit the office without seeing Bates. Mitchell would be used again a few years later in another Mark Rothman/Lowell Ganz sitcom called *Makin' It*, in the episode "The Art Auction."

In 1992, Mitchell married composer Jay Livingston, who, with Ray Evans, wrote "Silver Bells," "To Each His Own," "Tangerine," "Que Sera Sera (Whatever Will Be, Will Be)," and "Tammy," as well as the theme songs for TV's *Mister Ed* and *Bonanza*. Livingston and Evans also composed the music for a Broadway show called *Oh, Captain*, which starred Tony Randall as Captain Henry St. James, in 1958. Jay Livingston died October 17, 2001; he was 86.

Shirley Mitchell was seen most recently in an episode of *Desperate Housewives*, and was heard on an episode of the animated *Mad* series. Sadly, Mitchell died only a week after her 94th birthday, on November 11, 2013.

AL MOLINARO

Co-starred in 73 episodes from "The Laundry Orgy" (episode one) to "Felix Remarries" (episode 114) as Murray. Albert Francis Molinaro was born June 24, 1919, in Kenosha, Wisconsin, one of ten children. The big, Italian family moved to California in the early 1950s, and it was there that Al earned money as a musician (he got to play for real in Felix Unger's band, the Sophisticatos, on the series) and by starting his own collection agency. After a long time struggling in the business he found his first success in television in a couple of episodes of *Get Smart* as Agent 44, and then as a Jewish cop named Murray on *The Odd Couple*.

Garry Marshall discovered Molinaro doing improv onstage. His character's name, Murray, took on the surname Greshler—influenced by Abbey Greshler, who was Tony Randall and Jack Klugman's agent. ABC was against hiring Molinaro for the role (they thought he was too silly), but Garry was insistent and eventually got his way. As a policeman, Murray had almost no arrests, wasn't very aggressive, and had a rather pronounced proboscis, which was sometimes shown poking through the peephole of Felix and Oscar's apartment 1102 (and was the source of much ridicule). Murray had a wife, Mimi, played at various times, by Alice Ghostley and Jane Dulo. Molinaro's portrayal of Murray was quite different from Herb Edelman's approach in the movie version. Molinaro played him as a sweet, rather naïve guy.

Al was also offered the role of the owner of the drive-in on *Happy Days*, but he turned it down (Pat Morita ultimately took the role). When Morita left for his own series, the ill-fated *Mr. T. and Tina*, Al was his heir apparent, and this time he accepted. His character was named Al, and he was Italian (his last name was Delvecchio). He was fond of saying, "Yep, yep, yep, yep, yep" in place of a sigh when things weren't going well. He only intended to stay on for a season or two, but the show was such a success he continued to play Al in a total of 146 episodes of *Happy Days*, and 17 episodes of its spinoff, *Joanie Loves Chachi*.

Molinaro had a regular role in one more series in 1990—*Family Man*, starring Gregory Harrison. Molinaro portrayed another Italian, Joe Alberghetti, in this single-season sitcom. Another pilot starring Molinaro, *The Ugily Family*, was not sold. Except for commercials for On-Cor frozen dinners, Cortaid, Westbank, and Mr. Big toilet tissue, Molinaro all but retired from acting at this point in his career. He and his *Happy Days* co-star Anson Williams opened a chain of diners called "Big Al's." He reprised his role of Al Delvecchio for a music video for the song "Buddy Holly" by Weezer. As of this writing, he is a nonagenarian and lives in Glendale, California, with his second wife, Betty.

George Montgomery

Guest starred in "The Hollywood Story" (as Griff). George Montgomery Letz was born the youngest of 15 children August 27, 1916, in Brady, Montana. His major at the University of Montana was architecture, but his interest in boxing caused him to leave the school early. Shortly thereafter, he spent several years as a movie stuntman and came to the attention of 20th Century–Fox Studios, and was cast in numerous westerns. Likely, his most famous film role came when he was cast as Sergeant Duquesne in *The Battle of the Bulge* in 1965. He was also quite the ladies' man, and at one time or another was involved with the likes of Ginger Rogers, Dinah Shore (to whom he was married for 20 years), and Hedy Lamarr (to whom he was once engaged).

During the early days of live television, Montgomery guest starred on many of the anthology dramas of the day, such as *Studio One*, *Ford Television Theater*, and *GE True Theater*. He then landed a recurring role on an NBC-TV western called *Cimarron City*, as Mayor Matt Rockford. The series only lasted one season, so Montgomery returned to guest starring on episodic TV. After appearances on *Bonanza*, *Hawaiian Eye*, *Alias Smith and Jones*, and *The Six Million Dollar Man*, he took a stab at comedy on *The Odd Couple*. Montgomery portrayed the star of a film called *Home Run Kid*, about an aging baseball professional. (Oscar has a cameo role.)

Montgomery's original college major, architecture, served him well in his retirement years, as he became a devotee of furniture making and sculpting. For a time, he was the TV spokesman for Pledge furniture polish. On December 12, 2000, George Montgomery died of heart failure; he was 84.

Rita Moreno

Portrayed the slovenly Olive Madison in *The Female Odd Couple*, onstage, in 1985. Rita Moreno was born Rosito Alverio December 11, 1931, in Puerto Rico. Moreno is the surname of her stepfather. She wanted to be a dancer from a very young age, and by the time she was 13, she was performing on Broadway in *Skydrift*. She is probably best known for her portrayal of Anita in *West Side Story*. She won a Best Supporting Actress Oscar for her performance in the 1961 film adaptation.

Moreno has the rare distinction of having won a Tony (*The Ritz*), an Oscar (*West Side Story*), a Golden Globe (*West Side Story*), two Emmys (*The Rockford Files*, *The Muppet Show*) and a Grammy (*The Electric Company Album*).

In 1985, Moreno portrayed the disheveled Olive Madison to Sally Struthers's finicky Florence Ungar in Neil Simon's *The Female Odd Couple* at the Ahmanson Theater on West Temple Street, in Los Angeles, and, later, at the Broadhurst Theatre on West 44th Street, in Manhattan. The two actresses had previously worked on Broadway together in *Wally's Café*, in 1981.

She also starred in an unsold sitcom pilot called *The Rita Moreno Show*, from Mark Rothman and Lowell Ganz, who were head writers for the TV sitcom version of *The Odd Couple*. She got a couple of seasons out of the TV sitcom version of the hit motion picture, *Nine to Five*. As of this writing, Moreno's most recent TV role was that of Dori, on *Happily Divorced*, on the TV Land cable network.

JAYE P. MORGAN

Guest starred in "The Songwriter" (as herself). Mary Margaret Morgan was born December 3, 1931, into a large family (five brothers and one sister) in Mancos, Colorado. She began performing at the age of three, and the family's move to Los Angeles benefitted her career greatly. She went on to have a long string of hit singles, such as "That's All I Want from You," "The Longest Walk," and "Life Is Just a Bowl of Cherries." Her name was inspired by the famous banker J. P. Morgan, and she became a regular on TV on *Stop the Music* and the eponymous *Jaye P. Morgan Show*.

One of her most memorable TV appearances came in season four of *The Odd Couple*. In the episode, "The Songwriter," Felix was determined to write a song for Jaye P. Morgan, who was dating Oscar at the time, and the result was a silly-but-memorable composition titled "Happy and Peppy and Bursting with Love." Ms. Morgan recalled, "The show's talented writers came up with the tune. It was very funny and very silly. Believe it or not, for many, many years afterward, I got requests to perform it in concert. That really shows you the reach of that show."

About the experience, Ms. Morgan said, "Garry Marshall was extremely

Jaye P. Morgan, feeling "Happy and Peppy" in "The Songwriter," on *The Odd Couple* (courtesy the Mike Donaldson Collection).

nice to me. Jack Klugman and his wife, Brett Somers, were wonderful, too—so kind, so sweet, so considerate. Tony Randall was quite a bit like his character—he had a temper and could be a little bit short with you, but, once we got rolling, he was fine. I made a concerted effort not to look at Tony while I performed 'Happy and Peppy and Bursting with Love' on the show, because he talks and moves around a lot throughout my performance in that scene and I didn't want to be distracted. I don't think he liked Wolfman Jack, who was also a guest on that episode. Wolfman was a chain smoker, and Tony hated when anyone smoked around him. The one person with whom I had a problem was the director, Mel Ferber. He was very pushy, and I never let anyone push me around. The problem was they kept changing the dialogue right up until the day we shot the show. Ferber was very impatient with me, yelling things like, 'Why can't you learn your lines? I wish you could learn your lines.' Other than that, it was a whole lot of fun."

The clean-cut singer we knew in the 1950s reinvented herself in the 1970s with more of a bawdy persona, exhibited on popular game shows, such as *Rhyme and Reason*, hosted by Bob Eubanks, and especially on *The Gong Show*, and even *The Gong Show Movie*, with the show's producer/host, Chuck Barris.

Pat Morita

Guest starred in "Partner's Investment" (as Mr. Wing/Mr. Yamata).

Noriyuki Morita was born June 28, 1932, in Isleton, California. A spinal defect in childhood kept him in a body cast for long periods of time. He was told that he might never walk, but he bravely defied the odds. He began his career in show business as a stand-up comic. Redd Foxx saw him perform his comedy routine, liked him, and used him on several episodes of *Sanford and Son*. However, Morita's first regular role was on the short-lived Larry Storch/Billy DeWolfe sitcom titled *The Queen and I*, in 1968, on which Morita portrayed Barney. The program was cancelled after 13 weeks, and Morita spent the next several years guest starring in episodic TV programs, such as *Green Acres*, *McCloud*, *Blondie*, and *The Odd Couple*. In the latter, he portrayed the owner of a Japanese restaurant in which Felix and Oscar were investing (after a big win at the racetrack). Morita also owned a restaurant in his next role on a Garry Marshall show—Arnold's Drive-In, on *Happy Days*. In his later years, coincidentally, in 2003 Morita briefly portrayed Felix Ungar in a touring version of Neil Simon's *The Odd Couple* alongside Sherman Hemsley as Oscar Madison.

Morita left *Happy Days* for a starring role on *Mr. T. and Tina*—a James Komack show that only lasted for five weeks. Morita returned to Garry Marshall's stable, on *Blansky's Beauties*, starring Nancy Walker (he once again portrayed Arnold), but it, too, failed to catch on. In 2003, he played Felix Ungar in a touring show, opposite Sherman Hemsley as Oscar Madison. Morita's biggest role came on the big screen as the very wise Mr. Miyagi in *The Karate Kid* (1984), an Oscar-nominated role. Morita died of natural causes on November 24, 2005, at the age of 73.

Jessica Myerson

Guest starred in "You've Come a Long Way Baby" (as Mrs. Ferguson), "Natural Childbirth" (as the instructress), and "Take My Furniture Please" (as woman number two).

Jessica Myerson would have roles in two very famous motion pictures—*Billy Jack* (1971) and *Mrs. Doubtfire* (1993). However, she got her start making a guest appearance on Garry Marshall's first sitcom, *Hey, Landlord*, in an episode titled "Safari." She followed this appearance with a role in one of Marshall's first motion pictures, *The Grasshopper* (1970, as the owner of the wedding chapel). Of course, the ever-loyal Garry Marshall also used her talents in an episode of *Happy Days*, and three episodes of *The Odd Couple*.

Myerson's other TV appearances, though few in number, include episodes of *Mayberry RFD*, *Love, American Style*, *The Bob Newhart Show*, and *Midnight Caller*.

Frank Nelson

Provided the voice for Spiffy in 32 episodes of *The Oddball Couple*. Frank Brandon Nelson was born on May 6, 1911, in Colorado Springs, Colorado. He started in radio at the age of 15. Nelson's big break came on Jack Benny's radio show. The sarcastic character he created on radio, with his familiar "EEEE-Yesssssss" greeting endured for over a quarter of a century, and worked just as well on television when Benny made the successful transition to that new medium. Nelson also performed variations of that snippy persona occasionally on *I Love Lucy* and *The Lucy Show*.

Along with dozens upon dozens of guest appearances on sitcoms, Nelson also lent his dulcet tones to animation. He became a very prolific voice actor, and can be heard in episodes of *The Flintstones*, *Mister Magoo*, *Foofur*, *Monchhichis*, *Garfield and Friends*, and *The Oddball Couple*. The latter was the cartoon version *The Odd Couple*, and it debuted on ABC-TV just weeks after the sitcom version was cancelled in 1975. Nelson played a tidy tabby named Spiffy (modeled after Felix Unger), and Paul Winchell provided the voice for Fleabag, the unclean canine (patterned after Oscar Madison). A total of 32 11-minute cartoons were produced, and ABC aired two episodes back-to-back every Saturday morning for two seasons.

Frank Nelson's familiar voice was silenced on September 12, 1986, in Hollywood. The 75-year-old actor had been suffering from cancer.

Cliff Norton

Guest starred in "The Odd Decathlon" (as Lloyd of "Lloyd's of Lubbock") and "The Dog Story" (as Barry Fishkin). Clifford Charles Norton was born March 21, 1918, in Chicago, Illinois. He got his start in radio. It was then that Norton met Dave Garroway, who hired him for his *Garroway at Large* TV show. Norton later became a regular panelist on the short-lived ABC game show, *What's Going On?* He also had his own five-minute show, in 1952, titled *The Public Life of Cliff Norton*, and, in 1960, a syndicated sketch show called *The Funny Manns*.

Norton also made numerous TV guest appearances on *Dr. Kildare, Pete and Gladys, The Dick Van Dyke Show, The Jack Benny Program, My Favorite Martian, The Farmer's Daughter, The Andy Griffith Show, Hogan's Heroes, Bewitched, I Dream of Jeannie, That Girl, The Lucy Show,* and *The Odd Couple,* to name but a few. He also guest starred on Tony Randall's other two sitcoms, *The Tony Randall Show* and *Love, Sidney.*

Norton had numerous roles in famous films such as *Harry and Tonto* (1974), *Funny Lady* (1975), *The Russians Are Coming the Russians Are Coming* (1966), and *Suppose They Gave a War and Nobody Came?* (1970). His final TV credit came in an episode of *Murphy Brown.* Cliff Norton died on January 25, 2003, at the age of 84.

SAM NUDELL

Guest starred in "Being Divorced Is Never Having to Say I Do" (as Mr. Parsley), "The Moonlighter" (as the foreman), and "New York's Oddest" (as the neighbor). Sam Nudell was born March 19, 1911. He was rather a late bloomer, and earned his first TV credits in 1970 when he was pushing 60.

Among his first TV credits were three guest appearances on *The Odd Couple.* Nudell's other credits include *Bridget Loves Bernie, Cagney and Lacey, The Blue Knight,* and *Starman.* He also had roles in small films such as *The Frisco Kid* (1979), *Dr. Black, Mr. Hyde* (1976), *Your Three Minutes Are Up* (1973), and *Brothers* (1977). Sam Nudell died on September 2, 1988, at the age of 77, in Los Angeles.

DONEY OATMAN

Guest starred in "The Odd Father," "The Paul Williams Story," and "Felix Remarries" (as Edna Unger). After Pamelyn Ferdin left the role of Edna Unger on *The Odd Couple* for a regular part on *The Paul Lynde Show,* the void was filled by young actress Doney Oatman.

Oatman's TV career was short-lived, lasting only about five years. Other guest appearances include roles on *The Waltons, James at 16, Eight Is Enough, Maude,* and *The Rockford Files.* She also appeared in several *ABC Afterschool Specials* and a mini-series titled *Little Vic.*

Today, she is the senior interpreter for the Rochester Institute of Technology.

JO MARIE PAYTON

Co-starred on *The New Odd Couple* (as Mona). Jo Marie Payton was born August 3, 1950, in Albany, Georgia. She graduated from Albany State University, and, upon graduating, tried to break into the acting field.

Her first recurring role on TV came

in 1982 when she was cast as "Big-Hearted" Mona on *The New Odd Couple*. She appeared in the following episodes: "The New Car," "Bachelor of the Year," "A Grave for Felix," and "The Night Stalker."

Bigger things lay ahead for Payton—as Harriet Winslow for nine seasons on the ABC sitcom *Family Matters*. Among Payton's other conquests: *Moesha*, *Will and Grace*, and most recently, *The Proud Family*.

E. J. PEAKER

Guest starred in "Bunny Is Missing, Down by the Lake" (as Julie). Edra Jane Peaker was born February 22, 1944, in Tony Randall's hometown—Tulsa, Oklahoma. She appeared in numerous high school plays and studied drama at the University of New Mexico. She may be best known for her portrayal of Minnie Fay in the 1969 motion picture version of *Hello, Dolly!* On Broadway, she appeared in *Bye, Bye Birdie*, and co-starred with Robert Morse in a weekly ABC-TV series called *That's Life*, which was an attempt to bring the feel of a Broadway musical comedy to the small screen every week.

Peaker played a lost camper named Julie on *The Odd Couple* in the single-camera first-season episode, "Bunny Is Missing, Down by the Lake." In the episode, a downpour leads her and her young scouts to seek refuge in Felix and Oscar's cabin. Peaker also guest starred in numerous episodes of another Paramount Television program, *Love, American Style*.

Peaker is married, has one daughter, and lives in the Los Angeles area.

ED PECK

Guest starred in "The Odd Monks" (as Brother Horace), "The Flying Felix" (as Bill), and "The Rent Strike" (as Mr. Ralston). Peck was born March 26, 1917, in New York. He had roles in numerous popular films, such as *Bullitt* (1968), *The Comic* (1969), *The Last Unicorn* (1982), *I Love You, Alice B. Toklas* (1968), and *The Prisoner of Second Avenue* (1975, a Neil Simon film). Peck's TV credits date back to the very early 1950s, and among the highlights were appearances on *Surfside 6*, *Leave It to Beaver*, *The Untouchables*, *Perry Mason*, *The Jack Benny Program*, *The Munsters*, *Get Smart*, *The Dick Van Dyke Show*, *Star Trek*, *I Dream of Jeannie*, *That Girl*, *All in the Family*, and *The Odd Couple*. For *The Odd Couple*, Peck guest starred in three episodes as three totally different characters (none more unique than Brother Horace, the monk). His deep, gravelly voice was his stock in trade.

Peck was often cast as a policeman, and he earned a recurring role (nine episodes) on *Happy Days*, as Officer Kirk. After *Happy Days* came to an end in 1984, Ed Peck decided to retire. His retirement lasted almost a decade: he died on September 12, 1992, in Los Angeles.

ED PLATT

Guest starred in "Oscar's New Life" (as Bill Connelly). Edward Cuthbert

Platt was born February 14, 1916, on New York's Staten Island. He majored in the romance languages at Princeton University, and also attended the Juilliard School, with aspirations of becoming an opera star. World War II delayed that quest.

In the early 1950s he earned a few roles on Broadway, and also worked on radio (his deep, booming voice was a definite advantage). His role as one of the juvenile officers in *Rebel Without a Cause* (1955), and a stint on the daytime soap opera *General Hospital* led to his biggest break—that of the Chief of Control on Mel Brooks's *Get Smart*.

When *Get Smart* came to an end, Platt found more work in episodic TV, guest starring on numerous episodes of *The Governor and J. J.* (as Orrin Hacker). On *The Odd Couple*, he portrayed Bill Connelly, Oscar's boss at the *New York Herald*, in the episode "Oscar's New Life," in 1971.

On March 19, 1974, Platt was found dead in his apartment. The original diagnosis of a heart attack was changed to suicide (for many years he suffered from depression). Platt left behind four children from two failed marriages.

JOHN QUALEN

Guest starred in "A Taste of Money" (as Sam), "A Grave for Felix" (as the groundskeeper), and "Sometimes a Great Ocean" (as Mr. Larson). John Qualen had an interesting history. He was a Canadian-American character actor of Norwegian descent, who specialized in Scandinavian dialects. He was born December 8, 1899, in Vancouver, as Johan Mandt Kvalen. His father, a minister, Anglicized their last name to Qualen when the family moved to Illinois. Young John attended Northwestern University, and caught the acting bug in the 1930s, appearing often on Broadway.

Qualen parlayed his Broadway successes into roles in dozens of films, including *The Three Musketeers* (1939), *Casablanca* (1942), *His Girl Friday* (1940), *Knute Rockne All American* (1940), *The High and the Mighty* (1954), and the highlight of his career, *The Grapes of Wrath* (1940).

Qualen also found work in the new medium of television, beginning in the 1950s. He guest starred on *Dragnet*, *Father Knows Best*, *Cheyenne*, *Maverick*, *Dr. Kildare*, *Ben Casey*, *Green Acres*, *Mister Ed*, *The Streets of San Francisco*, and *The Odd Couple*. By this time, Qualen was well into his 70s, and his career was winding down. After his appearances on *The Odd Couple*, his health began to fail. He went blind in his final years, and died of heart failure on September 12, 1987, at the age of 88. He and his wife, Pearle, were married for 53 years and had three daughters together.

BILL QUINN

Guest starred in "Oscar's Ulcer," "Lovers Don't Make House Calls," "Sometimes a Great Ocean," and "The Ides of April" (as Dr. Melnitz). Bill Quinn was born William Tyrell Quinn May 6, 1912, in New York City. He was Bob Newhart's father-in-law in real life (and guest starred on a couple of

Newhart episodes in the 1980s). In fact, many other comedians attended Bob Newhart's wedding, and while Quinn was walking his daughter down the aisle, one of them said out loud, "Look who they got to play the father." Quinn was often cast as a father, a doctor, or a judge. Quinn got his start in silent films at the age of six, billed as Billy Quinn. His film credits include Alfred Hitchcock's *The Birds* (1963), *Twilight Zone—the Movie* (1983), *Star Trek V: The Final Frontier* (1989), and *It Happened at the World's Fair* (1963) with Elvis Presley. His TV credits span five decades in *The Virginian, The Loner, A Man Called Shenandoah, Mister Ed, My Three Sons, The Fugitive, The Man from UNCLE, Bonanza, The Wild Wild West, Judd for the Defense, The Big Valley, Ironside, The Mod Squad, Mannix, The Mary Tyler Moore Show* (on which he played Walter Richards, Mary's doctor dad), and *The Odd Couple*. On the latter, he portrayed poor Dr. Melnitz, who was called upon frequently for house calls because of Felix's hypochondriacal ways.

Quinn died just days shy of his 83rd birthday, on April 29, 1994. He was the father of three, and grandfather of four.

Tony Randall

Co-starred as Felix Unger in summer stock, the original series, and the 1993 TV reunion movie. Born as Leonard Rosenberg February 26, 1920, in Tulsa, Oklahoma, he developed an affinity for acting at a very early age, and began as a radio actor (alluded to in an episode of *The Odd Couple* titled "The Big Broadcast"), and played the role of Reggie on *I Love a Mystery*. His career was put on hold when he was drafted into the army in 1942 during World War II. Upon his return to civilian life in 1946, he made frequent appearances on Henry Morgan's radio program, and also worked on Broadway in *Antony and Cleopatra*.

With the advent of television, Randall quickly found a regular role as Mac on the TV version of *One Man's Family*. The program was much more successful on radio, but it did have a decent run on television as well. A short time later, Randall was cast as a teacher who worked with and befriended *Mister Peepers*, played by Wally Cox on that live sitcom. The series ran for four seasons. Tony was also a frequent panelist on the long-running *What's My Line?* Contrary to his own persona and the fastidious character he portrayed, Tony Randall was really quite a sports fan, and he loved beer.

Randall then moved to the silver screen and, even though he could play Shakespeare and heavy drama proficiently (check out a film he did titled *No Down Payment*), he became best known for light comedies, such as *Pillow Talk* (1959), *Lover Come Back* (1961), and *Send Me No Flowers* (1964), in which he played second banana to Doris Day and Rock Hudson. Not only was he a great supporting actor in light comedies, but also a great leading man in *Will Success Spoil Rock Hunter?* (1957) and *The Mating Game* (1959). In 1970, he was cast as Felix Unger for the sitcom version of Neil Simon's *The Odd Couple*. Randall really wanted Mickey Rooney to portray Oscar Madison (they had appeared in the play together in summer stock), but instead Jack Klugman was chosen. Klugman had already played the role on Broadway when he replaced Walter Matthau. Tony had seen the original stage production with Walter Matthau and Art Carney. Initially, Randall and Klugman nearly came to loggerheads because Klugman loved to smoke, and Randall was fervently anti-smoking. Despite this, a great and lasting friendship between the two actors evolved and the series lasted for five seasons and a total of 114 episodes. Even though the program never finished in the Top Thirty in any season, it endured and became an even bigger success in reruns. To this day, these are the roles which define Tony Randall and Jack Klugman.

One year after the cancellation of *The Odd Couple*, Randall had his own eponymous sitcom, *The Tony Randall Show*, from MTM Productions. This very funny show struggled through two seasons and two networks (first ABC, and then CBS) before disappearing altogether. Randall tried one more sitcom in 1981—a two-season wonder on NBC called *Love, Sidney* on which he portrayed Sidney Shorr, a lonely homosexual who lives with a single mother and her young daughter.

There were a lot of similarities between Tony Randall and his most famous role, Felix Unger. Both loved the opera and classical music. Both were natty dressers. Both were very particular about language and diction. Both had the same friend—Jack Klugman. Especially in the years after the series ended, Tony Randall and Jack Klugman became extremely close, and that friendship and reverence for one another is documented in Klugman's book, *Tony and Me: A Story of Friendship*. After Klugman's cancer surgery, which all but destroyed his voice, Tony and Jack reprised their most famous roles on stage and in an *Odd Couple* TV reunion movie in 1993 titled *The Odd Couple: Together Again*.

Randall's legacy is the National Actors Theater (NAT), which he started in 1991. The NAT produced plays, first at the Belasco Theater on West 44th Street in Manhattan, then at the Lyceum Theater on West 45th Street, and finally at the smaller Pace University's Michael Schimmer Center for the Arts. The NAT didn't always get stellar reviews, and often operated in the red, but Randall fought to make it a success for the last 13 years of his life. Heather Harlan, an intern for the NAT, became the second Mrs. Tony Randall (they had two children together—Julia and Jefferson). Harlan was almost 50 years younger than Randall. They were married by Mayor Rudy Guiliani in New York City.

Tony Randall died on May 17, 2004, at the age of 84, after a bout with pneumonia that was brought on by heart bypass surgery. He is buried at Westchester Hills Cemetery in New York. On the night of his passing, the lights on Broadway were dimmed in his honor. He received a star on the Hollywood Walk of Fame in 1998.

William Redfield

Guest starred in "Shuffling Off to Buffalo" (as Felix's brother, Floyd Unger). William Redfield was born January 26, 1927, in New York City, into a show-business family—his father was a musical conductor, and his mother was part of the Ziegfield's Follies. He was performing on Broadway before his tenth birthday. By the middle 1950s, he had moved into television and had a recurring role in *The Marriage*—a live color sitcom starring Hume Cronyn and Jessica Tandy on NBC. Redfield also worked occasionally on *Mister Peepers*, where he first met Tony Randall. It's only fitting that years later they portrayed brothers on *The Odd Couple*. Redfield played Floyd Unger, a bubble-gum magnate from Buffalo, New York, who hired his brother to be a manager within the company (only to quickly come to the realization that they were getting on one another's nerves). Besides "Shuffling off to Buffalo," the episode could have been titled "Unger Management."

Redfield's TV credits are enviable, but just as his movie career was gaining steam (*One Flew Over the Cuckoo's Nest* [1975]), he was diagnosed with leukemia and died at the age of 49, on August 17, 1976. His son, Adam, is also an actor.

Joe Regalbuto

Joseph Regalbuto was born in New York City August 24, 1949. He graduated from New Milford High School in New Jersey in 1967. After years of theater work, he got his first movie credit in Neil Simon's *The Goodbye Girl* (1977). In 2002, he appeared onstage at the Geffen Playhouse in Los Angeles in *The Odd Couple*, as Felix Ungar to John Larroquette's Oscar Madison. Coincidentally, Martin Short, Regalbuto's co-star on the short-lived sitcom, *The Associates*, has also portrayed Felix Ungar onstage.

Regalbuto is best known for his long run as Frank Fontana on the CBS sitcom *Murphy Brown*. In recent years, his interests have turned to the director's chair, and among his directorial credits are numerous episodes of the popular Betty White TV Land sitcom, *Hot in Cleveland*.

Richard Reicheg

Richard Reicheg was born May 26, 1937, in Brooklyn, a few blocks from Ebbets Field. After graduating from Erasmus Hall High School, he served active duty in the army, stationed in Weisbaden, Germany. He attended Brooklyn College, earning a BA and MA in speech and theatre. Reicheg exemplifies the term multi-tasker, having enjoyed a 50-plus-year career as a folk singer/guitarist, recording artist, stand-up comic, comedy writer, doo-wop singer/bass player, Grammy-nominated songwriter, improviser, and actor.

Of his lengthy résumé of featured TV, film and theater appearances, the following anecdotes are *Odd Couple*–related. Reicheg shared, "I was living in New York. At that point I was a comedy writer, but anxious to get back to performing. My only connection to *The Odd Couple* was a 'fumetti' piece I had co-written with Harvey Kurtzman for *Playboy* magazine in 1970 that featured Tony Randall. It was a spoof of Spaghetti westerns, called *The Good, the Bad and the Garlic*. Tony portrayed the Clint Eastwood character. An agent named Eddie Blum was the theatrical agent at the agency I was with and I kept asking him to submit me for an acting role. One day he called with an audition for a stage show, with the encouraging words, 'Don't embarrass me!' I got the job, a comedy, slated for Broadway! It was directed by Harvey Medlinsky (who would later direct numerous MTM sitcoms, including *The Tony Randall Show*), a wonderful man who became a lifelong friend. Harvey had been stage manager on *An Evening with Nichols and May*, and the early Neil Simon plays that Mike Nichols went on to direct—*Barefoot in the Park*, *The Odd Couple*, etc. He was now directing productions himself. This was a comedy called *Even Steven*, and while heading for Broadway, it closed in Paramus, New Jersey. For those who drive through New Jersey and experience that bad odor, this play may be, in a small part, responsible. On the bright side, I got my equity card, and Harvey's managers saw the play and offered to represent me. Soon, Harvey called and cast me as the telephone man in Neil Simon's *Barefoot in the Park* in Chicago at the Arlington Park Theatre (the role my friend from Brooklyn College, Herb Edelman, created on Broadway and again in the film). While no one could fill Herb's shoes, I received a Joseph Jefferson nomination. As a footnote, while working on the 2007 film *Charlie Wilson's War*. I mentioned Herb Edelman to Mike Nichols, who was directing. Mike recounted the anecdote about Herb—who was driving a cab for a living, double-parked his taxi to run in to audition for his role in *Barefoot in the Park*. I also mentioned Harvey Medlinsky and Mike asked for his phone number. After all those years, they had a long conversation, which was meaningful to Harvey, who was ill and passed away shortly thereafter. Next Harvey cast me in the touring company of *The Odd Couple* with Klugman and Randall. I was to play Roy, one of the poker players. The others were Al Molinaro as Murray, Larry Gelman as Vinnie, and Garry Walberg as Speed. The ABC series was already a big hit, but Jack and Tony were touring major cities with the stage version during hiatus. Tony Randall was vehemently anti-smoking, but also a perfectionist. I remember him orchestrating the amount of smoke that was supposed to hover over the poker table when the curtain rose for act one. We poker players puffed our cigars and cigarettes and only when Tony was satisfied, the curtain came up. I also remember that one actor was stepping on one of Tony's laughs—not waiting long enough before speaking his next line. Tony resolved that by holding on to the actor's knee, instructing the actor not to say his line until the laugh crested and Tony released his grip."

Reicheg recalled an offstage event: "One morning, while playing in Hamilton, Ontario, Canada, Tony and I had breakfast together. Tony, busy looking at the menu, ordered a very precisely detailed breakfast, with eggs cooked just so, toast just so, etc. The young man, who was taking our order, had recognized him and was now in a semi-catatonic state, mouth agape. He never heard a word Tony said. Tony's disdain was priceless. You had to be there.

"One of the great experiences was watching Jack and Tony do *The Odd Couple*'s argument scene. While Jack hurled Felix's spaghetti against the wall and said, 'Now it's garbage,' Tony, as Felix, demonstrated his anger by picking up a chair and shaking it—a great choice for his character. What a privilege to watch those masters from the wings, night after night. Another stage production of *The Odd Couple* was again in Chicago at the Arlington Park Theatre, and again directed by Medlinsky. This time it was with Art Carney as Oscar and Don Knotts as Felix. I played Speed this time, as Sid Armus, who had played Roy on Broadway, was available. Gelman was Vinnie and Al Checco was Murray. For Art Carney to play Oscar was a switch, since he had played Felix on Broadway. It was great fun to spend six weeks with that cast. I remember Art playing piano in the theatre lobby—he played beautifully. Art's wife, Barbara, played one of the Pigeon sisters. I asked Art how he started and he said on radio, doing impressions. He then launched into a spot-on Franklin D. Roosevelt, Winston Churchill, etc. I also did a production of Neil Simon's *Chapter Two*, directed by his brother, Danny Simon. My character, Leo, was based on Danny—so I was actually directed by the man whom I was portraying. Weird! Jack Klugman was very encouraging and offered to help if I ever decided to move to L. A. So, in 1973, I came to Los Angeles, slept on Larry Gelman's couch for a couple of nights, and the moved in with Herb (Edelman) in Santa Monica for a couple of months. I got a job as a staff songwriter with Warner Bros. Music. Meanwhile, the acting bug still itched, and Jack, true to his word, recommended his and Tony's agent, Abbey Greshler. (Greshler's story would be great fodder for a book.) I signed with Greshler, starting my TV and film career with a small role in an *Odd Couple* episode ('The Rain in Spain Falls Mainly in Vain'), and here we are reminiscing some forty years later."

As of this writing, Reicheg is a series regular on the popular hidden-camera TV show, *Betty White's Off Their Rockers*.

CHARLES NELSON REILLY

Charles Nelson Reilly was born January 13, 1931, in the Bronx, New York, but raised in New Haven, Connecticut. An only child, Reilly sought attention on the stage beginning at age nine. By the early 1960s, he had won a Tony Award for his role in Broadway's *How to Succeed in Business Without Really Trying*. He was nominated again for *Hello, Dolly!* and *The Gin Game*.

On television, he garnered an Emmy nomination for his portrayal of Claymore Gregg on the sitcom version of *The Ghost and Mrs. Muir*, and played a TV chef on the early 1970s sitcom, *Arnie*. However, Reilly is likely best known for occupying the seat next to Brett Somers for many years on the *Match Game*. Being seated next to Mrs. Jack Klugman all those years was not Reilly's only connection to *The Odd Couple*—he also portrayed Felix Ungar in the Burt Reynolds Dinner Theater production of the play, alongside Darryl Hickman's Oscar Madison. Reilly and Burt Reynolds were longtime friends. One of the head writers of the TV sitcom version of *The Odd Couple*, Mark Rothman, says that, despite the brilliance of Tony Randall, Charles Nelson Reilly was the best Felix Ungar he has ever seen.

Reilly died on May 25, 2007, due to complications from pneumonia.

ROB REINER

Guest starred in "The Rain in Spain Falls Mainly in Vain" (as Sheldn). Robert Reiner was born March 6, 1947, and followed in the footsteps of his brilliant, trailblazing father, Carl Reiner. Rob Reiner is the reason the main character on *The Dick Van Dyke Show* was named Rob. Like his dad, Rob Reiner became a famous actor, writer, producer, and director. Rob used to hang around the set of *The Dick Van Dyke Show*, and had a mad crush on Mary Tyler Moore, like most young men in America at the time. One day, however, the brazen young man grabbed Mary's posterior, and Rob was called into his father's office for a "talking to." As a teenager, Rob's first experiences performing on a sitcom came in Garry Marshall and Jerry Belson's *Hey, Landlord*—Rob had small roles in three of the program's episodes, and he studied at the UCLA Film School. He also guest starred on *Gomer Pyle, USMC*, *The Beverly Hillbillies*, and one *Mothers-in-Law* episode, which was titled "The Career Girls." Rob loved to improvise, but when he attempted that on *The Mothers-in-Law*, a hot-tempered Desi Arnaz called him on the carpet (grabbing him by the lapels).

Rob quickly became a star when *All in the Family* caught on in its second season on CBS, late in 1971. As Mike "Meathead" Stivic, he was the perfect counterpart to Archie Bunker's archaic ways of thinking. While still with *All in the Family*, Reiner guest starred on *The Odd Couple*'s first episode of the fifth and final season. Reiner portrayed a character named Sheldn (they left out the "O" on his birth certificate), the love interest of Penny Marshall (his then wife in real life). Penny's Myrna Turner character married Sheldn in that episode, and Penny left the show for a larger role in *Paul Sand in Friends and Lovers*, a short-lived MTM sitcom. Reiner and Marshall divorced in 1979.

Reiner found even greater success on the silver screen with movies he wrote, produced or directed, such as *The Bucket List* (2007), *A Few Good Men* (1992), *Misery* (1990), *The Princess Bride* (1987), *This Is Spinal Tap* (1984), *Stand by Me* (1986), and *When Harry Met Sally...* (1989). In the latter, Rob's mother, Estelle Reiner, delivered the movie's funniest and most memorable line in the restaurant scene: "I'll have what she's having."

Today, Rob Reiner, not unlike his Mike Stivic character, is very active in liberal political causes.

BARBARA RHOADES

Guest starred in "I Gotta Be Me" (as Marie) and "Our Fathers" (as Lucy). Barbara Rhoades was born March 23, 1947, in Poughkeepsie, New York. This tall and comely redhead's first credits date back to the late 1960s when she was in her early twenties. Movie roles included *The Shakiest Gun in the West* (1968), *Harry and Tonto* (1974), and *The Goodbye Girl* (1977).

Rhoades guest starred in two episodes of *The Odd Couple*—one, a flashback episode ("Our Fathers") which showed that Felix and Oscar's fathers had crossed paths during prohibition. Rhoades continued to find consistent work as Carrie in *The Blue Knight*, as Melody Feebeck on *Busting Loose* (from the head writers of *The Odd Couple*, Mark Rothman and Lowell Ganz), as Maggie Chandler on *Soap*, and, most recently, as Irene Manning on *One Life to Live*. Rhoades has been married to writer/executive producer Bernie Orenstein since 1979 (the "O" in Toy Productions). Rhoades, as Maggie Davis, worked again with Jack Klugman on the short-lived sitcom, *You Again?*, in 1986.

BOBBY RIGGS

Guest starred in "The Pig Who Came to Dinner" (as himself). Robert Larimore Riggs was born February 25, 1918, in Los Angeles. He played in his first professional tennis match only days after the attack on Pearl Harbor, in December 1941. At one time, he was the World's number-1 tennis player, and later the co-world number-1 player.

Riggs garnered a reputation for braggadocio and male chauvinism. His cocky persona led to the extremely popular "Battle of the Sexes," in 1973, with Billie Jean King. Riggs was already in his mid-fifties at the time, and King was the victor of the $100,000 prize in that highly publicized event. Both Riggs and King guest-starred as themselves on an episode of *The Odd Couple*, "The Pig Who Came to Dinner." Riggs had a much larger role in the episode, and at the end of the show, he and King have a rematch, of sorts, on a Ping-Pong table. Riggs wasn't much of an actor, and Klugman and Randall took him under their respective wings and aided him in finding his mark in each scene. He and Billie Jean King are also mentioned in the episode "The Rain in Spain Falls Mainly in Vain."

Despite the media's portrayal of Riggs and King as rivals, the two remained on friendly terms until Riggs's death from prostate cancer, on October 25, 1995. In recent years, rumors have surfaced that Bobby Riggs purposely lost his storied "Battle of the Sexes" tennis match with King to pay off a huge gambling debt.

RODNEY ALLEN RIPPY

Guest starred in "The Rent Strike" (as himself). Rodney Allen Rippy was born July 29, 1968, in Long Beach, California. Rippy became a media darling in the early 1970s in a series of TV commercials for Jack in the Box restaurants. This led to a role as young Sheriff Bart in Mel Brooks's *Blazing Saddles*, in 1974. Before long, Rippy was making 45 rpm records, and making the rounds on episodic TV shows, such as *Marcus Welby M. D.*, *The Six Million Dollar Man*, and *The Odd Couple*. On the latter, we discovered that he owned the building in which Felix and Oscar lived, and helped to settle the tenants' rent strike.

Rippy's success was short-lived, and for the most part, he abandoned acting to get a degree from California State University. In 2013, Rippy made news when he attempted a run for mayor of Compton, California, but quickly backed out when early polling showed he had little chance of winning.

Pernell Roberts

Guest starred in "Strike Up the Band or Else" (as Billy Joe). Pernell Elven Roberts, Jr., was born in Waycross, Georgia, May 18, 1928. He attended the University of Maryland and participated in several plays performed by the school's theatrical group. He was also very musical—he sang and played several instruments. His first big break came onstage in the early 1950s when he performed in numerous off–Broadway shows, many of which were Shakespearean.

He got his first TV breaks on dramas such as *Sugarfoot*, *Whirlybirds*, *Have Gun, Will Travel*, *Zane Grey Theater*, and *77 Sunset Strip*. Then came his biggest break—the role of the eldest Cartwright son, Adam, on *Bonanza*. He stayed with the western for six years before opting to move on—a decision many considered unwise.

Roberts remained very active in episodic TV after leaving *Bonanza*, and though he was known as a dramatic actor, he took a turn at comedy in *The Odd Couple*. In the episode, "Strike Up the Band or Else," he portrayed a sports team owner to whom Oscar loses a large amount of money in a poker game. Felix's band then performs country music for Billy Joe's hoedown, gratis, to help Oscar pay down his debt.

Roberts found TV success again, beginning in 1979, in *Trapper John, M. D.* and enjoyed a seven-year prime-time run as Dr. John McIntyre in this dramatic sequel to *M*A*S*H*. Wayne Rogers had originated the role on TV, and this sequel series was set in present day 1979, and followed the Trapper John character in his medical practice.

Roberts's last TV appearances came in the 1990s on Dick Van Dyke's *Diagnosis: Murder*. Roberts was nicknamed "the liberal Cartwright" because of his activism in liberal causes. He died from pancreatic cancer on January 24, 2010, at the age of 81.

Esther Rolle

Guest starred in "The Ides of April" (as Mrs. Gibbs on *The New Odd Couple*). Esther Rolle was born November 8, 1920, in Pompano Beach, Florida. (Yes, Florida Evans was born in Florida.) She was the tenth of 18 children, born to Bahamian immigrants. Her first job was in New York's garment district, but a keen interest in the theater and dance led to a career as an actress.

Early on, she could only find work with the Negro Ensemble Company, but eventually her talent led to the important role of Miss Maybell in the staging of *Don't Play Us Cheap*. This opened the door to her being cast as the housekeeper on *Maude*, and the eventual spinoff, *Good Times*. She was almost 20 years older than her on-screen husband, James Evans (John Amos).

In 1982, Rolle guest starred in the debut episode of *The New Odd Couple* as Mrs. Gibbs, of the IRS, who audits Felix's and then Oscar's tax returns.

Rolle won her only Emmy Award for her performance in the TV-movie, *The Summer of My German Soldier*, in 1979. Although she was nominated for a Golden Globe for *Good Times*, she did not win. Due to complications from diabetes, Esther Rolle died just days after her 78th birthday, on November 17, 1998.

VERN ROWE

Guest starred in "Engrave Trouble" (as man number one), "A Different Drummer" (as Vern), and "Strike Up the Band or Else" (as the trumpet player). Vern Rowe (sometimes credited as Vernon Rowe, and sometimes Vern E. Rowe) was born Laverne Edward Rowe July 2, 1921, in Washington State. Rowe was a character actor who could also sing and play instruments. Some of the numerous motion pictures in which he appeared include (1967), including *The Big Mouth*, with Jerry Lewis, *The Shaggy D. A.* (1976), and *Pandemonium* (1982).

Vern's TV roles included guest appearances on *The Doris Day Show*, *Columbo*, *The Rookies*, *Police Woman*, *The Bob Newhart Show*, *Starsky and Hutch*, *CHiPs*, *Alice*, *Happy Days*, and *The Odd Couple*. His was not a household name, but he is likely best known for his portrayal of Vernon Taylor on numerous episodes of *Fernwood Tonight*.

Rowe died at the age of 60, on September 4, 1981, in Los Angeles, California.

ANDY RUBIN

Guest starred in "Oscar's Birthday" and "Sometimes a Great Ocean" (as Monroe Hernandez). Andrew Harold Rubin was born in New Bedford, Massachusetts, June 22, 1946. His father operated a bedding factory, and his mother wrote about international travel. He developed the acting bug early in life, and he eventually attended the American Academy of Dramatic Arts in New York. After a brief stint as an NBC page, he picked up and moved to California to look for work.

He earned guest-starring roles on *Ironside*, *The Jeffersons*, *Mary Hartman, Mary Hartman*, *Cannon*, and *The Odd Couple*. Rubin was of Jewish descent, but often found work portraying Hispanic characters. Such was the case in his two appearances on *The Odd Couple* as the superintendent's son, Monroe Hernandez (on the program, he is said to be of Puerto Rican descent). He was featured rather prominently in those two episodes, and thus, it's unclear why his character was never heard from again. He did have one more *Odd Couple* connection, however—he portrayed Walter Matthau's son in the motion picture *Casey's Shadow* (1978). After this, he appeared in the hit film *Police Academy* as George Martin. Rubin has co-starred in three short-lived TV series—*Jessica Novak*, *Hometown* and *Joe Bash*.

Debra Jo Rupp

Co-starred in the 1993 TV reunion movie, *The Odd Couple: Together Again*, as the assistant hotel manager. Debra Jo Rupp was born February 24, 1951, in Glendale, California, but was raised in Massachusetts. She graduated from the University of Rochester and opted to pursue a career in acting. Among her early TV roles was that of a topless dancer on ABC's *All My Children*.

Rupp's first big break was on Broadway, as Cynthia in *A Girl's Guide to Chaos*, in 1986. At this point, Rupp turned to co-starring roles in motion pictures such as *Big* (1988) and *Death Becomes Her* (1992), and guest-starring roles on episodic television programs, such as *Spenser for Hire*, *Kate and Allie*, *Newhart*, *Family Matters*, *Blossom*, and *Evening Shade*. In 1993, Rupp could be seen in *The Odd Couple: Together Again*. As the frustrated hotel manager, she becomes impatient with finicky Felix's unreasonable plans for his daughter's wedding, and expresses profound relief when Felix opts to hold the ceremony elsewhere.

Rupp had recurring roles in numerous short-lived TV sitcoms in the 1990s, and eventually enjoyed a long run as Kitty Forman, alongside Ashton Kutcher and Topher Grace, in *That 70s Show* on the Fox Television Network. She also appeared as Phoebe's sister-in-law, Alice, in numerous episodes of *Friends*, and co-starred in the single-season ABC sitcom *Better with You*. As of this writing, she is single and has no children.

Pat Sajak

He was born Patrick Sajdak October 26, 1946, in Chicago. He later dropped the "D" from his professional name. Sajak was a real-life Adrian Cronauer—a broadcaster in Vietnam on Armed Forces Radio during the war. In later years, he became the owner of several radio stations in Maryland. He was also a TV weatherman, and eventually received the opportunity of a lifetime to take over for game-show host Chuck Woolery, who was leaving *Wheel of Fortune* in 1983. Sajak and letter-turner Vanna White made the program more popular than it had ever been. Sajak also briefly hosted his own late-night talk show.

Sajak also enjoyed acting, and has made guest appearances on such TV programs as *The Commish*, *Days of Our Lives*, and *The Larry Sanders Show*. Onstage, Sajak appeared as Felix Ungar in a Hawaiian production of *The Odd Couple*, at the Manoa Valley Theater, in 2001. Sajak is a huge baseball fan and historian. He is also an investor in the Golden Baseball League.

BILLY SANDS

Guest starred in "Being Divorced Means Never Having to Say I Do" (as groom-to-be and milk magnate Roger J. Doctor), "The Princess" (as a tailor), "New York's Oddest" (as Mr. Bennick), "The Subway Story" (as the "sandwich man"), and in "Our Fathers" (as a federal agent). William F. Sands was born January 6, 1911, in New York. He got his first break in 1946 when he was cast in a play with Spencer Tracy, *Rugged Path*, on Broadway. Sands was already 40 when he got his first TV credit for *Lux Video Theater*. He had a recurring role on two anti-militaristic sitcoms—*The Phil Silvers Show* (as Private Dino Paparelli) and *McHale's Navy* (as Harrison "Tinker" Bell). He also guest starred on a bevy of other sitcoms, including *Car 54, Where Are You?*, *All in the Family*, *Love, American Style*, *Big Eddie*, *Laverne and Shirley*, *Webster*, and *The Jeffersons*. Sands guest starred in five *Odd Couple* episodes spread over five years, and was a favorite of the cast and crew. He also guest starred in one episode of *The New Odd Couple*, "The Perils of Pauline." Mark Rothman and Lowell Ganz used Sands as often as they could, and they found him guest starring roles on many of their shows, including *Busting Loose* and *The Ted Knight Show*.

Sands also had a small role in the original *Rocky* (1976), as the club fight announcer. Sands, a longtime smoker, died of lung cancer on August 27, 1984, at the age of 73.

JOHN SCHUCK

Co-starred in "The Ides of April," "Frances Moves In," "The New Car," "The Cordon Blues," "Opening Night," "My Strife in Court," "Murray's Hot Date," "The Perils of Pauline," "The only Way to Fly," and "The Night Stalker" (as Murray the cop in the 1982 TV remake series, *The New Odd Couple*). Conrad John Schuck was born in Boston, Massachusetts, February 4, 1940. He graduated from Denison University and, after performing in plays up and down the East Coast of the U.S., he was discovered by director Robert Altman while working at ACT (the American Conservatory Theater),

A big smile from John Schuck, who played Murray the cop on *The New Odd Couple* (courtesy John Schuck).

in San Francisco. Altman cast Schuck in the movie version of *M*A*S*H*, as Painless. Soon after, Schuck attained one of his biggest TV successes as Sergeant Charles Enright in the Leonard Stern–produced show, *McMillan and Wife*.

Schuck's next venture with Stern, however, was a funny single-season sitcom, *Holmes and Yoyo*, in which he portrayed Gregory Yoyononvich—a human-looking robot cop who weighed over 400 pounds and printed photographs through his shirt pocket. Schuck's next show was *Turnabout* (loosely based upon the 1940 Hal Roach–directed comedy of same name) from Stephen Bochco and Sam Denoff.

In 1982, Schuck co-starred in yet another sitcom, *The New Odd Couple*. "I recall auditioning for the role of Murray, the cop," Schuck said recently. "Garry Marshall was present, and when I got the job, I was very grateful to be working since I was having a very slow year. It's interesting that I was playing a cop for the third time. Actors do tend to get boxed in because in television, actors play professions, [e.g., cops and lawyers], and the character evolves out of whoever has been cast in the show. I attempted to bring my own personality to the role that had been portrayed previously by Herb Edelman [in the movie] and Al Molinaro [in the original TV series]. Height-wise, I was somewhere in between the two. I loved the character of Murray—he wasn't the sharpest tool in the shed, but he had a good heart." Schuck co-starred in ten of the series' 18 episodes.

He added, "Unlike my previous two sitcoms, it was fun and refreshing to film a program with three cameras in front of a live audience. It was very much like a stage performance, and the response was immediate."

About his co-stars on the series, Ron Glass and Demond Wilson, Schuck recalled, "They weren't exactly friends—they were two very different people, but they had a sort of détente for the good of the show. They each had a lot riding on this program as both were coming off big hit shows—Ron from *Barney Miller* and Demond from *Sanford and Son*. We all went into the project highly hopeful, but writing became the issue. If the producers hadn't recycled so many of the scripts from the original series, we might have had a fighting chance. The problem was, those scripts were already done, and were written for two white, New York guys. And even when the writers attempted to revamp these scripts for the black cast, Ron and Demond had difficulty making them work. However, Garry Marshall was always very cheerful, upbeat and supportive." About actress Liz Torres, who portrayed Oscar's secretary, Maria, on the show, Schuck shared, "Liz is one of the funniest women I've ever met. She was so much fun to work with."

All but one of the 18 episodes were directed by Joel Zwick, of whom Schuck said, "Zwick was great to work with, and luckily I got to work with him twice more, later on—first in a film titled *Second Sight* [1989], and then in a play called *Cyrano* that was written by Madeline Sunshine," (who had written an episode of *The New Odd Couple*, "The Only Way to Fly"). *Cyrano* was a bawdy retelling of Edmond Rostand's *Cyrano de Bergerac*, and John portrayed a mobster in New York's Little Italy.

Schuck's height and deep, booming voice also made him the perfect choice to take the reins from Fred Gwynne in the role of Herman in *The Munsters Today*. This syndicated remake ran from 1988 to 1991 and actually lasted one season longer than the original. Schuck has also appeared in several *Star Trek* motion pictures and TV series, and, mostly recently, portrayed Carl on the TV series *Zeke and Luther*. He was Daddy Warbucks in the 2006 Broadway revival of *Annie*. In fact, most of John's work these days is in theater. He recently closed on Broadway in *Nice Work if You Can Get It* with Matthew Broderick, and as of this writing, he is performing in *A Funny Thing Happened on the Way to the Forum* in Sag Harbor, Long Island, New York. He lives in Nashville, Tennessee, with his wife.

Rebecca Schull

Co-starred in *The Odd Couple II* (as Wanda, the vixen). Rebecca Schull was born Rebecca Wattenberg February 22, 1929, in New York City. She graduated from New York University, but studied acting in Dublin, Ireland.

Schull was rather a late TV bloomer. Her first credits are from the early 1980s, including a stint on the daytime soap opera *One Life to Live*. She is best known as the dizzy, oft-widowed receptionist/sometimes stewardess Fay Evelyn Cochran on the long-running NBC sitcom *Wings*. Schull played quite a similar role in Neil Simon's *The Odd Couple II* in 1998—a thrice-widowed flirt.

Schull most recently completed a run on the USA Network series *Suits*, when her character passed on.

Vito Scotti

Guest starred in "Felix, the Calypso Singer" (as Pepe). Vito G. Scotti was born January 26, 1918, in San Francisco, California. An extremely prolific character actor, he portrayed a variety of ethnic roles on Broadway, in movies, and on television. In the early days of television, he played a Frenchman on the short-lived live ABC sitcom *Mama Rosa*, and an Italian-American as the second Luigi Basco on the early live CBS sitcom *Life with Luigi*. His list of guest-starring roles, almost always as an Italian or Spanish character, is miles long. On *The Odd Couple*, he portrayed the multi-tasking Pepe, who was the tipsy pilot, the cab driver, and the musical entertainment for the tiny island of Hockaloma, on which Felix, Nancy, and Oscar were vacationing.

Scotti also found work in major motion pictures (never in a starring role), such as *The Godfather* (1972), *Get Shorty* (1995), and *Cactus Flower* (1969). He also lent his voice as the Italian Cat in Walt Disney's *The Aristocats*, in 1970. Scotti continued to find consistent work well into the 1990s. He died of lung cancer on June 5, 1996, at the age of 78.

Reta Shaw

Guest starred in "Maid for Each Other" as (Claire Frost). Reta Shaw was born September 13, 1912, in Maine. Because of her tough, no-nonsense, matronly appearance, she was usually cast as a housekeeper, a nanny, a military official, a manager, or a school principal. In fact, her best-known role is that of the housekeeper, Martha Grant, on the TV version of *The Ghost and Mrs. Muir*.

Reta Shaw had previously worked with Tony Randall as Mister Peepers's Aunt Lil. In the *Odd Couple* episode "Maid for Each Other," she portrayed Oscar's caretaker, Claire Frost (nicknamed "Frosty"). Shaw also portrayed a domestic in the mega-hit 1964 motion picture *Mary Poppins*—a film which is mentioned in that particular episode as an inside joke.

Shaw also guest starred on another Garry Marshall sitcom, *Happy Days*, as Mrs. McCarthy. She died on January 8, 1982, at the age of 69.

Dick Shawn

Portrayed Felix at the Westbury Music Fair in 1967. Dick Shawn was born Richard Schulefand in Buffalo, New York, December 1, 1923. Shawn was proficient as both a dramatic and a comedic actor, but it is the latter for which he's best known—mostly for *It's a Mad, Mad, Mad, Mad World* (1963) and *The Producers* (1968). On Broadway, he replaced Zero Mostel in *A Funny Thing Happened on the Way to the Forum*. At the Westbury Music Fair in 1967, Shawn portrayed Felix Ungar to Jack Carter's Oscar Madison in a production directed by Jack Klugman (who had just wrapped up portrayals of Oscar on Broadway as well as London's Queen's Theatre).

Shawn's stand-up act was way ahead of its time. Billing himself as "The Second Greatest Entertainer in the World," one never knew what to expect (except to expect the unexpected). His performances were a zany mix of songs, pantomime, philosophy, satire, sketches, jokes, and props. He was "out there" in a big way. He was known to lie totally motionless on stage during his intermission, thus on April 17, 1987, while performing in San Diego, he collapsed face first onstage and the audience thought it was part of the act. After a considerable and uncomfortable amount of time had lapsed, someone finally ran up to check on him. It was too late—he had suffered a heart attack while, ironically, discussing "lying down on the job." Shawn was only 63.

Christopher Shea

Guest starred in "You've Come a Long Way, Baby," "A Taste of Money," and "Trapped" (as Phillip Wexler). Christopher Dylan Shea was born February 5, 1958, in Los Angeles, California. He was the eldest of three acting Shea brothers. Christopher is best known as the voice of Linus Van Pelt in numerous *Peanuts* holiday specials. His younger brother Stephen took over as the voice of Linus in the 1970s.

Christopher also appeared regularly

in the short-lived ABC series based upon the classic 1953 movie *Shane*. In episodic TV, he had supporting roles on *That Girl*, *Bonanza*, *The Invaders*, *Green Acres*, *My World and Welcome to It*, and *The Ghost and Mrs. Muir*. In *The Odd Couple*'s first season Shea portrayed the mischievous neighbor boy, Phillip, in three episodes.

Christopher Shea died at the young age of 52 on August 19, 2010, in Honeydew, California. He is survived by his wife Sara, and two daughters, Nicea and Teal.

Carole Shelley

Guest starred in the original Broadway production, the original motion picture, and the original TV series in "The Laundry Orgy," "It's all over now Baby Bird," "The Breakup" and "The Jury Story" (as Gwendolyn Pigeon). Carole Shelley was born August 16, 1939, in London. She came from a family of performers—her mother was a singer, and her father a composer. Although she was born in Great Britain, most of her theatrical success has come about in the U.S. In fact, she was cast in several plays as American characters in the UK before Neil Simon cast her as a British lass in *The Odd Couple* on Broadway. She (as Gwendolyn), and fellow Pigeon Sister Monica Evans (as Cecily) have the distinction of playing the same roles in *The Odd Couple* play, movie, and TV series. (Oddly enough, Shelley had to audition for the TV version.) The Pigeon sisters didn't work well in the TV version, and only appeared in four early episodes. Both Shelley and Evans provided voices for the Disney animated movies, *The Aristocats* (1970) and *Robin Hood* (1973).

Shelley's biggest successes came on Broadway. She was nominated for a Tony for her role as Jane in *Absurd Person Singular*; she won a Tony as Mrs. Kendall in *The Elephant Man*; and she was nominated again for playing Maxine in *Stepping Out*. She also played Madame Morrible in the original Broadway cast of *Wicked*. As recently as 2009, she received another Tony nomination for *Billy Elliott*. She has also performed in the American Shakespeare Festival in Stratford, Connecticut.

Among Shelley's other film credits are *Bewitched* (2005), *Quiz Show* (1994), and *The Boston Strangler* (1968). It's interesting to note that this long-time "Pigeon" sister is not at all a fan of birds of any kind.

Joshua Shelley

Guest starred in "The Ides of April" (as an accountant), "Two Men on a Hoarse" (as burglar number two) and "Felix the Horse Player" (as the race announcer). Joshua Shelley was born January 27, 1920, in New York City. He was one of the unfortunate recipients of blacklisting during the McCarthy Era, and couldn't find work for a time. In fact, Shelley has very few credits between 1952 and the early 1970s, and did mostly stage work during that period. To that end, Shelley landed a great role, as Sam, in the 1976 motion picture *The Front*, which starred Woody Allen and Zero Mostel. The movie is about the effects of McCarthyism, and much of the cast consisted of formerly blacklisted actors. Once Shelley's career was rolling again, however, he worked non-stop, guest starring on programs such as *All in the Family, Love, American Style, Happy Days, Police Woman, McCloud, Police Story, The Streets of San Francisco, B. J. and the Bear, Hunter,* and *Family Ties.* On *The Odd Couple,* Shelley guest starred in three episodes (one with "horse," and another with "hoarse" in the title).

Shelley's movie credits include *All the President's Men* (1976), *Funny Lady* (1975), *The Front Page* (1975, with Lemmon and Matthau), *The Apple Dumpling Gang* (1975), and *Little Miss Marker* (1980, with Matthau). Shelley also reconnected with Jack Klugman in an episode of *Quincy, M. E.* titled "The Hot Dog Murder." Shelley died February 16, 1990, at the age of 70.

Martin Short

Played Felix to Jason Alexander's Oscar in the "Reprise! Production" of *The Odd Couple* at the Wadsworth Theatre in Los Angeles. Martin Short was born in Hamilton, Ontario, Canada, March 26, 1950, the youngest of five children. Short graduated from McMaster University with a degree in social work in 1971. Some of his classmates there (Eugene Levy and Dave Thomas) encouraged him to pursue comedy and acting, and, luckily, he heeded their suggestions.

Short co-starred in a couple of short-lived sitcoms early in his career: *The Associates* and *I'm a Big Girl, Now.*

His TV successes include *Second City TV, Saturday Night Live, The Completely Mental Misadventures of Ed Grimley* (one of his looniest characters), and *Primetime Glick* (as his smarmy agent character Jiminy Glick). Much like Nathan Lane and Matthew Broderick, Short teamed with Jason Alexander in productions of both *The Producers* and *The Odd Couple.* Short also had success starring in the Broadway production of Neil Simon's *The Goodbye Girl.* He won a Tony Award in Simon's revival of *Little Me.*

Among Short's film successes are: *Three Amigos!* (1986), *Father of the Bride* (1991), and *Mars Attacks!* (1996). In 2010, Short lost his wife of 30 years, Nancy, to ovarian cancer. As a result, he now campaigns for a charity called the Women's Research Cancer Fund. The Shorts had three adult children, two boys and a girl.

Johnny Silver

Guest starred in both "Felix Is Missing" and "What Does a Naked Lady Say to You?" (as the bum), "Good Bad Boy" (as the chaplain), "That Was No Lady" (as the coach), and "Felix the Horseplayer" (as the man at OTB). Not to be confused with actor Joe Silver or Jonathan Silverman, Johnny Silver was born John Silverman April 16, 1918, in Indiana. He got his start winning a singing contest on the radio, and when his family moved to Los Angeles, his career really began to blossom. He is likely best known for playing Benny Southstreet in *Guys and Dolls,* but also made a name for himself in over 40 years of episodic television appearances, beginning in 1950 with *NBC Television Opera Theater*. Then came guest-starring roles on *Leave It to Beaver*, *Alfred Hitchcock Presents*, *The Jack Benny Program*, *The Danny Thomas Show*, *The Dick Van Dyke Show*, *The Joey Bishop Show*, *Get Smart*, *The Munsters*, *My Three Sons*, and *Here's Lucy*. He guest starred in five episodes of *The Odd Couple*. He was very adept at portraying scruffy, unkempt characters and hobos, and was usually seen wearing a beret.

Silver continued to get work through the 1980s, on *Barney Miller*, *Alice*, and *Diff'rent Strokes*. In the 1990s, he portrayed a character on the *Seinfeld* episode titled "The Understudy," with guest star Bette Midler. His movie credits include *Spaceballs* (1987), *History of the World—Part One* (1981), and *The Great Race* (1965).

Silver died on February 1, 2003, in Woodland Hills, California, from heart and kidney failure, at the age of 84.

JONATHAN SILVERMAN

Co-starred in *The Odd Couple II* (as Oscar's soon-to-be-wed son, Brucey). Not to be confused with Johnny Silver, Jonathan Silverman was born August 5, 1966, in Los Angeles. His father and grandfather were rabbis. Jonathan initially had aspirations to wait tables, but, luckily, he followed his passion for acting.

His first regular role on TV came on the Nell Carter sitcom, *Gimme a Break* (on which he portrayed Jonathan Maxwell). He is best known as Richard Parker in the motion picture *Weekend at Bernie's* (1989) and the sequel, *Weekend at Bernie's II* (1993). Then came his starring role on TV in *The Single Guy*, as Jonathan Elliott, with co-star Ernest Borgnine.

In 1998, Silverman portrayed Oscar's son, Brucey Madison, in *The Odd Couple II*. In real life, he is married to actress Jennifer Finnigan, whom he met while doing a brief stint on *The Bold and the Beautiful*. He recently filmed another chapter in the *Beethoven* series (*Beethoven's Treasure*) with writer/director Ron Oliver, in Canada, for Universal Pictures.

JEAN SIMMONS

Guest starred in "The Princess" (as Princess Lydia). Jean Merilyn Simmons was born January 31, 1929, in Crouch Hill, London, England. She was the youngest of four children and began acting at the age of 14. She got her start in British films, and eventually found success in Hollywood. In 1948, her role as Ophelia in Sir Laurence Olivier's *Hamlet* earned the teenager an Oscar nomination. In 1950, she married actor Stewart Granger, and they appeared together in several films. Among her most famous movies were *Guys and Dolls* (1955), *Spartacus* (1960), and *Elmer Gantry* (1960). While married to her second husband, Richard Brooks, he directed her in yet another Oscar-nominated performance, as Mary Wilson, in *The Happy Ending* (1969).

In the 1970s, Simmons turned to

television, and guest starred on an episode of *The Odd Couple* as a visiting princess who has a short-but-memorable fling with Oscar Madison (and finds his "everyman ways" somewhat refreshing). Simmons found great success in TV miniseries such as *North and South* and *The Thorn Birds*, the latter earning her an Emmy Award. Simmons died of lung cancer on January 22, 2010, just days short of her 81st birthday. She is survived by two children—one from each marriage. Those who worked on *The Odd Couple* with her say that she was every bit as sweet and gracious as the princess she portrayed.

RICHARD X. SLATTERY

Guest starred in "The Fight of the Felix" (as Splint McCullough). Richard X. Slattery was born June 26, 1925, in the Bronx, New York. He was an officer in the New York Police Department for a dozen years, and when things broke his way as an actor, he was usually cast as either a policeman, a military officer, or (because of his gravelly voice) a tough guy.

Slattery garnered co-starring roles in numerous short-lived TV series, such as *The Gallant Men*, *Mister Roberts*, *Switch*, and *CPO Sharkey*. He guest starred on the second episode of *The Odd Couple* as an irate, jealous hockey pro who punches Oscar. He later challenges Felix to a boxing match for flirting with his girl, Irma (played by future *Rowan and Martin's Laugh-In* regular, Ann Elder). Slattery was already 45 at the time, but looked older and was not, therefore, very credible in the role of a professional athlete.

Slattery also found parts in motion pictures such as *Walking Tall* (1973) and *Herbie Rides Again* (1974). He died at the age of 71, on January 27, 1997, in Woodland Hills, California.

JEAN SMART

Co-starred in *The Odd Couple II* (as Holly, one of the flirtatious girls in the bar with very jealous boyfriends). Jean Smart was born in Seattle, Washington, September 13, 1951. After graduating from the University of Washington, she quickly became active performing Shakespearean works in Ashland, Oregon, and eventually made it to Broadway in *Piaf*.

Smart's early attempts at TV were less than successful. After several failed sitcoms, she finally landed her "role of a lifetime"—that of dizzy Charlene on the long-running CBS series *Designing Women*. However, it was her recurring role on *Frasier* that garnered her not one, but two, Emmy Awards. She won yet another Emmy for her role, as the mother, on the short-lived sitcom, *Samantha Who?*, in 2008. Her scenes as Holly with Christine Baranski as Thelma in *The Odd Couple II* are among the film's highlights.

BUBBA SMITH

Guest starred in "Take My Furniture, Please" (as himself). Charles Aaron "Bubba" Smith was born February 28, 1945, in Orange, Texas. He first made his mark playing defense for the Michigan State Wolverines. Even though he was immensely popular, his career in the NFL was relatively short. He began with the "Baltimore" Colts, then the Oakland Raiders, and finally with the then Houston Oilers.

Smith also had the acting bug, and appeared in most of the *Police Academy* movies, as well as several short-lived TV series, such as *Semi-Tough*, *Open All Night*, and *Blue Thunder*. He guest starred on *Taxi*, *McGyver*, and *Good Times*. He portrayed himself on an episode of *The Odd Couple*. Bubba, totally out of character, discussed window treatments and decorating with Felix while Oscar was attempting to conduct an interview with him for a book.

Smith died at the age of 66 in his Los Angeles home, from heart failure, on August 3, 2011.

Hal Smith

Guest starred in "Oscar's Birthday" (as Arthur O'Reilly) and "Surprise, Surprise" (as Sherman, the clown). Harold John Smith was born in Petoskey, Michigan, August 24, 1916. He began as a disc jockey in the 1930s in Utica, New York, but his radio career was interrupted by World War II (he was in Special Services).

Immediately after the war, Smith began one of the most lucrative animated-voice careers in history—supplying his myriad tones to Walt Disney's Goofy, Goliath the dog (and Davey's conscience) in *Davey and Goliath*, and Owl in *Winnie-the-Pooh* (and we've only scratched the surface).

He was also proficient at portraying bums and drunks (he guest starred in dozens of episodes of *The Andy Griffith Show* as the oft-locked-up lush, Otis Campbell).

On *The Odd Couple*, he played Sherman, the poker-loving, heavy-betting hired clown at Edna's birthday party on "Surprise, Surprise," and (of course) the drunk at Oscar's *This Is Your Life* moment in "Oscar's Birthday."

Smith's voice acting career kept him busy, literally until the day he died, on January 28, 1994, at the age of 77.

Howard K. Smith

Guest starred in "The Odd Candidate" (as himself). Howard Kingsbury Smith was born May 12, 1914, in Ferriday, Louisiana. He studied German and journalism at Tulane University. He became one of Edward R. Murrow's "Boys" at CBS in the 1940s, while stationed overseas. In the early 1960s, he moved over to the perennial last-place network, ABC. Smith later teamed with Frank Reynolds as co-host of the *ABC Evening News*, and then with Harry Reasoner.

Smith also appeared in several films, including *Close Encounters of the Third Kind* (1977) and *The Best Little Whorehouse in Texas* (1982). On TV, Smith was a guest star on a couple of ABC series, including *The Bionic Woman* and *The Odd Couple*. On the latter, in an episode titled "The Odd Candidate," Felix disrupts Smith's lunch at a local Manhattan eatery to discuss the closing of a local playground (and sticks Smith with the bill for his iced tea). To

Felix and Oscar's pleasure, Smith mentions the issue on his nightly newscast.

Smith published his memoirs in 1996, and died on February 15, 2002.

BRETT SOMERS

Guest starred in "Being Divorced Is Never Having to Say 'I Do,'" "The Odd Holiday," "The Odd Couples," "A Night to Dismember," and "This Is the Army Mrs. Madison" (as Blanche Madison). Brett Somers was born Audrey Johnston July 11, 1924, in New Brunswick, Canada. She grew up in the Portland, Maine, area, but moved to New York's Greenwich Village at the age of 18 to pursue a career as an actress. The name "Brett" was inspired by the character Brett Ashley in Ernest Hemingway's *The Sun Also Rises*.

Brett started in live television, performing on dramatic programs such as *Playhouse 90*, *Philco Playhouse*, and *Robert Montgomery Presents*. In 1953, she also made a couple of appearances on *Bonino*, a short-lived NBC sitcom, which starred Ezio Pinza.

Brett married Jack Klugman in 1954, and they worked together onstage in 1958 in Clifford Odets's *The Country Girl*. They united on television in the 1970s in five episodes of *The Odd Couple*, during which time she was being credited as Brett Somers Klugman. Brett portrayed Jack's ex-wife, Blanche Madison, in those five episodes (and she was alluded to in countless others). In real life, Jack and Brett separated during the show's run, in 1974, but never divorced. They reunited onstage at Fairfield University, in 2005, in a show called *Danger, People at Large*.

Brett's biggest claim to fame came on the 1970s version of *The Match Game*, on which she became a regular panelist (seated on the top row, in the middle, to the left of Charles Nelson Reilly). Although she denied it for many years, Brett had a long battle with cancer. She died on September 15, 2007, in Westport, Connecticut, at the age of 83. It was only after her passing that Jack Klugman remarried.

JACK SOO

Guest starred in "Oscar's Promotion" as Chuk Mai Chin. Jack Soo was born as Goro Suzuki October 28, 1917, in Oakland, California. After World War II, he became a popular nightclub entertainer, and that paid the bills until his big break in Rodgers and Hammerstein's *Flower Drum Song* (the 1958 Broadway production, and the 1961 motion picture).

Then came television. In 1964, Soo earned a role as the valet Rockwell "Rocky" Sin on the single-season sitcom *Valentine's Day*, with Tony Franciosa and Janet Waldo. Also on ABC, Soo guest starred on one episode of *The Odd Couple*, as a visiting red Chinese wrestler whom Felix talked into retiring (because of a bad shoulder) — a move that almost cost Oscar his job. However, it was his co-starring role on an ABC sitcom a few years later for which he became famous—Detective Sergeant Nick Yemana on the long-running *Barney Miller*. Yemana was the deadpan, wise-cracking Detective

Sergeant who developed a reputation for making terrible coffee. Sadly, Soo took ill and died on January 11, 1979, during the program's fifth season, leaving behind a huge void. His *Barney Miller* coffee cup is housed in the Smithsonian Institution, in Washington, D.C.

RICHARD STAHL

Guest starred in "I Do I Don't," "Oscar in Love," and "Being Divorced Is Never Having to Say I Do" (all three as the minister), "Engrave Trouble" (as the florist), "Murray the Fink" (as a cop/prison guard), "The Odd Monks" (as Brother Ralph), "This Is the Army Mrs. Madison" (as the Justice of the Peace/Fireman), "Cleanliness Is Next to Impossible" (as Dr. Bates), and "The Frog" (as Buck, the pet shop owner). Richard Stahl was born January 4, 1932, in Detroit. He was a student of the American Academy of Dramatic Arts in New York City. He later relocated to San Francisco, where he became a member of The Committee, an improvisational group. Something of a late bloomer, Stahl's earliest credits are from the late 1960s, when he was already in his middle-to-late 30s. His film credits include *Nine to Five* (1980), *High Anxiety* (1977), *Ghosts of Mississippi* (1996), and *Five Easy Pieces* (1970). His TV credits include mostly sitcoms, such as *The Golden Girls*, *Barney Miller*, *Soap*, *WKRP in Cincinnati*, *Laverne and Shirley*, *Night Court*, *All in the Family*, and *Turnabout*. He made nine guest appearances on *The Odd Couple*, and was never the exact same character twice (even though he was thrice cast as a minister). Garry Marshall loved his work, and used him as often as he could. Stahl's most famous guest appearance on the program was in the episode titled "The Odd Monks," as Brother Ralph.

Stahl's wife, Kathryn Ish, also acted and guest starred in numerous sitcoms, and was a regular on the game show, *Oh, My Word*. Stahl succumbed to Parkinson's Disease on June 18, 2006. Ish died one year later, on December 31, 2007. They are survived by two children, a son, Oliver, and a daughter, Allegra.

FLORENCE STANLEY

Co-starred in *The Odd Couple II* (as Hattie). Florence Stanley was born as Florence Schwartz July 1, 1924, in Chicago. After graduating from Northwestern University, Florence traveled to Germany as a civilian actress technician, right after World War II. There she toured in John Willard's popular "old dark house" play, *The Cat and the Canary*. Upon returning to the U.S., she scored a role in the 1948 production of Oscar Wilde's *The Importance of Being Earnest*. While in *Bury the Dead*, she met the man who would become her husband—Martin Newman.

She performed in numerous Shakespearean works throughout the 1950s and 1960s, but it is her comedy roles for which she is best known. In the early 1970s, Stanley found work in Neil Simon's *The Prisoner of Second Avenue* (the play and the movie). She also portrayed Hattie, one of the card players, in *The Odd Couple II* in 1998.

On television, Stanley was a regular fixture on numerous sitcoms, including *Joe and Sons*, *My Two Dads*, *Cybill*, and of course, *Barney Miller* and the spin-off, *Fish*, on which she portrayed Bernice Fish. Stanley died on October 3, 2003, in Los Angeles, at the age of 79.

DAVID STEINBERG

Guest starred in "The Odd Couple Meets Their Host" (as himself). David Steinberg was born August 9, 1942, in Winnipeg, Manitoba, Canada. He studied English literature at the University of Chicago and, inspired by Lenny Bruce, decided to pursue comedy. His diverse career has included stand-up, acting, directing and writing. He also hosted his own talk show, *The David Steinberg Show*. It was during this time that he guest starred as himself on an episode of *The Odd Couple*. Oscar is a guest on Steinberg's TV show, and tells the audience all about his roommate's peculiar idiosyncrasies. An embarrassed Felix demands equal time, and after a severe bout of stage fright, ends up singing old radio theme songs on Steinberg's show.

In recent years, Steinberg has directed numerous episodes of *Curb Your Enthusiasm*, *Mad About You*, *Seinfeld*, *Friends*, and over 30 episodes of *Designing Women*. In 2012, he also hosted *Inside Comedy* on the Showtime Network.

SALLY STRUTHERS

Co-starred in *The Female Odd Couple* (as Florence Ungar). Sally Ann Struthers was born July 28, 1947, in Portland, Oregon. She studied at the Pasadena Playhouse College of Theater Arts. In 1970, she had a nude scene with Jack Nicholson in *Five Easy Pieces*. Shortly thereafter, she was cast as Gloria Stivic on the groundbreaking sitcom *All in the Family*. (Gloria in the show's pilot was portrayed by actress Candy Azzara.) Struthers won two Emmys for her role on the show, and only got to read for the part after the advantageous cancellation of *The Tim Conway Comedy Hour*, on which she was a regular. She also starred in a short-lived *All in the Family* spinoff, *Gloria*, in 1992.

Struthers has also provided the voice for numerous cartoon characters, including the grown-up Pebbles Flintstone. Her commercials for Child Fund were very popular, but soon became fodder for *South Park*, and many late-night comedy skits. She made her Broadway debut co-starring with Rita Moreno in *Wally's Café*, in 1981. Just four years later, she and Moreno became *The Female Odd Couple* at the Ahmanson Theatre, on West Temple Street in Los Angeles, and then the Broadhurst Theatre on West 44th Street in Manhattan. This new spin on the old classic received mixed reviews.

Her most recent TV credits were in recurring roles on the long-running *Gilmore Girls* and the sitcom *Still Standing*.

GRADY SUTTON

Guest starred in "The Flying Felix" (as Pop Belkin). Grady Sutton was born April 5, 1906, in Chattanooga, Tennessee. While still a teenager, he got his first Hollywood break as an extra in the 1925 motion picture *The Mad Whirl*. Among his crowning glories were appearances in four films with W. C. Fields. He also found roles in such classics as *White Christmas* (1954), *A Star Is Born* (1954), and *Anchors Aweigh* (1945).

On television, Sutton had a recurring role as Jed on *The Egg and I*, Swann on *The Ann Sothern Show*, and Sturgis on *The Pruitts of Southampton/The Phyllis Diller Show*. On *The Odd Couple*, Sutton portrays the elderly pilot of a chartered plane containing Felix and Oscar. Head writer Mark Rothman said, "That funny double-take of his as he is initially headed in the wrong direction to get aboard that chartered flight was totally his doing. No one told him to do that. He had amazing comedy chops. He is one of the reasons that 'The Flying Felix' is one of my favorite episodes."

Sutton's final motion picture appearance, capping off a long career, was as the school board president in *Rock 'n' Roll High School* (1979). Sutton died in Woodland Hills, California, on September 17, 1995, at the age of 89.

OGDEN TALBOT

Guest starred in "Scrooge Gets an Oscar" (as the messenger), "Natural Childbirth" (as Howard), "The Ides of April" (as the postman), and "Gloria Moves In" (as the bellboy). Ogden Talbot also had small roles in several motion pictures—*The Reivers* (1969, with Steve McQueen), *How Sweet It Is* (1968, with James Garner and Debbie Reynolds), and *Young Doctors in Love* (1982, with Michael McKean and Sean Young)—the latter two were Garry Marshall vehicles.

Talbot found quite a bit of work on TV shows such as *The Dick Van Dyke Show* (his first credit), *That Girl*, *Good Morning, World*, *Love, American Style*, *Serpico*, and *Hey, Landlord* (Garry Marshall and Jerry Belson's first show). Talbot had small roles in four episodes of *The Odd Couple*, encompassing both the single-camera and multi-camera eras. Talbot was well liked by Marshall and Belson, and was also used in episodes of *Happy Days* and *Laverne and Shirley*.

LIZ TORRES

Guest starred in "The New Car" and "The Odd Triangle" (in the 1982 remake series, *The New Odd Couple*) and *The Odd Couple II* movie sequel (all as Maria). Elizabeth Torres was born September 27, 1947, in New York City. This Puerto Rican-American got one of her first breaks in an episode of *Love, American Style*. A short time later, a regular role on *Phyllis* cropped up when series regular Barbara Colby (who had only appeared in three episodes) was murdered. Liz Torres then assumed the role of Julie Erskine, the manager of the photography studio. That lasted one season. Torres then took on the role of Teresa Betancourt on *All in the Family*, in 1976.

In 1982, Torres guest starred in a couple of episodes of *The New Odd*

Couple, as Oscar's secretary, Maria. She had the same role in the 1998 movie, alongside Walter Matthau and Jack Lemmon.

One of Torres's biggest successes came in the 1990s as Mahalia Sanchez, the sassy assistant manager of the bus station on *The John Larroquette Show*. The program ran for four seasons, and Torres was nominated for an Emmy and a Golden Globe. Most recently, she could be seen occasionally on *The Gilmore Girls* and *Ugly Betty*.

GEORGIO TOZZI

Guest starred in "Our Fathers" (as the Big Boss). Georgio Tozzi was born January 8, 1923, in Chicago, Illinois. He studied at DePaul University and, shortly thereafter, garnered big roles as Figaro in Mozart's *The Marriage of Figaro*, and as Phillip II in Verdi's *Don Carlos*. Several of his opera recordings of the 1960s won Grammy Awards, and he was nominated for a Tony for his performance in *The Most Happy Fella*. He was also the singing voice for Emile de Becque in the 1958 motion picture version of *South Pacific*.

In the 1970s, Tozzi broadened his horizons and also took on some straight (non-singing) dramatic roles. He was a guest star on TV's *Baretta*, *Knight Rider*, and *Kojak*. He also tried his hand at comedy in an episode of *The Odd Couple*, set in his native Chicago. Although he originally performed a number *a cappella* in the episode, that part was cut when the DVD set was released.

Tozzi, in his later years, was a voice professor at the Juilliard School of Music. He died of a heart attack at the age of 88, on May 30, 2011.

JOAN VAN ARK

Guest starred in "A Night to Dismember" (as tipsy tennis pro Trudy Wells). Joan Van Ark was born June 16, in New York City. She was accepted to the Yale Graduate Drama School straight out of high school and quickly accrued a long list of credits. Van Ark got her start in Neil Simon's national tour of *Barefoot in the Park*, and she recalled, "What an exciting way to get started! The great Myrna Loy played my mother, and Dick Benjamin played my husband. A Neil Simon play directed by the amazing Mike Nichols! It was a very heady experience. I re-

Joan Van Ark guest starred as Trudy Wells in *The Odd Couple* episode titled "A Night to Dismember" (courtesy Joan Van Ark).

member auditioning and I was told instantly that I got the part. I then ran all the way down 57th Street to my see my agent, I was so excited. My agent thought I'd maybe gotten the understudy role, but I told him, 'No I got the actual lead part!' How rewarding it was to later guest star on Neil Simon's *The Odd Couple* on television." In the episode, Van Ark was the cause of the breakup of Oscar and Blanche Madison (seen from three totally different perspectives on New Year's Eve) and Van Ark shared, "I had to kiss Jack Klugman numerous times in those three *Rashomon*-type scenes, but I didn't mind—he was a pretty good kisser. However, because of the repetition of those three scenes it was psychologically a little bit ... confining. I get a little intimidated by three-camera shows filmed before a live audience. In some ways, it's like the theater, but, again, in many ways it's not. All the last-minute rewrites and the cameras all around you, and I always want it to be perfect. And so did they, because I recall working long hours on that episode—we did it over and over until we got it just right." It wasn't too long after this particular episode aired that Jack and Brett broke up in real life, and Joan reflected, "They were still together at that time, but I could tell that maybe something was amiss there. But we were all so busy doing the work ... it didn't register until later."

About Tony Randall, Van Ark said, "When you are doing a guest shot on a series, you can often feel like a stranger—a bit of an outsider. However, coming from the theater, being a real theater person, Tony Randall made me feel very comfortable, less alone and grounded. He was extremely helpful to me. I never got to work with him again, but I did go to see Lynn Redgrave and him in a play in New York for his National Actors Theatre, and they were both magnificent. I went backstage to see them after the performance, and it was a wonderful experience. I got to work with Jack Klugman again, on *Quincy, M. E.*, in an episode called 'Gone but Not Forgotten.'"

Van Ark added, "I still see Garry Marshall occasionally. I have always gotten a wonderful vibe from him. He's what I call 'a hugger.' A funny, unique and wonderful man, and his New York accent is so special and endearing."

Joan is likely best known for her brilliant portrayal of Val Ewing, first on *Dallas*, and then on the long-running spinoff, *Knots Landing*. She recently reprised that role in the 2013 updated version of *Dallas* on the TNT Network. She supplied the voice for the animated version of *Spider Woman*, and, as of this writing, she can be seen as Miss Senior Someone in the popular web series *Pretty*. She portrays Momma in the upcoming film, *Watercolor Postcards*. After reminiscing about *The Odd Couple*, Van Ark smiled and said, "I want to do another sitcom character next. That would be fun."

Van Ark is still married to her childhood sweetheart, John Marshall. Their daughter, Vanessa Marshall, has followed in her mother's footsteps and is an accomplished voice-over actress, director and comedienne (and mom couldn't be more proud).

DICK VAN PATTEN

Guest starred in the 1993 TV reunion movie (as Roy). Richard Vincent Van Patten was born December 9, 1928, in New York City. He began as a child actor and was on Broadway at a very young age. Van Patten shared, "I was seven when I started on Broadway alongside Melvyn Douglas in *Tapestry in Gray*, in 1935. It closed after only four weeks, but I later performed in three great shows which won Pulitzer Prizes—*The Best Years of Our Lives*, *The Skin of Our Teeth*, and *The American Way*. Fredric March was one of the nicest people I've ever worked with. I worked with him in *The Best Years of Our Lives*. In *The Skin of Our Teeth*, I worked with Tallulah Bankhead, and I have a great story about her. I was 14 at the time, and after about two weeks of doing the play, she called me into her dressing room. She was stark naked, and this was the first time I had ever seen a naked woman. She called me in to tell me that one of my lines should be performed as a statement and not a question. Well, I wanted to be called into her dressing room again, so I continued to say the line as a question, and she called me into her dressing room the same way for four consecutive nights."

Van Patten was seemingly never out of work. In television's infancy he was Nels Hansen on the long-running *Mama* (often called *I Remember Mama*) from 1949 to 1956 (Dick has a son, Nels, named after that character). Dick recalled, "The show was done live every week, and one time, Judson Laire forgot to come back after our daytime rehearsal. He had gone home and it just totally slipped his mind. In a panic, a member of the crew performed all of Papa's lines from offstage. It was the only thing we could do to save the show that week. That was the fun of live television. The show must go on." Although a great dramatic actor, Van Patten appeared most often in situation comedies, and had regular roles on many, including *The Partners*, *The New Dick Van Dyke Show* (Van Patten says that Van Dyke is the nicest person he has ever worked with), and *When Things Were Rotten* (the latter for his good friend Mel Brooks). In fact, Van Patten reprised his role from *When Things Were Rotten* in a Mel Brooks theatrical film, *Robin Hood: Men in Tights* (1993).

Van Patten's sister, Joyce, guest starred as a spurned bride-to-be in the *Odd Couple* episode "I Do, I Don't" from the first season of the original series. Dick said, "Not because she's my sister, but she truly is my favorite actress of all time." Brother Dick's association with *The Odd Couple* came about in 1993 in the TV reunion movie, *The Odd Couple: Together Again*. He resurrected Roy—a character who hadn't appeared since season one of the original series. This reunion movie was done single camera, and Van Patten shared, "I prefer filming that way, without an audience. I know it's fun for the audience, but I like the single-camera method. That's the way we did *Eight*

Is Enough for all those years." About Tony Randall and Jack Klugman, Van Patten recalled, "I also did the play with them. They were both terrific guys—very real. I remember admiring them and being so impressed with how funny, talented, and natural they were. They were always very nice to me. Jack, of course at that time had problems with his voice, but worked through it all. They were brilliant as Felix and Oscar." Coincidentally, as a child, Van Patten had a pet alligator named Oscar.

Dick Van Patten's biggest claim to fame is his role as Tom Bradford in a five-season run of ABC's *Eight Is Enough*. Eight decades in television is not enough for Van Patten, however, as he still makes guest appearances in episodic programs, such as *Hot in Cleveland*, and he continues to tout Natural Balance Pet Products.

JOYCE VAN PATTEN

Guest starred in "I Do, I Don't" (as Phyllis). Joyce Benignia Van Patten was born March 9, 1934, in New York City. She is Dick Van Patten's younger sister, and she was once married to Martin Balsam. Before she was ten she was performing on radio and on Broadway. This led to work as a model several years later, and, eventually, a long and successful career as a stage, TV, and movie actress.

After a season on *As the World Turns* (as part of the original cast), Joyce's first really big TV break came as a regular on *The Danny Kaye Show* from 1964 to 1967. Shortly after that, she was cast as Claudia Gramus in Leonard Stern's *The Good Guys* sitcom on CBS, which starred Herb Edelman and Bob Denver. Van Patten said, "I did a guest shot on *The Andy Griffith Show*, which still has the most loyal fans, and I also did a *Movie of the Week* with Andy called *Under the Influence*. That was Keanu Reeves's first union job." She remained very active in episodic TV on such programs as *The FBI, Family Affair, Cannon, Medical Center, Hawaii Five-O, The Bob Newhart Show, Mannix, The Rockford Files,* and *Columbo*. On *The Odd Couple*, she portrayed a would-be bride who was spurned at the altar (because of Felix). Van Patten recalled, "Tony Randall and I worked and toured together on the Florida circuit, where he opened up to me about having a very strained relationship with his father. I also knew Jack Klugman and his wife, Brett, very well. When Tony and Jack landed the series, I got to play the bride who was stood up at the altar in the 'I Do, I Don't' episode, which was shot single-camera style. Tony and Jack were seasoned stage performers and not getting an audience reaction was uncomfortable for them. Luckily, that changed the following season with three cameras and a studio audience. I was surrounded by friends on the episode I did—Tony and Jack were such great guys. Tony had such a great sense of humor. He and his first wife, Florence, were so devoted to one another—one of the great Hollywood marriages." Being in a Neil Simon work was nothing new to Van Patten, "I was in the original company of four Neil Simon hits—*Brighton Beach Mem-*

oirs, *I Ought to Be in Pictures*, *Jake's Women*, and *Rumors*."

About her co-stars in *The Odd Couple* episode, Van Patten said, "George Furth was a wonderful actor, as was Richard Stahl, who played the minister. Richard was great, but just a little bitter that his wife, actress Kathryn Ish, was having trouble finding steady work. It's a tough business, and I have been so very fortunate to have worked with so many greats. In fact, it was nice to be reunited with producer Jerry Davis on *The Odd Couple*. I worked with Jerry for two seasons on *The Good Guys*, and he was so adorable and easy-going."

In the 1990s, Van Patten remained active, with recurring roles in programs such as *Brooklyn Bridge* and *Unhappily Ever After*. Later, she guest starred on *The Sopranos* and *The Good Wife*, and the most recent Joyce Van Patten sightings were in a 2013 motion picture titled *Angel's Perch*, and a film directed by her son-in-law, John Slattery, called *God's Pocket*, which co-stars the late Philip Seymour Hoffman and John Turturro.

Herb Vigran

Guest starred in "Engrave Trouble" (as Louie, the jeweler/engraver). Herb Vigran was born June 5, 1910, in Fort Wayne, Indiana. He was a law school graduate who changed his focus to acting and, beginning in 1934, accumulated among the most impressive lists of credits in Hollywood history. He began in radio and parlayed that into motion pictures, such as *The Noose Hangs High* (1948), *Bedtime for Bonzo* (1951), *The Long, Long Trailer* (1954), and *Abbott and Costello Meet the Invisible Man* (1951).

However, his list of TV credits could fill a book by themselves. Among the highlights: *Make Room for Daddy, I Love Lucy, The George Burns and Gracie Allen Show, The Adventures of Superman, Dragnet, Perry Mason, The Donna Reed Show, The Dick Van Dyke Show, Alfred Hitchcock Presents, Bonanza, The Jack Benny Program, Bewitched, Gunsmoke, The Flintstones*, and *The Jeffersons*. On *The Odd Couple*, he portrayed Louie, the jeweler/engraver. Louie's jewelry shop was robbed, he was tied up and gagged, and the watch Felix left there to be engraved was gone (it was to be a special gift for Gloria so that Felix could get back on her good side).

The ubiquitous Vigran accrued almost 350 credits by the time of his passing on November 29, 1986, in Los Angeles.

Edward Villella

Guest starred in "Last Tango in Newark" (as himself). Edward Villella was born October 1, 1936, in Bayside, New York. He became the lead dancer for the New York City Ballet Company, even though he had a marine science degree, and lettered in baseball and boxing. He danced in *A Midsummer Night's Dream* and *The Nutcracker*, and became the first male dancer for the Royal Danish Ballet.

In 1973, Villella portrayed himself in a memorable episode of *The Odd*

Couple. Tony Randall was always rallying to get ballet and opera stars on the show, and this was one of his triumphs. In the episode, Felix is cast as the huntsman in Villella's local production of *Swan Lake*. When Villella shows up late for the performance, Felix starts on time in the lead role, against the wishes of all others involved. Villella's real-life son, Roddy, also makes a cameo appearance in the episode.

The year 1997 was a great one for Villella—he was a Kennedy Center Honors recipient, and was awarded the National Medal of Arts by then-president Bill Clinton. Villella currently resides in Southern Florida.

GARRY WALBERG

Guest starred in "The Laundry Orgy," "Felix Gets Sick," "The Breakup," "Oscar's Ulcer," "Felix Is Missing," "Scrooge Gets an Oscar," "The Blackout," "What Does a Naked Lady Say to You?," "Murray the Fink," "Where's Grandpa?," "Let's Make a Deal," "Gloria Moves In," "Oscar in Love," and the 1993 TV reunion movie (as Speed). Garry Walberg was born June 10, 1921, in Buffalo, New York, and became a very prolific character actor, primarily in television. He guest starred on everything from *Lassie* to *Rawhide* to *Star Trek*. He has the distinction of performing in the very first episode of *Twilight Zone*, "Where Is Everybody?," in 1959.

Walberg was one of two Garrys associated with *The Odd Couple* series with that unusual double-r spelling (Garry Marshall being the other). Walberg appeared in a lucky 13 episodes, and later followed Jack Klugman over to his next series, *Quincy, M. E.*, as Lieutenant Frank Monahan. He would reunite with Klugman one more time in 1993 for *The Odd Couple: Together Again*, in which he reprised his role as Homer "Speed" Deegan. Like Jack Klugman, he also was involved in breeding race horses.

Walberg died of congestive heart failure at the age of 90, on March 27, 2012.

GEORGE WENDT

Portrayed Oscar Madison in Chicago at the Northlight Theatre. George Wendt was born in the Windy City October 17, 1948. He was a Notre Dame dropout who then joined The Second City comedy troupe. His first regular role was in the short-lived 1982 sitcom, *Making the Grade*, as Gus. A short time later, he got his biggest break by being cast as the slovenly, beer-swilling everyman Norm Peterson on the long-running sitcom *Cheers*, on NBC. He even briefly had his own eponymous sitcom on CBS, but it never did find an audience.

After years of seeing Wendt as Norm, he was a natural to assume the role of Oscar Madison in the successful 2012 production of *The Odd Couple*, in his native Chicago. When illness (chest pains) forced Wendt to leave the role, he was replaced by understudy Marc Grapey. Grapey was also a cast member in the 2005 Nathan Lane/Matthew Broderick production at the Brooks Atkinson Theatre. Wendt made a full recovery, and was seen most recently on the TV series *Portlandia*.

JOHN WHEELER

Guest starred in "Does Your Mother Know You're Out, Rigoletto?" (as Herbert Murphy), and "The Roy Clark Show," "The Hustler," and "Vocal Girl Makes Good" (all as Mr. Felscher/Flescher). John Wheeler was born June 20, 1930, in Texas. He attended the University of the Pacific, in Stockton, California. He spent over 40 years in episodic TV and movie roles. He was Gav in the "Journey to Babel" episode of *Star Trek*, and his sitcom credits include *Love, American Style*, *Here's Lucy*, *Happy Days*, *The Brady Bunch*, and *Rhoda*. He guest starred four times on *The Odd Couple*, and usually sang an aria or two (as a member of Felix's opera club). He also performed with the City Center Opera in New York, and was seen in numerous Broadway musicals, including *Carousel* and Neil Simon's *Sweet Charity*.

Wheeler's movie career includes roles in the Elvis Presley film *Live a Little, Love a Little* (1968), *Tell Them Willie Boy Is Here* (1969), *Support Your Local Gunfighter* (1971), *Mame* (1974), *Apollo 13* (1995), and *The Apple Dumpling Gang Rides Again* (1979). Wheeler has also performed in dozens of TV commercials. As of this writing, he is enjoying his retirement.

BETTY WHITE

Guest starred in "Password" (as herself). Betty Marion White was born January 17, 1922, in Oak Park, Illinois. She became interested in acting in high school, leading to a seven-decade career in television. She's hosted talk shows, a variety show, a game show, and she's starred (or co-starred) in many sitcoms—*Life with Elizabeth*, *A Date with the Angels*, *The Mary Tyler Moore Show*, *The Betty White Show*, *Maybe This Time*, and *The Golden Girls*. She was a favorite of Jack Paar and appeared frequently on his shows. She also guest starred as herself, along with then-husband Allen Ludden, on the single most popular episode of *The Odd Couple*. Felix and Oscar are paired up and pitted against Betty White and her teammate on Allen Ludden's legendary game show, *Password*. Felix's bizarre, eclectic clues cause him to lose the game, and he is escorted off the set while having a tantrum.

From the most popular *Odd Couple* TV episode, "Password," the amazing Betty White in a treasured photograph she autographed for the author, Bob Leszczak.

Betty's enduring popularity led to a popular TV commercial for Snickers candy bars and her first stint as host of *Saturday Night Live* (encouraged by a Facebook campaign). The nonagenarian, as of this writing, stars in a very popular TV series, *Hot in Cleveland*, on TV Land, and she was also recently the host of *Betty White's Off Their Rockers* on NBC—kind of a modern-day *Candid Camera*. She has garnered six Emmy Awards, and continues to do yeoman's work for numerous animal-related charities.

DAVID WHITE

Guest starred in "Felix Directs" (as Phil). Daniel David White was born April 4, 1916, in Denver, Colorado. During World War II he was in the Marine Corps, and afterwards began getting work on Broadway. Coincidentally, he guest starred in an episode of *Appointment with Adventure*—the very same summer-replacement series on which Jack Klugman and Tony Randall first appeared together.

His credits on episodic TV are impressive. He appeared in two episodes of *The Twilight Zone*—"I Sing the Body Electric" and "A World of Difference." He is likely best known for portraying Darrin Stevens's perplexed boss, Larry Tate, on *Bewitched*. Few know his name, but everyone knows his face and his wavy shock of white hair. In 1973, he guest starred on *The Odd Couple* in the episode "Felix Directs." Unbeknownst to Felix and Oscar, he attempts to turn Felix's G-rated film into an X-rated one.

He also appeared in numerous famous films, such as *Brewster's Millions* (1985), *The Great Impostor* (1961), and *The Apartment* (1960, with future Felix Ungar, Jack Lemmon). White was married twice, and when he died of a heart attack on November 27, 1990, in North Hollywood, he left behind a daughter, Alexandra.

PAUL WILLIAMS

Guest starred in "The Paul Williams Story" (as himself). Paul Hamilton Williams, Jr., was born September 19, 1940, in Omaha, Nebraska. Small in stature, but big in songwriting talent, Williams penned many immensely popular songs from the early 1970s, including "Rainy Days and Mondays" and "We've Only Just Begun" for the Carpenters, "An Old-Fashioned Love Song" for Three Dog Night, and "You and Me Against the World" for Helen Reddy. Williams performs the latter two songs in a season-five episode of *The Odd Couple*, in which Felix's daughter, Edna, runs away to follow Williams after Felix imposes too many strict rules upon her. Williams wrote a song especially for the episode called "The One Who Loves Ya." Because of constant script changes, he waited until the day of the filming to complete the song—the writers kept changing the way the episode was to end, and the song had to mesh with the plot. John Denver was the original choice for the episode, but when he bowed out, Paul Williams got the nod.

The guest appearance on *The Odd Couple* led to more acting roles in

Smokey and the Bandit (1977) and *Phantom of the Paradise* (1974). Williams continued to write popular music, including the theme song for TV's *The Love Boat*, and "The Rainbow Connection" for *The Muppet Movie*. He is a member of the Songwriter's Hall of Fame, and won an Oscar for the song *Evergreen* from the motion picture *A Star Is Born* (1976). Paul's brother, Mentor Williams, wrote the famous song "Drift Away," which was a big hit for both Dobie Gray and Uncle Kracker.

Demond Wilson

Co-starred in the 1982 remake series, *The New Odd Couple* (as Oscar Madison). Grady Demond Wilson (yes, his real first name was Grady) was born October 13, 1946, in Valdosta, Georgia, because Demond's mother, in her third trimester, didn't wish to climb four flights of stairs to her Harlem apartment. She wisely stayed at her mother's house until Demond was born, and then returned to the apartment in New York. Demond began his acting career, at age four, in a Broadway play titled *Green Pastures*. As a child, a ruptured appendix almost cost him his life, but he pulled through. He was drafted into the army in the middle 1960s and served a tour of duty in Vietnam. Upon returning to civilian life, his big television break came in an episode of *All in the Family*, "Edith Writes a Song." That guest appearance led to his being cast as Lamont on *Sanford and Son*.

In Wilson's next series, the very short-lived *Baby, I'm Back* on CBS, he portrayed a character named Ray Ellis, who attempts to work his way back into the family unit he left behind seven years earlier. A very young Kim Fields (long before she was Tootie on *The Facts of Life*) portrayed his daughter, Angie, on the show. Not long after that, he was on ABC in *The New Odd Couple*—an updated, mostly African American take on the original series. Mark Rothman, who had worked on the original version, attempted to make a go of the new version as well—sometimes even reworking favorite scripts used in the original. In all, 18 episodes were produced, but the program was not a ratings winner and was canceled.

In 1984 Wilson became an ordained minister, and significantly curtailed performing.

Paul Winchell

Provided the voice for Fleabag in 32 episodes of the cartoon series *The Oddball Couple*. Paul Wilchinsky was born December 21, 1922, in New York City. He modified his last name and became Paul Winchell and, inspired by Edgar Bergen, became one of the most famous ventriloquists of all time. His dummies included Knucklehead Smiff, Tessie, and Jerry Mahoney. After a win on *Major Bowes' Original Amateur Hour*, Winchell was offered his own, eponymously titled show. He was also a fine dramatic actor, but is best known for entertaining the younger set, on *Winchell-Mahoney Time*, a program which aired over Metromedia stations five days a week. Winchell was also the voice of Tigger in numerous Winnie-the-Pooh animated shorts (he even won a Grammy for a song called "The Wonderful Thing about Tiggers"); he was the voice of "the scrubbing bubbles" (a virtual imitation of the late comedian Hugh Herbert) in the Dow Chemical commercials, Dick Dastardly in the *Dastardly and Muttley* cartoons, and Fleabag, the Oscar Madison–esque canine in *The Oddball Couple*. This DePatie/Freleng Saturday morning cartoon series debuted on ABC just weeks after the original sitcom version was cancelled by the same network. Frank Nelson provided the voice for Spiffy, the Felix Unger–like feline in that series.

Winchell was also quite the accomplished inventor. The artificial heart and the disposable razor blade are just two of the many inventions to which he made claims. His nickname was "Winch," and that was also the title of his autobiography. The original Tigger's voice was permanently silenced on June 24, 2005, in Moorpark, California, just one day prior to the death of the voice of the original Piglet, John Fiedler.

Legendary DJ Wolfman Jack guest starred in *The Odd Couple* episode titled "The Songwriter," and is pictured here (left) with the author, Bob Leszczak. Wolfman and Bob worked together at WXTR-FM in Washington, D.C.

WOLFMAN JACK

Guest starred in "The Songwriter" (as himself). Wolfman Jack was born Robert Weston Smith on January 21, 1938. His Wolfman persona was derived from a love for horror films. He started his radio career on a high-powered radio station just south of the California border—XERF in 1963. He was a lover of rhythm and blues music, and would accentuate his banter with occasional Wolfman howls and mildly suggestive words and phrases.

While with 66 WNBC-AM in New York City, he solidified his popularity and legendary status with one of the most memorable scenes in the wildly popular George Lucas 1973 film classic, *American Graffiti* (as himself, a disc jockey who loved popsicles). This led to a cameo appearance, again as himself, in an episode of *The Odd Couple*. Jaye P. Morgan also guest starred in that episode, in which Felix and Oscar bring Wolfman a copy of Felix's composition, "Happy and Peppy and Bursting with Love" for a critique. Wolfman doesn't like it, but luckily for Felix, Jaye P. Morgan does, and agrees to perform it.

Wolfman last worked on a weekly live "oldies" radio show (1993-1995) broadcast live from the Washington, D.C., Hard Rock Café, and aired on D.C.'s XTRA 104.1 (WXTR-FM), where this writer was also working at the time as the morning-show host. Sadly, Wolfman was a chain smoker with a nagging and hacking cough, and died of a heart attack not long afterward, on July 1, 1995, at the age of 57.

He was inducted into the National Radio Hall of Fame in 1996, and into the NAB Broadcasting Hall of Fame in 1999.

WILLIAM WOODSON

Narrated the opening credits for the original TV series (seasons one, two, and three). William T. Woodson was born July 16, 1917, in San Bernardino, California. His dulcet tones served him well as a Shakespearean actor/voice-over announcer, but he is most famous for narrating *The Odd Couple*'s opening credits. Woodson recalled, "I was in Las Vegas when I got that job. I

Narrator and nonagenarian William Woodson, who uttered the immortal, "On November 13th, Felix Unger was asked to remove himself from his place of residence" (courtesy William Woodson).

was visiting singer Giselle McKenzie, who was doing a show there, and I got a call from my agent, who said, 'Get back here. You've got the job.' It was something I had auditioned for, and I quickly got back home. We used so many studios in those years, but I believe it was recorded at Radio Recorders on Santa Monica Boulevard. My agent said they were looking for a very stuffy guy, but when they called me back, they wanted me to tone it down a little bit. It was a time when the ad agencies flew you out and put you up at the very best hotels. Those days are long gone."

Regarding his pay for that memorable voiceover, Woodson said, "I got scale, whatever it was at that time, plus ten percent. I've always had a fond spot in my heart for that show. Because of it, advertisers would say, 'I'm looking for someone like the guy who does the intro for *The Odd Couple*. In fact, I was in Berlin with my wife watching an operetta when I got tapped on the shoulder to take a call from my agent in New York. It was for ABC's *The View*. They wanted me to read with the same kind of intonation, and they rented a studio and hired a limo. That came about because of that one reading for *The Odd Couple*, for which I'm eternally grateful. I also did something similar for *Family Guy*."

Was he aware of the significance of the date—November 13—mentioned in the show's intro? Woodson said, "No, not until you just told me. I had no idea that was Garry Marshall's birthday. That is an interesting bit of significance. It's amazing that I never got to meet Garry, nor did I ever talk to him, as far as I can recall. I had worked with Tony Randall in New York—I knew him in advance. I did *Inherit the Wind* with Tony on Broadway. Eventually, I got another job and left that show. I met Jack Klugman somewhere along the line, but we weren't talking acquaintants. I wasn't really close to either one of them."

Mr. Woodson also recalled, "I read one line in a very special way—'he knew one day ... he would return to her' in a very stiff, stalwart and ponderous fashion." Little did he realize that the line would prove prophetic in the 114th and final episode of the series, "Felix Remarries."

Three
The Crew

Nick Abdo

Nick Abdo was born in Los Angeles, and his long and successful TV and movie career began with *The Odd Couple*. He was quickly promoted from production assistant to associate producer for seasons four and five. He recalled, "There was a lot of generosity in front of the cameras. The guest stars and supporting actors always had jokes. There was a lot of sharing. Nobody left a scene without a laugh."

There were different writer's levels at the writer's table, Abdo explained: "As apprentice writers, we were told if we had a joke, to write it down, keep quiet, and give it to Garry Marshall. Garry was great—if the joke got a laugh and was used, we got the credit, but if it bombed Garry took the heat." Speaking of writing, Abdo said, "The show's tag—or closing scene—was rarely written ahead of time. On several occasions the stars were given a premise with a beginning and end, and they would ad-lib the scene. There was a lot of room for creativity and fun on that set. Our 'gag reels' were outrageously funny. Even during some of the lesser episodes of the show, it was always a fun, fun time."

Even though the show was filmed in Hollywood, it was set in New York City. Abdo shared, "The cast would go to Manhattan for two weeks each year and shoot all the outdoor scenes for that entire season. They would already know what was needed for that year's scripts—happy scenes, sad scenes, scenes in the rain, scenes for the opening credits, etc. All of the topics for that season would be covered in those two weeks on location."

About the show's cast, Abdo reminisced, "Jack was very warm and sweet. His loud demeanor sometimes made it seem like he had a bad temper. Tony Randall was a very refined man, and was very much a perfectionist. He insisted on maintaining the quality and integrity of the show, along with the humor. Although Garry Marshall did the live audience warm-ups, he was always joined by Tony, who not only got the audience's energy up, but also

The Odd Couple's associate producer, Nick Abdo (courtesy Nick Abdo).

pumped up his own. Tony and Jack always participated in the rewrite sessions after the run-throughs. They were amazing pros, too. We would sometimes do retakes weeks later, and they could immediately duplicate the action and attitude of the scene. Al Molinaro (Murray, the cop) was rather quiet and private. They used to say that he was the highest-paid-per-line actor in Hollywood. He had few lines, most of them being jokes. Al was involved in one of the show's funniest moments. There was a knock on the door. The peephole popped open and Murray's rather pronounced nose appeared in the opening; it got a huge laugh from the audience. Everyone knew who it was. It's not well known, but Al's character, Murray Greshler, got his last name from Tony and Jack's agent, Abbey Greshler, who was there at every single filming."

After *The Odd Couple*, Nick Abdo produced *Happy Days* and *Laverne and Shirley*, and served as executive producer for the *Leave It to Beaver* sequel series, *Still the Beaver*. His impressive résumé also includes work on such Garry Marshall–directed motion pictures as *Beaches* (1988), *Frankie and Johnny* (1991), and *Overboard* (1987). When asked if he ever had the itch to be an actor, Abdo said, "No, thank you. I'll leave that to the pros."

BILL ANGELOS

Often teamed with Buz Kohan, Bill Angelos began writing for King Features cartoon shows *Beetle Bailey*, and *Snuffy Smith & Barney Google*. His only sitcom-writing credits are for *The Odd Couple*: "Old Flames Never Die," "Vocal Girl Makes Good," and "The Songwriter." The latter two have a musical theme and big-name guest stars—Marilyn Horne and Jaye P. Morgan, respectively.

Angelos and Kohan found their biggest series writing success with *The Carol Burnett Show*. Angelos was involved in writing over 100 episodes of Carol's variety show, and he won a Primetime Emmy in 1973 for "Outstanding Writing Achievement in Variety and Music." Angelos also produced more than 20 episodes of the program.

ART BAER

Art Baer was born September 17, 1925. He wrote some sketch material for stand-up comics such as Flip Wilson, Victor Borge, and Jonathan Winters. Teamed with Ben Joelson, Baer wrote for many TV programs.

Baer and Joelson also wrote material

for a couple of game shows: *Picture This*, hosted by Jerry Van Dyke; *Make a Face*, starring Bob Clayton; and *Fractured Phrases*, hosted by Art James. The duo's sitcom credits include *Car 54, Where Are You?*, *The Andy Griffith Show*, *Gomer Pyle, USMC*, *The Dick Van Dyke Show*, *Hogan's Heroes*, *The Partridge Family*, and *Happy Days*. Their *Odd Couple* collaborations are, "The Dog Story," "New York's Oddest," and "Big Mouth" (the latter with Howard Cosell). Baer also wrote and/or produced dozens upon dozens of episodes of *The Love Boat*.

Baer, along with Ben Joelson, won their only Emmy Award for *The Carol Burnett Show* in 1972. Sadly, Art Baer died on his birthday in 2006, at the age of 81.

Norman Barasch

Norman Barasch was born February 18, 1922, in Rockville Center, New York. Usually paired with Carroll Moore, Barasch wrote and/or produced many famous television shows, including *The Danny Kaye Show*, *Rhoda*, *Chico and the Man*, *The McLean Stevenson Show*, *Fish*, and *Lotsa Luck*. For *The New Odd Couple*, Barasch wrote the episode "The Odd Triangle," and he also produced many of the short-lived series' episodes.

It's interesting to note that, even though Barasch didn't work on the original *Odd Couple* series, he did write a screenplay, *Send Me No Flowers* (1964), in which Tony Randall co-starred (with Doris Day and Rock Hudson). Barasch also penned the Bobby Darin and Sandra Dee comedy *That Funny Feeling* (1965).

Barasch has been nominated for three Primetime Emmy Awards, for *The Danny Kaye Show*, *Rhoda*, and *The Kraft Music Hall*. After *The New Odd Couple*, Barasch was already in his early 60s and went into semi-retirement.

Jerry Belson

Jerry Belson was born July 8, 1938, in El Centro, California. Before his career in television, Belson found work as a magician, a drummer, and a comic-book writer. Once he got his TV break, he did it all—writing, producing, and directing. Belson has writing credits on *The Dick Van Dyke Show*, *Gomer Pyle, USMC*, *I Spy*, *The Lucy Show*, and *The Joey Bishop Show*. For *The Odd Couple*, he wrote and/or co-wrote (with Garry Marshall) "The Laundry Orgy," "Oscar the Model," "They Use Horseradish Don't They?" and "Security Arms." Belson was never afraid to try risky things and jokes that not everyone would get. He was also the executive producer for 70 of the program's 114 episodes, and he directed numerous others. The episode titled "Our Fathers" includes an elderly character named Belson. Belson's father was occasionally used as an extra on the program. His movie credits include writing the screenplay for *Smokey and the Bandit* (1977), *The End* (1978), and *Fun with Dick and Jane* (1977).

Belson's brother is radio personality Gordon Belson, and his sister, Monica Johnson, was the typist for *The Odd Couple* scripts; she later became a prolific writer in her own right, with scripts for *The Mary Tyler Moore Show*, *Laverne and Shirley*, and *It's Garry Shandling's Show*. Monica also wrote several Albert Brooks films (*Mother*, *The Muse*, and *Lost in America*). Monica died at the age of 64, on November 1, 2010.

Much like the character of Oscar Madison, Jerry Belson was a long-time ulcer sufferer. Despite his health issues, he remained very busy in television. However, while working as a consulting producer for *The Drew Carey Show*, Jerry Belson took ill and succumbed to prostate cancer, on October 10, 2006. Belson had three children—Kristine, Julie and Will.

DICK BENSFIELD

Richard Edward Bensfield was born June 18, 1926, in Los Angeles, California. He began writing for television when it was still in its infancy. Often paired with Perry Grant, he is credited as co-writer of 188 episodes of *The Adventures of Ozzie and Harriet*. His other sitcom credits include *The Andy Griffith Show*, *Mayberry RFD*, *I Dream of Jeannie*, *Love, American Style*, *Happy Days*, *Good Times*, *The Partridge Family*, *Diff'rent Strokes*, *227*, *One Day at a Time*, and *Hello, Larry*. Actor/comedian John Femia, who played Tommy on the latter show, recalled working with Dick Bensfield and Perry Grant: "Their scripts were funnier and definitely more in tune with the times than other writers. They were also responsible for some of the funniest lines my character ever said, and they were always nice and very accessible to everyone around them." Bensfield, with Perry Grant, wrote seven episodes of *The Odd Couple*: "The Big Brother," "Murray the Fink," "Myrna's Debut," "Good Bad Boy," "The Frog," "Felix the Calypso Singer," and "A Grave for Felix." ("A Grave for Felix" was reworked for *The New Odd Couple* in 1982.)

Bensfield also served as co-executive producer on *227*, *One Day at a Time*, and *Hello, Larry*.

BRUCE BILSON

Bruce Bilson was born in Brooklyn, New York, May 19, 1928. He is a graduate of the UCLA School of Theater, Film and Television. During the 1950s, he worked his way up from assistant film editor to assistant director, and finally got his directorial break on *The Patty Duke Show*, in 1964. All in all, he's directed over 400 television shows, garnered an Emmy Award for directing *Get Smart*, and received a Director's Guild nomination for *The Odd Couple*. Bilson directed five episodes of *The Odd Couple* during the single camera first season ("The Fight of the Felix," "Oscar's Ulcer," "I Do I Don't," "The Big Brothers," and "Lovers Don't Make House Calls"), and one in the multi-camera second season ("Being Divorced Is Never Having to Say 'I Do'"). When asked about the single vs. multi-camera approach, Bilson stated, "Using three cameras with a live audience is actually less expensive than just one, and it's not as difficult as it seems—there are just more marks on the floor. The single-camera shows were good,

Director Bruce Bilson (center) is sandwiched between Jack Klugman (left) and Tony Randall (right) during a first-season rehearsal (courtesy Bruce Bilson).

but Jack and Tony wanted to play to a live audience, like when they were on stage." During those multi-camera shoots, Bilson reflected, "Garry used to throw penny candy into the audience between takes and scene changes. The audience absolutely loved it, and it killed some time while cast and crew got set for the next scene and the cameras could roll again."

Even though Felix and Oscar's apartment number was always 1102, Bilson said, "The apartment setup in the laugh-track shows was almost identical to the movie, but that needed to change drastically for the three-camera approach. It needed to be more open to accommodate the live audience."

As far as getting the job, Bilson remembered, "I was called in by Paramount, and the producer at that time, Jerry Davis, told me they were doing a TV version of *The Odd Couple* and they wanted me to direct the first two episodes. Jerry gave me six scripts to read and told me to pick the ones I wanted to do. 'The Laundry Orgy' was the best one, but they told me to select another because that would be the debut episode, and they wanted the actors to get an episode or two working together before shooting the first one to go on the air. I chose 'Fight of the Felix.' I had the great privilege of being in the room when Jack and Tony came in for the first reading of the script. Tony Randall entered, removed his perfectly pressed blue sport coat, hung it carefully on the back of a chair and sat down. Meanwhile, Jack Klugman took a seat across the table, threw his sweater on the chair next to him, and took out a cigar. Tony's head snapped up, a look of disapproval on his face, 'Are we smoking?' It was not a question. A moment passed. Jack put the cigar in his pocket. The Odd Couple was in the room. Three or four times during the first reading, there were lines similar to those in the play, and at that moment each time, Tony and Jack went right into the scene from the play. Both had done it before, but never together and they were feeling each other out. It was marvelous. And, initially, Oscar's messy bedroom looked much too organized, so Jack said, 'I'll handle this,' and within minutes it looked just perfect. Stuff was strewn everywhere."

Regarding specific episodes, Bilson remembered, "We used Clint Howard for an episode called 'The Big Brothers.' I knew Clint very well. I was assistant director on *The Andy Griffith Show* with Ron Howard, and his little brother was often there, too, behind the scenes. I also directed him in the short-lived sitcom, *The Baileys of Balboa*."

Two of the six episodes Bilson directed focused upon weddings. "That was purely coincidental," he insists. "I especially loved the 'I Do, I Don't' episode. Joyce Van Patten and George Furth were brilliant in it. Throughout that episode there are references to 'jellyfish' and 'jelly doughnuts,' so, even though I don't usually do such things, I ended that episode as Joyce and George exited happily together, racking focus to a tight close-up of a partially-eaten jelly doughnut for effect. I almost scrubbed the idea at first, but in retrospect, I'm glad I left it in. Now, on the other wedding episode, 'Being Divorced Means Never Having to Say 'I Do,'' we didn't have a funny tag to close the show after the wedding scene. Tony and Jack thought it would be amusing if they stayed around at the chapel for a funeral. This led to one of the show's funniest lines. Totally ad-libbed, Felix muses about the funeral he would want with a beautiful carriage pulled by a team of white horses while the band played the grand march from *Aida*. 'And what would you like, Oscar?' to which Oscar replies, 'I'd like to be there.' Sheer brilliance."

Many directors, from Garry Marshall to Ezra Stone to Jerry Paris to Alfred Hitchcock have also appeared on camera, but Bilson isn't one of them. "No, I never did that," he says. "I never appeared on camera. I never wanted to. Never had the urge."

Talent runs in the Bilson family. Bruce is married to actress Renne Jarrett; his son is writer/director Daniel Bilson; his daughter is producer Julie Bilson Ahlberg; and his granddaughter is actress Rachel Bilson.

Robert Birnbaum

Robert Birnbaum was born in 1938 in New York City. Often known simply as Bob Birnbaum, he began to have success in television and film in the 1960s. He became a prolific assistant director, director, and unit production manager for such TV programs as *Love, American Style*, *The Brady Bunch*, *Cagney and Lacey*, *Happy Days*, *Sledge Hammer*, and *The Les Crane Show* (on which *The Odd Couple*'s future head writer, Mark Rothman, was a page). On *The Odd Couple*, Birnbaum was the director for "Partner's Investment," "The Pen Is Mightier than the Pencil," "A Barnacle Adventure," and "The Ides of April." He was also assistant director for the famous "Felix, the Calypso Singer" episode, which produced the popular "Oscar, Oscar, Oscar" song. Birnbaum was twice nominated for Emmys (once for *Pee-Wee's Playhouse* and once for the limited 1985 series *Space*). He was also credited as assistant director for two immensely popular motion pictures—*Reds* (1981) and *Oh, God!* (1977).

Birnbaum died on May 12, 2007, at the age of 68.

Bob Brunner

Robert Brunner was born August 3, 1934, in New York City. Brunner began as a copyboy for *The New York Daily News*. It was there that he first met Garry Marshall. Brunner entered show business as a publicist for Tony Bennett and Louis Armstrong.

In the 1970s, Brunner began working in television with his old friend Garry Marshall as writer and/or producer. For *The Odd Couple*, Brunner wrote "The First Baby," "Oscar's Birthday," "The Odyssey Couple," and "This Is the Army, Mrs. Madison." Brunner also penned episodes of *Diff'rent Strokes*, *Love Sidney*, *Alice*, *Laverne and Shirley*, and *Happy Days*, including the infamous "Jump the Shark" episode of the latter, titled "Hollywood Part 3." (The term "Jump the Shark" became part of the vernacular, and signifies a program which has been on the air too long, or has taken an ill-advised direction.)

Brunner also produced numerous episodes of *Happy Days*, and was executive producer for many episodes of *Diff'rent Strokes*. Brunner died suddenly of a heart attack, brought on by severe hypertension, October 28, 2012, in Northridge, California. He is survived by three children and six grandchildren.

Frank Buxton

Frank Buxton was born in Wellesley, Massachusetts, February 13, 1930. He attended Northwestern and Syracuse Universities, and, after returning from active duty in the Korean War, he tried his hand at stand-up comedy. From there he joined the legitimate stage, appearing in *Bye Bye Birdie*, *Brigadoon*, and *The Tender Trap*. He also had roles in three Garry Marshall–directed films, *Overboard* (1987), *Beaches* (1988), and *Frankie and Johnny* (1991). He hosted a cultural show for kids on ABC called *Discovery* (with co-host Virginia Gibson), and the Peabody Award–Winning NBC kids' show *Hot Dog*, of which he is understandably very proud. Buxton also hosted *Get the Message*, a short-lived game show on ABC based in New York City (taped in the Elysee Theater). He was also the voice for the 1960s cartoon character, *Batfink*, a Batman parody.

Buxton also has ample experience working behind the camera. On *The Odd Couple*, Buxton directed nine episodes (including the memorable "Let's Make a Deal"), and wrote four scripts (including one for the show's most popular episode, according to *TV Guide*, "Password"). Actually, to be totally accurate, he wrote *five* episodes— "Laugh, Clown, Laugh" was penned under his alias, Fred Bernard. Buxton also produced seven *Odd Couple* episodes and even had a small part in one: he was the TV announcer in "The Insomniacs."

One of Buxton's biggest claims to fame was co-writing and providing a voice for the Woody Allen classic, *What's Up, Tiger Lily?* Buxton is the co-author of two books about radio, *Radio's Golden Age* and *The Big Broadcast*. As of this writing, he has a culinary internet program titled *Cookus Interruptus*.

Gerry Chiniquy

Germaine Adolph Chiniquy was born June 23, 1912, in Illinois. Chiniquy was an animator who worked closely with Friz Freleng at Warner Bros., beginning in the 1940s. Chiniquy's work is most prevalent in dance scenes in "Looney Tunes" and "Merrie Melodies" cartoons.

In the early 1960s when Warner Bros.' cartoon division folded, Chiniquy followed Friz Freleng and David DePatie to their new venture, DePatie/Freleng Enterprises. Chiniquy was promoted to animation director at DFE, and one of his first credits under his new title was *The Oddball Couple*— DFE's animated version of *The Odd Couple*, featuring Fleabag, a sloppy dog, and Spiffy, a fussy feline. *The Oddball Couple* ran for two seasons on ABC beginning in 1975, immediately after the cancellation of the ABC sitcom.

Among Chiniquy's other credits as animation director are *Spiderman, GI Joe, Dungeons and Dragons, Muppet Babies, The Transformers*, and *Jem*. Chiniquy died on November 22, 1989, at the age of 77, in Ventura, California.

Martin Cohan

Unlike George M. Cohan, who was born July 3 but claimed Independence Day as his birthday, *this* Cohan was actually born on the Fourth of July (in 1932) in San Francisco. After graduating from Stanford University, Cohan sought work in the burgeoning medium of television. After working on documentaries for ABC, Cohan turned to sitcom writing, a move which would prove very fruitful. Sometimes paired with Blake Hunter, Cohan wrote for such programs as *All in the Family, The Mary Tyler Moore Show, The Bob Newhart Show*, and *The Bob Crane Show*. Cohan's *Odd Couple* episodes are "And Leave the Greyhound to Us" (the title is a take-off on the Greyhound Bus TV commercials' "And leave the driving to us"), and "Oscar's

Promotion." He was also the producer of Mark Rothman and Lowell Ganz's *The Ted Knight Show*, in 1978.

Cohan's biggest successes came in the 1980s, writing and/or producing countless episodes of *Silver Spoons*, *Diff'rent Strokes*, and *Who's the Boss?* He won a Writer's Guild Award for *The Mary Tyler Moore Show* in 1972. Cohan died at the age of 77, on May 19, 2010, due to complications from lymphoma. Cohan's sister was actress Rhoda Gemignani, who was married to famed conductor Paul Gemignani.

HAL COOPER

Not to be confused with the hockey player of same name, Hal Cooper, the director and sometimes producer, was born February 23, 1923, in New York City. He got his first TV credits in the 1960s on shows such as *The Dick Van Dyke Show*, *Gidget*, *I Dream of Jeannie*, *I Spy*, *That Girl*, *Mayberry RFD*, *Death Valley Days*, and *The Courtship of Eddie's Father*.

Cooper remained extremely busy throughout the 1970s, and directed eight episodes of *The Brady Bunch*, 126 episodes of *Maude* (for which he was nominated for several Director's Guild Awards), and 11 episodes of *The Odd Couple*—including several in the single-camera first season, and quite a few multi-camera/studio-audience episodes. Cooper, in fact, directed the very first episode filmed before a studio audience, "Natural Childbirth" (starting off season two). Cooper was not against appearing on camera, and he did just that (in bit parts) on *The Courtship of Eddie's Father*, *I Dream of Jeannie*, *That Girl*, and *Mayberry RFD*.

Hal Cooper remained active as a director and producer until the late 1990s. He died at the age of 91 on April 11, 2014.

DAN DAILEY

Daniel James Dailey was born December 14, 1913, in New York City. He was a child performer, and got his start in vaudeville. In 1937, he made his Broadway debut in *Babes in Arms*—the Rodgers and Hart musical which spawned memorable songs such as "Where or When" and "My Funny Valentine." His first credited movie role was in *The Mortal Storm* (1940). He was later signed by 20th Century–Fox for a series of memorable musicals (although Dailey liked to refer to the studio as 20th Penitentiary Fox).

In 1969, he starred in his own TV sitcom, *The Governor and J. J.*, which lasted for two seasons on CBS. He won a Golden Globe Award for his role as Governor William Drinkwater on that series, and he also directed four episodes. Another series in which he starred, *Faraday and Company*, had an even shorter prime-time life. Dan Dailey also ties into *The Odd Couple* in three different ways. He directed one episode of the original TV program—"Vocal Girl Makes Good," on which opera star Marilyn Horne made a guest appearance in 1974. He's also mentioned in the Edward Villella episode "Last Tango in Newark." Dailey had also previously portrayed Oscar Madison to Richard Benjamin's Felix Ungar at the Blackstone Theatre in Chicago, in 1966. Dailey reprised the role of Oscar years later and, while performing *The Odd Couple* onstage in California, Dailey fell and broke his hip. A year later, Dailey died during surgery to replace that hip, on October 16, 1978.

Jerry Davis

Jerome L. Davis was born on September 16, 1917, in New York City. He wrote the Dean Martin and Jerry Lewis motion picture *Pardners* (1956), and then began his TV career as a writer and producer for numerous Warner Bros. TV shows, such as *Maverick*, *77 Sunset Strip*, *Room for One More*, *Hawaiian Eye*, and *Surfside 6*. His later credits as both writer and producer focused mainly on situation comedy, and that includes producing the first 63 of 114 episodes of *The Odd Couple*, including the immensely popular "Password" episode. For his work, Davis was nominated for no less than five Emmys.

Early in his career Davis was married to actress Marilyn Maxwell, with whom he had one child. He kept very busy throughout the 1970s and early 1980s, producing programs such as *House Calls* and *Harper Valley PTA*. Jerry Davis died of a stroke on April 11, 1991.

David H. DePatie

David Hudson DePatie was born May 26, 1935, in Shiprock, New Mexico. He was in charge of the Warner Bros. cartoon division until they closed up shop in 1963. At that time, DePatie and fellow Warner Bros.'s alumnus, Friz Freleng, opted to start their own company—DePatie/Freleng Enterprises.

Along with cartoons, DePatie/Freleng Enterprises, or DFE Films, produced the Starkist Tuna TV commercials featuring Charley, the tuna (voiced by character actor Herschel Bernardi). DFE also animated the opening credits for some of the *Pink Panther* movies, which led to the popular and long-running *Pink Panther* Saturday morning cartoon series. Other animated shows such as *The Super Six*, *The Fantastic Four*, and *The Oddball Couple* had runs on Saturday mornings. The latter was an animated take on *The Odd Couple*. Paul Winchell and Frank Nelson provided the voices for Fleabag the dog and Spiffy the cat (respectively) in the 32 episodes that were produced and aired between 1975 and 1977.

DePatie/Freleng Enterprises was later absorbed by Cadence Industries and rebranded as Marvel Productions. DePatie served as executive producer for the new company.

Howard Deutch

Howard Deutch was born in New York City September 14, 1950. He attended Ohio State University and began in the advertising department for United Artists Records. His directorial career began with music videos for a couple of rock stars named Billy (Joel and Idol).

From there, Deutch graduated to film directing, and achieved instant success with two scripts from the pen of John Hughes—*Pretty in Pink* (1986) and *Some Kind of Wonderful* (1987). During the filming of the latter, Deutch met his bride-to-be, actress Lea Thompson. They worked together on the small screen on her hit sitcom, *Caroline in the City*.

Movie sequels (in which the original was directed by someone else) became one of Deutch's signatures. He directed *The Whole Ten Yards* (2004), *Grumpier Old Men* (1995), and *The Odd Couple II* (1998). The latter reunited Walter Matthau's Oscar and Jack Lemmon's Felix, who take a meandering road trip on the way to their children's wedding.

Of late, Deutch has directed mostly television series, such as *Harry's Law* and *CSI: New York*.

Jack Donohue

John Frances Donohue was born in Brooklyn, New York, November 3, 1908. He was originally an iron worker, and broke both of his legs on the job. His doctor recommended dancing as a way to strengthen those legs after the injury, and Donohue later found work as part of the Ziegfeld Follies and in vaudeville. He was the dance director for several Shirley Temple films, numerous MGM film musicals, and several Broadway musicals. Child actress Sherry Alberoni Van Meter worked with Donohue years later on *The Ed Wynn Show* on television, and recalled, "He was great with kids, and he loved to dance. He would often do a soft shoe between takes. I loved working with him."

After being the dance director for numerous films, Donohue took on an entire picture, *Close Up* (1948). He also directed Doris Day in *Lucky Me* (1954). When he broke into the new medium of television, he directed many of the live Frank Sinatra and Red Skelton shows. He was not a fan of the live shows, and was much more at ease directing filmed sitcoms in the 1960s, such as *The Lucy Show* (he also had bit parts in two episodes), *The Brady Bunch*, *Chico and the Man*, *The Paul Lynde Show*, and *The Odd Couple*. Donohue directed 14 episodes of *The Odd Couple*, including an especially popular entry, "The Sleepwalker" (in which Oscar hits Felix with rolled-up newspapers in the middle of the night), "The Pig Who Came to Dinner" (with guest stars Bobby Riggs and Billie Jean King), and "Felix Remarries" (the final episode).

Donohue died of a heart attack at the age of 75, on March 27, 1984, in Marina Del Rey, California. He had one daughter, Jill, and a stepson, Tom.

Martin Donovan

Martin Donovan was born Carlos Enrique Valera Y Peralta-Ramos in Buenos Aires, Argentina, January 21. He was still quite young when he began writing with William Windom and Inger Stevens in *The Farmer's Daughter* on ABC (he wrote over 20 episodes, and was associate producer on numerous others). Donovan was seemingly never out of work: he jumped to *The Second Hundred Years*, *That Girl*, *My World and Welcome to It*, *The Mary Tyler Moore Show*, *The Courtship of Eddie's Father*, *Room 222*, *Alice*,

Tabitha, The Jeffersons, and The Love Boat. For The Odd Couple, he penned "Our Fathers" (a flashback episode) and "Two Men on a Hoarse" (in which both Felix and Oscar develop laryngitis).

In the 1990s, Donovan began writing for the movies, his most famous being Death Becomes Her (1992, with Meryl Streep, Bruce Willis, and Goldie Hawn).

DAVID W. DUCLON

David Warren Duclon became David W. Duclon in TV credits. He got his break working for Garry Marshall on The Odd Couple. The episodes Duclon co-wrote are "I Gotta Be Me," "Let's Make a Deal," and "Felix Remarries." Duclon wore many hats on the program—he was assistant producer on the "Password" episode, and assistant consultant on "Felix Remarries." He even had small on-camera roles in "Oscar, the Model" (as a messenger) "Laugh, Clown, Laugh" (as a bee handler) and "Fat Farm" (as a waiter). "Fat Farm" was voted one of the show's best episodes, second only to "Password."

The Odd Couple was a springboard for Duclon. He went on to write and/or produce numerous episodes of Happy Days, Laverne and Shirley, Punky Brewster, Silver Spoons, The Jeffersons, The Ted Knight Show, Busting Loose, Eve, Family Matters, Yes, Dear, and Malcolm and Eddie.

Duclon's niece, actress Cherie Johnson, had regular roles in two of the programs for which he wrote—Punky Brewster and Family Matters.

PEGGY ELLIOTT

She was born Margaret Elliott Krutilek, but is known professionally as Peggy Elliott. Thanks to Garry Marshall, she was paired with writer Ed Scharlach and they instantly clicked as a team. Peggy recalled, "We quickly became like brother-and-sister and are still great friends after all these years." Their sitcom credits include Captain Nice, The Ghost and Mrs. Muir, That Girl, Love, American Style, and Hey, Landlord. Peggy reflected, "Hey, Landlord was so much fun, and I got to work with so many of those wonderful people (Garry Marshall, Jerry Belson, Jerry Paris) again on The Odd Couple." Peggy and Ed penned five episodes of The Odd Couple together: "Engrave Trouble," "Fight of the Felix," "What Does a Naked Lady Say to You?," "Speak for Yourself," and "Don't Believe in Roomers." Concerning the titles, Peggy Elliott said, "I think Ed loves puns more than I do, and spends more time thinking of them, but right from the start, we got into the habit of using puns for titles." Some of those episodes were filmed in the single-camera first season, and some were filmed in the multi-camera era. As Peggy insists, "I love three-camera shows as a writer. It's fun to see them unfold as a play. With single-camera it is so chopped up, but with three-camera shows there are run-throughs and you can see little things that can be tweaked."

Peggy was quite a trailblazer in a time when there were very few female sitcom writers. "There was Madelyn

Pugh Davis, of course, from *I Love Lucy*," she recalls. "I worked with her on *The Mothers-in-Law*. There was Peggy Chantler Dick and also Selma Diamond. Treva Silverman (*The Mary Tyler Moore Show*) became active a couple of years after us. I used to make a joke that I was the only unbearded writer."

About the people behind the scenes of *The Odd Couple*, Peggy has nothing but praise: "Garry Marshall and Jerry Belson were the ultimate class act. I loved working for them. And the producer, Jerry Davis, was one of the nicest people in the world. Ed Scharlach and I had worked with him on *That Girl*. Writers weren't welcomed on most sets, but Jerry Davis always made us feel welcome and asked for our opinion. With such well-defined characters, however, coming up with fresh ideas and covering territory that Neil Simon had not was quite a challenge. Quite often, Garry and Jerry turned toward situations where Oscar and Felix were thrust into roles the complete opposite to their well-defined types, such as in 'The Fight of the Felix.' In that episode, Felix steps in to the ring to fight a hockey pro who has been bullying Oscar. I'm so proud that it was recently named in *TV Guide's* list of the '100 Best Written Shows,' as number 77."

Peggy was married to Samuel Goldwyn, Jr., for some 35 years, and they started Samuel Goldwyn Films together, which produced *The Madness of King George* (1994), and brought many foreign films and talent to the U.S. As of this writing, she lives in

Odd Couple **Scriptwriter Peggy Elliott (courtesy Peggy Elliott).**

Idaho, is very active in women's causes, and runs film festivals. She has authored her own book, *A Small Part of History*, from Headline Publishing, and has a popular *Huffington Post* blog featuring memories of her TV comedy writing career at http://www.huffingtonpost.com/peggy-elliott/.

Peggy Elliott shared a bit of wisdom passed down to her from Garry Marshall, "Never throw anything away. You never know when you'll need to use it."

Friz Freleng

Isadore Freleng (sometimes credited as simply I. Freleng) was born August

21, 1905, in Kansas City, Missouri. Nicknamed "Friz" (a shortened form of his original nickname—Congressman Frizby) he had little or no formal training in drawing, but found work with Disney as an animator in his late teens. His success story began in 1929 with Warner Bros., and his work on "Merrie Melodies" and "Looney Tunes" cartoons is legendary. Freleng helped introduce Bugs Bunny, Tweety, Sylvester, Porky Pig, and was himself the inspiration for Yosemite Sam (Freleng was short, had a red moustache, a gruff voice, and a similar temperament). Bugs Bunny would later be introduced as "the Oscar-Winning rabbit" on *The Bugs Bunny Show* and that Oscar was for a cartoon titled "Knighty Knight, Bugs" in 1947.

The golden age of Warner Bros. cartoons came to an end in the early 1960s when the studio opted to close its animation department. At that time, Freleng teamed with the head of the Warner Bros. cartoon division, David H. DePatie, to form DePatie/Freleng Enterprises. Their biggest success was *The Pink Panther Show*, on which some of their other creations—*The Inspector* and *The Ant and the Aardvark*—were also featured. Freleng was awarded a "special Oscar" for "The Pink Phink" in 1965. In 1975, DePatie and Freleng created the animated answer to *The Odd Couple*—*The Oddball Couple*, featuring a messy dog named Fleabag and a fastidious feline named Spiffy.

Freleng died of natural causes on May 26, 1995, at the age of 89. Upon his passing, Warner Bros. created a moving tribute lithograph featuring all of the "Looney Tunes" characters with very sad faces gathered around Freleng's empty drawing table.

RON FRIEDMAN

Ron Friedman was born in Pittsburgh, Pennsylvania, and attended Carnegie Tech (as did Jack Klugman—in fact, they both experienced a tough-as-nails acting professor there named Henry Boettcher, the professor who told Klugman he'd make a better truck driver than an actor). Friedman's major was architecture, and he worked successfully in that field, but he wanted to earn a lot more money so that he could afford a great education for his children, and he relied upon his many talents to achieve this. Friedman had been born into a very musical family—his mother was quite a proficient opera singer and classical pianist. Ron was a good actor and also quite an impressive writer, and got his start writing comedy for Vaughn Meader (best known for his JFK impersonations and comedy albums). After the death of President Kennedy, Friedman wrote Meader's new act. Impressing the powers-that-be at CBS, Friedman began writing for *The Danny Kaye Show*. This led to scripts for sitcoms such as *Get Smart, Love on a Rooftop, The Andy Griffith Show, Bewitched, The Second Hundred Years, The Ghost and Mrs. Muir, Bridget Loves Bernie, The Partridge Family*, and *The Odd Couple* (he penned seven episodes for the latter). Friedman said, "*The Odd Couple*'s producer at the time, Jerry Davis, wanted me to write a script for the show, and wanted me to include a believable girlfriend because ABC was afraid people were thinking these two middle-aged Jewish men living together might be gay. Out of that came my first of seven scripts for the show, 'Lovers Don't Make Housecalls,' which introduced Joan Hotchkis as Dr. Nancy Cunningham—a love interest for Oscar. In fact, Nancy was a perfect match for Oscar because both of them were big boxing fans. I purposely threw in a few lesser-known boxers into the script, and we got some amazing fan mail from boxing devotees as a result. For 'Felix's Wife's Boyfriend,' they wanted me to create a history for Dr. Nancy Cunningham, so I came up with Fred Bier as her ski-bum brother, Raymond, who begins dating Felix's ex-wife, Gloria. Because of my musical background, I wrote 'Does Your Mother Know You're Out, Rigoletto?' Originally, opera singer Sherill Milnes was to guest star in that episode, but he backed out and Richard Fredricks agreed to do it instead. Tony was thrilled about my knowledge of opera and the ballet, and told me I was the only writer who wasn't a Philistine. I also penned the 'Last Tango in Newark' episode. I originally called it 'Swine Lake,' but that was changed. That's the wonderful episode with Edward Villella. Then they asked for a script about Murray the cop, since he hadn't been featured in a while, so I came up with 'The Murray Who Came to Dinner,' in which Murray and Mimi have a quarrel, and Murray moves in with Oscar and Felix, making for an even *odder* coupling. For 'Psychic Shmychic' we cast my friend, the wonderful Bernie Kopell, to debunk Felix's notion that he had psychic abilities. I also wrote the program's only holiday episode, 'Scrooge Gets an Oscar,' based upon Charles Dickens's *A Christmas Carol.* Garry Marshall and Jerry Belson called me in a frenzy, needing a Christmas episode, and even though it was hurriedly written, it came out really good. I worked on both the single-camera and multi-camera scripts. Tony and Jack liked my writing, and very little rewriting was necessary."

Why was he sometimes credited on *The Odd Couple* as Ronald I. Friedman, and other times as Ron Friedman? Ron stated, "I was way too busy to give a hoot." (Okay, so he didn't say "hoot.") Friedman added, "I loved working with those guys. It was a lot of fun and I had a great relationship with both Tony Randall, Jack Klugman, and even Jack's wife, Brett. When Klugman started doing *Quincy, M. E.*, I wanted to write for that show, too, but I was turned down because I was known as a comedy writer."

After a few more years of writing for sitcoms, such as *Love, American Style, That's My Mama,* and *Chico and the Man,* he switched gears. A newfound love for superheroes emerged while writing for *Wonder Woman.* Friedman recalled, "My longtime friendship and work with the great Stan Lee and my writing an animated, prime-time CBS special called *The Romance of Betty Boop* with producer Lee Mendelson (*Peanuts* and *Garfield*), and the sensational animator, the incomparable Bill Melendez, certainly helped (as did my lifelong experience as an artist, sculptor, and scenic designer), and this led to a long association with *G. I. Joe* (the animated 1987 movie), *The Bionic Six, Zorro, Iron Man, The Transformers* (a 1986 animated theatrical film) and *The Fantastic Four* (from *The Marvel Action Hour*)." Friedman provided the voice of Blastarr in *The Fantastic Four*.

Friedman shared, "I have a motion picture coming soon called *The Devil's Commandment* from West Coast Film Partners, and a play titled *Uprising*. I'm extremely busy—just the way I like it."

JIM FRITZELL

James Gustave Fritzell was born February 19, 1920, in San Francisco, California. Frequently paired with Everett Greenbaum, Fritzell wrote multiple episodes of many popular TV sitcoms, such as *Make Room for Daddy, Mister Peepers, The Real McCoys, M*A*S*H, The Doris Day Show*, and *Sanford and Son*.

His one and only script for *The Odd Couple* came about in 1971—"Surprise, Surprise," in which Felix's daughter, Edna, has a surprise party, which is ruined by Oscar's big poker game, a torrential downpour, and an uncooperative clown. Fritzell and Greenbaum liked to take credit for creating Tony Randall's effervescent, eccentric persona on *Mister Peepers* (which followed him throughout his movie career and even into *The Odd Couple*).

Fritzell also penned a couple of movie scripts for Don Knotts (*The Reluctant Astronaut* [1968] and *The Ghost and Mr. Chicken* [1965]), as well as one for Andy Griffith (*Angel in My Pocket* [1969]). Fritzell died shortly after his 59th birthday on March 9, 1979, in Los Angeles.

LOWELL GANZ

Lowell Ganz was born August 31, 1948, in New York City. As a TV writer and producer he was often teamed with either Mark Rothman or (later) Babaloo Mandel. In their youth, Ganz and Rothman wrote several skits and shows for school productions. How did they parlay this into writing for *The Odd Couple*? Ganz recalled, "We actually aspired to be variety show writers. We had never written a sitcom before, but we were devotees of *The Dick Van Dyke Show*, and that was a great tutorial. We even knew the blocking and the camera angles. Meanwhile, as luck would have it, Mark Rothman's father, Abe, was a limo driver and always knew at least two days in advance who his celebrity passengers were to be. Well, together, Mark and I wrote an episode of *The Odd Couple*, and when Abe was to have Jack Klugman and Tony Randall in his limo (separately), we had Abe present each of them with our script. A couple of weeks later, we got a call to come out to Los Angeles—we were to be hired as writers for the show. It was a bit overwhelming at first, and we were actually fired after about six weeks, along with several other writers (we were collateral damage). At the time, Mark and I were sharing an apartment, much in the manner of Felix and Oscar, except we were *both* untidy. With nowhere else to go, we still showed up at the Friday filmings anyway. Garry took notice, and eventually we submitted another draft for a possible script for the show—the most important one of our respective careers, 'The Ides of April.' It was inspired by an episode of *The Honeymooners*, 'The Worry Wart.' Garry liked it, and we were welcomed back and got to stay for the show's last three seasons."

Among the many other finely crafted scripts Ganz and Rothman penned—"The New Car," "Gloria Moves In," and "The Flying Felix" (the latter is one of Ganz and Rothman's favorites)—Ganz shared, "Yes, I concur with Mark on that. I trust his opinions. He always had great taste and judgment." Many of their scripts were later reworked by Mark for *The New Odd Couple*. Ganz added, "The episode titled 'My Strife in Court' was actually inspired by an actual event in the life of writer Barry Rubinowitz (still one of my closest friends). Barry was once arrested for what a policeman thought was ticket scalping. That was great fodder for a very memorable episode of the series. And, the episode's famous 'When you assume, you make an ass of you and me' line came from the genius that was Jerry Belson. When I spoke at his funeral, I told the story of how, when I got into the comedy writing business, with introspection I tried to compare myself to Belson and said, 'If this is how funny I'm supposed to be, I'm in big trouble.'"

Ganz shared a memory about the first of two times Howard Cosell guest starred on the program, in "The Big Mouth" episode: "Big mouth is appropriate. This was very early in my *Odd Couple* tenure. For some reason, for a long period of time I was alone with Cosell on stage at one of the rehearsals. I was painfully shy at the time, but I tried to conjure up a conversation with the man and brought up the schedule for that season's *Monday Night Football* broadcasts. Well, Howard instantly went into broadcast mode and listed the entire Monday Night schedule at the top of his lungs, as if the cameras had just gone live and the teams had taken the field. Much like our show's title, that was very 'odd.'"

About working with Tony Randall and Jack Klugman, Ganz reflected, "It was a very scary experience, especially at first. To be honest, I was scared shitless. Jack would be right in your face—he had a temper, but he also had a good 'writing brain.' In fact, years later, his words still have great weight and meaning in my writing. There was one time when Jack was yelling four words, 'What do I want?' Basically, that meant 'What is my motivation?' To this day, with my writing partner Marc Babaloo Mandel, we utter those four words, or simply say, 'Jack Klugman' to point out when we need to clarify a character's motivation. Because of the numerous times Jack shouted at Mark and me, I feel partly responsible for his later throat problems. Now, Tony Randall was about 90 percent charming and 10 percent childish. Collectively, Tony and Jack thought they were performing on the funniest show on television, and I'd like to think they were right, and I'm very proud of my contributions to the program."

Ganz worked with some incredibly talented directors on the show, but his favorite: "Jerry Paris. He was extremely warm and talented. Some people didn't 'get him' because when he spoke, he had absolutely no filter. He said exactly what was on his mind. But because of his brilliance on *The Dick Van Dyke Show*, and then the experience of working with him on both *The Odd Couple* and *Happy Days*, he is my favorite. And, we became great friends, too."

Ganz and Rothman went on to write for other Garry Marshall shows, such as *Happy Days* and *Laverne and Shirley*. About the lessons Garry bestowed upon him, Ganz remembered, "I learned so very much from the man. He used to say that if an idea started writing itself, there was a good chance it was writing itself poorly. Another of his pearls of wisdom was, 'The road to a joke is more valuable than being able to write a joke.'" In 1981, Ganz teamed with Babaloo Mandel and made the transition to writing for the big screen. This new partnership led to many monumentally successful motion pictures: *Parenthood* (1989), *A League of Their Own* (1992), *Mr. Saturday Night* (1992), *Forget Paris* (1995), *City Slickers* (1991), *Gung Ho* (1986), *Night Shift* (1982), and *Splash* (1984). The latter earned Ganz an Oscar nomination for Best Original Screenplay.

A large majority of *The Odd Couple*'s writers hailed from New York. About that subject, Ganz mused, "It was a great immigrant city. It had this 'outsider element' to it. People just 'grew up funny.' There's a funny sound to the manner in which New Yorkers speak. Most of those writers had no formal training, either. It was much more of an informal, instinctive and 'wildcat' thing."

As of this writing, Ganz lives in the Los Angeles area with his wife, Jeanne. They have three talented children, Scott, Allie, and Simon, all of whom are following in their famous father's footsteps, and Lowell couldn't be more proud.

Carl Gottlieb

Carl Gottlieb was born March 18, 1938, in New York City. Studying drama at Syracuse University served him well—he would later become involved in every aspect of motion pictures and TV. He became an actor, producer, and director, but, most notably, a writer. He had a hand in performing all four duties on Garry Marshall's shows. He had a small role on Marshall's first series, *Hey, Landlord* (and later *Mork and Mindy* and *Laverne and Shirley* as well). Gottlieb also directed one *Laverne and Shirley*, and wrote an episode of *The Odd Couple*, "Oscar in Love." This guest starred Dina Merrill as Oscar's harp-playing fiancée, Anita (with two children who take quite a while to warm up to Oscar).

Gottlieb is best known for writing the screenplay for both *Jaws* (1975) and its sequel *Jaws 2* (1978), *The Jerk* (1979) as well as *The Jerk, Too* (a TV version), and *Caveman* (1981). As of this writing, Gottlieb lives in the Los Angeles area.

NORM GRAY

Norm Gray wore many hats on Garry Marshall programs, and he worked on most of them—*Happy Days, Laverne and Shirley, Angie, Mork and Mindy,* and *The Odd Couple*. Gray was the assistant director for numerous episodes of the latter and was also listed as the unit manager on "Felix Remarries"—the show's final episode. Gray got directorial credits on another four episodes: "Maid for Each Other," "The Subway Story," "The Rent Strike," and "Laugh, Clown, Laugh."

Gray's final credit was as unit production manager on a TV-movie, *Skyward*, which was directed by Ron Howard. The movie starred Bette Davis, Howard Hesseman, and Marion Ross. Anson Williams (Potsie on *Happy Days*) received credit as the film's co-writer.

EVERETT GREENBAUM

Everett Greenbaum was born December 20, 1919, in Buffalo, New York. He and his writing partner, Jim Fritzell, penned multiple episodes of many famous sitcoms, such as *Mister Peepers, The Real McCoys, M*A*S*H, Sanford and Son, The Andy Griffith Show,* and *The New Andy Griffith Show* (Greenbaum even made a cameo appearance in an episode of the latter show). The writing duo penned only one episode of *The Odd Couple*: "Surprise, Surprise," in which Felix's surprise party for his daughter, Edna, is disrupted by Oscar's big poker game, and vice-versa. Greenbaum and Tony Randall had a big falling out over changes Tony made to the original script and they didn't speak to one another for over a decade.

Greenbaum and Fritzell also wrote some memorable movie scripts for Don Knotts, including *The Ghost and Mr. Chicken* (1965), *The Reluctant Astronaut* (1967), and *The Shakiest Gun in the West* (1968). Greenbaum died on July 11, 1999, at the age of 79.

NEAL HEFTI

Neal Paul Hefti was born in Hastings, Nebraska, October 29, 1922. A gift of a trumpet on his tenth birthday changed his life. His musical prowess led to an amazing career as a jazz trumpeter, as well as composer and arranger for Woody Herman and Count Basie. Hefti occasionally produced records for the likes of Frank Sinatra, Doris Day, Mel Torme and Tony Bennett. He penned numerous memorable tunes, including "Girl Talk" and "Cute."

However, it is movie scoring and theme songs for which Hefti is best known. He scored Neil Simon's *Barefoot in the Park* (1967) and *Last of the Red Hot Lovers* (1972). Unquestionably, *The Odd Couple* theme is one of the two compositions for which he is best known. This theme received exposure over and over again—in the original 1968 film, in the 1970–75 TV series, in *The New Odd Couple* in 1982, in the 1993 TV movie *The Odd Couple: Together Again,* and even in the 1998 sequel for the big screen, *The Odd Couple II.* (It was not used, however, in the animated series, *The Oddball Couple.*) The popularity of *The Odd Couple* theme is eclipsed only by the universality of Hefti's *Batman* TV show theme. Writing the *Batman* theme was tough—Hefti had to find a quality sound that was also child-friendly. The *Batman* theme garnered him his only Grammy Award.

Neal Hefti died at the age of 85, on October 11, 2008, in Toluca Lake, California. The epitaph on his tomb at Forest Lawn in Hollywood reads, "Forever in Tune."

The Odd Couple theme had lyrics, too (although they were never used), written by Sammy Cahn.

Kenyon Hopkins

Kenyon Hopkins was born January 15, 1912, in Coffeyville, Kansas. Hopkins became a respected jazz arranger and composer, and scored many films, including *The Hustler* (1961), *Wild in the Country* (1961, starring Elvis Presley), *Baby Doll* (1956), and *12 Angry Men* (1957). Jack Klugman was one of the jurors in the latter, and, coincidentally, Hopkins was the music supervisor on *The Odd Couple* TV series.

Hopkins also composed and worked in a supervisory capacity on other TV programs, such as *The Cara Williams Show, The Brady Bunch, Mannix, Love, American Style, Mission: Impossible,* and *East Side, West Side*. He received an Emmy nomination for the latter.

Hopkins died in Princeton, New Jersey, on April 7, 1983, at the age of 71.

Bill Idelson

Bill Idelson was born August 21, 1919, in Forest Park, Illinois. Bill got his start as a radio actor, playing Rush on *Vic and Sade*. He also performed on television in *One Man's Family,* and is probably best known for playing Sally Rogers's nerdy on again/off again boyfriend, Herman Glimscher, on *The Dick Van Dyke Show*. Besides acting on that show, Idelson also wrote several episodes.

Writing, in fact, was Idelson's true calling. He penned brilliantly funny scripts for *The Andy Griffith Show, Get Smart, That Girl, Bewitched, Gomer Pyle, USMC, Happy Days, The Bob Newhart Show, M*A*S*H,* and *Love, American Style*. For *The Odd Couple*, Idelson wrote "The Blackout," "The Odd Couple Meet Their Host," "Win One for Felix," "Partner's Investment," "The Princess," and the first multi-camera episode filmed before a studio audience, "Natural Childbirth." Idelson also stepped in front of the cameras as a judge in "The Dog Story," in which Felix steals a collie away from its cruel owner, only to be arrested and brought to trial (and, as per usual, defends himself in court).

Idelson won two Writer's Guild Awards (for *Get Smart* and *The Andy Griffith Show*). In the late 1970s, Idelson successfully turned to producing. He authored three books: *The Story of Vic and Sade, Gibby* (about his experiences in World War II), and *Bill Idelson's Writing Class*. Sadly, Idelson died on New Year's Eve 2007, from complications after having had hip surgery.

Ben Joelson

Benjamin Aaron Joelson was born October 1, 1925, in Paterson, New Jersey, and began by writing material for *Candid Camera* and *The Robert Q. Lewis Show*. It was there at CBS that he met with his future writing partner, Art Baer. Their early work was on the game shows *Picture This*, *Make a Face*, and *Fractured Phrases*, but they later penned scripts for *The Carol Burnett Show*, as well as some of the biggest sitcoms of the day, including *Car 54, Where Are You?*, *The Dick Van Dyke Show*, *Gomer Pyle, USMC*, *The Andy Griffith Show*, *Hogan's Heroes*, *The Partridge Family*, and *Happy Days*. For *The Odd Couple*, Joelson and Baer's contributed "Big Mouth," "The Dog Story," and "New York's Oddest."

Benjamin Aaron Joelson later connected with another Aaron (Spelling), and found steady work on ABC's *The Love Boat*, on which Joelson was writer and/or executive producer for some 200 episodes of the series. Joelson garnered his only Emmy Award (with Art Baer) for Outstanding Writing Achievement in Variety or Music in 1972 (for *The Carol Burnett Show*).

Ben Joelson died of complications from lung disease on August 24, 1996, at the age of 70.

BRUCE JOHNSON

Bruce Johnson was born July 7, 1939, in Piedmont, California. He majored in drama at USC. He began his show business career as an intern on *The Andy Griffith Show*, and parlayed that into the title of associate producer on *Gomer Pyle, USMC*, *Arnie*, and *Hey, Landlord*. While with the latter, Johnson worked with Garry Marshall, who was obviously impressed with his work. Marshall used Johnson as a producer in many of his other shows, including *Angie*, *Mork and Mindy*, *Blansky's Beauties*, and *The New Odd Couple*.

Johnson continued his prolific output throughout the 1980s and 1990s, producing *Webster*, *Hangin' with Mr. Cooper*, and *All-American Girl*.

Bruce Johnson died young, at the age of 66, on September 27, 2005, in Encino, California.

SHELDON KELLER

Sheldon Bernard Keller was born August 20, 1923, in Chicago, Illinois. While attending the University of Illinois, he began writing comedy with the great Allan Sherman. After World War II, Keller got married, borrowed some money, and moved the family to New York, with aspirations of becoming a comedian.

When that didn't come to fruition, Keller settled for writing comedy for television. He was soon writing for some of the biggest names in television, such as Dinah Shore, Sid Caesar, Danny Kaye, Dick Van Dyke, Art Carney, and Frank Sinatra. He won an Emmy for writing a TV special titled *An Evening with Carol Channing*.

His talents were later expanded to that of executive producer on *The Odd Couple* in 1974—a position he maintained for all 22 episodes of the program's final season.

Keller remained active as a television writer into the 1980s. Sadly, he was later diagnosed with Alzheimer's Disease, and his name began to disappear from TV credits. Sheldon Keller died on September 1, 2008.

ROBERT KLANE

Robert Klane was born in 1941, and found success as a writer, producer, and director. His biggest successes were in feature films: *Weekend at Bernie's* (1989), *Weekend at Bernie's II* (1993, as director), *National Lampoon's European Vacation* (1985), *The Man with One Red Shoe* (1985), and *Unfaithfully Yours* (1984, as writer); *Thank God It's Friday* (1978, as director).

However, Klane found considerable success on the small screen, too. He wrote several episodes of *M*A*S*H* and *Tracey Takes On* (which he also produced). Klane penned and directed the Tony Randall and Jack Klugman TV-reunion movie, *The Odd Couple: Together Again*, in 1993. Along with Randall and Klugman, Garry Walberg returned as Speed, and Penny Marshall was back as Myrna. They were all reunited because Felix's daughter, Edna, was about to walk down the aisle.

This TV movie takes place after Klugman's throat surgery, and his raspy voice and victory over cancer are addressed in the script.

DENNIS KLEIN

Writer Dennis Klein was born in the Bronx, New York. Throughout the 1970s, he rarely wrote more than one or two scripts for any series (*Getting Together*, *The Partridge Family*, *The New Dick Van Dyke Show*, *Fay*, *Doc*, and *Sirota's Court*). For *The Odd Couple*, he penned "The Odyssey Couple" (in which Oscar invents a girlfriend to appease his mother), and "Sometimes a Great Ocean" (in which Oscar and Felix take a cruise with senior citizens—an attempt by Felix to heal Oscar's ulcer).

There are two programs, however, on which Klein had a longer association—*Buffalo Bill*, with Dabney Coleman (now available on a DVD box set), and, especially, *The Larry Sanders Show*, with Garry Shandling. Klein had a hand in writing 89 of the latter program's episodes. He also served as executive producer of *Cosby* on CBS, and creative consultant for *Grace Under Fire* on ABC.

CARL KLEINSCHMITT

Carl Kleinschmitt was still in his twenties when he broke into TV writing, with then-partner, Dale McRaven. Together, they penned most of the episodes for the final season of *The Joey Bishop Show*, and an episode of *The Dick Van Dyke Show*, "Br-room Br-room," which garnered them a Writer's Guild Award.

The credits for most of *The Odd Couple* episodes are phrased "written by," but a select few use the words "story by" and "teleplay by." Kleinschmitt clarified this by saying, "Usually that particular credit is the result of the first writer coming up with the basic story, but failing to deliver a script that satisfied the show runners, who then rewrote it and claimed credit. The final credits were, and I assume still are, the result of a Writers

Guild arbitration in which all drafts of the script are submitted to a panel of three anonymous Guild members who determine who gets credit for what."

Kleinschmitt then began writing solo, and penned scripts for *That Girl, Gomer Pyle, USMC, The Doris Day Show, The Courtship of Eddie's Father, Love, American Style, Welcome Back, Kotter, The Love Boat,* and *M*A*S*H*. Regarding his work on *The Odd Couple*, Kleinschmitt said, "I'm very fond of the episode I wrote titled 'I Do, I Don't,' and I also love 'It's All Over Now, Baby Bird,' written by my former writing partner, Dale McRaven." Kleinschmitt's other duties? He recalled, "Meeting with freelance writers, listening to the stories they pitched, helping them work out the specifics of a script, guiding them through a rewrite, then polishing the finished product, if necessary."

Before *The Odd Couple*, Kleinschmitt worked on the first show Garry Marshall and Jerry Belson produced, *Hey, Landlord*, and reflected, "It presented a lot of pressure for Marshall and Belson as it was their first time running a show. That said, we had a lot of fun on *Hey, Landlord*—all of us in an old house across the street from the Desilu Cahuenga lot where we played touch football in the driveway. Marshall and Belson, however, probably had a lot more riding on *The Odd Couple*, it being such a successful play and movie, and bearing the name of Neil Simon."

Kleinschmitt worked closely with *Odd Couple* producer Jerry Davis,

A photograph of *Odd Couple* scriptwriter Carl Kleinschmitt from back in the day (courtesy Carl Kleinschmitt).

about whom he recalled, "In addition to producing *The Odd Couple*, Jerry became the executive producer of a Paramount show I created and produced, *Funny Face*, which starred Sandy Duncan. Jerry had a long and checkered career, and he knew virtually everybody. He was a charming man, a dapper dresser, and a great raconteur. Many of his stories featured himself as the punch line, but he was friends with people like Groucho Marx and Sidney Sheldon, and his tales of his years in Hollywood were endless."

Kleinschmitt fondly recalls another Jerry who worked on *The Odd Couple*—Jerry Paris: "He was not just a fine director but also a fine human being. I'd known him since *The Dick Van Dyke Show*, on which he directed most of the later episodes. Of course, he also played [Dr. Jerry Helper,] Rob and Laura's next-door neighbor. Jerry was a free spirit whose enthusiasm for life in general, and his craft in particular, were contagious. He left us much too soon."

About the stars of the show, Kleinschmitt said, "I don't think I ever exchanged more than a word or two with Al Molinaro. I had virtually no interaction with Jack Klugman, but Tony was a very social guy. One day Tony went to lunch with Garry, the two Jerrys (Belson and Davis), and me. We ended up at some dive on Melrose Drive that advertised nude dancers. A young woman seated us, took our food orders, served us, then mounted a small stage, took off all of her clothes and gyrated to some cheesy music for a few minutes before gathering up her duds, putting them on again, and going back to wait tables. As we left, Tony, ever the show business professional, shook the woman's hand and told her (as sincerely as if she'd just done a scene from Shakespeare) how much he admired her performance. That always marked him as a good guy in my book, and he was never anything but pleasant to me."

Did Carl Kleinschmitt follow Garry Marshall on to his other projects? Kleinschmitt said, "No, that was my last official job with Garry, who was responsible for getting me into the business in the first place. I just thought it was time to try my own wings. We've remained friendly all these years, and get together semi-regularly with the other surviving members of the 'Sunset Six' (Garry, Arnold Margolin, Jim Parker, Dave McRaven, myself) who all shared an office on the Sunset Strip in the 1960s."

He did submit a script for *The Odd Couple: Together Again* TV reunion movie, but Kleinschmitt recalled, "Klugman didn't want to do it. He'd just had a battle with throat cancer and wanted the story to be about that. Since I didn't see throat cancer as a particularly amusing subject, I withdrew from the project—as did NBC, which originally backed the project. It eventually made its way to CBS, with a cancer script, and, as I remember, was not a laugh riot."

Kleinschmitt kept very busy throughout much of the 1980s, as supervising producer for *Pryor's Place* and the creator of the long-running *First and Ten*.

Buz Kohan

Alan W. Kohan was born August 9, 1933, in the Bronx, New York. He was nicknamed "Buz" as a baby for a sound he made in his crib, and it stuck. Kohan said, "Originally it was Buzzer, then Buzz, and then it was shortened even more to simply Buz (with one "Z"). In fact, my publishing company is appropriately called 'One Zee Music.'"

He is a graduate of the Eastman School of Music of the University of Rochester (with a master's degree in composition). This writer/producer/composer/arranger is best known for writing TV specials, particularly awards shows (Oscars and Emmys), and for his Emmy-winning run writing for *The Carol Burnett Show* (well over 100 episodes). Over the years, he has won 13 Emmy awards for various shows and in various capacities.

Kohan was usually paired with his high school friend Bill Angelos through 1975, and, together, they wrote a few scripts for sitcoms. Kohan said, "I was in the army with Garry Marshall, and years later while I was busy writing for TV variety shows, Garry contacted me and said that 'variety shows were dying' and that 'I should come learn a trade (sitcoms) so that I'd have a profession for life.' I did that for six weeks but, while it was fun, I thought that sitcom writing was the most destructive form of writing. A writer is lucky if six of his original lines remain in the script after all of the rewrites and the punch-ups, and if his name is still on the screen as the writer. I did it for a while, but my niche was variety and awards shows. I was most comfortable there, and it has served me well." For *The Odd Couple*, Kohan penned "Old Flames Never Die," and two others focusing on music ("The Songwriter," with Jaye P. Morgan, and "Vocal Girl Makes Good," with Marilyn Horne.) Kohan recalled, "Marilyn Horne was so sweet and so good on *The Odd Couple*, I used her again in an episode of *The Carol Burnett Show*, where, along with Eileen Farrell and Carol, they became the Three Little Pigs, and with Harvey Korman as the Big Bad Wolf, it was a genuine mini-opera, with every word sung in true operatic style."

About the Jaye P. Morgan episode, Kohan shared, "The 'Happy and Peppy and Bursting with Love' song seemed to take on a life of its own. I've been

A photograph of 13-time Emmy winner Buz Kohan, who wrote "The Songwriter," "Vocal Girl Makes Good," and "Old Flames Never Die" (courtesy Buz Kohan).

told that Billy Joel loved to sing it with his band in the dressing room before concerts to get into a happy and peppy frame of mind."

Writing for TV is truly in the Kohan genes—his son David achieved great success as the co-creator and executive producer of *Will and Grace*, and his daughter, Jenji, created and executive produced the award-winning *Weeds*, and currently does the same for the much-lauded Netflix series *Orange Is the New Black*. She also worked on numerous episodes of the Paul Reiser/Helen Hunt sitcom *Mad About You*. For the Kohans, writing is a family affair. Buz's wife of over half a century, Rhea, is also a writer, having penned a number of novels and having been on staff for a number of TV specials and series. Buz's other son, David's twin brother, Jono, also had a career in the entertainment business, serving as

A&R man for MJJ Records, which was Michael Jackson's record company.

It's not well known, but there was also an *Odd Couple* opera. Kohan explained, "We did a four-episode network series called *Imagination* with producer/director Marty Pasetta, each with a topic, and for one of the episodes about music, we wrote an *Odd Couple* opera for Jack and Tony. Once again, it was in true operatic form with the two stars singing all the words. It became so popular that it was included on *The Odd Couple Album* on the London Record label (on side two). Jack and Tony performing an opera in front of an 85-piece orchestra—that really took 'imagination.'"

Years later, Garry Marshall asked Buz to take a crack at a musical episode of *The Odd Couple* for one of the final segments of the series. "I wrote six original songs and the script for the episode, but I was very busy with other projects, and by the time I finished the work and it got to the table read and a first rehearsal, we all realized that there would never be enough time to learn it, prepare it, and do it justice. It was shelved at the last minute."

Over the years, Kohan has worked with the giants of the industry—Bob Hope, Neil Diamond, Sammy Davis, Jr., Shirley MacLaine, Bette Midler, Frank Sinatra, Cher, Dolly Parton, Diana Ross, Judy Garland, and Perry Como. But perhaps Buz's biggest musical achievement was co-writing songs with a very young Michael Jackson. Kohan reflected, "I get asked about that constantly. Writers are always seeking quotes about Michael. He was amazing. I wrote the song, 'Gone Too Soon' with Larry Grossman, which Michael recorded for the *Dangerous* album as a tribute to his friend Ryan White, the teenager who died of AIDS, and it went platinum many times over. Michael also sang it at the Presidential Gala for Bill Clinton, and it was performed by Usher as a tribute to Michael himself at his memorial service at Staples Center."

Buz Kohan has mastered the fading art of people skills, and shared this bit of wisdom with his famous children: "Always treat the people under you with the utmost respect, care and love because they can make or break you. It takes very little effort to be very nice to these people. Someday, you might be working for them."

Michael Leeson

Michael Leeson was born May 6, 1947, in Tucson, Arizona. His father, Louis, an upholsterer, was born in Canada, and his mother, Ada, a bookkeeper, was born in Dublin, Ireland. Leeson earned his bachelor of arts degree at the University of Arizona, with a major in English literature.

Leeson co-wrote three scripts for *The Odd Couple:* "A Different Drummer" (the second of two episodes with guest star Monty Hall), "The Odd Father," and "The Exorcists." His other television credits include scripts for *All in the Family, The Partridge Family, Happy Days, The Mary Tyler Moore Show, Rhoda, Phyllis, Taxi, The Associates, Best of the West, The Cosby Show, I Married Dora,* and *Grand.* Leeson is credited on screenplays for *The Survivors* (1983), *I. Q.* (1994), *The Tuxedo* (2002), *What Planet Are You From?* (2000), and *The War of the Roses* (1989).

He garnered an Emmy Award and Humanitas Prize for his writing for *Taxi*, and won a second Emmy Award for *The Cosby Show*, which he created with Ed. Weinberger. Leeson said, "I planned to be a high school English teacher."

ALBERT E. LEWIN

Not to be confused with director/producer Albert Lewin, Albert E. Lewin studied at the Chicago School of Art Institute and Los Angeles Valley College. Immediately after serving in the military during World War II, he began writing for television—mostly sitcoms. Some of his early scripts were for *Meet Mr. McNutly*, *The Brothers*, *The Life of Riley*, and *My Little Margie*. Then came *Gilligan's Island*, *My Favorite Martian*, *The Ghost and Mrs. Muir*, and *The Brady Bunch*. Lewin also penned six great scripts over the first three seasons of *The Odd Couple*—"Felix Gets Sick," "Felix Is Missing," "The Fat Farm" (one of the most popular), "Where's Grandpa?" (in which Tony Randall portrays his own grandfather), "Felix's First Commercial" (with NFL star Deacon Jones), and "Oscar's Birthday." He wrote both single-camera and multi-camera episodes.

Lewin remained very busy throughout the 1970s, writing for *The Facts of Life*, *Diff'rent Strokes*, *All in the Family*, *Nanny and the Professor*, *Maude*, and *All's Fair*.

Albert E. Lewin died of heart failure on April 23, 1998, at the age of 79.

CARL MAHAKIAN

Carl Mahakian's name is most often associated with video editing, sound-effects editing, cinematography, and post-production. He is credited thusly in countless TV shows, including *12 O'Clock High*, *The Brady Bunch*, *Love, American Style*, *Happy Days*, *Laverne and Shirley*, *Mork and Mindy*, and *Knight Rider*.

For all 22 episodes of the final season of *The Odd Couple*, however, Mahakian is credited as associate producer. That includes the program's final episode, "Felix Remarries."

Mahakian was also a highly respected sound editor for numerous TV mini-series, for which he was nominated for two Emmy Awards (he won for "Outstanding Film Sound Editing for a Limited Series" for the 1983 nuclear war mini-series *The Day After*). While working on *Miami Vice*, he won another Emmy, also for "Outstanding Film Sound Editing." Mahakian's editing work in films encompasses titles such as *Mannequin* (1987) and *The Manchurian Candidate* (1962). As of this writing, Mahakian resides in Palm Springs, California.

ALAN MANDEL

Alan Mandel was born in 1945 in Chicago, Illinois. Many of his early collaborations were with Charles Shyer, including scripts for *Love, American Style*, *Barefoot in the Park*, *Getting Together*, and *The Partridge Family*. For *The Odd Couple*, Mandel and Shyer penned "Bunny Is Missing Down by the Lake" and "Trapped" in the show's single-camera first season.

Mandel's later achievements in TV writing include scripts for *Hotel*, *Who's the Boss?*, *Perfect Strangers*, and *Punky Brewster*.

Alan Mandel is not to be confused with Babaloo Mandel, who also co-wrote many scripts for Garry Marshall and Paramount, as well as numerous popular screenplays (with Lowell Ganz).

ALEX MARCH

Alex March was born in New York City February 4, 1921. He began as an actor, and his only TV acting credit was as a chauffeur on a 1950 episode of *The Philco-Goodyear Television Playhouse*, "Nocturne." When acting didn't pan out, March turned to producing, and directing—attaining most of his success in the latter.

March's TV-directing credits include *Naked City*, *The Untouchables*, *The Defenders*, *Ben Casey*, *The Man from UNCLE*, *NYPD*, *Police Story*, *Barney Miller*, and *The Paper Chase*. It's interesting to note that March only directed two episodes of *The Odd Couple*, but one of them, "Password," is the show's most popular episode, voted the number-five all-time TV episode by *TV Guide*. March also directed "The First Baby," a flashback episode that shows the birth of Felix's daughter, Edna. March worked with Jack Klugman again, years later, when he directed four episodes of *Quincy, M. E.*

March also directed some memorable motion pictures: *Paper Lion* (1968, with Alan Alda), *The Big Bounce* (1969, with Ryan O'Neal), and *Mastermind* (1969; released in 1976, with Zero Mostel). He retired in the middle 1980s, and died on June 11, 1989, in Los Angeles, California.

GARRY MARSHALL

Garry Kent Maschiarelli was born in the Bronx, New York. The Garry with two R's was inspired by sportswriter Garry Schumaker, who spelled his first name that same way. By pure coincidence, actor Garry Walberg (also with two "R's") became a semi-regular on *The Odd Couple* as "Speed." Garry "Marshall" (his father shortened the family surname) attended Northwestern University, and wrote a sports column for the school paper. His writing talents then expanded to writing jokes for Phil Foster and Joey Bishop, and before long he was teamed with longtime associate Jerry Belson. Together, they wrote for *The Joey Bishop Show*, *The Lucy Show*, *The Danny Thomas Show*, *The Bill Dana Show*, and *The Dick Van Dyke Show*. Their first shot at creating and producing their own program came in 1966 with the single-season sitcom called *Hey, Landlord*, which starred Will Hutchins and Sandy Baron. Unfortunately, NBC scheduled the program on Sunday nights against *The Ed Sullivan Show*, and it was gone by the fall of 1967.

After the *Hey, Landlord* experience,

Marshall and Belson moved over to motion pictures, and produced *How Sweet It Is!* (1968) and *The Grasshopper* (1970). Neither was a whopping success, but it proved to be a great training ground for the duo.

Marshall and Belson's next big venture was bringing Neil Simon's *The Odd Couple* to television. For Garry Marshall, *The Odd Couple* truly became a family affair—he raised nepotism to an art form. His father, Tony Marshall, was the show's producer; Garry's sister Penny became an important member of the cast as Oscar's secretary, Myrna Turner; Garry's mother, Marjorie (a tap-dance teacher in real life) tap danced in "The Rain in Spain Falls Mainly in Vain" and "Oscar's Birthday"; Garry's other sister Ronny Hallin had an uncredited cameo in "The Rain in Spain Falls Mainly in Vain"; Garry's brother-in-law, Rob Reiner, also guest starred (as Sheldn—they forgot an "O" on his birth certificate) in that very same episode; and Garry's daughter, Lori, played piano, badly, in "This Is the Army, Mrs. Madison."

While *The Odd Couple* was never a ratings bonanza (it never finished in the Top 30 for any of its five seasons), it was popular enough and there was enough of a devoted fan base to keep it in primetime for 114 episodes (it was most popular during the summer reruns). It was also a great stepping stone for Garry Marshall, as he expanded his successful horizons with *Happy Days, Laverne and Shirley, Mork and Mindy, Angie, The New Odd Couple,* and *Blansky's Beauties*. On those programs, he wore a myriad of hats— producer, executive producer, director, writer, and even actor (he was also Stan Lansing, the network boss, on numerous episodes of *Murphy Brown*).

Garry then returned to feature films in the 1980s, producing and/or directing such hits as *The Flamingo Kid* (1984), *Overboard* (1987), *Beaches* (1988), *Nothing in Common* (1986), *Pretty Woman* (1990), *Runaway Bride* (1999) and *The Other Sister* (1999). Harking back to his days as a sports columnist, Garry loves using sports scenes (especially involving baseball) in his films. His production company is named Henderson Productions after a sitcom character named Wendell Henderson featured in a 1963 episode of *The Danny Thomas Show* written by Garry and Jerry Belson and titled "Linda's Crush." Garry Marshall has a star on the Hollywood Walk of Fame. He and his wife, Barbara, have three children and, as you'd expect, all of them have been used in Garry's movies. He has written two highly readable memoirs, the latest being *My Happy Days in Hollywood*, from Crown, and *Wake Me When It's Funny*, from Adams. He also owns the Falcon Theater in Burbank, where several plays are staged each year.

Some interesting Garry Marshall factoids: he made cameo appearances on *The Odd Couple* in "I Do, I Don't," "The Rain in Spain Falls Mainly in Vain," "A Different Drummer" (and got to show off his percussion prowess) and "The Subway Story." He appeared in the latter when the actor who was supposed to play the role took ill at the very last moment. He, in real life, has the same nasal issues as Felix Unger. He has a fixation with the number 13, and that's why the apartment number for Felix and Oscar is 1102 (11 + 2 = 13). That's also why the clock during the closing credits of every season (except season five) shows a clock with the little hand on the 11 and the big hand on the 2. Garry's birthday is November 13, the day mentioned in the opening narration—the date Felix Unger was asked to remove himself from his place of residence (that request came from his wife). Garry and his family lived on Arcola Street in Toluca Lake, California, and that's why the name Arcola is used often as a character surname. It was utilized on *The Odd Couple,* and it was used on *Happy Days* and *Joanie Loves Chachi* (as Chachi's surname).

George Marshall

George E. Marshall was born December 29, 1891, in Chicago, Illinois. He was expelled from Chicago University, and drifted from job to job. While visiting his mother in Los Angeles, he sought out work in the burgeoning film industry and was soon working as a stunt actor. He didn't really enjoy being in front of the camera, so he hastily parlayed that "foot in the door" into a lengthy career as a writer, producer, and, especially, a director. He started in silent films, and when sound came in, he found work at Hal Roach Studios and worked on two of Laurel and Hardy's films. Comedy was his forte, and after leaving Roach, he worked with W. C. Fields, Betty Hutton, and Bob Hope. He also directed numerous Dean Martin and Jerry Lewis films.

In the late 1940s, Marshall was president of the Screen Director's Guild. While continuing to direct movies, Marshall found work directing television programs, such as *Valentine's Day, Here's Lucy, Tarzan, The Wackiest Ship in the Army,* and *Daniel Boone.* Already in his early 80s, some of his final directing work came on two episodes of *The Odd Couple*—"Oscar's Birthday" and the flashback episode titled "A Night to Dismember" (which showed three differing perspectives of Oscar and Blanche's breakup).

Marshall died on February 17, 1975. Just three days earlier, he was inducted into the Motion Picture Arts and Sciences Hall of Fame. He has a star on the Hollywood Walk of Fame on Hollywood Boulevard. He was not related to the bevy of other Marshalls on *The Odd Couple.*

Tony Marshall

Tony Marshall was born Anthony W. Maschiarelli on March 29, 1906, in New York City. Tony's son, Garry, Anglicized the name to Marshall and encouraged his sister Penny, his other sister, Ronny, his mother, Marjorie, and father, Tony, to do the same. Before joining his son in Hollywood, Tony worked in advertising and public relations.

Tony has credits on almost all of son Garry's shows—*Happy Days, Laverne and Shirley, Mork and Mindy, Angie,* and *The Odd Couple.* Tony was listed as the producer for 89 episodes of *The*

Odd Couple, and 76 episodes of *Happy Days*. However, for *Laverne and Shirley*, his title was supervising producer, and, for *Mork and Mindy*, he was elevated to executive producer.

Tony Marshall died on July 12, 1999, in Toluca Lake, California, at the age of 93.

ROBERT MCKIMSON

Robert Porter McKimson was born October 13, 1910, in Denver, Colorado. He studied art, and then got a job with Disney. After a short stay, McKimson moved over to Warner Bros., where he was eventually promoted to animator, and worked on many classic "Merrie Melodies" and "Looney Tunes" cartoons. McKimson is credited with streamlining and defining Bugs Bunny's look.

McKimson followed David DePatie and Friz Freleng over to DePatie/Freleng Enterprises when Warner Bros. abandoned its cartoon production in the early 1960s. He was eventually named director of *The Bugs Bunny/Road Runner Hour*, *The Super Six*, *The Pink Panther Show*, and *The Oddball Couple*.

McKimson died at the age of 66 on September 29, 1977, in Burbank, California, only two weeks before his 67th birthday.

RICHARD MICHAELS

Not to be confused with Michael Richards, Richard Michaels was born February 15, 1936, in Brooklyn, New York. He began his career as a script supervisor in the 1950s on such films as *Friendly Persuasion* (1956) and *Damn Yankees* (1958). He also held the title of script supervisor on a variety of TV programs: *Sea Hunt*, *Hennesey*, *The Ann Sothern Show*, *Peyton Place*, and *Bewitched*.

As a director, his credits include *The Brady Bunch*, *Love, American Style*, *Room 222*, *Bewitched*, and *The Odd Couple*. Michaels only got one crack at *The Odd Couple*—an episode from season one, "The Hideaway," in which Oscar lets a promising young football prospect hide out in his apartment to avoid the media. Felix, meanwhile, wants the boy to pursue his other dream instead—becoming a concert cellist.

While working on the final season of *Bewitched*, Michaels had an affair with Elizabeth Montgomery—a move which led to the end of her marriage to producer/director William Asher. Michaels retired young, and, at last report, was living in Maui.

HARVEY MILLER

Born Harvey Skolnik in 1935, he grew up in Plainfield, New Jersey, and found work as a social worker in the Catskills. There, in the legendary vacation resort known as The Borsht Belt, he became enamored with stand-up comedy, and the fact that comics, regardless of their looks, could pick up pretty girls just by telling them jokes. Before long, he was writing jokes for Dick Gregory, Alan King, Shecky Greene, and Sandy Baron. He, in fact, became Sandy Baron's manager, and while Baron was co-starring on the sitcom *Hey, Landlord*, Harvey Miller connected with the program's producers, Garry Marshall and Jerry Belson. After writing a few scripts for *The Mothers-in-Law*, *That Girl*, *The Ghost and Mrs. Muir*, and *Gomer Pyle, USMC*, Miller teamed with Garry Marshall and Jerry Belson on *The Odd Couple*. Miller also guest starred in one of the eight episodes he wrote, playing the "rubber ducky" under his real name, Harvey Skolnik (in "What Does a Naked Lady Say to You?"). He was also the maître d' in "Gloria Hallelujah." In "The Odd Couple Meet Their Host," actor Frank Corsentino portrayed a comedy writer named Harvey Skolnik (an inside joke). Miller was also the executive producer for over 20 episodes of the program, and had a lifelong fascination with celebrities and having his photograph taken with them. He is credited with enticing Monty Hall, Howard Cosell, Bobby Riggs, Allen Ludden, Betty White, Paul Williams, Roy Clark, and Richard Dawson to guest star on the program.

In later years, Miller turned to writing for the big screen, and had a hand in penning two big vehicles for Goldie Hawn, *Private Benjamin* (1980) and *Protocol* (1984). He was nominated for an Emmy for producing *Love, American Style*, but lost to *All in the Family*. He was the creator and executive producer of the short-lived NBC sitcom, *Sirota's Court*. Miller also had a small role as Dr. Hegler in the 1993 TV-reunion movie, *The Odd Couple: Together Again*. Harvey was always "on," and was usually the funniest guy in the room. At the writer's table, he would often entertain those present by assuming the role of his alter ego, Jackie Hitler—Adolf's comedic brother.

Miller's magnetic personality and spirit were silenced on January 8, 1999, due to heart failure.

Phil Mishkin

Phil Mishkin was often teamed with Rob Reiner. Mishkin was a member of Reiner's improvisational troupe called "The Session," in Los Angeles, and he also wrote several scripts for *All in the Family,* including the introduction of Bea Arthur as Maude in the episode titled "Cousin Maude's Visit." Mishkin was also involved in a few of Reiner's other TV ventures, such as *The Super*, *Morton and Hayes*, and *Free Country*.

Among Mishkin's other TV credits—*The Mary Tyler Moore Show*, *Sanford and Son*, *Happy Days*, and *Matlock*. He was also a story editor, and wrote "The Odd Holiday" (the episode which shows how Felix and Gloria broke up) and co-wrote "The Moonlighter" (in which Oscar takes on a job as a short-order cook to pay off his debts). Mishkin served as associate producer for 22 episodes of the program, and was later the supervising producer for *Laverne and Shirley*.

Gordon Mitchell

Gordon "Whitey" Mitchell was a multi-tasker. He had two careers—musician and TV writer, and he was proficient at both. He was born February 22, 1932, in Hackensack, New Jersey, and during his musical career he toured with Benny Goodman, he played Carnegie Hall with Gene Krupa, and he appeared with Buddy Rich, Ella Fitzgerald, and Dizzy Gillespie. In the early 1960s, he played stand-up bass guitar on Ben E. King's legendary recording of "Stand by Me." He comes from a musical family—his brother was bassist Red Mitchell.

During his TV-writing career, Gordon was usually paired with Lloyd Turner. Mitchell is credited with penning dozens of episodes for such sitcoms as *My Mother, the Car, Get Smart, The Doris Day Show, Gomer Pyle, USMC, The Good Life, The Partridge Family, All in the Family, The Mary Tyler Moore Show, Maude, The Jeffersons, Good Times, Mork and Mindy,* and *Diff'rent Strokes*. Both episodes he co-wrote for *The Odd Couple*—"The Jury Story" and "A Taste of Money"—came about in the show's single-camera laugh track–laden first season.

Mitchell wrote two books—*Hackensack to Hollywood: My Two Show Business Careers*, and *Star Walk: A Guide to the Palm Springs Walk of Stars*. He was a board member for the Palm Springs Walk of Stars, and was honored with his own Golden Palm Star.

After a brief battle with prostate cancer, Mitchell died on January 16, 2009, at the age of 76.

Rick Mittleman

Richard Mittleman was born in Brooklyn, New York, on April 18, 1930, but he said, "Having to contend with being drafted during the Korean War, there were times I felt like I was issued, not born." Beginning in his twenties, he kicked off a long and very prolific career, writing for many popular TV shows, including *The Dick Van Dyke Show, Bewitched, Get Smart, I Spy, The Courtship of Eddie's Father, That Girl, The Doris Day Show, Gomer Pyle, USMC, The Mary Tyler Moore Show, Sanford and Son, What's Happening?, The Love Boat,* and *Murder, She Wrote*. For *The Odd Couple*, he wrote six scripts—"Gloria Hallelujah," "Strike up the Band, or Else," "The Paul Williams Story," "Being Divorced Means Never Having to Say 'I Do,'" and "A Night to Dismember" (the latter two featured the real-life married couple, Brett Somers and Jack Klugman), and "The Rain in Spain Falls Mainly in Vain" (which featured the real-life couple of Penny Marshall and Rob Reiner). Mittleman said, "I was unaware that the couples (Jack and Brett, and Penny and Rob) were actually married in real life. Garry Marshall and Jerry Belson didn't mention it."

Rick Mittleman was nominated for three Emmy Awards (*The Red Skelton Show, Arnie,* and *Van Dyke and Company*), and he won the Writer's Guild of America Morgan Cox Award in 1997.

Mike Nichols

Michael Igor Peschkowsky was born November 6, 1931, in Berlin, Germany. His father changed the family name to Nichols, and Michael attended the University of Chicago as a pre-med student. He quickly lost interest in medicine and gravitated toward acting. He then studied under Lee Strasberg at the Actors Studio. He and a girl named Elaine May joined the Compass Players—a troupe that would later evolve into Second City. Nichols and May became a comedy sensation, performing on Broadway, and winning a Grammy for a comedy album. Nichols got used to winning awards—Emmys, an Oscar, a Golden Globe, and several Tonys—if possible, finding even more success as a director than as a comedian. He was also named *Cue* magazine's "Entertainer of the Year," in 1966.

Several of the Tony Awards Nichols garnered were for directing Neil Simon plays—*Barefoot in the Park*, *The Prisoner of Second Avenue*, *Plaza Suite*, and, of course, *The Odd Couple*. Nichols famously changed the blocking for *The Odd Couple* only days before previews were to begin so as to keep the actors on their toes. With Walter Matthau and Art Carney in the Oscar and Felix roles, respectively, the original Broadway production debuted at the Plymouth Theater, on March 10, 1965. Even though the cast and venue changed during this original run, the play enjoyed a 964-performance run, and dozens upon dozens of revivals have followed. A short time later, Nichols directed Richard Burton and Elizabeth Taylor in the motion picture version of *Who's Afraid of Virginia Woolf?* (1966).

In 2003, Nichols was honored by the Kennedy Center. He also won an American Film Institute Lifetime Achievement Award in 2010. Nichols's most recent triumph was winning a Tony Award in 2012 for "Best Direction of a Play" for Arthur Miller's *Death of a Salesman*.

JERRY PARIS

Jerry Paris was born William Gerald Grossman in San Francisco, California, July 25, 1925. Early in his career, he had roles in such films as *Marty* (1955), *The Naked and the Dead* (1958), *The Caine Mutiny* (1954), and *The Wild One* (1954). His first recurring TV role was on a Desilu sitcom called *Those Whiting Girls* that took over for *I Love Lucy* during the summers of 1955 and 1957. Paris had a role in the 1957 version of that program as Artie, and that led to parts on *The Untouchables*, *Michael Shayne*, and *Steve Canyon* before earning a long run as dentist/neighbor Dr. Jerry Helper on *The Dick Van Dyke Show*. Paris was really playing against type here—Jerry Helper was a very secure, confident character, but in real life Jerry Paris was anything but. While portraying Jerry Helper, Paris always had directing in the back of his mind, and after pestering Carl Reiner for over a year, Paris got his shot. He wound up directing 83 episodes of the program, and preferred that end of the business for the rest of his prolific career. Paris got to direct Carl Reiner again on Reiner's short-lived 1970s sitcom, *Good Heavens*. Reiner portrayed an angel on that show.

Among Paris's other TV triumphs, he directed memorable episodes of *The Mary Tyler Moore Show*, *Happy Days*, *The New Dick Van Dyke Show*, and

Laverne and Shirley. Between 1970 and 1975, Paris directed 18 episodes of *The Odd Couple*, including the debut episode, "The Laundry Orgy," and "My Strife in Court," which yielded the famous line, "When you assume, you make an ass of you and me." Paris directed Jack Klugman again years later on the short-lived sitcom, *You Again?*

Paris also had directorial success onstage with the West Coast Tour of another Neil Simon work, *Barefoot in the Park*. He also conquered the big screen, especially with parts two and three of the *Police Academy* series. Paris accomplished so much in his all-too-brief 60 years of life. He was felled by a brain tumor on April 1, 1986, in Pacific Palisades, California. He had three children—two sons, Tony and Andy, and a daughter, Julie.

ALAN RAFKIN

Alan Rafkin was born July 23, 1928, in New York City. He studied at Syracuse University and started as a stand-up comedian and actor. He also worked, off-camera, on some early episodes of *Captain Kangaroo*. His first TV credits as a director came in the 1960s on *The Patty Duke Show*, *The Dick Van Dyke Show*, *My Favorite Martian*, *Gomer Pyle, USMC*, *I Dream of Jeannie*, *The Andy Griffith Show*, *The Donna Reed Show*, and *The Governor and J. J.*

He found steady work throughout the 1970s, directing *The Mary Tyler Moore Show*, *The Partridge Family*, *Lotsa Luck*, *Alice*, *M*A*S*H*, and *The Bob Newhart Show*. For *The Odd Couple*, he directed three single-camera first-season episodes—"A Taste of Money," "Engrave Trouble," and "Oscar's New Life."

Rafkin won an Emmy for directing *One Day at a Time*, and received another nomination for *It's Garry Shandling's Show*. He wrote his memoirs, *Cue the Bunny on the Rainbow: Tales from TV's Most Prolific Sitcom Director*, in 1998 for Syracuse University Press. In the book, he reflected about the *Odd Couple*, branding Tony Randall as "a pain in the ass." He liked Klugman more, and said Jack was a lot of fun to be around, but also stated that both of the program's stars were tough to direct; they were *very* opinionated. Rafkin does state, however, "They were marvelous in their roles, and to get marvelous you can put up with a lot."

Rafkin remained active into the new millennium, directing episodes of *Suddenly Susan* and *Veronica's Closet*, until his death from heart disease on August 6, 2001, in Los Angeles.

JOHN RAPPAPORT

John Rappaport was born on August 26. A Chicago-area native and graduate of Indiana University, he originally had designs on becoming a major radio personality. He had an exceptionally quick wit and a great voice, but became sidelined by another avenue of show business—script writing and producing. In his early 20s, after working on Los Angeles radio as a character voice and comedy foil for his still-lifelong friend, the legendary Gary Owens, he ended up on the writing

Odd Couple, *M*A*S*H* and *Rowan and Martin's Laugh-In* scriptwriter John Rappaport (courtesy John Rappaport).

staff of the number one TV program in the U.S., *Rowan and Martin's Laugh-In*, for four seasons (he was a credited writer on over 80 episodes). From there, Rappaport moved to writing for TV sitcoms, including *All in the Family*, *Maude*, *The Bob Newhart Show*, numerous pilots, *Night Court*, and *M*A*S*H*. He served on the writing staff for *The Odd Couple*'s season five as Executive Consultant and penned two episodes for the show's final two seasons—"Your Mother Wears Army Boots" (with Howard Cosell, Roone Arledge, Jack Carter and Martina Arroyo) and "One for the Bunny" (with a cameo appearance by Hugh Hefner). Rappaport recalled, "When I wrote for *All in the Family*, I was the youngest writer on the staff by 15 years, but on *The Odd Couple*, I was the oldest guy, and I was only in my late 20s. There were many young, extremely talented people involved in *The Odd Couple*."

"One for the Bunny" is a flashback episode about Felix's doomed stint as a photographer for *Playboy* magazine. Rappaport related, "The reason Murray and Myrna are huddled in the kitchen for the opening and closing scenes is that the living room set had been retooled as the guys' apartment in the middle 1950s when the flashback takes place. Hugh Hefner had done *Playboy After Dark* on TV, so he was able to hold his own pretty well in his cameo role on the show. 'Your Mother Wears Army Boots' is an interesting episode. We had constructed a script that was to bring Howard Cosell back for an encore performance. He and Oscar had a love/hate relationship, and Oscar was very excited about having a shot at becoming the new color announcer to join Howard and Frank Gifford on *Monday Night Football*. But he was also very nervous because of a derogatory column he had written about Cosell. My first draft was a breeze, and a lot of fun. But after it was written, I was told that a major rewrite was needed because Tony, a huge opera buff, wanted us to work in Martina Arroyo, a renowned opera singer whom he had gotten to commit to doing the show. Of course, everyone knows that football and opera go hand-in-hand. So we had to shoehorn her into the script somehow, and connected the two threads by arranging for Cosell to meet Arroyo, 'his favorite opera singer.' In reality, Cosell wasn't an opera fan, but somehow we made it work. In addition to the broadcasting scene, a highlight for me was the scene where Oscar practices a *Monday Night Football* broadcast in the apartment with the always-brilliant Al as Murray playing Frank Gifford."

Rappaport added, "In the *Playboy* episode, Felix steals the show, no surprise, by representing himself in his trial scene against *Playboy*. I think that every season they tried to do an episode where Felix goes to court and acts as his own attorney, because he was always hilarious doing it. During my year there, our writers' office sessions were a ball. And, in final preparation on the set for each show on punch-up night, it would be Garry, the brilliant Jerry Belson, Harvey Miller, Mark Rothman, Lowell Ganz, David Duclon, and me. And those sessions were absolutely terrific, no matter how long they took."

About the cast and crew, Rappaport reflected, "Tony Randall was sensational in his role. Much like the brilliance of Jack Benny's character, Tony, as Felix, brought so much to the table—he added so many wondrous little nuances to Neil Simon's original creation. And it would seem that Jack was born to play Oscar. I'll bet that when he was a baby, his diaper was always rumpled. And then there's the incomparable Murray, so different from the character in the play. Al Molinaro and I are longtime friends. He's a fabulous guy but opts to remain out of the spotlight nowadays. The ironic thing is, he's an extremely intelligent man, who is unbelievably fabulous at playing a dumb guy, and, together, we wrote a couple of pilots. He was also a brilliant businessman." And Garry Marshall, "You will never hear a bad thing said about Garry. And that's a rarity in our business. He's a total delight—a great human being. And, an amazing all-around creative talent. I still see him a lot (he's hard to miss—his license plate simply says 'Bronx'). Garry is also a terrific athlete. I don't think we were ever more than a few feet away from a basketball hoop either on the Paramount lot or in his huge backyard every Saturday morning for a couple of decades or more for legendary basketball games. And he still pitches regularly in a softball league that we're in."

While discussing Garry Marshall, Rappaport reflected on "a couple of 'Garry-isms.' They remain with me after all these years. Words like 'chuffa,' that Garry used to express too much time being taken to set up the premise of an episode or getting into a scene or bit. There was also the 'Hey, May!,' which Garry wryly invented, referring to something just before the act breaks that gives the story a teaser for TV networks to hook viewers on what was coming up after the commercial break. It was intended to keep the audience tuned in or to get new viewers being called in to watch the show."

I learned something fascinating about writer's credits per WGA rules from Rappaport, who shared, "When you see an ampersand between the names of writers, such as Lowell Ganz & Mark Rothman, that means they wrote the episode together as a team, but when you see the word 'and' actually spelled out, that means each of the writers wrote or rewrote the script separately."

A few years later, Rappaport had a long, award-winning association with the TV version of *M*A*S*H*, as head writer and supervising producer for its final four seasons, including the record-setting (which still stands today) viewership of the two-and-a-half hour final episode, "Goodbye, Farewell, and Amen." He said, "*M*A*S*H* was extremely rewarding and the experience of a lifetime.... But *The Odd Couple* was right up there as the most fun and the funniest." Rappaport remained active through 2000 as executive producer for the TV version of *Gung Ho*; he was the creative consultant for a season of *Night Court*; and he wrote and produced numerous pilots before turning his attention to feature writing.

Bob Rodgers

Bob Rodgers wrote mostly for sitcoms, and mostly from the middle–1960s through the early–1970s. His first credited script was for the short-lived *Bing Crosby Show* in 1964 (on which Beverly Garland played Bing's wife). After that, he penned most of the episodes of *Camp Runamuck* (from Screen Gems), and several for *Gilligan's Island*, *I Dream of Jeannie*, *The Partridge Family*, *The Courtship of Eddie's Father*, *The Mary Tyler Moore Show*, *Love, American Style*, and *Funny Face*. For *The Odd Couple*, he wrote one for the single-camera first season, "Oscar's Ulcer," and one for the multi-camera studio-audience era—the popular "You Saved My Life."

Rodgers liked to "think young," and proved it by also writing several *ABC Afterschool Specials*, as well as kid-friendly episodes of *Room 222* and *Batman*.

Charles R. Rondeau

Charles R. Rondeau was born July 14, 1917, in Worcester, Massachusetts. Rondeau had a long and successful run as a TV director. In the 1960s, he leaned more toward drama, working on programs such as *Hawaiian Eye*, *The Gallant Men*, *Perry Mason*, *Ben Casey*, *The Man from UNCLE*, and *Mannix*.

Heading into the new decade of the 1970s, he tended to direct more comedies, including *Love, American Style*, *Room 222*, *The Partridge Family*, *The Red Hand Gang*, and *Tabitha*. His two *Odd Couple* episodes—"The Blackout" (with some innovative lighting to resemble a real blackout) and "The Break-Up"—came in the single-camera first season, when the series bore more of a resemblance to the original movie version.

When the 1980s came around, Rondeau's career began winding down. Charles Rondeau died on August 27, 1996, in Carson City, Nevada, at the age of 79.

Mickey Rose

Michael "Mickey" Rose was born May 20, 1935, in the Bedford-Stuyvesant section of Brooklyn, and he was a lifelong friend of Woody Allen. Rose co-wrote Woody's early stand-up routines and also some of his early films, such as *What's Up, Tiger Lily?*, *Bananas*, and *Take the Money and Run*. Allen introduced Rose to his future bride, Judy, on a blind date. It was love at first sight, and Mickey and Judy were married for over 40 years. Woody was Mickey's best man, and the two friends dreamed of one day owning a pharmacy together. Mickey and Woody spent many days together watching the Brooklyn Dodgers at Ebbets Field.

The pharmacy idea never came to fruition, but both Woody and Mickey did pretty well for themselves. On his own, the prolific Rose penned material for Shari Lewis and Lamb Chop, Johnny Carson, Dean Martin, Sid Caesar, and the Smothers Brothers.

Rose also wrote for episodic TV. Most notable are his scripts for *Love, American Style*, *Happy Days*, *The Love Boat*, *Too Close for Comfort*, and *227*. He was a story editor for *The Odd Couple*. He also penned "The Pig Who Came to Dinner" (with Bobby Riggs and Billie Jean King), "The Insomniacs," "The Sleepwalker" (the last two involving sleep, or the lack thereof), "To Bowl or Not to Bowl," and he co-wrote (with Phil Mishkin) "The Moonlighter."

Rose died of colon cancer on April 7, 2013, in Beverly Hills, California.

Mark Rothman

Mark Rothman was born in the Bronx, New York. He got his start in show business in a rather unusual manner. Mark's father, Abe Rothman, was a limo driver and had dozens upon dozens of celebrity accounts. Abe knew in advance who would be riding in his limo, and he took advantage of having both Jack Klugman and Tony Randall (separately) as his fare. Abe presented each of them (without the other one knowing) with an *Odd Couple* script his son Mark (and Lowell Ganz) had written. Rothman recalled, "*The Odd Couple* had just finished its second season and they were on hiatus before starting the third. My writing partner, Lowell Ganz, and I wrote something we thought even Neil Simon would be proud of. A week later, Jack Klugman called my house. He didn't want to buy the script, he wanted to hire us as staff writers." When asked about his biggest influence in the comedy writing realm, Rothman said, "Nat Hiken. Hiken was my comedy writing god. He had the best story mind in the business and his use of repetitive phrases was nothing short of brilliant. His work on *The Phil Silvers Show* and *Car 54, Where Are You?* is legendary. I often used Hiken's work as an example of what I wanted out of my writing staff when I worked on *She's the Sheriff* a few years later."

Because of Tony Randall's influence, several episodes of the sitcom contained clumsy guest appearances by stars of the opera stage. Rothman remembered, "Working in Marilyn Horne, Martina Arroyo and Richard Fredricks wasn't an easy undertaking. None of them were great actors. However, conversely, when we used opera great Georgio Tozzi in the 'Our Fathers' episode, we had a wholly different problem. He was actually a very good actor, but he couldn't stay on-key when singing a cappella, and we scrapped his musical number because of it. One of us said to the other, 'We finally got an opera singer who can act ... but he can't sing!' That was truly a memorable occurrence."

Every TV program has a budget, and it is someone's job to keep the program within the parameters of that budget. This was the job of Garry Marshall's father, Tony, and as Rothman recalled, "'My Strife in Court' was a very funny episode. Every year I was there we would try to do a courtroom scene where Felix acted as his own attorney. These courtroom shows remain some of my favorite episodes, and Tony loved doing them, too. In each courtroom episode, we figured out a unique way for Felix to humiliate Oscar on the witness stand. In this particular one, he portrayed Oscar as 'a slob and a loser who can't get a date.' But, we had also written something that really would have been icing on the cake. While he had Oscar on the witness stand, Felix got him to admit that he couldn't get any of the women in his 'little black book' to go with him to see the Broadway musical, *Kiss My Face*. At that point, Felix was to ask all of the women in the gallery who rejected Oscar to please rise. A motley array of women would then stand up, check each other out, and then stare at Oscar, heightening his embarrassment tenfold. Because of the additional cost for the extras in the gallery, the kibosh was put on what I now call 'the $500 joke.' The show was still really good, but this would have made it great. When that script was reworked for *The New Odd Couple* in 1982, we got to include 'the $500 joke,' and the audience howled. It got an incredible response. That was a very gratifying payoff." Speaking of *The New Odd Couple*, others scripts which were adapted for the "new" show were "The New Car," "The Hustler," "The Ides of April," "That Was No Lady," and "Gloria Moves In" (now known as "Frances Moves In").

About the scripts he co-wrote for *The Odd Couple*, Rothman said, "Lowell was very much the

Odd Couple, Laverne and Shirley and *Happy Days* head writer Mark Rothman.

joke writer. I was very much the storyteller and character writer. My main contribution to that series was to make the show more mature and reality-based. Garry Marshall used to refer to the kind of shows I liked to write as 'internal shows'—shows about the real problems of two middle-aged Jewish divorced men, rather than cartoons about them going on *Let's Make a Deal* for no good reason. For the last three seasons, Lowell and I were really the guts of the writing staff." About the writing, Rothman recalled, "Inspired by something Carl Reiner used to do, Garry Marshall would often write 'BR' or 'RR' on a script. Humorously, 'BR' stood for 'better writing,' and 'RR' stood for 'rotten writing.'"

Rothman shed light on a couple of the show's fifth and final-season episodes. "In 'The Bigger They Are,' Jack had to wear a fat suit," he recalls. "Well, Jack had a large head to begin with. In the fat suit, anybody else's head would've appeared too small, but he looked just right. In 'Two on the Aisle' we had a script that sat on the shelf for about a year—it needed an ending. In the episode, Oscar gets a mandate from the newspaper to cover theater reviews, and he tricks Felix into writing the reviews for him. Oscar is then invited on a talk show to participate in a forum about theater. Because he knows nothing about theater, he appears in bandages (unable to speak under the guise of dental surgery) and solicits Felix to be his interpreter. This part of the script was inspired by a classic episode of *The Phil Silvers Show*. Oddly enough, years later while visiting New York City, I saw both the Phil Silvers episode and our episode on TV on different channels at the exact same time. Mind you, at that time there were only seven channels. It's not like today, with 500-plus cable channels. What are the odds of both episodes running concurrently?" About his personal favorite episode, Rothman shared, "'The Flying Felix' is my second favorite. It was originally to end with Oscar and Felix finding themselves booked on a gay chartered flight, but it was too soon for that subject matter. We had problems with the censors on that one. Tony Randall actually came up with a replacement premise—a charter flight for a parachute club. Tony was great in that episode. I was always in awe of his talent. He could take great material and make it even better. However, my all-time favorite is 'Two on the Aisle.'" Rothman recalled another incident with a censor named Elaine Newman: "We received a letter about our episode titled 'To Bowl, or Not to Bowl.' In the episode, Leonard Barr portrays Arnold, the 'faith healer.' We were ordered to change his title to 'belief healer,' lest we insult a lot of faith healers. I have to give Tony credit once again for taking that disappointment well, and still making it all work." However, Rothman stated, "The best Felix Ungar I ever saw was Charles Nelson Reilly on stage. Just awesome."

Rothman humorously recalled, "Outside Stage 20, where *The Odd Couple* was filmed, there was a sign which said, 'In case of fire, push red buttons.' My response to that sign was always, 'Isn't that the job of his agent?'"

Rothman and Ganz enjoyed a long association with Garry Marshall, wearing many hats, from executive producer to writer to director to creator to show runner for *Happy Days* and *Laverne and Shirley*. Rothman and Ganz also found success on their own with *Busting Loose*, *The Ted Knight Show*, and *Makin' It*. Rothman was solo at the helm for the sitcom *She's the Sheriff*, starring Suzanne Somers, and *The New Odd Couple*. About *The New Odd Couple*, Rothman shared, "Unlike Tony Randall, Ron Glass was never open to being portrayed as a fool on screen. Tony openly sought 'the fool' in his characterization of Felix Unger, and that's why it worked so brilliantly. It's the same reason Glass's Felix was not successful."

A talented actor himself, Rothman is a big proponent of the "actors must think" school. He says, "In the episode titled 'Not with My Wife,' actor Johnny Silver (who guest starred in five *Odd Couple* episodes) portrays Alex Karras's character's coach. Johnny Silver, in real life, was fond of wearing a beret, but he chose to wear that same beret while trying to convince an audience that he was a football coach. It never occurred to him that this might be inappropriate. Actors must think."

Today, Rothman is a very active playwright (*Who Wants Fame?* and *The Wearing of the Greens*, which have been produced very successfully on both coasts), author of several books—*Mark Rothman's Essays*, and a novel (his first), *I'm Not Garbo* (available in paperback), and blogger about classic TV, movies and more (www.markrothmansblog.

blogspot.com). Mark also has four books available through the Amazon Kindle Store (*Show Runner*, *Show Runner II*, *The Man Is Dead*, and *Report Cards*). Mark's books are available through his blog site, and this author whole-heartedly recommends them all.

Gene Saks

Gene Saks was born November 8, 1921, in New York City. He studied at Cornell University; he also studied drama at the Dramatic Workshop of the New School for Social Research. Saks directed many anthology programs from television's infancy, such as *Omnibus* and *Kraft Theater*. A lifelong friendship with Neil Simon proved mutually beneficial. Saks directed many of Neil Simon's best works, such as *Barefoot in the Park*, *Last of the Red Hot Lovers*, *Brighton Beach Memoirs*, and, in 1968, *The Odd Couple* movie. Billy Wilder was the first directorial choice, but his salary was simply not in keeping with the budget. When *The Odd Couple* became a television series, the first season was directed much in the manner of the film.

Saks was first and foremost a director, but he also did garner acclaim as an actor on Broadway, in *South Pacific* and *A Shot in the Dark*. In feature films, Saks had roles in *Cactus Flower* (1969), *The Prisoner of Second Avenue* (1975), and *A Thousand Clowns* (1965).

Saks won Tony Awards for *I Love My Wife*, *Brighton Beach Memoirs*, and *Biloxi Blues*. He was nominated for numerous others, and won a Director's Guild Award for "Outstanding Directorial Achievement in a Movie" for *The Odd Couple*. From 1950 to 1980, Saks was married to Bea Arthur. Saks directed Arthur in *Mame*, and they had two sons together.

JAY SANDRICH

Jay Sandrich was born in Los Angeles, California, February 24, 1932. He came from a show business family—his father, Mark Sandrich, had directed several Fred Astaire and Ginger Rogers musicals. Mark died when his son Jay was only 13, but directing was in the genes. Jay first directed training films for the Signal Corps while he was in the service. A lucky break came about when Jay wrote a letter to Desilu Productions. Although only 25 at the time, he was given the job as an assistant director on several episodes of *I Love Lucy*; this experience led to jobs on other programs, such as *The Danny Thomas Show*. He was, simultaneously, working as associate producer for *The Andy Griffith Show*.

By the middle–1960s, the "assistant" part of his title was gone, and he kicked off a very lucrative career as a TV director and producer on such programs as *Get Smart*, *The Ghost and Mrs. Muir*, *The Bob Newhart Show* pilot episode, *The Mary Tyler Moore Show* (for which he won several Emmys), *Soap*, and *The Odd Couple*. Sandrich said, "When *The Odd Couple* went to three cameras, Garry Marshall called and wanted me to direct a few episodes. I loved working with Garry—truly one of the finest comedy minds. And because *The Mary Tyler Moore Show* started their new season closer to the fall, I said yes. Working on *The Odd Couple* was so much fun." Sandrich directed numerous episodes—"Murray the Fink," "Last Tango in Newark" (with Edward Villella), "The Odd Decathlon," "To Bowl or Not to Bowl," "Strike up the Band, or Else" (with Pernell Roberts), "Two on the Aisle," and "The Bigger They Are" (with John Byner). Sandrich shared, "I vividly remember the one in which Felix represents Oscar in court ('Murray the Fink'). It took a while for a director to earn Tony's trust, but later we became good friends. He was so creative, too. Both Tony and Jack were very generous to one another. Tony would be given a funny line to say, and he would tell the writers, 'Give it to Jack.' Those writers, with the help of Garry, Tony and Jack, were constantly rewriting and rewriting. The original script was more like an outline on that show. The other episode I vividly recall is the one with ballet star Edward Villella ('Last Tango in Newark'). His son appears at the end of the episode, and during the whole episode, Villella was so concerned about his son. What a good dad, and a good guy. He couldn't possibly have been nicer."

Sandrich tried his hand at directing movies, such as *Seems Like Old Times* (1980), with Goldie Hawn and Chevy Chase, but disliked the slow pace and returned to television, where he directed the pilot episode of *The Golden Girls* and all the episodes of *The Cosby Show* in the first three seasons. Now in semi-retirement, Sandrich has opted to become, at his leisure, a theater director in Aspen, Colorado. Thus far, he has directed *Rounding Third, Same Time Next Year*, and *Chapter Two*—another amazing "chapter" in an amazing life.

ED SCHARLACH

Edmund Norman Scharlach was born March 12, 1943, in San Francisco, California. His stepfather was prolific screen and TV writer Harry Crane. Teamed with Peggy Elliott, Scharlach wrote scripts for some of television's most famous programs. Among their early TV credits are *Please Don't Eat the Daisies, The Doris Day Show, Room 222, That Girl,* and *The Ghost and Mrs. Muir.*

Scharlach and Elliott wrote *Odd Couple* scripts for both single-camera and multi-camera episodes. As Scharlach recalled, "For *The Odd Couple*, the multi-camera approach worked much better. *The Odd Couple* was, of course, originally created as a play to be performed in front of a live audience, so it thrived when done that way on TV. This allowed the writers to go much stronger with jokes and humor. By the way, we experienced a similar situation with *Happy Days*."

Scharlach and Elliott's episodes had some very clever, pun-laden titles such as "Engrave Trouble," and "Don't Believe in Roomers." Scharlach said, "Peggy and I did name our episodes and the titles were often puns. Our favorite, the year after *The Flight of the Phoenix* was a major hit movie, was the episode titled 'The Fight of the Felix.' The Writer's Guild of America and *TV Guide* named that episode among the '101 Best Written TV Episodes of All-Time.' Ann Elder guest starred in that episode and, I didn't know her then, but five years later we were paired as a writing team, and did several variety series, sitcoms, and pilots together. On 'Engrave Trouble,' I worked with Michael Constantine. He's a terrific and charismatic character actor. He was a favorite of Marshall and Belson. When he was in a scene, it gained several dimensions. I also wrote for his short-lived series *Sirota's Court*, created and produced by Harvey Miller, where Michael again stole every scene he was in. My fondest memory of Michael, however, was years later, watching him rave about the wonders of Windex in *My Big Fat Greek Wedding*. On the episode titled 'Don't Believe in Roomers,' I worked with Marlyn Mason—an amazing and touching actress. I was a

Odd Couple **scriptwriter Ed Scharlach (courtesy Ed Scharlach).**

fan of hers from her stage comedy and musicals. She had previously appeared in one of the episodes of *Hey! Landlord* that Peggy and I wrote. Peggy and I were freelance writers on *The Odd Couple*, therefore our experiences were mostly with Garry Marshall and Jerry Belson, and often with producer Jerry Davis. We were only on the set to watch rehearsals and the final filming of the show."

Among the scripts Scharlach and Elliott wrote for the show is "Speak for Yourself"—a flashback episode. Is there ever a problem maintaining continuity with flashback episodes? Scharlach reflected, "Flashback episodes can be a fun departure for TV episode writers. Any complexity would only be in production and post."

Inspired by the hit 1970 film, *What Do You Say to a Naked Lady?*, Scharlach and Elliott penned the funny episode titled "What Does a Naked Lady Say to You?" It's not well known, but frequent *Odd Couple* writer/producer/director Harvey Miller portrayed 'The Rubber Ducky' in that episode, and Scharlach recalled, "Miller was an original. He was great to know and colorful to work for on *Sirota's Court*. It was fun having him cast as kind of an inside joke in that episode." Miller appeared in the credits on that episode under his real name, Harvey Skolnik.

About *The Odd Couple*'s directors, Scharlach commented, "I loved the work of Jerry Paris—he directed lots of Marshall-Belson shows. Alan Rafkin was a friend, and I also enjoyed working with him when he was briefly a producer on *Love, American Style*."

What was it like working for Garry Marshall? Scharlach stated, "Garry Marshall has always been a treasured teacher, mentor, producer, brilliantly funny mind, and friend. He introduced Peggy Elliott and me to be writing partners—which kicked off our television careers. I learned more about writing and putting on a TV show from Garry than anybody else I ever worked for. Peggy is one of my closest friends and is like my sister. We are still in constant touch. Peggy spent many years married to Samuel Goldwyn, Jr., and is now writing books, blogs, running film festivals, and working with great dedication for women's causes, significantly in various parts of Africa, where she spends much of her time."

About the show's stars, Tony Randall and Jack Klugman, Scharlach said, "Tony and Jack were always very nice to us, and complimentary of our work."

CHARLES SHYER

Sometimes credited as "Chuck" Shyer, Charles Richard Shyer was born October 11, 1951, in Los Angeles, and got his start as Garry Marshall and Jerry Belson's personal assistant on the single-season Sandy Baron and Will Hutchins sitcom *Hey! Landlord*. Shyer recalled, "At that time my job was basically going for fudgsicles, getting Garry and Jerry's cars washed and doing their Christmas shopping. But by the early '70s, when I was promoted to co-script consultant on *The Odd Couple*, Jerry, Garry, and I had become pretty much inseparable. At first, I was kind of shy and, frankly, intimidated by these Emmy-winning writers, but Garry and Jerry believed in me and were incredibly supportive. I also learned a tremendous amount from Dale McRaven and Carl Kleinschmitt, who were head writers on *The Odd Couple* ... and just wonderful to me. From the start, I was nurtured as a writer, and all the guys were always open to my sometimes idiotic ideas, opinions, and suggestions. I was also credited as associate producer for those single-camera first-season episodes and supervised the post-production on most of those shows. Back then, I did my best to learn absolutely everything I could about writing, acting, directing, and, of course, comedy. It was also during that time that I was first introduced to Ernst Lubitsch, Billy Wilder, Preston Sturges, Howard Hawks and writers like Ben Hecht, Charles MacArthur, George S. Kaufman, and Moss Hart. I'd been given an incredible opportunity and there was no way I was going to squander it."

Surrounded by so much talent and creativity, Shyer's career blossomed quickly. He is credited as co-writer for two of those first season *Odd Couple* episodes—"Trapped," and the cleverly titled "Bunny Is Missing, Down by the Lake." Shyer recalled, "Those episodes were an eye-opener for me because I quickly realized writing 'one-liners' wasn't really my forte. In those days nobody entered or exited Felix and Oscar's apartment without a joke. But Tony and Jack's characters were so well drawn, that I had a great time helping construct the stories, adding character touches and coming up with physical comedy bits."

What was it like working with the brilliant Tony Randall and Jack Klugman? Shyer remembered, "To be honest, I was the youngest guy on the creative team and I don't believe they took much notice of me. I mean, they were cordial.... Tony especially could be nice, but Jack would kind of nod and look straight through me ... which was actually a kind of a relief because I probably would've been tongue-tied if he'd tried to engage me. But those guys were amazing talents ... and born to play those roles. I mean, they surely gave Lemmon and Matthau a run for the money."

When *The Odd Couple* became a multi-camera, live-audience show in season two, Shyer decided to move on. About that decision, Shyer said, "The whole dynamic of the show changed. The comedy became broader—less character-centric and more audience driven. It also became a much bigger hit, but I felt it was time for me to try some different things.... And I was dying to get into film." Shyer did, however, return to direct one of the live-audience episodes and shared, "That was an episode titled 'Two Men on a Hoarse' near the end of season five. It was really the first thing I ever directed, and my best friend, Jerry Belson, backed me up on the set for the whole shoot. I realized the poor guy was going nuts—absolutely stir-crazy that week, because if any adult ever had A.D.D., it was Belson ... but he hung in there with me, which is something I'll never forget."

Chuck Shyer really found his niche writing and directing many wildly popular and memorable motion pictures, including *Father of the Bride* (1991), *Private Benjamin* (1980), *Baby Boom* (1987), *The Parent Trap* (1998), *Smokey and the Bandit* (1977), *Irreconcilable Differences* (1984), and *Alfie* (2004), to name but a few. At one time, Shyer was married to film director Nancy Meyers.

Neil Simon

Marvin Neil Simon was born July 4, 1927, in the Bronx, New York. Simon is an amazingly successful screenwriter, author and playwright—perhaps the most successful playwright of all time. Many think his nickname is "Doc," because of his glasses, but it is actually because of his penchant for playing doctor as a kid (he carried his toy stethoscope everywhere with him). So much of what "Doc" wrote for the stage enjoyed a second life as a feature film. A few of his works were even launched as TV series.

Simon's childhood coincided with the Great Depression, and financial woes put a strain on his parents' relationship. Neil and his brother, Danny, were sometimes sent to live with relatives when problems surfaced between their parents, Irving and Mamie (Irving was gone for long periods of time). Neil would frequently seek refuge at the movies, and big-screen comedies made him yearn to be a comedy writer. He attended both NYU and the University of Denver through the Air Force Reserve Training Program. His earliest credits came about in radio (writing for Goodman Ace of *Easy Aces*). Then, in television's infancy, he was a writer for *Your Show of Shows* and *Caesar's Hour*, both with Sid Caesar. Next came a live NBC sitcom called *Stanley*, which starred Buddy Hackett, Carol Burnett, and Paul Lynde. Simon wrote the debut episode titled "The Opera Tickets," and also made a non-speaking cameo appearance in another episode at a lunch counter. He also penned 17 episodes of the classic *Phil Silvers Show* (Sgt. Bilko). Shortly after that, however, his focus became the Broadway stage. Simon had found his niche, and what followed was to become legendary. He became a master at exposing human frailties and foibles, and making audiences laugh at themselves. He then had us rooting for these flawed, albeit mostly good-hearted characters.

Come Blow Your Horn got the ball rolling. Simon's next plays, *Barefoot in the Park*, *Little Me*, and *The Odd Couple* really put him on the map. They were huge Broadway successes, and huge motion picture successes. They also both debuted on Thursday, September 24, 1970, as back-to-back ABC sitcoms. *Barefoot in the Park*, with an African American cast aired at 9 p.m. and *The Odd Couple*, with Jack Klugman (who had played Oscar on Broadway) and Tony Randall (who had portrayed Felix in summer stock) aired at 9:30 p.m. After 13 weeks, the struggling *Barefoot in the Park* was given the axe, but *The Odd Couple* (at this time, a single-camera show with a laugh track) was given a full-season commitment. Simon was not in favor of *The*

Odd Couple becoming a series—his deal with Paramount did not include this. The TV rights to *Odd Couple* and the stage rights to *Barefoot in the Park* were combined into something called Ellen Enterprises. After initial hesitance, Simon sold Ellen Enterprises for $125,000. His reluctance was warranted, as the deal cost him millions from the TV version of *The Odd Couple*, and all future stage performances of *Barefoot in the Park*. Even after the ill-advised financial move, he eventually warmed up to Randall and Klugman's portrayal of his characters (because his daughter loved the program). It was then that he realized and appreciated the quality of the show. Simon even agreed to do a cameo appearance in an episode titled "Two on the Aisle." Simon and Garry Marshall have remained friends ever since.

Even though they didn't always receive good reviews, the hits just kept on coming for Neil Simon: *The Out-of-Towners, The Sunshine Boys, Murder by Death, The Goodbye Girl, California Suite, Chapter Two, Brighton Beach Memoirs, Broadway Bound, Biloxi Blues,* and *Lost in Yonkers* (the latter garnering him his only Pulitzer Prize and Drama Desk Award; it is also Simon's favorite). He could do it all—he even wrote the books for hit musicals *Sweet Charity* and *They're Playing Our Song.* Simon even gambled with a female stage version of *The Odd Couple* in 1985 with Florence Ungar and Olive Madison (Sally Struthers and Rita Moreno, respectively). He is famous for his many rewrites—honing each scene of each play over and over again—his favorite part of the process has always been the rewrite (in fact, his autobiography is titled *Rewrites*). Almost all of his characters are loosely based upon real people he's known (writers are always urged to write about what they know). Neil's older brother, Danny, for example, is the inspiration for a character in *Broadway Bound, Brighton Beach Memoirs* and, of course, Felix in *The Odd Couple.*

Simon has garnered two Emmy Awards, four Tony Awards and a Pulitzer Prize (as well as countless Writer's Guild Awards). He was a Kennedy Center honoree in 1995, as presented by President Bill Clinton. He was honored with the Mark Twain Prize for American Humor in 2006. He has been married five times, twice to the same woman, Diane Lander. Shortly after the death of his wife of 20 years, dancer Joan Baim (his first wife), he then married the star of *The Goodbye Girl,* Marsha Mason (only 22 days after they met), and is currently (since 1999) married to Bobby Van's widow, Elaine Joyce. Simon has three daughters. He is a longtime New York Giants football fan.

Broadway's Alvin Theater was renamed the Neil Simon Theater in 1983. Simon received a successful kidney transplant donated by his publicist, Bill Evans (a match) in 2004. Eschewing modern technology, Simon is said to still write using a pen or typewriter to this day (no word processor, no laptop). Sitting alone in a writing room has to be difficult for a man with claustrophobia, but it hasn't hampered his creativity one iota.

LLOYD TURNER

Lloyd Gardner Turner was born August 14, 1924, in Winnemucca, Nevada, but he studied at the California College of Arts and Crafts in Berkeley, California. Turner lost one of his arms in a childhood accident. Usually paired on TV scripts with Gordon "Whitey" Mitchell, Turner began writing for Warner Bros. cartoons (primarily Bugs Bunny and Daffy Duck). With the advent of television, Turner teamed with Jay Ward and began writing for cartoon shows in the new medium, including *Crusader Rabbit*, *Time for Beany*, *Rocky and His Friends*, *The Dick Tracy Show*, and *George of the Jungle*. His dream was to become an animator for Disney.

From there, he teamed with Gordon Mitchell and penned episodes of the live-action programs, *The Doris Day Show*, *Get Smart*, *The Mary Tyler Moore Show*, *Bridget Loves Bernie*, *The Partridge Family*, *All in the Family*, *Mork and Mindy*, *The Love Boat*, and *The Jeffersons*. For *The Odd Couple*, the duo wrote two episodes for the single-camera first season: "The Jury Story" (which flashes back to one of the many times Felix and Oscar met), and "A Taste of Money" (in which the neighbor boy, Phillip, begins flashing a wad of cash, and Felix and Oscar attempt to find out its origin and worry that it might be stolen).

Lloyd Turner died of cancer on November 30, 1992, in Jackson, Oregon.

GEORGE TYNE

George Tyne was born Martin Yarus February 6, 1917, in Philadelphia, Pennsylvania. He had roles in many famous films, including *The Sands of Iwo Jima* (1949), *The Boston Strangler* (1968), and *Tell Them Willie Boy Is Here* (1969). His nickname was "Buddy," and he was one of the many show business professionals who was blacklisted during the McCarthy Era of the early 1950s. Tyne did appear very briefly in a Broadway show (with James Dean) titled *See the Jaguar*, which closed in less than a week.

Tyne's forte was directing TV comedy, and beginning in the 1960s, that career really flourished, with credits on such programs as *The Ghost and Mrs. Muir*, *The Governor and J. J.*, *Sanford and Son*, *Love, American Style*, *The Paul Lynde Show*, *The Bob Newhart Show*, *Happy Days*, *M*A*S*H*, and *The Love Boat*. Tyne also directed four episodes of *The Odd Couple*: "Oscar the Model," "Felix Is Missing," "Scrooge Gets an Oscar," and "Security Arms," and he co-directed (with Bob Birnbaum) one other, "Partner's Investment." In the early 1980s, Tyne pretty much called it a career and enjoyed a long retirement. He died on March 7, 2008, at the age of 91.

JACK WINTER

Jack Winter was born February 9, 1942, in New York City. The son of a violin virtuoso, he began in his twenties writing for TV sitcoms, such as *The Monkees*, *That Girl*, *The Dick Van Dyke Show*, *The Mary Tyler Moore Show*, *Hey, Landlord*, and *Barefoot in the Park*. Winter also wrote four episodes of *The Odd Couple*: "Oscar's

New Life," "The Pen Is Mightier than the Pencil," "The Odd Decathlon," and "Your Mother Wears Army Boots." He also directed one of the program's funniest episodes, "Take My Furniture, Please," in which Felix redecorates the apartment with some rather eclectic pieces, such as chairs shaped like hands.

Winter also directed five episodes of *Laverne and Shirley* (and wrote three), and was credited as a special advisor on the Penny Marshall–directed film, *Big* (1988).

At one point in his career, Winter was a very popular and highly paid "script doctor," one who is paid to fix up other people's scripts.

Winter often made light of the fact that Ted Kaczynski (the infamous Unabomber) was in his graduating class in Harvard. The future writer/director was the second youngest member of the graduating class of 1962. He is also said to have played tennis against a nine-year-old Pete Sampras, and beat the future champion.

Jack Winter died December 29, 2006, at the untimely age of 64.

Joel Zwick

Director Joel Zwick was born in Brooklyn, New York, on January 11, 1942. He attended Brooklyn College, and went on to become a director of some note, especially in comedy. He found his biggest successes on ABC, directing *Family Matters*, *Full House*, *Laverne and Shirley*, and *Perfect Strangers*.

Speaking of ABC, Zwick also directed 17 of the 18 produced episodes of *The New Odd Couple*, with Ron Glass as Felix Unger and Demond Wilson as Oscar Madison. Zwick not only directed the episodes, but was also listed as the supervising producer. Several of the original Klugman and Randall *Odd Couple* scripts were reworked for this new African American cast version, including "The Ides of April," "Frances Moves In," "That Was No Lady," "The New Car," "A Grave for Felix," "The Hustler," and "My Strife in Court." Zwick recalled, "We didn't really see any of the original episodes or scripts, but several of them were reworked for this new version of the show. However, we soon realized that a lot of adjustments needed to be made, especially to Ron Glass's character. Instead of the two Jewish 40-year-old men in the original, we had two good-looking black men in their 30s. At the time, the term 'metrosexual' didn't yet exist, and to keep Ron Glass's Felix from being perceived as gay, we had to constantly surround him with women. Also, Jewish men tend to settle things by yelling at one another, while black men tend to utilize their fists more, so we had to adjust a lot of the dialogue. It's interesting to note that Tony Randall and Jack Klugman were quite similar to their roles on the show, while Demond Wilson and Ron Glass were not. Demond, who portrayed Oscar on the show, always arrived to the studio nattily dressed, while Ron Glass, who portrayed Felix, was actually the sloppy dresser. However, it was their earlier TV characters (Glass on *Barney Miller* and Wilson on *Sanford and Son*) which typecast them. Glass and Wilson did

Director of 17 of 18 episodes of *The New Odd Couple*, Joel Zwick (up at bat), pictured here between Demond Wilson (left) and Ron Glass (right) (courtesy Joel Zwick).

not hang out together after work. They didn't bond in that way, but they did have a very nice professional relationship for the series."

One of Zwick's big-screen hits came in 2002, *My Big Fat Greek Wedding*. It was so popular, in fact, that it spawned a TV series version a short time later, and brought about a surge in the sale of Windex.

Four
The Episode Guides

The Odd Couple
(September 24, 1970–March 7, 1975)

"The Laundry Orgy" (1:1)
September 24, 1970

Writers: Jerry Belson and Garry Marshall; *Director:* Jerry Paris; *Guest Stars:* Al Molinaro as Murray Greshler, Larry Gelman as Vinnie, Ryan McDonald as Roy, Garry Walberg as Speed, Monica Evans as Cecily Pigeon, Carole Shelley as Gwendolyn Pigeon.

Complications set in when Oscar, eager to get newly divorced Felix back in the dating scene, arranges a date with the Pigeon sisters, only to realize it conflicts with his and Felix's regularly scheduled poker game. The song "Tiny Bubbles" is featured in the background while Felix, Oscar, and the Pigeon sisters are dancing in the laundry room. *The Odd Couple* debuted immediately after the premiere of another sitcom based upon a Neil Simon play and movie, *Barefoot in the Park*, on that same Thursday on ABC.

"Fight of the Felix" (1:2)
October 1, 1970

Writers: Peggy Elliott and Ed Scharlach; *Director:* Bruce Bilson; *Guest Stars:* Richard X. Slattery as Splint McCullough, Ann Elder as Irma, Fabian Dean as Feldman, and Peter Dawson as the bartender.

To settle a score, Felix challenges a hockey pro to a boxing match when it's discovered that the player falsely accused Oscar of flirting with his girlfriend and gave him a black eye. The title, concocted by writers Elliott and Scharlach, was a play on the movie title, *The Flight of the Phoenix* (1965). Actor Fabian Dean, who portrayed Feldman in the episode, was often confused with Al Molinaro, and vice-versa.

"Felix Gets Sick" (1:3)
October 8, 1970

Writer: Albert E. Lewin; *Director:* Hal Cooper; *Guest Stars:* Larry Gelman as

Vinnie, Ryan McDonald as Roy, Al Molinaro as Murray Greshler; Garry Walberg as Speed, Beryl Hammond as Mary Ann, and Bridget Hanley as Barbara Phipps.

Oscar's dilemma: care for a feverish Felix, who has come down with a 48-hour bug, or keep a date with a pretty stewardess. Why not both?

"THE JURY STORY" (1:4) October 15, 1970

Writers: Lloyd Turner and Gordon "Whitey" Mitchell; *Director:* Hal Cooper; *Guest Stars:* Bobby Baum as Mr. Welk, Barney Martin as Mr. Moss, Eva McVeagh as Mrs. Lachman, Peter Virgo, Sr. as the bailiff, Monica Evans as Cecily Pigeon, and Carole Shelley as Gwendolyn Pigeon.

Flashbacks are used to reveal how Felix and Oscar met as jurors on a case and how, after being sequestered, each received an early glimpse into the other's unbearable idiosyncrasies. The song playing in the background as Felix and Oscar discover each other's faults is Rodgers and Hammerstein's "Getting to Know You," from *The King and I*. Actor Barney Martin and Tony Randall reunited in a courtroom in 1976 as co-stars for two seasons of *The Tony Randall Show*. Jack Klugman had previously portrayed a juror in the classic 1957 drama *12 Angry Men*.

"THE BREAKUP" (1:5) October 22, 1970

Writer: Ruth Brooks Flippen; *Director:* Charles Rondeau; *Guest Stars:* Larry Gelman as Vinnie, Ryan McDonald as Roy, Al Molinaro as Murray, Garry Walberg as Speed, Alice Ghostley as Mimi Greshler, Monica Evans as Cecily Pigeon, and Carole Shelley as Gwendolyn Pigeon.

The "odd couple" uncouples, and Felix seeks a new place to call home after Oscar, unable to cope with him, throws him out (Murray and his wife, Mimi, learn just how difficult it is to live with Felix when he becomes their house guest). Mimi was later played by Jane Dulo.

"OSCAR'S ULCER" (1:6) October 29, 1970

Writer: Bob Rodgers; *Director:* Bruce Bilson; *Guest Stars:* Larry Gelman as Vinnie, Ryan McDonald as Roy, Al Molinaro as Murray Greshler, Garry Walberg as Speed, Bill Quinn as Dr. Melnitz, Timothy Blake as Marilyn, Marlene Tracy as Donna, Allan Kent as Joe McClosky, Marti Little as Lupe, and Ben Frommer as Gonzales.

Oscar makes an effort to abide by Felix's rules—no poker, girlfriends, or unhealthy foods—when he is diagnosed with an ulcer. Bill Quinn, who portrays Dr. Melnitz, also portrayed Mary Richards's doctor father, Walter Richards, on *The Mary Tyler Moore Show*. He was frequently typecast as a doctor or a judge.

"I DO, I DON'T" (1:7) November 5, 1970

Writer: Carl Kleinschmitt; *Director:* Bruce Bilson; *Guest Stars:* Joyce Van Patten as Phyllis Parker, George Furth as Harvey Bixley, Richard Stahl as the minister, Leonard Ross as Man number one, and Garry Marshall as man number two.

Oscar tries to comfort an angry would-be bride after Felix's talk with the groom about his own marriage woes causes him to call off the wedding. The song playing in the background is "A Man and a Woman."

"Oscar, the Model" (1:8) November 19, 1970

Writers: Jerry Belson and Garry Marshall; *Director:* George Tyne; *Guest Stars:* Albert Brooks as Rudy Mandel, Peter Brocco as Mr. Whitehill, Dee Gardner as Tracy, Timothy Near as Loretta, Victoria Thompson as Gabrielle, and David Warren Duclon as the messenger.

Oscar's unpolished look earns him a new career when an advertising agency head seeks him for a campaign. The man portraying the messenger, David Warren Duclon, later wrote three episodes of the series—"I Gotta Be Me," "Let's Make a Deal," and "The Roy Clark Show."

"The Big Brothers" (1:9) November 19, 1970

Writers: Richard Bensfield and Perry Grant; *Director:* Bruce Bilson; *Guest Stars:* Clint Howard as Randy Grainger, and Janice Carroll as Mrs. Grainger.

When Felix and Oscar join Big Brothers of America, Felix becomes crushed when a young man (Clint Howard), who needs a father figure, favors the company of Oscar. Director Bruce Bilson had previously worked with another Howard brother—Ronny—on several episodes of *The Andy Griffith Show*.

"It's All Over Now, Baby Bird" (1:10) December 3, 1970

Writer: Dale McRaven; *Director:* Jerry Paris; *Guest Stars:* Monica Evans as Cecily Pigeon, Carole Shelley as Gwendolyn Pigeon, Damian London as Dr. Schneider, James Millhollin as Mr. Humus, and Ken Swofford as the cop.

Felix drives Oscar batty after his beloved parrot passes on, and he can't decide on a fitting tribute. Jack Klugman considered this the best of the single camera episodes, and it's also one of Garry Marshall's favorites. There is an obscure reference in the dialogue to an old radio and TV sitcom titled *Ethel and Albert*. This was James Millhollin's first of three guest appearances on the show. His character's name, funeral director Mr. Humus, is a play on the word *posthumous*. The episode's title was inspired by the Bob Dylan and Leon Russell song, "It's All over Now, Baby Blue." Coincidentally, this episode about a bird was written by Dale Mc*Raven*.

"Felix Is Missing" (1:11) December 10, 1970

Writer: Albert E. Lewin; *Director:* George Tyne; *Guest Stars:* Larry Gelman as Vinnie, Ryan McDonald as Roy, Al Molinaro as Murray Greshler, Garry Walberg as Speed, Albert Brooks as Rudy Mandel, Therese Baldwin as Priscilla, Anitra Ford as Jennie, Lloyd Gough as Sergeant Flanagan, Jerry Jones as the attendant, and Johnny Silver as the bum.

Oscar and his friends worry about Felix's sudden disappearance—unaware that he left a note telling of an emergency photo shoot in Canada—a note that became lost in Oscar's room rubble. Johnny Silver made his first of five guest appearances in this episode.

"Scrooge Gets an Oscar" (1:12) December 17, 1970

Writer: Ronald I. Friedman; *Director:* George Tyne; *Guest Stars:* Larry Gelman as Vinnie, Ryan McDonald as Roy, Al Molinaro as Murray Greshler, Garry Walberg as Speed, and Ogden Talbot as the messenger boy.

Murray's police charity is staging Charles Dickens's *A Christmas Carol*, and Felix Unger is directing. All involved consider Oscar to be the ideal man to play Scrooge, but when Oscar refuses to participate, he experiences a Dickensian nightmare. (Coincidentally, Klugman died on Christmas Eve 2012.)

"THE BLACKOUT" (1:13) December 24, 1970

Writers: Bill Idelson and Harvey Miller; *Director:* Charles Rondeau; *Guest Stars:* Larry Gelman as Vinnie, Ryan McDonald as Roy, Al Molinaro as Murray Greshler, Garry Walberg as Speed, Herbie Faye as Mr. Lambretti, and Cynthia Lynn as Inga.

Oscar turns detective and reenacts an alleged crime to discover how, during a blackout, a fifty dollar bill disappeared from the jackpot at a poker game. This episode marks the first of seven episodes on which character actor Herbie Faye appeared. Some creative lighting techniques were needed during the blackout.

"THEY USE HORSERADISH, DON'T THEY?" (1:14) January 7, 1971

Writers: Jerry Belson and Garry Marshall; *Director:* Garry Marshall; *Guest Stars:* Marlyn Mason as Barbara Arcola, Francine York as Sharon, Margot Nelson as Dora, Walter Jankowitz as Judge number one, and Louis DeFarra as Judge number two.

Felix's psychosomatic issues, coupled with the theft of his gravy recipe, wreak havoc when he, assisted by Oscar, enters a cooking contest to win a brand-new kitchen. The title of this episode was inspired by the 1969 motion picture (which was based on Horace McCoy's novel), *They Shoot Horses, Don't They?* Garry Marshall made his single-camera directorial debut on this episode, in which Felix utters his first, "Oscar, Oscar, Oscar." Marlyn Mason's character, Barbara Arcola, was named after Garry Marshall's address on Arcola Avenue in Toluca Lake, California. It was also later used as Chachi's surname on *Happy Days* and *Joanie Loves Chachi.*

"THE HIDEAWAY" (1:15) January 14, 1971

Writers: Harry Winkler and Harry Dolan; *Director:* Richard Michaels; *Guest Stars:* Reni Santoni as Ernie Wilson, Cliff Osmond as Effram, and Dub Taylor as Slim.

Oscar's hopes for discovering a promising NFL quarterback are shattered when Felix, discovering the young man is a talented cellist, helps him pursue that career instead. After this episode, the series moved to Friday nights at 9:30.

"LOVERS DON'T MAKE HOUSE CALLS" (1:16) January 29, 1971

Writer: Ron Friedman; *Director:* Bruce Bilson; *Guest Stars:* Joan Hotchkis as Dr. Nancy Cunningham, Nora Marlowe as the nurse, and Bill Quinn as Dr. Melnitz.

Oscar meets the new love of his life, Dr. Nancy Cunningham, after she makes a house call to treat Felix, who suffered an allergic reaction after accidentally ingesting mayonnaise. This episode marked the first of eleven appearances for Hotchkis, and marked the debut of narrator William Woodson in the opening credits, with those immortal words, "On November 13th, Felix Unger was asked to remove himself from his place of residence. That request came from his wife." The program was now seen on Friday nights at 9:30.

"ENGRAVE TROUBLE" (1:17) February 5, 1971

Writers: Peggy Elliott and Ed Scharlach; *Director:* Alan Rafkin; *Guest Stars:* Michael Constantine as Bill Green, Richard Stahl as the florist, Herb Vigran as Louie, Vern E. Rowe as Man number one, and Frank Loverde as Man number two.

Felix's plans to reunite with Gloria are shattered when a specially engraved gold watch is stolen before he can present it to her. The title of this episode exhibits writers Ed Scharlach and Peggy Elliott's passion for puns. Michael Constantine had previously worked with Garry Marshall and Jerry Belson on *Hey, Landlord*.

"BUNNY IS MISSING DOWN BY THE LAKE" (1:18) February 12, 1971

Writers: Alan Mandel and Charles Shyer; *Director:* Jerry Paris; *Guest Stars:* E. J. Peaker as Julie Thompson, Lisa Gerritsen as Bunny, Pamelyn Ferdin as Cindy, and Gloria McCartney as Lois.

Felix is depressed—he found out Gloria is seeing another man. To get his mind off of the situation, Oscar invites Felix on a fishing trip. A downpour dampens their fishing plans—until the weather brings stranded women to their cabin. This episode's title is based upon the name of a popular British movie called *Bunny Lake Is Missing* (1965). Pamelyn Ferdin portrays Cindy in this episode, but was later cast as Felix's daughter, Edna.

"YOU'VE COME A LONG WAY, BABY" (1:19) February 19, 1971

Writer: Albert E. Lewin; *Director:* Garry Marshall; *Guest Stars:* Al Molinaro as Murray Greshler, Joan Hotchkis as Nancy Cunningham, Christopher Shea as Phillip Wexler, Lisa Lu as Mrs. Lee, and Jessica Myerson as Mrs. Ferguson.

After a photo shoot featuring babies, Felix discovers that one of the mothers left without hers. He leaves a note with his telephone number and address, and brings the infant home with him, on the same night as Oscar's "Toast and Roast Dinner." The title of this episode was inspired by the slogan from Virginia Slims cigarette commercials. This was the first of three episodes with guest star Christopher Shea as neighbor boy Phillip. Shea was also the voice of Linus Van Pelt in the *Peanuts* TV specials.

"A TASTE OF MONEY" (1:20) February 26, 1971

Writers: Lloyd Turner and Gordon "Whitey" Mitchell; *Director:* Alan Rafkin; *Guest Stars:* Christopher Shea as Phillip Wexler, Ed Belson as the bum, Queta DeAcuna as Alicia the maid, Howard Morton as Mr. Larkin, Peter Brocco as Max, John Qualen as Sam, and William O'Connell as Mr. Skyler.

Felix and Oscar turn detective to figure out where their 11-year-old neighbor, Phillip, acquired a large amount of cash. The title of this episode was inspired by the Beatles and Herb Alpert song "A Taste of Honey."

"OSCAR'S NEW LIFE" (1:21) March 5, 1971

Writer: Jack Winter; *Director:* Alan Rafkin; *Guest Stars:* Ed Platt as William Donnelly, Britt Leach as Morris Donnelly, John Astin as Beau "Buff" Buffingham, George Wyner as the art director, Dee Gardner as the model, Carolyn Stellar as the secretary, Liv Von Linden as beautiful girl number one, and Rena Horten as beautiful girl number two.

Oscar ditches an assignment to cover the Pan American Badminton Championships, instead opting to fabricate a story. Trouble ensues when his story does not mention the event's referee being shot in the leg. John Astin, whom Tony Randall discovered, guest stars as Buff.

"WHAT MAKES FELIX RUN?" (1:22) March 22, 1971

Writer: Bill Manhoff; *Director:* Jerry Paris; *Guest Stars:* Joan Hotchkis as Nancy Cunningham, and Johnny Scott Lee as Little Felix.

A flashback is first used to reveal Felix as a young boy ("Little Felix") with Tony Randall playing his own grandfather. A nightmare is later incorporated wherein Felix meets an angel (Oscar) who relegates him to "The Other Place," not Heaven, for his controlling ways. Johnny Scott Lee portrays Little Felix in this episode, but Sean Manning took over the role in the "Our Fathers" episode.

"WHAT DOES A NAKED LADY SAY TO YOU?" (1:23) March 19, 1971

Writers: Peggy Elliott and Ed Scharlach; *Director:* Hal Cooper; *Guest Stars:* Larry Gelman as Vinnie, Al Molinaro as Murray Greshler, Garry Walberg as Speed, Marj Dusay as Madelyn the librarian, Harvey Skolnik as the rubber ducky, Johnny Silver as the bum, and Frank Alesia as the producer.

Oscar and Murray seek a way to tell Felix that the lady he is seeing is not a librarian, but an actress who appears in the nude play *Bath Tub*. This episode's title was inspired by the Allen Funt motion picture, *What Do You Say to a Naked Lady?* (1970). Executive producer/writer/director Harvey Miller portrays the "rubber ducky" in this episode, credited under his real name, Harvey Skolnik—an inside joke.

"TRAPPED" (1:24) March 26, 1971

Writers: Charles Shyer and Alan Mandel; *Director:* Jerry Belson; *Guest Stars:* Joan Hotchkis as Nancy Cunningham, Christopher Shea as Phillip Wexler, Dave Ketchum as the cop, Ellen Corby as Florence, Russell Thorson as Herman, and Larry Kent as Vern the stick-up man.

Felix, Oscar, and Nancy become trapped in the basement of the apartment building, dressed in costumes they were to wear to a Women's Club Party. Felix, a devil, Oscar, in a suit of armor, and Nancy, dressed as a nurse, have additional bad luck—they are held up and robbed through the street grate on the basement window. Garry Marshall calls this a "stuck in it" show—a cost-cutting episode in which the cast is stuck somewhere, negating the need for a lot of scene changes and guest stars. This was the only season in which 24 episodes were produced. This was the final single-camera episode.

"Natural Childbirth" (2:1) September 17, 1971

Writers: Bill Idelson and Harvey Miller; *Director:* Hal Cooper; *Guest Stars:* Hilarie Thompson as Martha, Carolyn Payne as the Girl, Ogden Talbot as Howard, Lillian Adams as the woman, Shawn Michaels as the driver, and Jessica Myerson as the instructress.

Oscar's niece, Martha, is about to have a baby and has decided upon natural childbirth. Felix believes she should have her baby in a hospital. Trouble ensues when Felix tries to convince her to see things his way. This is the first multi-camera episode, filmed before a live audience, eliminating the laugh track. Beginning here, the look of Felix and Oscar's apartment changes drastically.

"Felix's Wife's Boyfriend" (2:2) September 24, 1971

Writer: Ron Friedman; *Director:* Jerry Paris; *Guest Stars:* Joan Hotchkis as Nancy Cunningham, Janis Hansen as Gloria, and Fred Beir as Raymond Cunningham.

Oscar and Nancy seek a way to tell Felix that Gloria has a new boyfriend—Nancy's handsome ski bum brother, Ray.

"Hospital Mates" (2:3) October 1, 1971

Writer: Garry Marshall; *Director:* Jerry Paris; *Guest Stars:* Joan Hotchkis as Nancy Cunningham, Janis Hansen as Gloria, Peggy Doyle as the nun, and Keg Johnson as the orderly.

Felix needs to have nasal surgery at the exact same time that Oscar needs an operation to repair his Achilles tendon. As luck would have it, they land in the same hospital room and, as per usual, they drive each other crazy. This episode was loosely based upon Garry Marshall's own hospital stay because of a torn knee cartilage.

"The Sleepwalker" (2:4) October 8, 1971

Writer: Mickey Rose; *Director:* Jack Donohue; *Guest Stars:* Al Molinaro as Murray Greshler, and Joan Hotchkis as Nancy Cunningham.

Upon Nancy's insistence, Oscar attempts to become more tolerant of Felix—only to find his suppressed hostilities lead to bouts of sleepwalking, during which he wanders into Felix's bedroom and hits him over the head with rolled-up newspapers in the middle of the night.

"A Grave for Felix" (2:5) October 15, 1971

Writers: Dick Bensfield and Perry Grant; *Director:* Hal Cooper; *Guest Stars:* Joan Hotchkis as Nancy Cunningham, Ken Samson as Mr. Twitchell, John Qualen as the groundskeeper, Dan Tobin as the cemetery salesman, and Ivor Francis as Bengstrom.

Oscar elicits his roommate's anger when he uses the money Felix gave him for the down payment on a cemetery plot to bet (and lose) it on "a sure thing" at the race track. This was one of the scripts reused for *The New Odd Couple*.

"Murray, the Fink" (2:6) October 29, 1971

Writers: Dick Bensfield and Perry Grant; *Director:* Jay Sandrich; *Guest Stars:* Larry Gelman as Vinnie, Al Molinaro as Murray Greshler, Garry Walberg as Speed, Richard Stahl as the prison guard, George O'Hanlon as the drunk, Tim Herbert as Freddie, Curt Conway as the judge, and Mark Russell as the bailiff.

In an effort to win a promotion to the vice squad, Murray arrests Felix, Oscar, and their poker pals. As Oscar attempts to implicate Murray as a fellow card player, Felix begins a defense to make Murray look good in front of his superiors. George O'Hanlon, who portrays the prison drunk, previously provided the voice for George Jetson on *The Jetsons*. Curt Conway makes his first of three appearances as a judge.

"Does Your Mother Know You're Out, Rigoletto?" (2:7) November 5, 1971

Writer: Ron Friedman; *Director:* Jack Donohue; *Guest Stars:* Richard Fredricks as himself, John Wheeler as Herbert Murphy, Janice Carroll as Agnes, Dee Gardner as Dee Dee, and Annik Borel as Monica.

Oscar comes home early from a softball game and disrupts Felix's "Opera Day." To make amends, Oscar attempts to get his first baseman, Richard Fredricks (the leading baritone for the New York City Opera Company), to play Rigoletto in the opera club's local production. The title of this episode is a play on the old song, "Does Your Mother Know You're Out, Cecilia?" Opera singer Sherill Milnes was the first choice for the episode, but he opted not to do it.

"The Fat Farm" (2:8) November 12, 1971

Writer: Albert E. Lewin; *Director:* Mel Ferber; *Guest Stars:* Joan Hotchkis as Nancy Cunningham, Dave Ketchum as Jock, Thelma Pelish as the lady, Norbert Schiller as Dr. Burger, David Warren Duclon as the waiter, and Edward Fury as the patient.

To appease Felix, Oscar, who is gaining weight, agrees to spend time at a "fat farm" and hopefully change his poor eating habits. But a lack of "real food" causes Oscar to cheat. Occasional *Odd Couple* scriptwriter David Warren Duclon guest stars as the waiter.

"The Odd Couple Meet Their Host" (2:9) November 19, 1971

Writers: Bill Idelson and Harvey Miller; *Director:* Hal Cooper; *Guest Stars:* Al Molinaro as Murray Greshler, David Steinberg as himself, and Frank Corsentino as Harvey Skolnik.

When Oscar appears on a talk show hosted by David Steinberg and begins talking about Felix's idiosyncrasies, Felix is allowed equal time—and attempts to lambaste Oscar for his equally strange ways. This episode features a character named Harvey Skolnik—the real name of co-writer Harvey Miller (an inside joke).

"Win One for Felix" (2:10) December 3, 1971

Writers: Bill Idelson, Harvey Miller and Arthur Julian; *Director:* Jack Donohue; *Guest Stars:* Janis Hansen as Gloria Unger, Willie Aames as Leonard Unger, and Randy Whipple as Chubby.

Oscar attempts to help Felix become a hero in his son Leonard's eyes, by teaching him to coach his football team. Future teen idol Leif Garrett later replaced Willie Aames in the role of Leonard Unger.

"BEING DIVORCED IS NEVER HAVING TO SAY 'I DO'" (2:11) December 10, 1971

Writer: Rick Mittleman; *Director:* Bruce Bilson; *Guest Stars:* Brett Somers Klugman as Blanche Jefferson Madison, Richard Stahl as the Reverend Wright, Sam Nudell as best man Charles Parsley, and Billy Sands as Roger J. Doctor the groom.

Oscar is ecstatic—his ex-wife, Blanche, is getting remarried (no more alimony), but he's also about to kill Felix when, at the wedding, Felix responds with "I do" when the minister asks "Does anyone object...?" Richard Stahl guest starred as a minister three separate times during the run of the show. This episode also marks the first of five guest appearances by character actor Billy Sands. The title is a turn on a line from the wildly popular 1970 movie (and the source novel by Erich Segal) *Love Story* "Love means never having to say you're sorry."

"SURPRISE, SURPRISE" (2:12) December 17, 1971

Writers: Jim Fritzell and Everett Greenbaum; *Director:* Jerry Paris; *Guest Stars:* Pamelyn Ferdin as Edna Unger, Hal Smith as Sherman the Clown, Peter Dawson as Big Al, David Fresco as Charley, Frank Loverde as Harry, Tom Stewart as Man number one, Cindy Eilbacher and Serrina McLendon as the party girls, and Cindy Henderson as Billy Amanda.

Oscar is enjoying his big sportswriter's poker game—until Felix, his daughter, Edna, and her friends invade the apartment when a downpour forces the celebration of Edna's birthday indoors instead of in the park. Cindy Eilbacher had previously portrayed Cindy Crabtree on *My Mother, the Car.* Her brother on that series, Randy Whipple, guest starred on "Win One for Felix" in this same season.

"FELIX, THE CALYPSO SINGER" (2:13) December 24, 1971

Writers: Dick Bensfield and Perry Grant; *Director:* Jack Donohue; *Guest Stars:* Joan Hotchkis as Nancy Cunningham, Barbara Colby as Bartender Monique, Vito Scotti as Pepe, Jack Perkins as Jesse Skolnik the drunk man, Sandra Caron as the drunk girl, and Guillermo DeAnda as the musician.

The popular song, "Oscar, Oscar, Oscar" is performed by Felix calypso style as Felix becomes a third wheel in a Caribbean vacation for Oscar and Nancy. Jesse, the drunk in this episode, has the surname Skolnik (script consultant Harvey Miller's real last name—an inside joke).

"AND LEAVE THE GREYHOUNDS TO US" (2:14) December 31, 1971

Writer: Martin Cohan; *Director:* Hal Cooper; *Guest Cast:* Phil Leeds as Salty Pepper; Buddy Lester as the kennel owner; Herbie Faye as the track official; and John McCartt as the race announcer.

After Oscar wins a greyhound named Golden Earrings in a poker game, he seeks to overcome Felix's objections about dog racing being cruel, and sneaks the dog down to Miami to make post time. The episode's title is a play on the Greyhound Bus commercials which stated, "Leave the driving to us." This episode marks the first of three guest appearances by character actor Phil Leeds. This was the second consecutive episode that mentioned greyhound racing.

"SECURITY ARMS" (2:15) January 7, 1972

Writer: Jerry Belson; *Director:* George Tyne; *Guest Stars:* Al Molinaro as Murray Greshler, Janis Hansen as Gloria Unger, and John Fiedler as G. Martin Duke of Security Arms.

After a robbery in their apartment, Felix demands that he and Oscar move into a safer building. They settle upon the Security Arms, and initially all is well, until the excessive rules, regulations and paranoia drive them back to their old apartment. John Fiedler plays the security building's manager, and also guest starred in the episode "The Dog Story." Fiedler also appeared in the Broadway production and the 1968 *The Odd Couple* movie, portraying Vinnie, the poker player. This script was later reworked as "Security" on *The New Odd Couple*.

"SPEAK FOR YOURSELF" (2:16) January 14, 1972

Writer: Peggy Elliott and Ed Scharlach; *Director:* Hal Cooper; *Guest Stars:* Al Molinaro as Murray Greshler, Janis Hansen as Gloria Unger, and Ronda Copland as Mitzi Ferguson.

This is a flashback episode set in the early 1950s. It relates how Felix and Gloria first met. Ronda Copland reprised her role as Mitzi in the famous "Password" episode. The old song playing in the background when the flashback begins is "You Belong to Me."

"YOU SAVED MY LIFE" (2:17) January 21, 1972

Writer: Bob Rodgers; *Director:* Jack Donohue; *Guest Stars:* Al Molinaro as Murray Greshler, and Penny Marshall as Myrna Turner.

Felix, feeling obligated to repay Oscar for saving his life, becomes even more of a pest than usual. Penny Marshall as Oscar's inept, nasal secretary, Myrna Turner, is introduced in this episode.

"WHERE'S GRANDPA?" (2:18) January 28, 1972

Writer: Albert E. Lewin; *Director:* Jack Donohue; *Guest Stars:* Larry Gelman as Vinnie, Al Molinaro as Murray Greshler, Garry Walberg as Speed, Madge Kennedy as Mimi Unger, and Ann Doran as Loretta Spoon.

Believing he has the apartment to himself after Felix leaves for a vacation in Acapulco, Oscar receives a visit from Felix's Grandpa Unger, who has just separated from his wife. Oscar feels as though Felix never left as Grandpa has all of the same idiosyncrasies and quirks. Tony Randall portrays his own grandfather in this episode, and Madge Kennedy portrays the grandmother, Mimi. The name Mimi was used frequently on *The Odd Couple*, possibly inspired by the lead female character in the opera *La Boheme*.

"Partner's Investment" (2:19) February 4, 1972

Writers: Bill Idelson and Harvey Miller; *Directors:* George Tyne and Bob Birnbaum; *Guest Stars:* Al Molinaro as Murray Greshler, Pat Morita as Mr. Yemana/Mr. Wing, H. W. Gim as Cho San, Dale Ishimoto as Man number one, Guy Lee as Man number two, and Hiroko Watanabe as Woman number one.

When Oscar discovers that Felix has been creating a little nest egg for him, he uses the money to bet on a horse named Redneck. When the horse wins, Oscar and Felix find more headaches than usual when they invest in a Japanese restaurant and get back a dim sum.

"Good, Bad Boy" (2:20) February 11, 1972

Writers: Dick Bensfield and Perry Grant; *Director:* Hal Cooper; *Guest Stars:* Jimmy Van Patten as Michael Robert Callahan, Jr., Johnny Silver as Chaplain Muldoon, Pamelyn Ferdin as Edna Unger, and Gerald Michenaud as Eddie.

Felix becomes extremely overprotective of Edna when a boy from a correctional institution takes a liking to her. This was Pamelyn Ferdin's swan song on the program. She moved on to *The Paul Lynde Show*, and Doney Oatman assumed the Edna role.

"A Night to Dismember" (2:21) February 18, 1972

Writer: Rick Mittleman; *Director:* George Marshall; *Guest Stars:* Brett Somers Klugman as Blanche Madison, Joan Van Ark as Trudy Wells the tennis champion, and Arch Johnson as Billy Jack.

Exactly what happened on the night Oscar and Blanche broke up is told from three perspectives: that of Oscar, Blanche, and Felix. This kind of episode, with multiple perspectives of the same event, is called a "Rashomon."

"Oscar's Promotion" (2:22) February 25, 1972

Writer: Martin Cohan; *Director:* Jack Donohue; *Guest Stars:* Jack Soo as Mr. Chuk Mai Chin, Peter Hobbs as Nathaniel Talbot, Bobby Baum as Buzzy Allen, and Virginia Ann Lee as Miss Hong Kong.

Oscar regrets his decision to hire his roommate as a photographer when Felix convinces the subject of Oscar's story, a red Chinese wrestling champion, to retire because of a bad shoulder. This was the first of four guest appearances on the program for Peter Hobbs.

"Psychic, Schmychic" (2:23) March 3, 1972

Writer: Ron Friedman; *Director:* Mel Ferber; *Guest Stars:* Al Molinaro as Murray Greshler, Bernie Kopell as Professor Faraday, Mal Alberts as the event host, Dee Gardner as the lab girl, and Herbie Faye as the man.

Oscar finds his life changing for the better when Felix, who has developed psychic powers while running a fever, begins to envision good things happening to his roommate, with one big exception.

"Gloria, Hallelujah" (3:1) September 15, 1972

Writer: Rick Mittleman; *Director:* Garry Marshall; *Guest Stars:* Elinor Donahue as Miriam Welby, Penny Marshall as Myrna Turner, Janis Hansen as Gloria Unger, and Harvey Skolnik as the maître d.'

Unredeemed ticket to a 1972 TV filming (courtesy Joel Tator).

At Myrna's insistence, Oscar joins a dating service and uses the pen name Andre La Plume. Trouble ensues when Felix discovers that the computer has matched Oscar with Felix's ex-wife, Gloria. This episode marks the first of 17 appearances by Elinor Donahue as Felix's girlfriend, "Upstairs Miriam" Welby (named Welby because she used to co-star with *Marcus Welby, M.D.*'s Robert Young on *Father Knows Best*). Oscar meets Miriam for the first time in this episode. Myrna Turner uses the alias Lena Molinaro in this episode—another inside joke. Speaking of inside jokes, Harvey Miller once again has a small role as the maître d' in this episode, under his real name, Harvey Skolnik.

"THE BIG MOUTH" (3:2) September 22, 1972

Writers: Ben Joelson and Art Baer; *Director:* Jerry Paris; *Guest Stars:* Penny Marshall as Myrna Turner, Howard Cosell as himself, Susan Moffat as Phyllis, Michael Morgan as Charley DiMazzo, Ray Ballard as Mr. Crane, and Shawn Michaels as the reporter.

Guest star Howard Cosell finds himself locking horns with both Oscar and Felix: first in an argument with Oscar; then with Felix when he makes sport of Cosell's nasal twang and attempts to correct it. Cosell returned to guest star in another episode, "Your Mother Wears Army Boots," in 1975. The New York Giants play the Philadelphia Eagles and later the Giants play the Dallas Cowboys on *Monday Night Football* in this episode.

"THE PRINCESS" (3:3) September 29, 1972

Writer: Bill Idelson; *Director:* Jerry Paris; *Guest Stars:* Jean Simmons as Princess Lydia of Lichtenberg, Peggy Rea as Miss Rykof, Billy Sands as the tailor, and James Millhollin as the barber.

Felix becomes a teacher of sorts when he and Oscar are invited to a dinner party for Princess Lydia of Lichtenstein and Felix must transform Oscar from a slob to a man of distinction, à la *Pygmalion*. Peggy Rae, who portrays Miss Rykof, was utilized again in Mark Rothman and Lowell Ganz's *Busting Loose*, in an episode titled "A Nut at the Opera."

"THE PEN IS MIGHTIER THAN THE PENCIL" (3:4) October 6, 1972

Writer: Jack Winter; *Director:* Bob Birnbaum; *Guest Stars:* Elinor Donahue as Miriam Welby, Wally Cox as Mr. Fegivny, Elliot Reid as instructor Gerard Ferguson,

Tracy Reed as Mrs. Flood, and Phil Leeds as Mr. Katleman.

Felix decides to take a creative writing course. His instructor provides an overabundance of encouragement, but it is painfully obvious that Felix lacks talent. Oscar suspects fraud and attempts to get Felix's money back. This episode reunited Tony Randall and Wally Cox who, two decades earlier, had worked together on the live NBC sitcom, *Mister Peepers*.

"THE ODD MONKS" (3:5)
October 13, 1972

Writer: Garry Marshall; *Director:* Jerry Belson; *Guest Stars:* Penny Marshall as Myrna, Richard Stahl as Brother Ralph Decker, Jack Collins as Brother Samuel, Robert Ball as Brother Lou, Ed Peck as Brother Horace, and Charles Lampkin as Brother Lowell.

Oscar and Felix seek a more serene life and, upon the advice of a monk, join his monastery. The hardest part for them, however, is keeping the vow of silence. This is one of Garry Marshall's favorite episodes; he wrote it to give the cast a break from learning numerous pages of dialogue.

"I'M DYING OF UNGER" (3:6)
October 20, 1972

Writer: Joe Glauberg; *Director:* Mel Ferber; *Guest Star:* Al Molinaro as Murray Greshler.

Felix's efforts to help Oscar overcome writer's block turn disastrous when he takes him to a remote cabin that is not only free of distractions but so remote that foraging for food becomes a problem. This episode contains a reference to a very popular Chiffon Margarine commercial with the catch phrase, "It's not nice to fool Mother Nature."

"THE ODD COUPLES" (3:7)
October 27, 1972

Writer: Harvey Miller; *Director:* Hal Cooper; *Guest Stars:* Al Molinaro as Murray Greshler, Janis Hansen as Gloria Unger, Brett Somers Klugman as Blanche Madison, and Jane Dulo as Mrs. Madison.

When Oscar and Blanche divorced, Oscar feared telling his mother. Now that she is coming for a visit, Oscar concocts a charade to convince his mom that he and Blanche (as well as Felix and Gloria) are still married. Prolific character actress Jane Dulo portrays Oscar's mother in this episode; she later played Murray's wife, Mimi, in the episode "The Murray Who Came to Dinner."

"FELIX'S FIRST COMMERCIAL" (3:8) November 3, 1972

Writer: Albert E. Lewin; *Director:* Jerry Paris; *Guest Stars:* Deacon Jones as himself, Herbie Faye as Mr. Faffner, Louise Troy as the agency woman, Arthur Batanides as the bartender, and Bob W. Hoffman as the assistant.

Oscar attempts to help Felix film a shaving commercial starring NFL defenseman Deacon Jones by convincing the shy and moody Jones that he has nothing to fear. This episode marks the first of three guest appearances for actor Arthur Batanides.

"THE FIRST BABY" (3:9)
November 10, 1972

Writers: Garry Marshall and Bob Brunner; *Director:* Alex March: *Guest Stars:* Al

Molinaro as Murray Greshler, Penny Marshall as Myrna Turner, Janis Hansen as Gloria Unger, Ric Carrott as Steve O'Connor, Tracy Rydell as Pat, Jim Boles as the minister, Paul Gale as Dr. Arnold, and Kathalynn Turner as the nurse.

A flashback sequence is used to recall the circumstances surrounding Edna's birth and why Felix was asked to remove himself from Mid-City Memorial Hospital. That request came from Mid-City Memorial. Penny Marshall is seen in a leg cast in this episode, but even though she did enjoy skiing at that time in her life, the leg cast and the crutches were only for comic effect.

"OSCAR'S BIRTHDAY"(3:10) November 17, 1972

Writers: Albert E. Lewin and Bob Brunner; *Director:* George Marshall; *Guest Stars:* Elinor Donahue as Miriam Welby, Al Molinaro as Murray Greshler, Penny Marshall as Myrna Turner, Andy Rubin as Monroe Hernandez, Mickey Fox as Judy Skelton, Hal Smith as Arthur O'Reilly, and Marjorie Ward as Irene Langley.

Oscar's surprise birthday party is *really* a surprise: Felix and Miriam have arranged a *This Is Your Life* theme, wherein friends pay homage to the guest of honor. This episode marks the first of two guest appearances by Andy Rubin as Monroe Hernandez, the superintendent's Puerto Rican son; actress Mickey Fox makes her first of four guest appearances. Marjorie Marshall, who plays tap-dancing Irene Langley, is Garry and Penny Marshall's mother, and Tony Marshall's wife. Judy Skelton, a character in this episode, is named after a longtime secretary for the program's writing staff.

"PASSWORD"(3:11) December 1, 1972

Writer: Frank Buxton; *Director:* Alex March; *Guest Stars:* Elinor Donahue as Miriam Welby, Penny Marshall as Myrna Turner, Allen Ludden as himself, Betty White as herself, Ronda Copland as Mitzy Ferguson, and Francine Greshler as Millicent.

Oscar and Felix appear as partners on the then-popular game show *Password*. The real comedy stems from Felix's off-the-wall clues, which cause them to lose. This immensely popular episode was also the favorite of Jack Klugman. It was written by former game show host Frank Buxton of ABC's short-lived game show *Get the Message*. Actress Francine Greshler is the daughter of Abner "Abbey" Greshler, the agent for both Tony Randall and Jack Klugman. Greshler had been incorporated into the show as Murray's last name.

"THE ODD FATHER"(3:12) December 8, 1972

Writers: Steve Zacharias and Michael Leeson; *Director:* Jack Donohue; *Guest Stars:* Al Molinaro as Murray Greshler, Doney Oatman as Edna Unger, Frank Delfino as Mr. Albertson, Sadie Delfino as Mrs. Albertson, and Stephen Liss as Wilfred Albertson.

Felix tries to win Edna's affections when he sees her bonding more with Oscar. Pamelyn Ferdin, the show's original Edna Unger, had moved on to ABC's *The Paul Lynde Show,* so beginning with this episode Doney Oatman assumed the role. The diminutive Mr. and Mrs. Albertson are portrayed by Frank and Sadie Delfino, who were married in real life. The episode's title is a mild pun on Mario Puzo's *The Godfather*, the film adaptation of which was then playing in theaters.

"DON'T BELIEVE IN ROOMERS" (3:13) December 22, 1972

Writers: Peggy Elliott and Ed Scharlach; *Director:* Jack Donohue; *Guest Stars:* Marlyn Mason as Lisa, and Joy Harmon as the waitress.

Both Oscar and Felix experience infatuation with a pretty homeless girl (Lisa) who mysteriously enters and disappears from their lives. Marlyn Mason portrayed a similar character on a similar episode of *Hey, Landlord*, "Same Time, Same Station, Same Girl."

"SOMETIMES A GREAT OCEAN" (3:14) January 5, 1973

Writer: Dennis Klein; *Director:* Hal Cooper; *Guest Stars:* Al Molinaro as Murray Greshler, Bill Quinn as Dr. Melnitz, Andy Rubin as Monroe Hernandez, Karl Swenson as Captain Potter, John Qualen as Mr. Larson, Queenie Smith as Mrs. Grapney, and Russell Thorson as Mr. Coswell.

Felix's efforts to get Oscar to relax and heal his ulcer backfire when he books passage on a cruise ship—for the elderly. Actor Bill Quinn (Dr. Melnitz) also portrayed a doctor (Mary's father) on *The Mary Tyler Moore Show*. The episode's title was inspired by Ken Kesey's mammoth novel *Sometimes a Great Notion*.

"I GOTTA BE ME" (3:15) January 12, 1973

Writers: David W. Duclon and Joe Glauberg; *Director:* Mel Ferber; *Guest Stars:* Elinor Donahue as Miriam Welby, Al Molinaro as Murray Greshler, Penny Marshall as Myrna Turner, Norman Shelly as Dr. Able, Barbara Rhoades as Marie, and Cliff Emmich as Harold.

A therapist's suggestion that Felix and Oscar try role reversal goes awry when they do become one another yet still continually bicker. The episode's title is borrowed from a popular song from the 1968 Broadway show *The Golden Rainbow*.

"THE IDES OF APRIL" (3:16) January 19, 1973

Writers: Mark Rothman and Lowell Ganz; *Director:* Bob Birnbaum; *Guest Stars:* Al Molinaro as Murray Greshler, Bill Quinn as Dr. Melnitz, Vivian Bonnell as Ms. Lee J. Ferret, Joshua Shelley as the accountant, Louis Guss as the man in waiting, and Ogden Talbot as the postman.

Oscar prepares for a tax audit thanks to Felix's slip of the tongue to the IRS that his sloppy roommate keeps haphazard files. This episode was inspired by an episode of *The Honeymooners* titled "The Worry Wart," and marks the first of five guest appearances by actor Louis Guss. It was later reworked as the debut episode for the 1982 series *The New Odd Couple*. The title, of course, is a turn on "The Ides of March," the date on which Julius Caesar was assassinated in 44 BC.

"MYRNA'S DEBUT" (3:17) February 2, 1973

Writers: Dick Bensfield and Perry Grant; *Director:* Jerry Paris; *Guest Stars:* Al Molinaro as Murray Greshler, Penny Marshall as Myrna Turner, Bob Hastings as Happy Greshler, Ralph Manza as Tony Magucci, Bella Bruck as Aunt Lucille, Arthur Batanides as Nino Babaloni, Inga Neilsen as Miss Jensen, and Bob Hoffman as the TV floor director.

Felix attempts to help Myrna pursue her dream of becoming a tap dancer by convincing Oscar to let her appear on his TV show, The *Sports Den*. In real life, Penny Marshall studied tap for many years. This was comic actress Bella Bruck's first of four very funny guest appearances.

"THE HUSTLER" (3:18) February 9, 1973

Writers: Mark Rothman and Lowell Ganz; *Director:* Jerry Paris; *Guest Stars:* Stanley Adams as Sure Shot Wilson, John Wheeler as Henry, Louis Guss as Arnold, and Sidney Clute as Barney.

Oscar, the authority on gambling, creates a Casino Night to help raise funds for Felix's Lexington Avenue Opera Club production of *Madame Butterfly*. This is one of the scripts which was revamped for *The New Odd Couple*. Stanley Adams, who portrayed "Sure-Shot" Wilson, the portly, heavy-smoking pool shark with the hacking cough died only a few years later. He also guest starred in "The Big Broadcast." The episode's title, "The Hustler," was borrowed from a classic 1961 film starring Paul Newman and Jackie Gleason.

"MY STRIFE IN COURT" (3:19) February 16, 1973

Writers: Mark Rothman and Lowell Ganz; *Director:* Jerry Paris; *Guest Stars:* Elinor Donahue as Miriam Welby, Al Molinaro as Murray Greshler, Jill Jaress as Beth Olam, Curt Conway as the judge, Mel Bishop as the bailiff, Frank Loverde as the policeman, Joseph Alfasa as the reporter, and Edmund Towers as the prosecutor.

Felix, falsely accused of ticket scalping for the Broadway musical *Kiss My Face,* has his day in court and utters one of the show's most famous lines, "When you assume, you make an ass of you and me." Jill Jaress's character in this episode, Beth Olam, was the name of a Jewish cemetery next to the Paramount lot. Jaress also guest starred in *The New Odd Couple* in an episode titled "The Hustler." Tony Randall did not like the name of the musical, *Kiss My Face,* and wanted it changed to *Rainy Days.* Tony's title was considered. In fact, on the poster outside the theater, if you look carefully you'll see a "cloud design" along with the words *Kiss My Face* emblazoned across it. On that same poster are the words "Denny Peeples Presents." Denny Peeples was one of *The Odd Couple*'s art directors. The name Andee Nealis on that same poster refers to the program's set decorator, Anthony D. Nealis.

"LET'S MAKE A DEAL" (3:20) February 23, 1973

Writers: Joe Glauberg and David W. Duclon; *Director:* Frank Buxton; *Guest Stars:* Elinor Donahue as Miriam, Al Molinaro as Murray Greshler, Monty Hall as himself, Garry Walberg as Speed, and Tom Scott as the producer.

In a harebrained scheme to win a brand new bed on the TV game show *Let's Make a Deal,* Felix and Oscar appear in a horse costume—a ruse to avoid detection as the show's host, Monty Hall, is Oscar's old college buddy (friends and family members are prohibited from being contestants). Former game show host Frank Buxton

The Full Monty (courtesy Monty Hall).

of *Get the Message* directed this episode. Monty Hall also guest stars in "A Different Drummer."

"The Odyssey Couple"
(3:21) March 2, 1973

Writers: Dennis Klein and Bob Brunner; *Director:* Jerry Paris; *Guest Stars:* Al Molinaro as Murray Greshler, Elvia Allman as Mrs. Elizabeth Madison, Titos Vandis as Aroestes Damaskopolous, Bobbi Jordan as Doris Atkins, Lynne Miller as Helen, and John Davey as Andreas.

To appease his mother, who feels he needs to find a nice girl and settle down, Oscar pretends to have one. Complications arise when he needs that girl to materialize for a dinner party date and Felix sets him up with Helen, a Greek girl who is looking for a husband.

"Take My Furniture, Please" (3:22) March 9, 1973

Writer: Harvey Miller; *Director:* Jack Winter; *Guest Stars:* Elinor Donahue as Miriam Welby, Al Molinaro as Murray Greshler, Penny Marshall as Myrna Turner, Bubba Smith as himself, Charles Lane as Sid, Bella Bruck as Woman number one, and Jessica Myerson as Woman number two.

Oscar's dilemma: how to live in a newly redecorated apartment that only Felix can love. NFL star Bubba Smith of the Baltimore Colts makes a cameo appearance in this episode and, completely out of character, discusses decorating with Felix. The title of the episode is a play on Henny Youngman's famous one-liner, "Take my wife, please."

"The Murray Who Came to Dinner" (3:23) March 23, 1973

Writer: Ron Friedman; *Director:* Jerry Paris; *Guest Stars:* Al Molinaro as Murray Greshler, Barbara A. Daitch as Lulu La Verne, Patty Regan as Chi Chi Caballero, and Jane Dulo as Mimi Greshler.

Oscar and Felix attempt to get the bickering Murray and his wife, Mimi, back together again. The theme from *Love Story* plays in the background during one scene. The title is a switch on *The Man Who Came to Dinner,* a famous play by George S. Kaufman and Moss Hart.

"Gloria Moves In" (4:1) September 14, 1973

Writers: Mark Rothman and Lowell Ganz; *Director:* Garry Marshall; *Guest Stars:* Larry Gelman as Vinnie, Al Molinaro as Murray Greshler, Garry Walberg as Speed, Janis Hansen as Gloria Unger, Archie Hahn as Roger, and Ogden Talbot as the bellboy.

Felix attempts to reconcile with Gloria, while Oscar contemplates a big poker game (two events which greatly conflict). William Woodson's narration during the opening credits is no longer used. The program was now seen an hour earlier on Friday nights, at 8:30 p.m.

"Last Tango in Newark" (4:2) September 21, 1973

Writer: Ron Friedman; *Director:* Jay Sandrich; *Guest Stars:* Elinor Donahue as Miriam Welby, Edward Villella as himself, Lark Geib, Jennifer Cheng, Denise Derns, Mary Jane Evans, Mimi Kirk, Anne Maier and Carolyn Weller are the dancers of the New York City Ballet Company.

Although Felix has been cast as the huntsman in Edward Villella's Ballet Appreciation Children's Class production of *Swan Lake,* he assumes the leading role when Villella fails to show up on time for the production. Dancer Dan Dailey, who directed an episode of the series, is mentioned in this episode. Writer Ron Friedman wanted to call the episode "Swine Lake," but it was retitled as a jokey reference to *Last Tango in Paris,* the most controversial film of the early 1970s.

"The Odd Decathlon" (4:3) September 28, 1973

Writer: Jack Winter; *Director:* Jay Sandrich; *Guest Stars:* Al Molinaro as Murray Greshler, Cliff Norton as Lloyd.

When Felix discovers that slovenly Oscar's insurance premium is less than his, he challenges him to a series of athletic events to prove he's in better physical condition.

"That Was No Lady" (4:4) October 5, 1973

Writer: Lee Kalcheim; *Directors:* Jerry Belson and Garry Marshall; *Guest Stars:* Penny Marshall as Myrna Turner, Alex Karras as Jake Metcalfe, and Patricia Harty as Melanie Metcalfe.

Felix invites a woman (Melanie Metcalf) to the opera, unaware that she is married to Jake Metcalfe—a football player with extremely violent tendencies. Alex Karras, who portrays the football pro, is also mentioned in the season five episode "Your Mother Wears Army Boots." This script was reworked for *The New Odd Couple*. The title is the punch line of an old joke: "Who was that lady I saw you with last night?" "That was no lady—that was my wife."

"THE ODD HOLIDAY" (4:5) October 12, 1973

Writer: Philip Mishkin; *Director:* Mel Ferber; *Guest Stars:* Al Molinaro as Murray Greshler, Brett Somers Klugman as Blanche Madison, Janis Hansen as Gloria Unger, and Victor Brandt as Ramon.

Murray is told, via flashback, about the time Felix, Gloria, Oscar, and Blanche all vacationed in San Dominguez. All four had to stay in the same hut, and Felix and Gloria's marriage came to an end. The outtakes from this episode (featuring the two couples in one bed) are alleged to be hilarious.

"THE NEW CAR" (4:6) October 19, 1973

Writers: Mark Rothman, Lowell Ganz and Michael Elias; *Director:* Garry Marshall; *Guest Stars:* Al Molinaro as Murray Greshler, Penny Marshall as Myrna Turner, Dick Clark as himself, John Byner as Bert the parking attendant, and Bella Bruck as Pushover Page Livingston.

A random contest on Dick Clark's radio show, featuring questions about opera, garners Felix and Oscar a new car. They decide to share ownership, but then encounter the problem of where to park it in Manhattan. John Byner makes his first of two guest appearances on the program. This is another of Garry Marshall's favorite episodes—he likes the intermingling of the multi-camera performances with the numerous single-camera exterior New York City scenes. It was an experimental episode that worked well.

"THIS IS THE ARMY, MRS. MADISON" (4:7) October 26, 1973

Writers: Garry Marshall and Bob Brunner; *Director:* Mel Ferber; *Guest Stars:* Al Molinaro as Murray Greshler, Penny Marshall as Myrna Turner, Brett Somers Klugman as Blanche Madison, Richard Stahl as the justice of the peace, Liam Dunn as Captain Wyatt, Britt Leach as Hobart, Lori Marshall as Crystal, and Eddie Garrett as Soldier number two.

This flashback episode recalls Oscar and Blanche's wedding, while Oscar was a private and Felix was a lieutenant. It's in this episode that Oscar first meets Felix's friend, Murray the cop. Actor Eddie Garrett made his first of seven guest appearances on the show; he followed Jack Klugman over to *Quincy M. E.*, on which he portrayed Eddie, the crime photographer. Garry Marshall's daughter, Lori, is Crystal, the inept young piano player at the wedding ceremony. The title is a switch on a well-known song from the World War II era, "This Is the Army, Mr. Jones."

"THE SONGWRITER" (4:8) November 2, 1973

Writers: Buz Kohan and Bill Angelos; *Director:* Mel Ferber; *Guest Stars:* Elinor Donahue as Miriam Welby, Jaye P. Morgan as herself, and Wolfman Jack as himself.

Felix attempts to write a song for Jaye P. Morgan. What results is "Happy, and Peppy and Bursting with Love," a pop tune that Jaye performs as a ballad (much to Felix's dismay). Radio legend Wolfman Jack makes a cameo appearance in this episode. At one time, comedienne Carol Leifer included the song "Happy and Peppy and Bursting with Love" in her stand-up act.

"FELIX DIRECTS" (4:9) November 9, 1973

Writer: Harvey Miller; *Director:* Jerry Paris; *Guest Stars:* Al Molinaro as Murray Greshler, Penny Marshall as Myrna Turner, David White as Phil, Louis Guss as Ed, Doris Cook as Christine, and Edward Faulkner as Harry.

Oscar's predicament: how to avoid Felix, who is filming a cinéma vérité documentary about him called *Mondo Filth*.

"THE PIG WHO CAME TO DINNER" (4:10) November 16, 1973

Writer: Mickey Rose; *Director:* Jack Donohue; *Guest Stars:* Elinor Donahue as Miriam Welby, Bobby Riggs as himself, Billie Jean King as herself, and Sandra Giles as both Roberta Riggs and Jacqueline Kramer.

Tennis pro Bobby Riggs is the male chauvinist pig who came to dinner. When Oscar loses every bet made with Riggs, Felix talks Riggs into giving Oscar a chance to win it all back in a Ping-Pong game. Billie Jean King makes a cameo appearance in this episode. In recent years, new evidence has surfaced which leads many to believe that Riggs threw the famous "Battle of the Sexes" tennis match in an attempt to pay off a number of huge gambling debts.

"MAID FOR EACH OTHER" (4:11) November 23, 1973

Writer: Marlene Barr; *Director:* Norm Gray; *Guest Stars:* Al Molinaro as Murray Greshler, Reta Shaw as Claire Frost, Janet Brandt as Mrs. Miller, Curt Conway as Dr. Gordon, Buddy Lewis as crony number one, Arlene Sinclair as the nurse, and Momo Yashimas as Mrs. Hanogi.

After a doctor recommends that Oscar eat only bland foods to control his ulcer, Felix seeks a nanny who will see that he does. His choice: Claire Frost—a female version of himself. Reta Shaw also played a housekeeper/nanny on the TV version of *The Ghost and Mrs. Muir* and in the 1964 motion picture, *Mary Poppins*. There is even a *Mary Poppins* reference in the dialogue. This was Marlene Barr's only writing credit. Actress Janet Brandt, who portrayed Mrs. Miller in this episode, was initially so impressive at rehearsals, she was given more lines. However, she took this approval as a license to steal every scene, and her role was then greatly pared back before the filming.

"THE EXORCISTS" (4:12) December 7, 1973

Writers: Frank Buxton and Michael Leeson; *Director:* Jack Donohue; *Guest Stars:* Elinor Donahue as Miriam Welby, Al Molinaro as Murray Greshler, Penny Marshall as Myrna Turner, Victor Buono as Dr. Clove, and Herbie Faye as Mr. Seltzer the fix-it man.

After hearing many strange things

that go bump in the night, Felix comes to the conclusion that the apartment is haunted. To bust said ghosts, Felix hires a shady exorcist named Dr. Clove. Actor Victor Buono later guest starred in "The Rent Strike," in season five. William Peter Blatty's novel *The Exorcist* (and William Friedkin's film thereof) created a sensation the year this episode was originally broadcast.

"A Barnacle Adventure" (4:13) December 21, 1973

Writers: Mark Rothman and Lowell Ganz; *Director:* Bob Birnbaum; *Guest Stars:* Al Molinaro as Murray Greshler, Penny Marshall as Myrna Turner, Janis Hansen as Gloria Unger, Malcolm Atterbury as Pop Abernathy, Val Avery as Dr. Elmo Most, John Mhyers as director number one, Wally Taylor as the repairman, and Erin O'Reilly as the nurse.

Oscar, Felix, and Miriam invest money in a new super glue made from barnacles, only to find out the hard way that the product, Elmo's Glue, is only effective when wet.

"The Moonlighter" (4:14) January 4, 1974

Writers: Phil Mishkin and Mickey Rose; *Director:* Frank Buxton; *Guest Stars:* Penny Marshall as Myrna Turner, Karl Lukas as Olaf, Phyllis Elizabeth Davis as Eve, Phil Leeds as the man, Bella Bruck as the woman, Mel Bishop as the hardhat, Clarence Landry as the truck driver, Sam Nudell as the foreman, Jocelyn Peters as Rusty, and Jannis Durkin as dog girl.

Oscar moonlights as a short-order cook to earn back the money he lost betting on a horse (the money belonged to Felix).

"Cleanliness Is Next to Impossible" (4:15) January 11, 1974

Writers: Mark Rothman and Lowell Ganz; *Director:* Frank Buxton; *Guest Stars:* Penny Marshall as Myrna Turner, Richard Stahl as Dr. Bates, Alan Arbus as Ernie the hypnotist, Janice Lynde as Phyllis, Adam Klugman as Little Oscar, and Shirley Mitchell as Alice the receptionist.

Oscar attempts to change his untidy ways by undergoing hypnosis when he meets a girl (Phyllis) who likes him—but not his sloppiness. Jack Klugman's real-life son, Adam, appears in this episode as "Little Oscar." The title is a clever switch on the axiom "Cleanliness is next to godliness."

"The Flying Felix" (4:16) January 18, 1974

Writers: Mark Rothman and Lowell Ganz; *Director:* Jack Donohue; *Guest Stars:* Al Molinaro as Murray Greshler, Penny Marshall as Myrna Turner, Teri Garr as the flight insurance saleswoman, George Furth as Mr. Belkin, Maggie Peterson as the stewardess, Ed Peck as Bill, Caryn Matchinga as Myrna's friend, Sondra Currie as the girl on the plane, Lee Duncan as the airline employee, Grady Sutton as Pop, and Mickey Fox as the passenger.

Felix's fear of flying is put to the test when he convinces Oscar to accompany him to a photo shoot in Houston and the charter flight they book doesn't actually land in Houston—it is for parachute enthusiasts only. Maggie Peterson, who portrays the stewardess in this episode, also played Ann in "The Bigger They Are." This was Tony Randall's favorite episode, and among head writers Mark Rothman and Lowell Ganz's favorite episodes.

"Vocal Girl Makes Good" (4:17) January 25, 1974

Writers: Buz Kohan and Bill Angelos; *Director:* Dan Dailey; *Guest Stars:* Penny Marshall as Myrna Turner, Marilyn Horne as Jackie Hartman, Janice Lynde as Phyllis, and John Wheeler as Mr. Felscher.

Oscar's co-worker, Jackie, has a lovely voice and Felix envisions her starring in his Opera Club's production of *Carmen*. The problem is, she is shy, and will only sing to the man she loves—Oscar. Opera star Marilyn Horne appears in this episode as Jackie Hartman. Oddly enough, a few years later the director of this episode, Dan Dailey, broke a hip while performing in a stage production of *The Odd Couple*.

"Shuffling off to Buffalo" (4:18) February 8, 1974

Writers: Mark Rothman and Lowell Ganz; *Director:* Frank Buxton; *Guest Stars:* William Redfield as Floyd Unger, Jack Collins as Albert, Beatrice Colen as Ivy the secretary, and Alice James as Mildred Unger.

Felix's little brother, Floyd, visits with a distinct purpose in mind: to get Felix to leave the rat race of Manhattan to become a company manager for his bubble gum company in Buffalo, New York. The title is a takeoff on "Shuffle Off to Buffalo," one of Harry Warren and Al Dubin's songs from the 1933 movie musical *42nd Street*.

"A Different Drummer" (4:19) February 22, 1974

Writers: Frank Buxton and Michael Leeson; *Director:* Mel Ferber; *Guest Stars:* Al Molinaro as Murray Greshler, Monty Hall as himself, Alan Copeland as Alan, Vern Rowe as Vern, Sid Gould as the comedian, Garry Marshall as the drummer, Morty Corb as the bass fiddler, Eddie Garrett as Oscar's co-worker, and Frances Gae as Mrs. Abernathy.

Felix seeks a way to convince Oscar to join his band so they can appear on a TV show hosted by Monty Hall. This is the second of two guest shots by game show host Monty Hall, appearing as himself. Garry Marshall gets to show off his percussion prowess in this episode.

"The Insomniacs" (4:20) March 1, 1974

Writer: Mickey Rose; *Director:* Jack Donohue; *Guest Stars:* Al Molinaro as Murray Greshler, Penny Marshall as Myrna Turner, Don Gazzaniga as Barney, and Frank Buxton as the TV announcer.

Felix's bouts of insomnia cause Oscar to take drastic measures so they can both get some much-needed sleep.

"New York's Oddest" (4:21) March 8, 1974

Writers: Ben Joelson and Art Baer; *Director:* Harvey Miller; *Guest Stars:* Elinor Donahue as Miriam Welby, Al Molinaro as Murray Greshler, Billy Sands as Mort Bennick, Lassie Ahern as Mrs. Bennick, Michael Lerner as Sergeant Chomsky, James Millhollin as the hiccup man, George Jordan as the narc, and Sam Nudell as the neighbor.

Felix and Miriam join the "civilian reserves" as an extra eye for the police. Felix goes overboard, and while guarding the eleventh floor of his apartment building cries wolf one too many times. The title is a switch on "New York's Finest," otherwise known as the NYPD.

"ONE FOR THE
    BUNNY" (4:22)
    March 22, 1974
Writer: John Rappaport; *Director:* Jerry Paris; *Guest Stars:* Penny Marshall as Myrna Turner, Janis Hansen as Gloria Unger, Hugh Hefner as himself, Lloyd Kino as Al Fisher, Curt Conway as the judge, Arthur Batanides as the plaintiff lawyer, Al Fisher as the art director, and Peggy Doyle as the woman juror.

Unredeemed ticket to a 1974 TV filming (courtesy Joel Tator).

This is a flashback episode that recounts what happened when Felix was a photographer for *Playboy* magazine—and Gloria turned out to be one of the nude models. Hugh Hefner makes a cameo appearance in the episode. Janis Hansen, the actress who portrayed Gloria was at one time a Playboy bunny in real life. The woman juror played by Peggy Doyle in Salvation Army attire was originally intended to be a nun, but censor Elaine Newman put the kibosh on that.

"THE RAIN IN SPAIN FALLS
    MAINLY IN VAIN" (5:1) September 12, 1974
Writer: Rick Mittleman; *Director:* Harvey Miller; *Guest Stars:* Penny Marshall as Myrna Turner, Rob Reiner as Sheldn Stimler, Bo Kaprall as the guy at the bar, Garo Yepremian as Zeeno Coricidin, Garry Marshall as Werner Turner, Ronny Hallin as Verna Turner, and Kapi Lindos as the belly dancer.

Myrna is distraught over her breakup with Sheldn (they forgot the "o" on his birth certificate). Sheldn eventually realizes the error of his ways and returns to marry Myrna. Sheldn is portrayed by Rob Reiner, Penny's real-life husband. Penny Marshall left the program after this episode to join the cast of *Paul Sand in Friends and Lovers*. Penny's real-life brother and sister, Garry Marshall and Ronny Hallin, have uncredited cameo roles in this episode as Myrna's siblings, Werner and Verna. Hallin was later the assistant to the producer on *Laverne and Shirley* and *Happy Days*. Kapi Lindos, the belly dancer, also guest starred as a gypsy in "The Odd Candidate." The closing credits for the season five episodes were shown on a plain blue background—gone were the scenes filmed on the streets of New York City. Here, in the final season, the program moved to Thursday nights at 8:00 p.m. The title is a switch on a lyric from Lerner and Loewe's *My Fair Lady*: "The rain in Spain stays mainly in the plain."

"TO BOWL, OR NOT TO BOWL"
    (5:2) September 19, 1974
Writer: Mickey Rose; *Director:* Jay Sandrich; *Guest Stars:* Al Molinaro as Murray Greshler, Larry Gelman as Vinnie, Leo-

nard Barr as Arnold the healer, Noam Pitlik as O'Herlihy, Bo Kaprall as Frank Klemble, and Beatrice Colen as the bride.

Oscar tries to convince Felix to rejoin his bowling team after he impulsively quits by showing Felix what a world without competition would be like. Beatrice Colen later became the waitress at Arnold's Drive-In in another Garry Marshall show, *Happy Days*. This episode contains a scene in which Oscar sprays room freshener into Felix's dinner—inspired by a similar scene in the 1968 motion picture. The title, of course, is a nod to Hamlet's soliloquy.

"THE FROG" (5:3) September 26, 1974

Writers: Dick Bensfield and Perry Grant; *Director:* Mel Ferber; *Guest Stars:* Al Molinaro as Murray Greshler, Leif Garrett as Leonard Unger, and Richard Stahl as the pet shop owner.

Felix's son, Leonard, is entering his pet frog in a jumping contest. When the amphibian escapes from his box, Felix and Oscar attempt to find a replacement without Leonard's knowledge.

"THE HOLLYWOOD STORY" (5:4) October 3, 1974

Writers: Al Gordon and Hal Goldman; *Director:* Mel Ferber; *Guest Stars:* Al Molinaro as Murray Greshler, Bob Hope as himself, Allan Arbus as the director, Leonard Barr as the stickman, George Montgomery as Griff, Alan Dexter as J. B Hofstetter, Alice James as the script girl, and Mickey Fox as Hannah.

Oscar has a cameo role in a movie to be filmed in Hollywood. Crazy Rhoda Zimmerman is supposed to go with him, but cancels at the last minute. Oscar then decides to ask star-struck Felix to tag along—a decision he will come to rue.

"THE DOG STORY" (5:5) October 10, 1974

Writers: Ben Joelson and Art Baer; *Director:* Frank Buxton; *Guest Stars:* Al Molinaro as Murray Greshler, Rona Barrett as herself, John Fiedler as Mr. Hugo, Cliff Norton as Barry Fishkin, Bill Idelson as the judge, Marguerite Ray as the forelady, Jennifer King as the receptionist, George Jordan as the prosecutor, and Buddy Lewis as the bailiff.

Felix, upset about the treatment of Silver, the Wonder Dog during a photo shoot, steals the dog and brings him to the apartment. He is soon arrested and has his day in court. Tony Randall loved doing scenes where he defended himself in court, and he got to do it yet again on this episode. Fittingly, in his next sitcom, *The Tony Randall Show* (1976–1978), he played a judge. Bill Idelson, who wrote six scripts for *The Odd Couple*, portrayed the judge, and Rona Barrett makes a cameo appearance.

"STRIKE UP THE BAND, OR ELSE" (5:6) October 17, 1974

Writer: Rick Mittleman; *Director:* Jay Sandrich; *Guest Stars:* Al Molinaro as Murray Greshler, Pernell Roberts as Billy Joe, Alan Copeland as the piano player, Vern Rowe as the trumpet player, Jim Boles as Sam, and Dick Curtis as Dick.

When Oscar loses $500 in a poker game, he finds that he has only 24 hours to pay off his debt. He then antes his one negotiating chip—paying off the debt by having Felix's band perform at the debtee's charity hoedown. This episode featured Pernell Roberts in a rare comic role.

"THE ODD CANDIDATE" (5:7) October 24, 1974

Writers: Mark Rothman, and Lowell Ganz; *Director:* Garry Marshall; *Guest Stars:* Elinor Donahue as Miriam Welby, Al Molinaro as Murray Greshler, Howard K. Smith as himself, Guy Marks as Igor, Peter Hobbs as Simpson, Kapi Lindos as the gypsy, and Filip Field as the TV director.

City Councilman Simpson, the longtime incumbent, is running again, and planning to eliminate a local playground in favor of office buildings. While away in Chicago on business, Felix throws Oscar's hat into the ring as an opponent. ABC newscaster Howard K. Smith appears as himself. This was the first of four guest appearances on the show for actor Filip Field, who would follow Jack Klugman to *Quincy M. E.,* on which he played a lab technician. Kapi Lindos, the gypsy, also guest starred as the belly dancer in "The Rain in Spain Falls Mainly in Vain."

"THE SUBWAY SHOW" (5:8) October 31, 1974

Writers: Mark Rothman and Lowell Ganz; *Director:* Norm Gray; *Guest Stars:* Elinor Donahue as Miriam Welby, Al Molinaro as Murray Greshler, Garry Marshall as the surly subway rider, Billy Sands as the sandwich man, Barney Martin as the suited man, Scatman Crothers as the blind man, Fritzi Burr as the angry woman, and Heather Lowe as Miss Rapid Transit.

When Oscar writes a scathing column about New York City, Felix aims to prove him wrong. His chance to accomplish this feat arises when he and Oscar become trapped on a dark, motionless New York Subway car. Tony Randall wanted to be certain that New York wasn't painted in a bad light in this episode. Featured are Felix's hand puppet named Harvey Hanky, and Garry Marshall as the sarcastic subway rider. Garry stepped into the role when the actor who was supposed to perform it was stricken with appendicitis.

"THE PAUL WILLIAMS SHOW" (5:9) November 7, 1974

Writer: Rick Mittleman; *Director:* Harvey Miller; *Guest Stars:* Paul Williams as himself, Doney Oatman as Edna Unger, William O'Connell as the hotel clerk, and Eddie Garrett as the body guard.

Edna, feeling she is being treated like a baby by her father, runs away to follow singer/songwriter Paul Williams in an act of defiance. Originally, the episode was to be centered on John Denver, but when he canceled, Paul Williams was the next choice. Williams performs two of his own compositions, "You and Me Against the World" and "An Old-Fashioned Love Song." As in the episode, Paul Williams was a glider enthusiast, a hobby he shared with fellow songsmith Jimmy Webb.

"OUR FATHERS" (5:10) November 21, 1974

Writer: Martin Donovan; *Director:* Harvey Miller; *Guest Stars:* Adam Klugman as Little Oscar, Sean Manning as Little Felix, Barbara Rhoades as Lucy the dancer, Billy Sands as the federal agent, Georgio Tozzi as the big boss, Elisha Cook as Heel,

Louis Guss as Moe, and Jack R. Clinton as the policeman.

Felix's father, Morris Unger, was an optometrist. Oscar's father, Blinky Madison, was a maître d' and ran a speakeasy. This information comes to light when Felix uncovers a story about Oscar's dad trying to kill his dad in Chicago because he squealed about a bribe. Adam Klugman, Jack's real-life son, reprised his role as "Little Oscar" in this episode. "Little Felix" had previously been portrayed by Johnny Scott Lee, but Sean Manning was used in this episode. The elderly gentleman seen leaving the doctor's office is referred to as "Belson"—an inside joke.

"THE BIG BROADCAST" (5:11) November 28, 1974

Writer: Frank Buxton; *Director:* Frank Buxton; *Guest Stars:* Al Molinaro as Murray Greshler, Graham Jarvis as Jim Antrobus, Tina Andrews as Tina, Stanley Adams as Ed, Filip Field as the director, Eddie Garrett as the irate listener, and John Thomas Lenox as the organist.

Oscar receives a tryout for his own radio talk show, but just can't seem to find his niche. Felix urges Oscar to bring back a live old-time radio adventure show complete with sound effects, but there are only two union actors to play all the parts. The writer and director of the episode, Frank Buxton, wrote a series of books about the history of radio, including one titled *The Big Broadcast*.

"OSCAR IN LOVE" (5:12) December 12, 1974

Writer: Carl Gottlieb; *Director:* Mel Ferber; *Guest Stars:* Al Molinaro as Murray Greshler, Garry Walberg as Speed, Dina Merrill as Anita, Richard Stahl as the minister, Kirby Furlong as Mark, and Shelly Hines as Laurie.

Oscar and a harpist named Anita are in a serious relationship, one that may lead to marriage. She has two kids, and as childless Oscar has very little experience in that department, he finds winning the kids over to be problematic.

"THE BIGGER THEY ARE" (5:13) December 19, 1974

Writer: David W. Duclon; *Director:* Harvey Miller; *Guest Stars:* Al Molinaro as Murray Greshler, John Byner as Mr. Lyle Hooper, Cliff Emmich as Ben, Peter Hobbs as the emcee, Maggie Peterson as Ann, and Eddie Garrett as Doyle.

Felix is about to receive a prestigious Dink Award for producing the "Best TV Commercial," but he has pangs of guilt because the fraudulent ad featured "before" pictures of Oscar wearing a fat suit. Maggie Peterson, who portrays Ann in this episode, also guest stars as the stewardess in "The Flying Felix."

"TWO ON THE AISLE" (5:14) January 16, 1975

Writers: Mark Rothman and Lowell Ganz; *Director:* Jay Sandrich; *Guest Stars:* Penny Marshall as Myrna Turner, Neil Simon as himself, John Barbour as the host, Joan Crosby as the female critic, John Simon as himself, and Dan Sullivan as himself.

While the *New York Herald*'s theater critic is out sick, Oscar is ordered to cover his theater review column. Without attending the shows, he gleans the information from Felix through trickery. Neil Simon makes a cameo appearance as himself in this episode, after initially eschewing the TV series. Head writer Mark Rothman claims this as his favorite episode.

"Your Mother Wears Army Boots" (5:15) January 23, 1975

Writer: John Rappaport; *Director:* Frank Buxton; *Guest Stars:* Al Molinaro as Murray Greshler, Howard Cosell as himself, Roone Arledge as himself, Martina Arroyo as herself, Jack Carter as Joey Birney, Mickey Fox as the Opera Club member, Eddie Garrett as the coach, and Filip Field as the production manager.

Oscar Madison's name is being bandied about to fill in for Alex Karras on *Monday Night Football,* but Oscar is convinced that he won't get the job. That is, until Felix guarantees Howard Cosell that he will get to meet his favorite opera singer, Martina Arroyo. The New York Jets play the Cincinnati Bengals on the *Monday Night Football* game in this episode.

"Felix, the Horseplayer" (5:16) January 24, 1975

Writer: Jack Winter; *Director:* Jerry Paris; *Guest Stars:* Al Molinaro as Murray Greshler, Fritz Feld as the maître d', Johnny Maren as Harry Tallman, Johnny Silver as the man number one at OTB, Don Diamond as man number two at OTB, Robert E. Ball as the waiter, Elizabeth Thompson as the showgirl, Frank Loverde as the hanger-on, and Joshua Shelley as the race announcer.

Oscar owes a lot of people a lot of money, and finally finds a race informant whose tips get him back into the black. In fact, the winning streak is so impressive, even Felix gets hooked on horse racing. Some of the scenes were filmed at Belmont Racetrack and others at Aqueduct Racetrack.

"The Rent Strike" (5:17) January 31, 1975

Writer: Martin A. Ragaway; *Director:* Norm Gray; *Guest Stars:* Elinor Donahue as Miriam Welby, Victor Buono as Hugo Lovelace, Rodney Allen Rippy as himself, Ed Peck as Mr. Ralston, Herbie Faye as Elmer, Fritzi Burr as Mrs. Perkins, Georgia Schmidt as Mrs. Osgood, and Peter Hobbs as the lawyer.

The new landlord is kinder to his plants than to his tenants, and wants to raise everyone's rent without making necessary improvements. A determined Felix organizes a rent strike, with disastrous results. Child star Rodney Allen Rippy appears as himself. As of this episode, the program returned to Friday nights at 8:30 p.m.

"Two Men on a Hoarse" (5:18) February 7, 1975

Writer: Martin Donovan; *Director:* Charles Shyer; *Guest Stars:* Al Molinaro as Murray Greshler, Dick Cavett as himself, Phil Foster as Dr. Krakauer, Louis Guss as burglar number one, Joshua Shelley as burglar number two, Eddie Garrett as the stage manager, Filip Field as the patient, and Kathalynn Turner as the nurse.

Oscar needs a throat operation just as he is scheduled to appear on *The Dick Cavett Show.* Felix then comes down with sympathetic laryngitis. While both are *sans* voice, their apartment is robbed and their whispers for help go unheeded. Phil Foster, who portrays Dr. Krakauer in this episode, a short time later earned a much bigger role in another Garry Marshall show, *Laverne and Shirley*, as Laverne's dad (owner of "The Pizza Bowl").

The episode's title was inspired by the play and movie called *Three Men on a Horse*. In the years after Klugman's throat surgery, Jack and Tony performed *Three Men on a Horse* for Tony's National Actors Theatre revival.

"THE ROY CLARK SHOW" (5:19) February 14, 1975

Writers: Bob Howard and David W. Duclon; *Director:* Frank Buxton; *Guest Stars:* Al Molinaro as Murray Greshler, Roy Clark as Wild Willie Boggs, Albert Paulsen as Kalnikov, and John Wheeler as Mr. Felscher.

Felix is not a fan of Oscar's old army buddy, an obnoxious banjo-playing prankster named Wild Willie Boggs (Roy Clark). That is, until Felix discovers that Boggs is also a proficient classical musician.

"OLD FLAMES NEVER DIE" (5:20) February 21, 1975

Writers: Buz Kohan and Bill Angelos; *Director:* Frank Buxton; *Guest Stars:* Al Molinaro as Murray Greshler, Tom Pedi as Louie Meninni, Leonard Barr as Sonny, Tina Andrews as Oscar's secretary, John Harmon as Ira, Jean Gillespie as Mildred Fleener, Christina Hart as Suzi, Marjorie Marshall as Mamie Etkins, and Kit McDonough as Jeannie.

Felix's first love, Mildred Fleener, is in town for a class reunion. When Mildred informs Felix that she is now a grandmother, Felix realizes that he's getting older. To allay that feeling, Felix and Oscar attempt a second childhood. Garry and Penny Marshall's real-life mother, Marjorie Marshall, portrays Mamie and tap dances in this episode. Actor John Harmon, who portrays the elderly man (Ira) who looks so out of place at the youthful nightclub, almost backed out of performing in the episode. He was embarrassed by the psychedelic clothing and long wig he was to wear, but was talked into staying.

"LAUGH, CLOWN, LAUGH" (5:21) February 28, 1975

Writer: Fred Bernard (aka Frank Buxton); *Director:* Norm Gray; *Guest Stars:* Al Molinaro as Murray Greshler, Richard Dawson as himself, Mark Wilson as himself, Nani Darnell as the magician's assistant, David Warren Duclon as the bee handler, and Georgia Schmidt as the old lady.

Oscar has been selected to co-host a new talk show with Richard Dawson. What Oscar doesn't know is that Felix and Dawson used to do an act together while in the army stationed in England, and their split was not an amicable one. Dawson's game show, *Masquerade Party*, is mentioned in this episode, the title of which is borrowed from a 1928 Lon Chaney film.

"FELIX REMARRIES" (5:22) March 7, 1975 (repeated July 4, 1975)

Writers: Sidney Resnick and Larry Rhine; *Director:* Jack Donohue; *Guest Stars:* Al Molinaro as Murray Greshler, Janis Hansen as Gloria Unger, Bartlett Robinson as the minister, Leif Garrett as Leonard Unger, and Doney Oatman as Edna Unger.

After countless attempts, Felix is finally able to prove to his ex-wife, Gloria, that he is a changed man—a "new Felix." This time Gloria does indeed take him back, and no one is more relieved than the long-suffering Oscar Madison. This was the last first-run episode. Initially, ABC didn't want a final episode providing closure, but Garry Marshall and the crew talked them into it. Larry Rhine and Sidney Resnick wrote the episode with two different endings—one in which Felix *doesn't* remarry (in case the program was renewed for another season), and one in which he *does* (in the event that the program was canceled). Sadly, the latter was chosen. Writer Larry Rhine was said to be unhappy with the final result because so much from the original script had been altered.

The Oddball Couple
(September 26, 1975–September 3, 1977)

Writers: Bob Ogle, Joel Kane, David Detiege, Earl Kress and John W. Dunn; *Directors:* Lew Marshall, Gerry Chiniquy and Robert McKimson; *Voices:* Paul Winchell as Fleabag, Frank Nelson as Spiffy, Joan Gerber as Goldie Hound; *Other Voices Provided by:* Joe Besser, Bob Holt, Sarah Kennedy, Don Messick, Ginny Tyler, and Frank Welker. *Animator:* Virgil Ross. *Music:* Doug Goodwin, Eric Rogers, George Rock, and Joe Siracusa.

Plot descriptions could only be found for the first few episodes.

"PILOT" (1:1) Unaired

"SPIFFY'S MAN FRIDAY" (1.2)
September 6, 1975

Fleabag loves to gamble, and when he loses a bet to Spiffy, he must be his servant for an entire month.

"WHO'S ZOO?" (1.3) September 6, 1975

When Spiffy and Fleabag visit the zoo, it becomes quite obvious to Fleabag that there's something about him the other animals just don't like. However, whenever an incident occurs, Spiffy is looking the other way.

"A DAY AT THE BEACH" (1.4)
September 13, 1975

What is intended to be a nice, relaxing day at the beach (with their paws in the sand) turns into a nightmare.

"FLEABAG'S MOTHER" (1.5)
September 13, 1975

When a prestigious *Better Homes and Gardens*–type of magazine arranges to do a photo shoot at their home, Spiffy conveniently sends Fleabag on a vacation to Hawaii. Trouble ensues when Fleabag's mother chooses that same time to pay a visit.

"TO HEIR IS HUMAN" (1.6)
September 20, 1975

Spiffy's tutorial on manners is all for

naught when he and Fleabag interview a wealthy couple who are just as slovenly as Fleabag.

"SPIFFY'S NEPHEW" (1.7) September 20, 1975

Spiffy's nephew pays a visit, but much to Fleabag's relief, he is nothing like his fastidious uncle.

"A ROYAL MIX-UP" (1.8) September 27, 1975

A visiting king bears an uncanny resemblance to Spiffy, and confusion "reigns."

"PAPER AIRPLANE" (1.9) September 27, 1975

Fleabag and Spiffy go snout-to-snout in a paper airplane–building contest. When Fleabag experiences difficulties, he seeks the assistance of a kid from the neighborhood.

"THE BIGHOUSE AND GARDEN" (1.10) October 4, 1975

The oddball couple is at odds over household chores and the pros and cons of planting a garden.

"THE TALKING PLANET" (1.11) October 4, 1975

"FAMILY ALBUM" (1.12) October 11, 1975

"HOTEL BOO-MORE" (1.13) October 11, 1975

"IRISH LUCK" (1.14) October 18, 1975

"WHO'S AFRAID OF VIRGINIA WEREWOLF?" (1.15) October 18, 1975

"DIVE DUMMERS" (1.16) October 25, 1975

"DO OR DIET" (1.17 October 25, 1975

"KLONDIKE OIL CAPER" (1.18) November 1, 1975

"OLD BUG EYES IS BACK" (1.19) November 1, 1975

"MUGSY BAGEL" (1.20) November 8, 1975

"TV OR NOT TV" (1.21) November 8, 1975

"ALL KAT" (1.22) November 15, 1975

"THE JOKER'S WILD" (1.23) November 15, 1975

"CINDERBAG" (1.24) November 22, 1975

"MOMMA FLEABAG" (1.25) November 22, 1975

"DO IT YOURSELF, FLEABAG" (1.26) November 29, 1975

"ROMAN DAZE" (1.27) November 29, 1975

"FLEABAG'S SUBMARINE" (1.28) December 6, 1975

"FOREIGN LEGION" (1.29) December 6, 1975

"BATS IN THE BELFRY" (1.30) December 13, 1975

"SUPERHOUND" (1.31) December 13, 1975

"JUNGLE BUNGLE" (1.32) December 20, 1975

"TALENT SCOUTS" (1.33) December 20, 1975

The New Odd Couple
(October 29, 1982–June 16, 1983 on ABC)

The New Odd Couple was a new spin on an old classic. Oscar Madison (Demond Wilson) is a divorced, untidy sportswriter, and his roommate is also divorced—the perfectionistic, fastidious Felix Unger (Ron Glass). This version (consisting of 18 episodes) was filmed before a studio audience, once again for Paramount, this time with a mostly African American cast. Several

The New Odd Couple cast—Clockwise from the top left—Liz Torres, John Schuck, Bart Braverman, Sheila Anderson, Ronalda Douglas, Demond Wilson, Ron Glass and Christopher Joy (center) (courtesy Christopher Joy).

of the scripts from the original version were reworked for the "New" show. Like the original version, most episodes aired on Friday nights on ABC.

"THE IDES OF APRIL" (1:1) October 29, 1982

Writer: Mark Rothman and Lowell Ganz; *Director:* Joel Zwick; *Guest Stars:* John Schuck as Murray, Bart Braverman as Roy, Esther Rolle as Mrs. Gibbs, Greg Finley as the postman, and Michael Prince as the priest.

Fastidious Felix, whose tax returns are flawless and impeccable, is surprised when he, and not Oscar, is audited by the IRS. This is one of the reworked scripts from the original series.

"THE HUSTLER" (1:2) November 5, 1982

Writers: Mark Rothman and Lowell Ganz; *Director:* Joel Zwick; *Guest Stars:* Ben Powers as "Sidepocket" Sidney, Jill Jaress as Vivian, Michael Rapport as Henry, and Wally Taylor as Barney.

Oscar is a good pool player, but not as good as a pool hustler who draws him into a big money contest at Ames Championship Pool Room. This is one of the revamped scripts from the original series. Jill Jaress also guest starred in "My Strife in Court" in the original series (as Beth Olam). Oscar's new nickname, "The Big O," appears first in this episode. The "Ames" name for the pool room was chosen because that was the name of the pool room in the 1961 motion picture *The Hustler*, which starred Paul Newman and Jackie Gleason.

"FRANCES MOVES IN" (1:3) November 12, 1982

Writers: Mark Rothman and Lowell Ganz; *Director:* Joel Zwick; *Guest Stars:* John Schuck as Murray; Bart Braverman as Roy, Christopher Joy as Speed, Telma Hopkins as Frances, and Malcolm Groome as Roger.

While her house is being painted, Frances moves into the apartment with Felix and Oscar, disrupting their regular poker game. This is one of the reworked scripts from the original series.

"THAT WAS NO LADY" (1:4) November 19, 1982

Writer: Lee Kalcheim; *Director:* Joel Zwick; *Guest Star:* Ernie Hudson as Moses Brown.

While Oscar gets quotes from a boxing champion for a book he's writing, Felix unwittingly falls for the boxer's girl. This is one of the reworked scripts from the original series, but the topic of Oscar's book in the original episode was football. In the original, the girl was a football player's wife. Initially, Ron Glass didn't want to do the episode because he felt that Felix would never date a married woman. It was then decided that she would be the boxer's girlfriend, and Ron Glass was placated.

"BROTHER, CAN YOU SPARE A JOB?" (1:5) November 26, 1982

Writer: Jerry Ross; *Director:* Joel Zwick; *Guest Stars:* Bart Braverman as Roy, Christopher Joy as Speed, Roy A. Firestone as Doug Richards, Robert Lesser as the stage manager, and Judy Pace as Brenda Gibson.

Felix, the busybody, urges Oscar to demand a raise—a move which takes Oscar from a byline to the unemployment line.

"THE NEW CAR" (1:6) December 3, 1982

Writers: Mark Rothman and Lowell Ganz; *Director:* Joel Zwick; *Guest Stars:* John Schuck as Murray, Liz Torres as Oscar's secretary Maria, and JoMarie Payton as Mona.

Oscar and Felix win a new car, but finding parking on the streets of Manhattan proves problematic. In this episode, Oscar answers theater questions to win the car. This is one of the reworked scripts from the original series. The topic was opera, not theater, in the original version.

"THE CORDON BLEUS" (1:7) December 10, 1982

Writer: Jeffrey Duteil and Ralph Farquhar; *Director:* Joel Zwick; *Guest Stars:* John Schuck as Murray and Henry Polic, II as Davies, and Gretchen Wyler as the restaurant owner.

A high-brow friend thinks Felix has what it takes to cut the mustard as manager of her classy restaurant. Actor Henry Polic, II, died at the age of 68 on August 11, 2013.

"THE ODD TRIANGLE" (1:8) December 17, 1982

Writer: Norman Barasch; *Director:* Joel Zwick; *Guest Stars:* Liz Torres as Maria, and Deborah Pratt as Sandra.

Fashion photographer Felix thinks that the model Oscar is dating is using him to get ahead in the fashion world.

"OPENING NIGHT" (1:9) December 31, 1982

Writers: Mary Cory Miller and Kurt Taylor; *Director:* John Tracy; *Guest Stars:* John Schuck as Murray, Bart Braverman as Roy, Carmen Argenziano as Tony, and Billy Van Zandt as the lab assistant.

A backer for a new Broadway play makes Oscar an offer he can't refuse—write a good review, or else.

"SECURITY" (1:10) January 7, 1983

Writer: Jerry Belson; *Director:* Joel Zwick; *Guest Stars:* Sheila Anderson as Cecily Pigeon, and Ronalda Douglas as Gwendolyn Pigeon.

After a robbery in the building, Felix takes no chances—he finds a more secure apartment and gets a guard dog. This episode is similar to "Security Arms" from the original series.

"BACHELOR OF THE YEAR" (1:11) January 14, 1983

Writers: Mary Cory Miller and Kurt Taylor; *Director:* Joel Zwick; *Guest Stars:* Sheila Anderson as Cecily Pigeon, Ronalda Douglas as Gwendolyn Pigeon, JoMarie Payton as Mona, and J. A. Preston as Mr. Walker.

It's *mano a mano* as both Felix and Oscar are considered for the title of "Bachelor of the Year" in a popular magazine.

"A GRAVE FOR FELIX" (1:12) January 21, 1983

Writers: Dick Bensfield and Perry Grant; *Director:* Joel Zwick; *Guest Stars:* JoMarie Payton as Mona and Ian Wolfe as Hanley.

Felix finds the ideal cemetery plot and gives Oscar the down payment to

PARAMOUNT TELEVISION PRODUCTIONS

THE NEW ODD COUPLE

"A GRAVE FOR FELIX"
60491-013

Return to Script Department
PARAMOUNT PICTURES CORPORATION
5555 Melrose Avenue
Los Angeles, California 90038

REVISED SHOOTING SCRIPT
NOVEMBER 17, 1982

An original script for "A Grave for Felix" from *The New Odd Couple*—one of the revamped scripts from the original series.

drop off. However, when that money is rerouted to Oscar's bookie, Felix loses out on his preferred final resting place. This is one of the reworked scripts from the original series.

"MY STRIFE IN COURT" (1:13)
January 28, 1983

Writers: Mark Rothman and Lowell Ganz; *Director:* Joel Zwick; *Guest Stars:* John Schuck as Murray, Sheila Anderson as Cecily Pigeon, Ronalda Douglas as Gwendolyn Pigeon, Jack Kruschen as the judge, Hope Clark as Beth St. Clair, John Isaac as the bailiff, Robert Lesser as Harry Price, Ernie Sabella as the policeman, and Jack Yates as the prosecutor.

When Oscar can't get a date for a Lena Horne concert, Felix gets them both arrested for ticket scalping. Felix then represents himself in court. This is one of the reworked scripts from the original series. Actor Jack Kruschen, who plays the judge, was among the many names bandied about to play Oscar in the original series. Kruschen had previously appeared as Mr. Markowitz on Mark Rothman and Lowell Ganz's sitcom titled *Busting Loose* in 1977.

"OSCAR DATES FELIX'S FRANCES" (1:14)
February 18, 1983

Writer: Stu Silver; *Director:* Joel Zwick; *Guest Stars:* Sheila Anderson as Cecily Pigeon, Telma Hopkins as Frances, Gloria Gifford as Rita, and Joe Mays as Eddie.

Oscar innocently accompanies Felix's ex-wife, Frances, to a lecture, but things become more complex when they begin dating.

"MURRAY'S HOT DATE" (1:15)
February 25, 1983

Writers: Madelyn and Steven Sunshine; *Director:* Joel Zwick; *Guest Stars:* John Schuck as Murray, and Kelly Bishop as Charity.

Under normal conditions, Oscar

giving money to Charity is encouraged, but not when Charity is the name of a hooker.

"THE PERILS OF PAULINE"
(1:16) May 13, 1983
Writers: Jeffrey Duteil and Barry O'Brien; *Director:* Joel Zwick; *Guest Stars:* John Schuck as Murray and Billy Sands as the man.

Borrowing the title of a 1914 silent movie serial, Pauline in this case is the nickname for Oscar's trusty old typewriter, which he prefers over his new word processor.

"THE ONLY WAY TO FLY"
(1:17) May 20, 1983
Writers: Madelyn and Steven Sunshine; *Director:* Joel Zwick; *Guest Star:* John Schuck as Murray.

When Murray has his palm read, he sees misfortune ahead for both Oscar and Felix.

"THE NIGHT STALKER" (1:18)
May 26, 1983
Writer: Ralph Farquhar; *Director:* Joel Zwick; *Guest Stars:* John Schuck as Murray, Bart Braverman as Roy, Sheila Anderson as Cecily Pigeon, Ronalda Douglas as Gwendolyn Pigeon, Christipher Joy as Speed, JoMarie Payton as Mona, Franklin Ajaye as Henry, and Tracy Reed as Celina.

A brick thrown through Felix's photography studio window bears a threatening message. That threat came from a jealous husband.

FIVE
The Odd Couple Extras, Flubs and Factoids

Cast: Jack Klugman (Oscar Madison), Tony Randall (Felix Unger), Al Molinaro (Murray Greshler), Elinor Donahue (Miriam Welby), Penny Marshall (Myrna Turner)

Basis: A divorced perfectionistic photographer/neatness freak, Felix Unger, and a divorced slovenly sportswriter/gambling addict, Oscar Madison, share an apartment and attempt to live together "without driving each other crazy." The roommates live in apartment 1102 at 1049 Park Avenue in Manhattan.

Sponsors: American Brands, Chesebrough Ponds, R. J. Reynolds Tobacco, and Procter and Gamble.

Oscar Madison: Oscar, middle name Trevor, is a Taurus and a sportswriter for the *New York Herald*. He was born at Our Lady of Angels Hospital in Philadelphia, and the doctor who delivered him was named Max Greenbaum. Oscar's brother was born in Toledo. As a child, Oscar threw his diapers all over the house. His best childhood friend was Chubby London. He attended the Langley Tippy-Tap Toe Dancing School and is a graduate of James K. Polk High School. His mother called him "Chicky" and his father, nicknamed "Blinky," worked in a speakeasy. Oscar had an uncle named Freddy, who carved roast beef with a switchblade. Oscar went to college with game show host Monty Hall and served a hitch in the army, where he was the perfect example of what not to do—"In any other army in the world he would have been shot on sight." The IRS claims Oscar has the worst tax returns they have ever seen ("Winos who throw their returns through the window have neater returns"). Oscar kicks things when he gets upset and yearns to be a great writer like Ernest Hemingway, but just doesn't seem to have the discipline to complete a novel.

Culturally, Oscar is like the proverbial bull in a china shop. His life is centered on sports and betting—he has little regard for his health or his ulcer. Neil Simon calls the Oscar Madison character his "Greek chorus"—his anchor, to whom the audience can best relate. At one time in his life, Oscar weighed 301 pounds. He smokes cigars, puts ketchup on everything and his usual source of nutrition is a can of beer. He frequents greasy spoons, such as Olaf's Diner (where he briefly "moonlights" as a cook named "Cookie"), Edible Eddie's, April Fools Tacos, Hessian Heidi's Nautical Nosh, and he often has dinner at the Press Box Steak House. Lasagna and French fries make up his favorite dinner; salami and jelly on rye is his favorite sandwich, and Boston cream pie is his favorite dessert. He also likes cookies shaped like horses' heads served with ketchup, chop suey with marinara sauce, and his own concoction—"goop melange." He has an affinity for creamed chipped beef on a doughnut, with raisins. He wears a size 11-D shoe and uses old beer cans and pickles as shoe trees, and shoehorns as spoons. He has a Pluto ashtray by his bed (stolen from Disneyland). He is a Mets baseball fan and was on a bowling team called The Bon Vivants.

Oscar first worked as a copyrighter for *Playboy* magazine, then as a sportswriter for the *New York Times* before acquiring his current position with the *Herald*. He was also very briefly in the employ of *Harem Magazine*. Oscar was the host of a radio program called *The Oscar Madison Sports Talk Show* (later *Oscar Madison's Greatest Moments in Sports*) and a TV show called *The Sports Den*. His favorite song is "Home on the Range," and he owns only one record album: *Gus Lesnevich Sings Lightweight Hits*. His most serious vice is gambling. Oscar acquired his current apartment after the death of its long-time occupant, Irving Cohen. Oscar's ex-wife, Blanche, divorced him because of their constant bickering and because of a misunderstood flirtation on New Year's Eve. They married on Christmas Day and went to a Rangers–Red Wings hockey game on their honeymoon. Oscar lost his car in the divorce. Oscar first met Felix Unger when they were jurors for the trial of Leo Garvey (a man accused of driving his roommate crazy).

Dr. Nancy Cunningham, who worked in Dr. Melnitz's office became Oscar's love interest. Oscar also had an ongoing liaison with Crazy Rhoda Zimmerman (whom we never got to see) and Nina the crane operator (also never seen). Myrna Turner, who called Oscar "Mr. M," was Oscar's nasal, slow-talking, inefficient secretary. She studied tap dancing for 12 years and danced at the Alabama–Mississippi football game half-time. Her siblings are Verna and Werner Turner, and her boyfriend is named "Sheldn" ("they forgot the 'o' on his birth certificate").

Felix Unger: The OCD-laden Felix, whose middle name is Alex, is a Pisces and an excessively neat, persnickety, neurotic perfectionist who owns a photography studio called Felix Unger Photography (also seen as F.U. Enterprises, at 380 Madison Avenue, located next to the Pottery Barn). His portraits of babies won him The Silver Nipple Award. Photographs of Oscar's room won him yet another award for starkly portraying slum conditions. Felix claims to have an IQ of 186, and mentions he was born in Chicago. As a youngster he frequently visited his grandmother, who owned a farm in Glenview, New York, where he became fond of a cow named Alice. He had a grandfather named Albert, who was married to "Grandmother Mimi." Felix was a tidy child, a perfect student in school, and acquired the nicknames "Felix the Pest" and "Felix the Cat" (the latter after the cartoon character). He was also voted "Cutest Boy," "Most Likely to Succeed," "Most Limber Boy," and "Most Likely to Interrupt." As a child, he had great admiration for clowns. He bakes every Monday and has a subscription to *National Geographic*.

Felix is an expert on old-time radio theme-songs; he became a radio actor (member of the Radio Actors Guild) as a teenager (he appeared on the radio series *Let's Pretend*). In college he hosted his own radio show and ran the station for three years. Following graduation, Felix enrolled in the army and was stationed in England during World War II (with the 22nd Training Film Platoon, Educational Division of the Special Services). He had an orthopedic cot and was teased by the other enlisted men. He starred in the army training film *How to Take a Shower* and originated the line, "Men, don't let this happen to you." He won the Silver Canteen Award (second place) for his song about Hitler, "To a Sour Kraut." Felix, a lieutenant at the time, was next transferred to Greenland and, two years later, retired as a captain. He won a good-posture medal there. He later served two weeks a year in the army reserves. He won the "concerned citizens medallion" for identifying a burglar. He is a great arm wrestler, developing a really strong grip from years of using nose and throat spray. He is deathly afraid of having surgery of any kind—in fact, his phobias are legion.

Felix's first job was as a photographer for *Playboy* magazine (he worked under the alias Spencer Benedict "because you don't think I'm going to use my real name to shoot nudies"). He was also engaged to his future ex-wife, Gloria Schaefer; at the time she worked as a Bunny in the Manhattan Playboy Club. He told her he loved her the first time they met. Felix and Gloria were married for seven years before she asked him for a divorce (he bought her clothes, recooked her meals, cleaned after she cleaned; he simply drove her to a point of not being able to tolerate him any longer, although she still loved him). Felix had the transcript of his divorce proceedings bound. Felix and Gloria became the parents of two children, Edna and Leonard. Gloria first called Felix "Honey Bear," and then "Mr. Clean"; their song was "Just One More Chance." Even after the divorce, Felix remained insanely jealous of Gloria's beaus. Before he met Gloria, Felix was dating a dietician named Dorothy, who left Felix for Kate Smith's drummer. He mourns every year on the anniversary of Eddie Fisher and Debbie Reynolds's divorce.

When Gloria asked Felix to leave, Oscar allowed him to share his apartment. Felix has an annoying and loud sinus problem, leading to a honking sound (caused by a deviated septum). He also makes "moose call" sounds to clear his ears. He claims to be allergic to animals (even of the plush variety) and says that, when he was a kid, he curled up with a sponge. Despite this, in addition to the aforementioned cow on his grandmother's farm, he had a pet parrot (Albert), a Pomeranian dog named Spot, and a teddy bear named Mr. Friend (which was never taken out of its cellophane). He has a general abrasion clause in his health insurance policy. For his fifth birthday, Felix asked for a wastepaper basket as a present and, since playing Hamlet in his junior high school play, he says, "I have been fascinated by ghosts."

Felix is a member of the Edward Villella Ballet Appreciation Club, the Lexington Avenue Opera Club, and a band called The Sophisticates (also known as the Sophisticatos). He subscribes to *Opera News* magazine and becomes embarrassed in public because he cries at those operas. Felix yearned to be a film director like Alfred Hitchcock and used his directorial ability to win a dubious Dink Award for a deceptive commercial for Fat-away Diet Pills. His overweight cousin Ben was supposed to be in the commercial, but he backed out of the production. Felix is allergic to mayonnaise, sour cream, flamingos, fog, and olives, and prides himself on knowing the best French restaurants in Manhattan. One of his favorite dishes is veal piccata.

Felix's boyhood friend was Orville Kruger ("the boy with the odd-shaped head"—his mother used to let out one side of his hat); his first girlfriends were "Big Bertha" and Mildred Fleener (who called Felix "Tiger"). He was potty trained at five months, and was training others at seven months. His father blamed him for the Great Depression. When they were kids, Felix and his brother, Floyd, were called "Spic and Span" (Floyd later owned the Unger Bubble Gum factory in Buffalo, New York). Felix called Floyd "Little F." and Floyd called Felix "Big F." Felix's mother, incidentally, liked Floyd best. Felix's father, Morris, was an optometrist, and he also has a sister (neither named nor seen, and only mentioned once). Felix had an uncle, Eric, who had six fingers on his right hand, and an unnamed aunt in Cleveland, who is mentioned numerous times (and is always notified when Felix is on TV), as well as an uncle Albert and an aunt Doris. Felix has a trick back (he hurt it during World War II, scrubbing a mess hall), and sometimes his arms lock (rendering them useless). He collects stamps, changes the kitchen cabinet shelf paper, and bangs his head against walls when upset; he is also one of a very select few who makes ladyfingers from scratch. He irons his neckties and puts shoetrees in his bedroom slippers, polishes those shoetrees, and uses the Waterpik on his toes. He won a grammar school spelling bee with the word *zeppelin*, and he also won the home economics medal. At one point in his life Felix gave up playing lacrosse because of a shoulder injury. He was a medal-winning boxer at Harvard Business School, but left the ring for the fine arts (he was also part of a two man song-and-dance act in the army). His favorite sport is squash. He can't shoot a basketball without kicking his right leg. "Upstairs" Miriam Welby was, for a time, Felix's regular romantic interest.

Gloria Unger: Gloria's maiden name was Schaefer. She lived at 145 Central Park West. Her measurements are 38-26-34, and 212-724-7069 was her phone number. She is five feet four inches tall. She was once fixed up with Oscar through a computer dating service. She is a former *Playboy* Bunny. She has a mole on her knee and a small scar on her right hand.

Blanche Madison: Hails from Kew Gardens, New York. She once had a boyfriend named Cecil Panch, and, had she married him, she would have been Blanche Panch. She married Oscar in Abnerville, Connecticut, while he was in the army, at Fort Ira Epstein. She has a brother, Sid, who was married to a girl named Molly (their children are Martha and Timmy). Blanche was hit by a puck on her honeymoon night. She almost married a milk farmer named Roger J. Doctor.

Myrna Turner: Has a boyfriend (eventually a husband) named Sheldn (they left out the "o" on his birth certificate). She has siblings named Werner and Verna Turner (both of whom laugh like her). She studied tap dancing for 12 years. She was the Alabama/Mississippi game half-time performer (she tap danced). Her belly button is an outie. She quit smoking by attending the Smoker's Institute, and has used a computer-dating service. She types seven words a minute, and has the habit of twirling her hair when she's nervous.

Murray Greshler: Has a poor arrest record as a policeman. He has been trying to become a sergeant for 11 years, without success. He deals cards for poker very slowly. His wife's first name is Mimi, and they were briefly separated. He is an animal lover. He plays ukulele in Felix's band, and sometimes piano, and, in one episode, the harmonica. Murray loves magic, and likes to pretend his nightstick is a magic wand and his police car, a pumpkin. He has a unique style of handwriting, called the "Murray curl." He is a whiz at playing casino and fish, and he loves to whistle. One of the most used nicknames for Murray is "Nosen-stein." He has an aunt, Goldie, from Teaneck, New Jersey, who was a manicurist with ESP.

Dr. Nancy Cunningham: Loves boxing and hockey, and is a trivia expert in both sports. She has a mole on her left hip. She worked in Dr. Melnitz's office and has a brother, Raymond, who is a skiing enthusiast. Nancy is a great cook and loves champagne.

Speed: His real name is Homer Deegan. He is always the first to the poker games, and always the last to leave. He placed a bet on Oscar's wedding (as did Oscar).

Vinnie: His last name is Barella. His wife is named Bibi. Vinnie and Bibi live at 220 East 60th Street, in Manhattan.

Miriam: Plays the bass fiddle and the fife. Lives upstairs from Felix and Oscar. Miriam takes umbrage at the chauvinistic views espoused by Bobby Riggs. She is in love with Felix, but is absent at the ceremony when he remarries Gloria. She loves musicals and the ballet. She is not a fan of Oscar and Felix's constant bickering.

Inconsistencies Galore/ Continuity Mishaps

Continuity was not *The Odd Couple's* strong point. In the opening monologue, the excision of the word *childhood* before the word *friend* begins with episode one of season two ("Natural Childbirth"). Through all of the second and third seasons, Felix, with nowhere else to go, now "appears at the home of his *friend* Oscar Madison." Also, to kick off the second season, the words *sometime earlier* are replaced by *several years earlier Madison's wife had thrown him out, requesting that he never return*. Madison and his ex-wife, Blanche, were said to have been married on the same day as baseball's All-Star Game in one episode; Christmas Day in another (the dates are almost six months apart). In the TV series, they went to a hockey game on their honeymoon, where Blanche was repeatedly hit by a puck, but in the 1968 film, she was hit by the puck at a game on their tenth wedding anniversary. Blanche's maiden name was given as Jefferson in one episode; Somers, in another. Oscar has two children in the movies and the Broadway play, but he is childless in the TV series. Oscar's son, Brucey, marries Felix's daughter, Hannah, in *The Odd Couple II*. Oscar and Blanche pretend they're still married in one episode so that Oscar's mother doesn't find out they've divorced, but in another episode it is stated that Oscar's mom was on the steps of the courthouse when they signed the divorce papers. Oscar said that he never returned the rented tuxedo from his wedding, but, in a flashback episode, we see that he was married in uniform while in the army.

In one early episode, Oscar acknowledges that alimony is tax deductible, but, in a later episode, he claims to be unaware that it is. The stuffed gorilla (important notes are left in his mouth) in Oscar's bachelor pad (in flashback episodes) is named Bruce, but in *The Odd Couple: Together Again* the gorilla was (inexplicably) named Stan. Oscar sometimes wears pajamas and sometimes sleeps in his underwear. He has New York Mets memorabilia all over the apartment and was seen in a vast majority of episodes with a Mets cap on his head—but in a few early episodes, and in the 1993 reunion movie, he dons a New York Yankees cap (something a true Mets fan would *never* do). He writes for the *New York Herald* in the TV series, and *The New York Post* in the movie. There is a disparity over Oscar's place of birth—one episode says Chicago, another says Philadelphia, and yet another says the Bronx. According to one episode, he attended James K. Polk High School, but, in another, it was Bayonne High School. In one episode, Oscar claims to despise creamed chipped beef (it conjures up bad memories of his army days), but, in another, he says it's one of his favorite foods (and he likes it served on a donut, with raisins). Oscar's apartment in the single-camera first season greatly resembled the one in the movie, but its layout changed drastically beginning in season two to accommodate the multi-camera format and the studio audience. In the multi-camera episodes, Oscar's bed is on the opposite side of the room from the single-camera first-season episodes. However, in flashback episodes, it is still the "new" apartment. In the 1993 reunion movie, however, the apartment once again resembled that of the first season and movie, with its long hallway and the gates. A peephole was added to the front door in the three-camera episodes (it was absent in the single-camera first season). Murray's nose is sometimes seen sticking through that peephole. In the opening monologue, we hear the line, "Madison's wife had thrown him out, requesting that he never return"—and yet, all flashbacks take place in the same apartment (number 1102), so he wasn't thrown out after all.

In the 1968 film, Felix claimed to be allergic to pillows, curtains, and perfume, but in the TV series it was flamingos, fog, olives, animals, sour cream, and mayonnaise. The name Albert is reused a lot in the series—as the name of Felix's parrot, as the first name of Felix's grandfather, and as the name of an unseen uncle. Felix's band is usually called the Sophisticates or the Sophisticatos, but in one episode they are known as the Unger Five Plus None. Felix claims in one episode that sleeping pills don't work for him, but in another, one little sleeping pill works *too* well. Felix claims to have the home version of *Password* in his car, but when he and Oscar win a car, both state that they haven't owned an automobile in years. In "The Subway Story," Oscar says he hasn't been on the subway in five years, but, in an earlier episode, he claims to have ridden the subway very recently.

Oscar has a poster of Felix in his office that has a balloon over Felix's head which says, "Thanks." In "You Saved My Life," that poster was given to Oscar for keeping Felix from falling 11 floors out the apartment window, onto the pavement below. However in "Two on the Aisle," Oscar says that it was given to him as a gift for letting Felix room with him. Oscar was already divorced when Felix moved in, but in "The Odd Holiday," Felix and Gloria were the first couple to divorce. (Felix and Frances were only separated in the original movie.) There is also disparity over which member of the Odd Couple was married first—in "The First Baby" it's Felix, but in "This Is the Army, Mrs. Madison," it's Oscar. The episode "One for the Bunny" contains an anachronism—it is a flashback to when Felix and Gloria were newly engaged, and Oscar uses a cassette recorder (they hadn't been marketed yet).

The address to their apartment was 1049 Park Avenue, Apartment 1102, but, in one episode, Felix gives the address as 74th and Central Park West. (The apartment was on Riverside Drive in the Broadway play.) In season four, the address for Oscar's place of business (at the *Herald*) changes inexplicably from number 235 to number 1501. One episode shows how Oscar and Felix met on jury duty, another shows them double dating in the 1950s (when Felix met Gloria), and, still another, shows them meeting as children in Chicago during Prohibition (which would make them much older than they claim to be).

In one episode, Felix states that he has never been a best man, but, in another, he serves as best man at Oscar and Blanche's nuptials. In the Broadway play and the original movie, Felix's wife was named Frances, but she was named Gloria in the original TV series. Her name became Frances again in 1982 when ABC broadcast *The New Odd Couple*. In the first series, Felix met Gloria on a double date in one episode, but, in another, it is stated that Felix met Gloria while she was part of the USO. In one episode of the original series, Gloria's maiden name was Schaefer, and Fleener in yet another. Fleener was also the surname of Felix's first girlfriend, Mildred Fleener (but, in another episode, his first girlfriend was named Big Bertha).

Felix is said to have been born in Philadelphia in one episode, Oklahoma in another, and Buffalo in still another. In one episode, Leonard is said to be the elder of Felix and Gloria's two children, but in another, Edna is. In one episode, Felix claims to have taken his own sister to the prom, but, in another, it was Mildred Fleener who accompanied him. This sister is never mentioned again (only his brother, Floyd. There is also conjecture about which brother is older: in "The Big Brothers," Felix is said to be the younger; in "Shuffle Off to Buffalo,"

Felix is the elder. Felix writes TV news stories in the movie and play, but is a photographer ("Portraits a Specialty") in both TV series. In the movie and play, Ungar is spelled with an "a," but in the TV sitcoms and the TV reunion movie, Unger has an "e." In the opening credits, the luggage Felix totes around on the street is different from the luggage he has with him in the elevator.

Felix and Oscar were supposed to have been in the service together, but, in one episode, Felix was said to have served in the UK, Greenland (in another), and Guadalcanal (in yet another). If Felix and Oscar were indeed in the army together, why doesn't Oscar know that Richard Dawson and Felix had a show business act? Felix is said to be allergic to all animals, real or stuffed, but in one episode he owns a parrot; in another, he is part owner of a greyhound named Golden Earrings; in another, we learn that Felix and Gloria had a Pomeranian named Spot, and, in yet another, Felix steals a dog (a collie named Silver) that he feels was being mistreated. Felix also handles his son, Leonard's frog, Max. Without explanation, Myrna Turner, who had left her job as Oscar's secretary months earlier, is back, only to disappear again the following week, this time for good.

The guest stars weren't immune from inconsistencies either. Actor Richard Stahl portrayed a total of nine different characters in different episodes. Actress Marlyn Mason portrayed two totally different girls in two different episodes (a chef, and a homeless woman). Victor Buono portrayed an exorcist in one episode, and the building's landlord in another. In "The Roy Clark Story" episode, the opera singing man portrayed by John Wheeler is called Mr. Felscher, but in the closing credits he's listed as Mr. Fletcher. In "Maid for Each Other," Reta Shaw is called Claire Frost and nicknamed "Frosty," but in the closing credits she's listed as Claire Foster. Murray's wife, Mimi, was portrayed by two different women—Alice Ghostley and Jane Dulo. Dulo also portrayed Oscar Madison's mother in another episode in the same season. Mimi was also the name of Felix's grandmother. Herbie Faye portrayed the building superintendent in different episodes under different names—Mr. Lambretti, Mr. Seltzer, and Mr. Faffner. Then again, in two other episodes, we see the super's son, whose last name is Hernandez. "Upstairs" Miriam lived downstairs from Felix and Oscar in one episode (on the 8th floor).

In *The New Odd Couple*, the character of Roy (Bart Braverman) magically reappears. He had only appeared in the first season of the original series (and was portrayed by Ryan McDonald). The Pigeon Sisters, who had been in the play, the movie and in some very early episodes of the original TV series, inexplicably reappeared on *The New Odd Couple*.

Real Life Parallels

Tony Randall's real first name is Leonard (the name of his son on *The Odd Couple*), and he had a sister named Edna (the name of his daughter on the show).

Tony Randall was a devotee of opera and the ballet, much like Felix Unger.

Tony Randall's real-life first wife was named Florence, as was the cow in his photography studio, and the elderly neighbor with the jealous husband.

Jack Klugman loved to bet on the horses, and listened to the racing results every day on the set, much like Oscar Madison.

Jack Klugman really was married to Brett Somers. They separated during the run of the series, but never divorced.

Jack Klugman and Tony Randall, as well as Walter Matthau and Jack Lemmon, were devoted friends on and off camera.

Jack Klugman and Jack Lemmon co-starred in the 1963 film, *The Days of Wine and Roses*.

Jack Klugman's throat surgery to remove part of a cancerous vocal cord was addressed in the reunion movie titled *The Odd Couple: Together Again*, in 1993.

Jack Klugman and Tony Randall both guest starred on the same 1955 TV episode of *Appointment with Adventure*.

Garry Marshall's birthday is November 13—the day Felix Unger was asked to remove himself from his place of residence.

Garry Marshall suffered from many of the same allergy and nasal maladies as Felix Unger.

- Garry Marshall lived on Arcola Avenue—Arcola was used as the last name of several characters on his shows.
- Murray the cop's surname is Greshler—inspired by Tony Randall and Jack Klugman's agent, Abbey Greshler.
- Penny Marshall (Myrna) and Rob Reiner (Sheldn) were married in real life.
- Penny Marshall and her character, Myrna Turner, had a dozen years of tap-dancing classes.
- Janis Hansen, like her character Gloria Unger, was a former *Playboy* bunny.
- Cicely and Gwendolyn (the Pigeon Sisters) are also the first names of the females in *The Importance of Being Earnest* by Oscar Wilde.

Broadcast and Cable TV Programs with Roommates as a Premise

The Big Bang Theory—Sheldon and Leonard are two brilliant but vastly different scientists who share an apartment and get on one another's nerves.

Bosom Buddies—When their building is demolished, Kip and Henry, desperate for cheap housing, masquerade as girls to share an inexpensive room in an all-female hotel.

Brother's Keeper—Porter (the neat one) and Bobby (the not-so-neat one) are brothers who share a home, and help raise Porter's motherless young son.

Committed—A 2005 NBC sitcom about a girl named Marni who rents out her closet to a dying clown known simply as "Clown" (portrayed by Tom Poston).

The Cop and the Kid—A policeman is granted custody of a troubled African American youth to set him on the straight and narrow.

Don't Trust the B--- in Apartment 23—A naïve blond woman moves in with a street-savvy brunette.

Exes—Three divorced men share an apartment owned by their divorce attorney. Airs on TV Land.

Four Kings—Four male childhood friends live together in Manhattan.

Frasier—Frasier Crane lives with his elderly father, Martin Crane, and they are nothing alike. Also sharing the apartment is Martin's British caretaker, Daphne.

Friends—Joey and Chandler, and Monica and Rachel share rooms across the hall from one another.

From a Bird's Eye View—Millie and Maggie are stewardesses who also room together (and sometimes compete for the same boyfriends).

Golden Girls—Four elderly, vastly different women share the same home in sunny Florida.

Harry's Girls—Three showgirls room together on the road while performing in small venues on a tour of Europe.

Hey, Landlord—A young man named Woody Banner inherits an apartment building, and he and his friend Chuck take up residence there and become the landlords.

Hot in Cleveland—Three "over 40" women find that Cleveland is more forgiving of age, and move in to-

FIVE : *THE ODD COUPLE* EXTRAS, FLUBS AND FACTOIDS • 231

gether with a caretaker who has an attitude.

How to Marry a Millionaire—Barbara Eden's first series. Three girls room together in a swanky penthouse apartment in an attempt to marry money.

I Dream of Jeannie—An astronaut who found a bottle on the beach containing a beautiful genie shares his home with her and her navel. (Barbara Eden's genie costume was considered to be too revealing for the censors. A compromise was reached by covering the actress's navel.)

It's About Time—Two astronauts who mistakenly travel back to prehistoric times share a cave and attempt to survive.

It's a Great Life—Bachelor veterans returning from World War II take up residence at a rooming house.

It's a Man's World—Four young guys live together on a houseboat called *The Elephant* on the Ohio River in the small town of Cordella.

Kate and Allie—Two divorcees and their kids share a Manhattan apartment to cut costs and friction ensues.

Laverne and Shirley—Laverne DeFazio and Shirley Feeney work at Shott's Brewery, and also live together in Milwaukee, and get into the wackiest predicaments.

Living Single—A popular show on the Fox Network, consisting of four single girls who live together, and two single guys who live together in the same Brooklyn, New York, brownstone.

Melissa and Joey—Melissa comes from a political family, and when a family scandal leaves her niece and nephew homeless, she takes them in and hires a male nanny named Joey.

Men Behaving Badly—Based upon the British show, the 1996 U.S. version featured two roommates, Kevin and James, who are both sloppy and immature. Kevin's girlfriend Sarah's attempts to make them change fail miserably. So did the show.

Mr. Terrific—A mild-mannered garage mechanic attempts to keep his secret superhero identity from his roommate and co-worker.

My Crazy Roommate—Two young African American women from vastly different backgrounds are forced together as roommates while each struggles to find her fame and fortune in Hollywood (on the Bounce Network).

My Favorite Martian—Tim O'Hara lives with a Martian whom he passes off as his "Uncle Martin."

My Friend Irma—From the days of live TV, Jane puts up with her extremely naïve roommate, Irma.

My Living Doll—A psychiatrist is forced to live with a female robot until her maker returns from a mission overseas.

New Girl—Jess placed an ad in Craigslist after breaking up with her boyfriend. She moves in with three guys (Nick, Schmidt and Winston), and predicaments ensue.

Perfect Strangers—Balky, an immigrant from Mykos, moves in with his distant cousin Larry in Chicago.

Roller Girls—A roller derby team takes up residence in their own locker room to cut costs and keep the team from folding.

Roomies—A short-lived 1987 NBC sitcom with a built-in creepiness factor—a 42-year-old man attempts to get his degree and shares a dorm with a 14-year-old genius at the same school.

Roommates—A 2009 ABC sitcom about two twenty-somethings, Kate and Mark, who move in together after college.

Room for Two—This short-lived 1992 ABC sitcom featured a recently widowed mother who moves from Ohio to New York City to live with her daughter. Linda Lavin starred.

San Pedro Beach Bums—A group of male friends makes a houseboat their home (named "Our Boat").

So This Is Hollywood—Queenie Dugan and Kim Tracy are roommates, friends, but also starving actresses competing for the same roles.

Three's Company—Jack, Janet and Chrissy live together under the guise that Jack is gay—a charade necessary for their old-fashioned landlord, Mr. Roper.

Twenty Good Years—Two totally opposite longtime friends, both of whom are past middle age and figure they have "twenty good years" left, share an apartment.

Two and a Half Men—Charlie, Alan and Jake live under the same roof in Charlie's Malibu home and drive one another mad.

Two Broke Girls—Max and Caroline live and work together. They also have a cupcake business, and a horse named Chestnut.

Two Guys, a Girl, and a Pizza Place—Pete and Berg are roommates, and the "girl" in the title lives in the apartment above them.

Will and Grace—An interior designer (Grace) shares an apartment with her best friend—a gay lawyer (Will) in New York City.

Zoe, Duncan, Jack and Jane—In season two, Zoe and Jane share an apartment in New York City.

Web (Internet) Programs with Roommates as a Premise

Bigfoot Roommate—While strolling through the woods, a man encounters Bigfoot, who has no place to stay. They decide to room together.

The Brodio—Havoc is wreaked when three conflicting and diverse male personalities room together because of small print in their lease, and call their home the "Brodio."

The Charlie Feldon Show—A bizarre concept show as an acerbic voice-over artist rubber duck and his human roommate try to get along.

The End—After a robot apocalypse, there are very few survivors. Those who remain live together and drive one another crazy.

The Ex-Box—Nate and Allie have aspirations to make it big in the movies in Hollywood, but when they break up, they decide to live out their nine-month lease anyway.

Flat 3—Lee, Jessica, and Perlina share an apartment while attempting to figure out who they are, and where their lives are going.

Flour—A pair of sisters, Tulip (the carefree one) and Violet (the older, more level-headed one), live together and drive each other to distraction.

Fresh off the Plane—A diverse group of immigrants live together in the same apartment, and their cultures clash.

Gentlemen's Dwelling—Two brothers, who are nothing alike, reside in the same apartment in Upper Manhattan.

Georgian Way—Steven is a meek accountant who lives with his freeloading, carousing older brother, Skippy.

A Girl, a Guy and Their Monster—Henry is a child's monster living under the bed. He is Jenn's best friend, and Jenn brings the monster with her when she moves in with her fiancé, Phil.

Grapes Roommate—Andy's roommate is a bunch of grapes. They often don't see eye-to-eye, which always leads to one of them "raisin" the roof.

The Guru—Supreme Mistress Looprah Woo with her Ugly-Betty-like intern Yessica have a dysfunctional working relationship, and an even worse personal relationship.

Hi, This Is Me John—Three vastly different, lazy roommates all share one common goal—becoming wealthy.

Hotel Reject—The Jensen Sisters take part in, and are ousted from, a reality show—until the reality show ends. They are then held against their will together in an undisclosed location.

The House on South Bronson—When ten people share a house, hilarity ensues.

It's Not You—Laura and Julia are flatmates with only one thing in common—they each have a unique talent for "bad dating."

Jake and Amir—A daily comedy at www.collegehumor.com, which shows the odd couple of Jake and Amir attempting to cope with each other's peculiar ways.

Just Moved In—Max and Camila are a romantically involved couple who take the next big step and share an apartment.

Kevin and Phebe—A show about the crazy antics of best friends and roommates.

Kole's Law—Terrence Kole attempts to open his own law firm, but relying on his lazy roommate and indifferent sister gets him nowhere.

Less Than Heroes—The story of three roommates with super powers who have the ability to save the world, but opt to play video games instead.

Life, with Zombies—Seven people share a house during a zombie apocalypse.

Living Together—A father moves back in with his son after a reversal of fortune and a divorce.

Living with Daniel—Greg and Daniel share a New York City apartment, but only one of them enjoys the arrangement.

Living with Frankenstein—Frankenstein's Monster shares an apartment with Mary Shelley, P. B. Shelley, and Lord Byron in modern-day Los Angeles.

Living with Friends—Two brothers live together, while dealing with friends and addressing their own demons.

Louis Grant—An unsavory character named Louis Grant lives in the attic of the woman he impregnated, and takes care of the baby when she's away.

Max and Melvin's Mortuary Madness—Two college students start a basement mortuary (they also live there).

Mermates—When he's kicked out by his girlfriend, Chris Anderson moves in with a merman who looks human.

Once Upon a Time in Brooklyn—Roommates in Brooklyn try to pay the bills and rent without murdering one another.

On Empty—Two hapless, child-like dreamers, Vince and Tyler, live together in Los Angeles.

Parker and Steve: a Bromcom—Two male thirty-somethings share the ups and downs of life in New York City. Their financial woes only strengthen their friendship.

Pat and Andy—Patrick Mulvey and Andrew Scott-Ramsey are best friends who room together.

Plus Utilities—A trio of friends—Elliot, Gary, and Sniffles—are on a journey to find the perfect roommate in Los Angeles. This proves difficult because all three are impossible to live with.

Riddled with Anxiety—The very uptight Tim butts heads with his wacky, free-spirited roommate, Shilly.

Roomies—Not to be confused with the NBC show of same name, three roommates with drastically differing personalities attempt to co-exist under the same roof.

Roomsies—This is the story of what happens when you live with someone far too long. Meagan and Jenny have lost all sense of boundaries and reality.

Saturday Special—Sarah and Katie, two lifelong friends who become roommates, have rummage sales every Saturday, and these invariably turn into undesirable situations.

Saving Rent—Six unlikely roommates in Los Angeles share a house in order to save money. The house belongs to Mike, who has lost his job (but doesn't divulge that piece of information). All the others have skeletons in their closets as well.

Second-Hand NY—Julie, Patrick, and Ariel room together to pay the bills. When they're together, they make everyone else's life appear normal.

Series—A true Southerner, a passionate New Yorker, and a crazy foreigner all reside under one roof. Trouble ensues.

Sibling Rivalries—Two brothers, opposites in nature, are forced to live under one roof for eternity.

Tenants—Chris is an intelligent loner whose life is turned upside-down when an obnoxious potato chip–making guy becomes his uninvited roommate.

This Day Sucks—The misadventures of New York City roommates Rudy and Rayzor, who attempt to live the "good life," but fail miserably.

Un-mate—Oblivious Jo shares an apartment with the undead—three of them (Rufus, Candy, and the dangerous Micus, who lives chained in the attic).

Vampire Mob—A hitman/vampire discovers that his mother-in-law is moving in to his place for eternity.

Others Who Have Portrayed Felix and Oscar Onstage

1966—Victor Spinetti (Felix) and Jack Klugman (Oscar)—The Queen's Theatre, London, England

1966—Victor Spinetti (Felix) and Ken Wayne (Oscar)—The Queen's Theatre, London, England

1966—Richard Benjamin (Felix) and Dan Dailey (Oscar)—The Blackstone Theater, Chicago

1967—George Gobel (Felix) and Phil Foster (Oscar)—The Fisher Theater Detroit, Michigan

1967—Dick Shawn (Felix) and Jack Carter (Oscar)—The Westbury Music Fair, Westbury, New York. It's interesting to note that this production was directed by Jack Klugman.

1970—Martin Short (Felix) and Eugene Levy, and later Dave Thomas (Oscar)—The McMaster Shakespearean Players

1981—Charles Nelson Reilly (Felix) and Darryl Hickman (Oscar)—The Burt Reynolds Dinner Theater

1985—Sally Struthers (Florence) and Rita Moreno (Olive), *The Female Odd Couple*—The Broadhurst Theatre in New York City, and the Ahmanson Theatre in Los Angeles

1994—Gerard Kelly (Felix) and Craig Ferguson (Oscar)—The Scotland Tour

1997—*M*A*S*H* meets *The Odd Couple* with William Christopher (Felix) and Jamie Farr (Oscar)—Troupe America Tour (played mostly in Canada)

1997—Billy Crystal and Robin Williams were supposed to perform in an *Odd Couple* remake, but when their highly anticipated motion picture *Father's Day* tanked, the idea was tabled.

2001—Pat Sajak (Felix) and Hawaiian TV personality Joe Moore (Oscar)—at Hawaii's Manoa Valley Theater.

2002—Joe Regalbuto (Felix) and John Larroquette (Oscar)—The Geffen Playhouse in Los Angeles. *Oscar and Felix: A New Look at the Odd Couple*—this was the updated, modernized version. The dialogue and jokes were more current, and the Pigeon Sisters were now Hispanic (Julia and Ynez).

2003—Pat Morita (Felix) and Sherman Hemsley (Oscar)—The Stoneham Theatre in Stoneham, Massachusetts. Truly among the oddest of the odd pairings.

2005—Matthew Broderick (Felix) and Nathan Lane (Oscar)—The Brooks Atkinson Theatre on West 47th Street in New York City (249 performances)

2012—Tim Kazurkinsky (Felix) and George Wendt (Oscar)—The Northlight Theatre in Chicago.

The Odd Couple *Reviews*

"Mr. Matthau and Mr. Carney settle in as roommates, making as nice a couple as you'd care to meet if they could only get along. Mr. Carney is death on dust and a fast man with an aerosol bomb (one reason his wife threw him out is that he always insisted on re-cooking the dinner) and he drives Mr. Matthau stark staring mad. In short, both of them might just as well have wives, and that constitutes the meat, the moral, and the malicious merriment of this brief encounter."—Walter Kerr, *The New York Times* (March 11, 1965)

"Simon's skill is not only great, but constantly growing.... There is scarcely a moment that is not hilarious."—*The New York Times*

"Fresh, richly hilarious, and remarkably original. Wildly, irresistibly, incredibly, and continuously funny."—*The New York Daily News*

"The Neil Simon comedy that lit up Broadway for more than two years shines again in this flawed but still funny screen adaptation."—*Time* magazine

"A funny 'screen version' of a very funny (if not very significant) Broadway comedy. It does well as an evening's entertainment. But it begs the question of what might have resulted if Saks had flexed his muscles and insisted on a genuinely cinematic treatment."—Roger Ebert, *The Chicago Sun-Times*

"Comedy at its best."—Gary Brown, *Houston Community Newspapers*

"What's not to like about this classic film which features two of our most beloved actors at their best?"—Luanne Brown, *Chico Enterprise-Record*

"Two grown men sharing an apartment ... and not so much as a mention of the word homosexual? This could only be 1968."—James O'Ehley, *Movie Gurus*

"The only successful adaptation of a Neil Simon play."—*Film4*

"Truly classic comedy in Neil Simon school with superb Lemmon and Matthau."—Steve Crum, VideoReviewmaster.com

"Corny, not the least bit risqué, but really good fun."—Brian Webster, *Apollo Guide*

"Felix and Oscar are now part of the American mythos."—Marjorie Baumgarten, *Austin Chronicle*

"A durable classic. The sort of comedy that doesn't try to yank laughs by cramming its fist down our throats."—Mark Bourne, Film.com

"It's still the original movie that best captures the essence of the characters and story."—John J. Puccio, *Movie Metropolis*

"For all of its overfamiliarity, this is a good play, easily Simon's best, and Matthau and Lemmon inhabit it with grace and style."—Dave Kehr, *The Chicago Reader*

"As sitcom-style theater goes, *The Odd Couple* if often highly amusing, with Lemmon and Matthau ideally cast as prissy neatnik and unmitigated slob."—*TV Guide's Movie Guide*

"*The Odd Couple,* Neil Simon's smash legit comedy, has been turned into an excellent film starring Jack Lemmon and Walter Matthau. Simon's somewhat expanded screenplay retains the broad, as well as the poignant laughs together in the rooming together of two men whose marriages are on the rocks."—*Variety*

"Acting is all: Lemmon and Matthau are terrific in this highly amusing comedy, which is sharply written by Neil Simon, but poorly directed by theater helmer Gene Saks."—Emmanuel Levy, EmmanuelLevy.com

"An irresistible double act from Lemmon and Matthau."—Tom Milne, *Time Out*

"When critics discuss chemistry, that on-screen magic that occurs between perfectly paired actors, the electricity exemplified by Walter Matthau and Jack Lemmon is a textbook illustration of same."—Bill Gibron, Film critic.com

"The key to the movie is its stars ... it is Matthau's reserved-yet-committed man's man that gives the film its comedic edge."—Kevin Carr, *7M Pictures*

"Lemmon and Matthau's finest hour."—Kim Newman, *Empire* Magazine

"Of all of the versions of, and variations on Neil Simon's classic, *The Odd Couple*, from its original production on Broadway, to the celebrated television series starring Jack Klugman and Tony Randall, from the countless worldwide small theater productions to the always popular revival runs, the 1968 version is, arguably, the best representation of the titular twosome."—Christel Loer, *Pop Matters* (regarding the release of "The Centennial Collection" DVD set).

"*The Oddball Couple* was DePatie/Freleng Enterprises' funny animal take on Neil Simon's *The Odd Couple*, produced as a Saturday Morning cartoon for ABC. It ran for two seasons from 1975 to 1977. The main characters were Spiffy, a neat freak cat voiced by Frank Nelson, and Fleabag, an unkempt dog voiced by Paul Winchell. As in the play and the live-action sitcom, most of the comedy came from personality clashes between Spiffy and Fleabag, but turned up to eleven to take advantage of the animated format"—*TVTropes.org* (regarding *The Oddball Couple* cartoon series).

"*The Female Odd Couple* seems an archeological composite, neither *The Odd Couple* of 1965 nor a 1985 comedy with its own point of view. Simon might have done better to forget the original play entirely and start out afresh, with perhaps some technical advice on how two female housemates set up the rules these days and how they might bug each other. Instead, he has patched and padded, added new wrinkles, found the occasional line that gets under the surface—and yet is unable to turn this *Odd Couple* into a living experience. From Neil Simon—to quote *Plaza Suite*—we expect more."—Dan Sullivan, *The Los Angeles Times* (regarding the debut of *The Female Odd Couple* at the Ahmanson Theatre in 1985).

"The show is so fondly remembered, it would have been a cinch for this TV reunion movie from 1993 to rely on nostalgia and its stars to carry it. Fortunately for us, it doesn't, at least not for the first half. The quality of the writing isn't nearly up to the standard set by the series, but it's still funny and still a cut above other TV series reunions."—Rinkworks.com (regarding the 1993 TV reunion movie, *The Odd Couple: Together Again*).

"The idea of hiring Jack Lemmon and Walter Matthau fresh from their successes as grumpy old men to reinhabit the roles that established them as inspired comic sparring partners three decades ago sounds promising. But the movie turns out to be a dispiriting, flavorless travesty, the equivalent of moldy tofu mystery meat and rancid skim milk."—Stephen Holden, *The New York Times* (regarding the 1998 release of *The Odd Couple II*.)

"This movie has me torn. It's not very good, mostly because it's sort of pointless. The story is flimsy and worn out and ultimately inconsequential. Even comedies should go somewhere, but this one accomplishes nothing. On the other hand, Jack Lemmon and Walter Matthau are a delight, and the script has a copious supply of one-liners. I can't quite recommend the movie, but I can certainly recommend the ever-watchability of the stars. The movie could have been three times as long and not worn out its welcome, which is an 'odd' thing to say about a movie that isn't very good."—Rinkworks.com (regarding the 1998 movie sequel, *The Odd Couple II*).

"*The Odd Couple* was a rare television show, because, like *M*A*S*H*, it was able to equal or surpass the popular film version. Based on Neil Simon's 1965 Broadway hit, the 1968 film gave us Jack Lemmon as the fussy and fastidious Felix Ungar, who moved in with his slovenly and sloppy friend, Oscar Madison (Walter Matthau). But while those two made the perfect oil and water combination, Tony Randall and Jack Klugman settled just as comfortably into their roles as two men recently separated from their wives."—James Plath, *Movie Metropolis* (regarding the season one DVD release).

"Previously only available through a mail order *Time Life* DVD set, *The Odd Couple,* one of the top TV comedies of all time, is now available everywhere through CBS Paramount Video. Presented in the same format as the *Time Life* DVD set, this new CBS Paramount disc set contains all the same bonuses found on the *Time Life* set, as well, but with a substantial addition of a fifth disc containing four classic episodes from the series' four other seasons that were personal favorites of stars Tony Randall and Jack Klugman."—Paul Mavis, DVDTalk.com (regarding the re-release of the season one DVD set, with a bonus disc).

"Coming rapidly after the first season release, CBS DVD and Paramount have put out *The Odd Couple: The Second Season,* a bare bones set of all 23 episodes from the 1971-1972 season. I wrote extensively about the show for the fantastic first season release; this second season release, devoid of any extras, is still quite strong, due mainly to the sensational comedic acting of Tony Randall and Jack Klugman."—Paul Mavis, DVDTalk.com

"Randall and Klugman knock each episode out of the ballpark in this exceptionally strong season. Stability is the name of the game in this third go-round."—Paul Mavis, DVDTalk.com (regarding the release of season three on DVD).

"CBS DVD and Paramount have not abandoned fans in mid-stream, releasing the four-disc 22 episode set, *The Odd Couple: The Fourth Season*—another delightfully witty, energetic season of one of the best sitcoms ever to show up on the airwaves. With only one more season to go, it looks pretty certain dedicated fans of producer Garry Marshall's beloved series won't have to worry about their *Odd Couple* collections being incomplete."—Paul Mavis, DVDTalk.com

"One of television's funniest, classiest, wittiest sitcoms, comes to a fitting close. CBS DVD and Paramount have released *The Odd Couple: The Final Season*, a collection of the last 22 episodes of the series fifth and final 1974–1975 season. A theory that's often trotted out when discussing TV sitcoms stipulates that a show begins to show signs of noticeable decline in or around its fifth season, but *The Odd Couple: The Final Season* is as strong a showing of this delightful, sophisticated comedy as any of the other previous seasons."—Paul Mavis, DVDTalk.com

"The butchering of numerous episodes because of music rights issues is extremely unfortunate, but in this day and age there may be no other reasonable, viable option, which is a pity. But the brilliant performances of Klugman, and especially Randall still shine through such indignities, and this is a great sitcom waiting to be rediscovered and reappraised."—Stuart Galbraith, IV, DVDTalk.com (regarding *The Odd Couple* DVD sets cutting, fading, and replacing certain music because of exorbitant royalties).

"It's just these aren't my episode picks. And they should be my picks. I should be in charge of these things. I should select what's best for you from *The Odd Couple*. And if you think that sounds ridiculously egomaniacal, I'm only writing what you're thinking, too."—Paul Mavis, DVDTalk.com (regarding "Fan Favorites: The Best of *The Odd Couple*" eight episode DVD release).

"When Mr. Lane and Mr. Broderick show up, their self-consciousness tears the time warp. The impression is one of those latter-day sitcoms in which the characters dream they've been beamed into an earlier, vintage television series. Which means the talented stars of this *Odd Couple* are indeed odd men out."—Ben Brantley, *The New York Times*. (Regarding the Nathan Lane/Matthew Broderick *Odd Couple* on Broadway).

"Broderick just doesn't cut it. The 40-year-old *Odd Couple* has not aged terribly well and it doesn't help that its star power has been cut by half. Still, Nathan Lane is so good he could play both parts. Pity he can't tear himself in two."—Roma Torre, *TV One* (regarding the 2005 Nathan Lane/Matthew Broderick Broadway production of *The Odd Couple*).

Awards and Nominations for The Odd Couple

1965—Nominated. Neil Simon, Tony Award for Best Play.

1965—Won. Walter Matthau, Tony Award for Best Performance by a Leading Actor in a Play.

1965—Won. Mike Nichols, Tony Award for Best Direction of a Play.

1968—Won. Walter Matthau, Golden Laurel Award for Male Comedy Performance.
1968—Nominated. Jack Lemmon, Golden Laurel Award for Male Comedy Performance.
1969—Nominated. Frank Bracht, Oscar Award for Best Film Editing.
1969—Nominated. Neil Simon, Oscar Award for Screenplay Based on Material from Another Medium.
1969—Nominated. Frank Bracht, American Cinema Editors (ACE) Award for Best Edited Feature Film.
1969—Nominated. Gene Saks, Director's Guild of America Award for Outstanding Directorial Achievement in Motion Pictures.
1969—Nominated. Neil Simon, Golden Globe Award for Best Motion Picture, Musical or Comedy.
1969—Nominated. Walter Matthau, Golden Globe Award for Best Motion Picture Actor, Musical or Comedy.
1969—Nominated. Jack Lemmon, Golden Globe Award for Best Motion Picture Actor, Musical or Comedy.
1969—Nominated. Neal Hefti, Grammy Award for Best Original Score Written for a Motion Picture.
1969—Won. Neil Simon, Writer's Guild of America (WGA) Award for Best Written American Comedy.
1971—Won. Jack Klugman, Emmy Award for Outstanding Continued Performance by an Actor in a Leading Role in a Comedy Series.
1971—Nominated. Tony Randall, Emmy Award for Outstanding Continued Performance by an Actor in a Leading Role in a Comedy Series.
1971—Nominated. Jerry Belson, Jerry Davis, Garry Marshall, Emmy Award for Outstanding New Series.
1971—Nominated. Jerry Belson, Jerry Davis, Garry Marshall, Emmy Award for Outstanding Series.
1972—Nominated. Bruce Bilson, Director's Guild Award for Outstanding Directorial Achievement in a Comedy Series ("Being Divorced Is Never Having to Say 'I Do'").
1972—Nominated. Jack Klugman, Emmy Award for Outstanding Continued Performance by an Actor in a Leading Role in a Comedy Series.
1972—Nominated. Tony Randall, Emmy Award for Outstanding Continued Performance by an Actor in a Leading Role in a Comedy Series.
1972—Nominated. Jerry Belson, Jerry Davis, Garry Marshall, Emmy Award for Outstanding Series, Comedy.
1972—Nominated. Jack Klugman, Golden Globe Award for Best TV Actor—Musical or Comedy.
1973—Won. Jack Klugman, Emmy Award for Outstanding Continued Performance by an Actor in a Leading Role in a Comedy Series.
1973—Nominated. Tony Randall, Emmy Award for Outstanding Continued Performance by an Actor in a Leading Role in a Comedy Series.
1973—Nominated. Jack Winter, Writer's Guild of America (WGA) Award for Episodic Comedy ("The Pen Is Mightier Than the Pencil").
1974—Won. Jack Klugman, Golden Globe Award for Best TV Actor, Musical or Comedy.

1974—Nominated. Jack Klugman, Emmy Award, Best Lead Actor in a Comedy Series.
1974—Nominated. Tony Randall, Emmy Award, Best Lead Actor in a Comedy Series.
1974—Nominated. Garry Marshall, Tony Marshall, Harvey Miller, Emmy Award, Outstanding Comedy Series.
1975—Nominated. Jack Klugman, Emmy Award, Outstanding Lead Actor in a Comedy Series.
1975—Won. Tony Randall, Emmy Award, Outstanding Lead Actor in a Comedy Series.
2004—Won. Jack Klugman and Tony Randall, TV Land Award, Quintessential Non-Traditional Family.

The Odd Couple *Glossary*

Ace—The alias Felix used to appear young and hip
Albert—The name of Felix's parrot, and also the first name of Felix's grandfather.
Andre La Plume—Oscar's "pen" name for computer dating
Angel Haven—The location of Felix's cemetery plot
Aristophanes—Ridiculous
Arlene Patulski—Miss Rapid Transit of the Month
"Ask for Osc"—One of two campaign slogans when Oscar ran for city council
Assume—An action which makes an "ass" of "u" and "me"
Banana Dragon—The tropical drink Felix had in Hockaloma

Bath Tub—The name of the nude play in which Felix's girlfriend performs
Belkin Airlines—The small airline with the charter flight Felix and Oscar take to Houston
Bengals vs. Jets—The *Monday Night Football* game Oscar co-hosts with Howard Cosell
Beth Olam—the name of the woman accuser in "My Strife in Court," who is named after a Jewish cemetery next to the Paramount lot
"The Big O"—Felix's nickname for Oscar on *The New Odd Couple*
Bill Mazeroski—Hits into a rare triple play while Oscar is on the press box telephone discussing dinner plans (franks and beans) in the 1968 movie
"Blinky"—Oscar's father's nickname
The Bon Vivants—The name of Felix and Oscar's bowling team
"Buckle Down Winsocki"—A public domain song used in numerous episodes, including "The Odd Monks" (that time with different lyrics). The song was also used in a series of safety PSAs on TV in which the lyrics became "Buckle up for safety, buckle up."
Capezios—A brand of ballet shoes
Cecily and Gwendolyn—The first names of the Pigeon Sisters. They are also the names of female characters in *The Importance of Being Earnest* by Oscar Wilde
Chicken complex—Something from which Felix suffers when presented with a win or lose situation
"Chicky"—Mrs. Madison's nickname for her son, Oscar
"Cookie"—Oscar's moonlighting name at Olaf's Diner

Crazy Rhoda Zimmerman—Oscar's emergency, desperation date, never seen on camera

Cuffy Crabbe—The celebrity Felix met in the Hollywood hotel lobby

Dan Jenkins—The other sportscaster with a bit part in Oscar's Hollywood movie

Dean Jones—The actor saved by Silver, the Wonder Dog

Deviated septum—The main cause of Felix's honking

Dew Drop Inn—Where Paul Williams performed in Albany (in the Tippy Toe Room)

Dink Award—The award Felix wins for the Fat-away commercial

Double-O-Seven—The name of the Chihuahua belonging to neighbor boy Phillip

Douglas Dignity—One of Felix's many deluded nicknames for himself

Dr. Berger—The Fat Farm director

E—The letter accidentally typed on Leonard's frog, Max

Easy Unger—Another nickname Felix has for himself

Ein Seltsames Paar—Title of *The Odd Couple* when it played in Germany

Electric Eggplant—The nightclub Felix and Oscar visit to feel younger

F. U. Enterprises—Sign on the door to Felix's photography studio

Fat-away—The weight loss pill in Felix's advertisement

"The fault, dear Brutus, is not in our stars, but in ourselves"—Shakespearean line (*Julius Caesar*, Act I, Scene II) that made the hypnotized slovenly Oscar become neat

Felix "Red River" Unger and the Saddlesores—Felix's country band

52nd Street Irwin—Oscar's bookie; his last name was Weintraub

Flight 306—Felix's last-minute flight to Quebec for a photo shoot

Florence—The cow in Felix's photography studio, also the name of one of Felix's elderly neighbors, and the name of Tony Randall's first wife in real life

Franklin Lang—Theatrical producer for whom Myrna auditions, albeit unsuccessfully

Frederick Ungman—Felix's alias on "Let's Make a Deal"

The Friendly One—Another of Felix's nicknames for himself

GCA—The Glue Corporation of America

Garbage—What linguine becomes when thrown against a wall

The Gerard Ferguson School of Creative Writing—Where Felix took a writing class

Golden Earrings—The name of Felix and Oscar's greyhound, won in a poker game

The Goldfarbs—Oscar and Blanche's attorneys

Goop Mélange—Oscar's special dish

Graphite—Lead

The Gray Tornado—Nickname for Felix's neat freak grandfather

The Great Melman—The magician from whom Oscar learned the milk trick

Hacking around—Hanging around, goofing off

Harem—The name of the magazine by which Oscar was briefly employed

Harry Tallman—Oscar's diminutive racetrack informant

Harvey Hanky—Felix's subway puppet

"Home on the Range"—Oscar's favorite tune, played on the saxophone by Felix as a thank you for saving his life

Home Run Kid—The name of the Hollywood movie in which Oscar is to make his cameo appearance

Hoshina—A new religion requiring one to shave one's head

Huntsman—Felix's role (and later Oscar's role) in *Swan Lake*

"I knew he wouldn't clean it up"—The final line of dialogue of the original series

I'll Bark Tomorrow—The name of Silver, the Wonder Dog's most famous movie (a takeoff on the title of a 1955 Susan Hayward tear-jerker, *I'll Cry Tomorrow*.

"I'm Mad for Madison"—One of two campaign slogans used when Oscar ran for city council

Inane drone—Howard Cosell's nickname for Felix

Inga—A neighbor's sexy maid

Irving Cohen—The late former tenant of apartment 1102, a retired postman

Jersey City Jammers—The roller derby girls Murray picks up (Lulu, Boom Boom, and Chi Chi)

Jessie—The drunk who was very messy, messy, messy

John Barrymore—Felix's favorite actor

Judy Keller—The girl's name whose number is on the wall in the jail cell

Judy Skelton—The name of a character in "Oscar's Birthday," and a real person, a secretary for the program's writing staff

Kali Tihi—"Good luck," in Greek

Kick—The only English word Myrna's blind date knows (pronounced "keek").

King of Fun—One of the delusional nicknames Felix has for himself

The King Pins—The name of the opponents' bowling team

Knockout—The name of the book Oscar attempted to write

Kojeck—The female impersonator in Oscar's barracks

La Comedia e finite—"The comedy is ended" (last line of *Pagliacci*)

La Extrana Pareja—The Odd Couple film's title when shown in Spanish-speaking countries. It translates to "the strange pair."

La Forza Del Destino—The Force of Destiny, an Italian opera by Verdi

Ladle—Not to be confused with a spoon

Lead—Graphite

Leo Furth—The bowling alley manager

"Let's Kiss Kissinger Where He Lives"—The updated version of "Let's Hit Hitler Where He Lives"

Linguini—Not to be confused with spaghetti

Lizzari—The frog bested by Leonard's frog, Max

Ma Gump and her Tumbleweeds—The band that backed out of Billy Joe's hoedown

Mandar—The cologne company that wants to use Oscar in their advertisements. *Mandar* means *command* in Spanish

Max—The name of Leonard's frog (Max-a-Million, one-in-a-million)

Max Greenbaum—The doctor who delivered Oscar Madison

Max's Delicatessen—The name of the deli next to The Fat Farm

Mayonnaise—Something to which Felix is allergic, and something that Abraham Lincoln loved

Midtown Orphanage—Murray's Christmas charity

Miss Needlepoint—Nickname of Felix's grandmother

Mondo Filth—The name of the cinéma vérité film Felix directs about Oscar

Mr. Friend—Felix's teddy bear, still wrapped in its original cellophane

Mr. M.—What Myrna Turner calls her boss

Mr. Mind My Own Business—Another nickname Felix has for himself

Mr. Party Guy—Yet another nickname Felix has for himself

Mrs. Gossert—Lives directly above Felix and Oscar

Mrs. Johnson—Lives directly below Felix and Oscar

Monty's Hall of Memories—The Monty Hall TV talent show on which Oscar and Felix appear

The Murray curl—Murray's distinctive handwriting

961133F—The serial number on Felix's TV set

Omaka Paar—What *The Odd Couple* is called in Sweden

Oscar Madisoy—The way Oscar typed his name in a bet lost to Bobby Riggs

"Oscar, Oscar, Oscar"—Uttered by Felix Unger to express disapproval of his roommate. First heard in the episode, "They Use Horseradish, Don't They?" Also the title of the calypso song Felix performs in Hockaloma

Owah Tagoo Siam—Felix's exorcism chant. All together it's "Oh, what a goose I am"

Ozzie Malone—Oscar's alias on *Let's Make a Deal*

Pahrump, Nevada—The place where Oscar's Hollywood cameo role was to be filmed

Party with a Theme—The kind of birthday party Oscar despises

Peaches—The name of the guard dog at Security Arms

Pits—Something that doesn't belong in one's juice, juice, juice

Plié—A continuous, smooth bending of the knees in ballet

Plot number 204—Felix's chosen gravesite, next to the cellist for the Philharmonic, by the babbling brook and the shade tree

A pony—What Oscar wanted for Christmas as a child, but instead got a rubber ducky

Port de bras—A ballet exercise for the movement of the arms to different positions

"Portraits a Specialty"—A tag line Felix used to describe his photography business

"Prisoner of Love"—The 78 rpm record Felix finds when he's trapped in the basement

Pushover Paige—A used car buyer played by Bella Bruck. Her last name was Livingston

Queen of Hearts—The card missing from the deck in the debut episode

"Really, Fleabag"—A substitute for "Oscar, Oscar, Oscar," uttered by Spiffy in *The Oddball Couple*

Redneck—The winning horse which allowed Felix and Oscar to invest in the Japanese restaurant

Responsibility—Felix says it's his middle name

Ridiculous—Aristophanes

Riggs' Pigs—Bobby Riggs's male-chauvinist club

The Rock with a Heart—What Felix called himself in the army

Sam—The name of the man whose body at the morgue is mistakenly thought to be Felix

San Dominguez—The vacation spot where Felix and Gloria split up

Sarah Morgan—Gloria's alias for the computer-dating service

Sgt. Romero—Murray's superior at the police station

Sherman—The name of the poker-playing clown at Edna's birthday party

Silent Sam—Another of Felix's nicknames for himself

Silver, the Wonder Dog—The name of the collie Felix dognaps

A 602—A domestic squabble

"Skinny"—A nickname many women use for Felix

Slim Daniels—Pro sports team owner, played by Pernell Roberts

Sophisticates/Sophisticatos—Felix's band, consisting of Murray, Al (an interior decorator), Bob (a butcher), Vern (a gynecologist), and Felix. Once called the Unger Five Plus None

Spencer Benedict—Felix's alias when photographing nude models for *Playboy*

Split Carson—The championship bowler with a plot next to Felix's grave

Spring Cola—The product endorsed by Howard Cosell

Sutton—Edna Unger's married surname in *The Odd Couple: Together Again*

Swell Felix—What Felix calls himself after kidnapping Silver, the Wonder Dog

380 Madison Avenue—The address of Felix's photography studio

Tiger—Mildred Fleener's nickname for Felix

"To a Sour Kraut"—The song that won Felix the Silver Canteen award

Tossed Salad—The first horse Felix bet on and won

27604—Murray's badge number

Uncle Sloppy—The nickname given to Oscar by his niece, Martha, and nephew, Timmy

Unger Gum—The brand of bubble gum made by Felix's brother, Floyd, from Buffalo

Vichyssoise—The substance found in Felix's canteen

Wheels Unger—Another of Felix's high school nicknames

Wyoming—A place Felix has never been

WZAZ—The radio station from which Oscar wins a new car

Yawbus—The name of one of the puppies born on the subway (subway spelled backwards)

Zebras—Felix's brother Floyd's lodge brothers in Buffalo

Epilogue

Despite recent unsuccessful network attempts to resurrect TV classics such as *The Bionic Woman, Dragnet, Ironside, Knight Rider, The Munsters,* and *Wonder Woman,* it was announced shortly before this volume went to press that a new "coupling of the odd" was in its gestation period. The instant one hears that this reinvention of the stage, screen and TV classic will star, be produced and co-written by *Friends* alumnus Matthew Perry, one immediately envisions the man who portrayed the nervous, neurotic, fastidious, relationship-challenged and sarcastic Chandler Bing as Felix Unger's ideal heir apparent. However, playing very much against type (a challenge to which many great actors aspire), Perry will instead be fulfilling his lifelong dream of portraying the slovenly, cigar-chomping, nutritionally challenged, sports gambling–obsessed Oscar Madison.

Post-*Friends,* Perry has encountered a rocky road in his quest for another successful episodic series. Although well-conceived and reviewed, *Studio 60 on the Sunset Strip, Go On,* and *Mr. Sunshine* all failed to find an audience. *Mr. Sunshine* was Perry's lone ABC venture—the other two (like *Friends*) were NBC vehicles. *The Odd Couple* will prove to be his first go-round in a starring role for the Tiffany network, CBS (although he did recently have a recurring role as Mike Kresteva on that network's *The Good Wife*). *The Odd Couple* is slated for CBS' fall 2014–spring 2015 schedule after its new Thursday night football contract has been fulfilled. Interestingly, CBS was also the network that produced the 1993 Jack Klugman/Tony Randall TV reunion movie titled *The Odd Couple: Together Again.*

Details, as of this writing, are sketchy. What *is* known is that Perry will pen scripts alongside *Mad About You*'s Danny Jacobson for (Sarah) Timberman/(Carl) Beverly Productions and The (Eric and Kim) Tannenbaum Company. It will mark Perry's return to a multi-camera show with a studio audience (*Go On, Studio 60 on the Sunset Strip,* and *Mr. Sunshine* were all single-camera programs which did not employ a laugh track). After a long delay, names such as Sean Hayes, David Schwimmer and Tony Shalhoub were bandied about as the new Felix Unger, but as of March 2014 Thomas Lennon got the nod. Lennon was seen most recently as Max on the ill-fated *Sean Saves the World* sitcom on NBC, and has accrued a long list of recurring roles on series such as *Reno 911, MDs,* and *Funny or Die Presents.* Lennon has also provided voices for animation (*Mr. Peabody and Sherman, Archer, Bob's Burgers*), and has appeared in popular motion pictures such as *Hot Tub Time Machine, Herbie Fully Loaded,* and *Night at the Museum: Battle of the Smithsonian.* He is also the executive producer of Comedy Central's *At Midnight.* Perry and Lennon are not strangers—they worked together on the 2009 New Line Cinema motion picture *17 Again.*

Perry is no stranger to short-lived series. In the pre–*Friends* era, he co-starred in three—*Second Chance* (1987, as Chazz Russell), *Sydney* (1990, as Billy Kells), and *Home Free* (1993, as Matt Bailey).

Whatever becomes of this new take on the tumultuous twosome, it certainly is nice to know that we and CBS see "eye-to-eye"—*The Odd Couple* premise is proven and timeless. The "can't live with you and can't live without you" concept has no generation gap. Whether one is a baby boomer, gen X-er or millennial, two things remain true—the conflicts of cohabitation are universal, and Aristophanes is, indeed, still ridiculous.

Index

Numbers in ***bold italics*** indicate pages with photographs.

Aames, Willie 21, 54, 192, 193
Abbott and Costello Meet the Invisible Man 125
ABC Afterschool Special 95, 170
ABC Evening News 116
ABC World News 23
Abdo, Nick 4, 133–34, ***134***
Absurd Person Singular 112
Accidental Family 30
According to Jim 84
Ace, Goodman 179
Adam-12 21
Adams, Lillian 191
Adams, Stanley 21–22, 200, 210
Addams, Charles 24
Addams, Gomez 24
The Addams Family 24, 29
Adler, Jerry 16, 47
The Ad-Libbers 80
The Adventures of Hiram Holliday 39
The Adventures of Ozzie and Harriet 89, 136
Ahern, Lassie 206
Ahlberg, Julie Bilson 138
Airport 55, 61
Ajaye, Franklin 219
Alberts, Mal 13, 195
Albertson, Jack 17
The Alcoa Hour 27
Alesia, Frank 190
Alexander, Jason 22, 113
Alf 45
Alfasa, Joseph 200
Alfie 179
Alfred Hitchcock Presents 52, 114, 125
Alias Smith and Jones 91
Alice 39, 106, 114, 139, 143, 167
The All-American Girl 153

All Grown Up 56
All in the Family 46, 56, 57, 64, 65, 68, 78, 96, 103, 108, 113, 118, 119, 120, 129, 140, 158, 159, 164, 165, 168, 181
All My Children 107
All the President's Men 113
Allen, Steve 84
Allman, Elvia 201
All's Fair 159
Ally McBeal 78
Alpert, Herb 190
Altman, Robert 108, 109
Alvin and the Chipmunks: The Squeakquel 59
Amen 56, 64
American Bandstand 35
American Buffalo 73
American Graffiti 131
American Music Awards 35
Amos, John 106
Amsterdam, Morey 32
Anderson, Sheila 15, 48, 215, 217, 218, 219
Andrews, Tina 22, 210, 212
The Andromeda Strain 66
The Andy Griffith Show 34, 42, 68, 95, 116, 124, 135, 136, 138, 146, 151, 152, 153, 167, 175, 187
Angel 29, 56
Angel in My Pocket 148
Angelos, Bill 134, 157, 203, 206, 212
The Angel's Perch 125
Angie 151, 153, 161, 162
The Ann Sothern Show 5, 120, 163
Another World 62
The Ant and the Aardvark 31, 146
Antony and Cleopatra 98
Any Wednesday 88

Any Which Way You Can 66
The Apartment 80, 128
Apollo 13 68, 127
The Apple Dumpling Gang 113
The Apple Dumpling Gang Rides Again 127
Appointment with Adventure 11, 75, 128, 229
The April Fools 33, 40, 52
Arbus, Allan 23, 205, 208
Archer 248
The Archer 32
Archie 63
Arcola, Chachi 162, 188
Are You with It? 46
Argenziano, Carmen 217
The Aristocats 48, 110, 112
Arledge, Roone 13, 23, 168, 211
Armstrong, Louis 139
Armus, Sidney 7, 102
Arnie 103, 153, 165
Arroyo, Martina 13, 23–24, 168, 171, 211
Arthur, Bea 164, 175
Arthur Godfrey's Talent Scouts 38, 39
As the World Turns 124
Asher, William 163
Astaire, Fred 175
Astin, John 24, 52, 190
At Midnight 248
At War with the Army 73
Atterbury, Malcolm 205
Avery, Val 205
Awakenings 84

Babes in Arms 141
Baby Boom 179
Baby Doll 152
Baby, I'm Back 129
Baby's Day Out 27
Bachelor Father 5, 89
Backdraft 68
The Bad News Bears 86
Baer, Art 134–35, 153, 196, 206, 208
The Baileys of Balboa 68, 138
Baldwin, Therese 187
Ball, Lucille 61
Ball, Robert 197
Balsam, Martin 11, 75, 124
Banacek 52
Bananas 170
Baranski, Christine 24–25, 115
Barasch, Norman 135, 217
Barbour, John 13, 210
Barefoot in the Park 6, 7, 9, 11, 26, 27, 47, 101, 121, 151, 160, 166, 167, 174, 179, 180, 181, 185
Barella, Vinnie 225
Baretta 70, 121
Barnaby Jones 81
Barney Google 134

Barney Miller 15, 26, 54, 56, 78, 109, 114, 117, 118, 119, 160, 182
Baron, Sandy 160, 163, 177
Barr, Leonard 25, 173, 208, 212
Barr, Marlene 204
Barrett, Rona 13, 25, 208
Barrie, Barbara 16, 25–26
Barris, Chuck 93
Basie, Count 151
Batanides, Arthur 26, 197, 207
Batfink 140
Bath Tub 190, 241
Batman 10, 30, 32, 35, 53, 64, 65, 89, 140, 152, 170
Battle of the Bulge 66, 91
"The Battle of the Sexes" 74, 104, 204
Baum, Bobby 186, 195
Beaches 46, 78, 134, 139, 161
The Beatles 190
The Beauty Part 56
Because They're Young 35, 89
Bedtime for Bonzo 125
Beetle Bailey 134
Beir, Fred 147
Bell, Harrison "Tinker" 108
Belson, Ed 189
Belson, Gordon 135
Belson, Jerry 11, 15, 83, 103, 120, 135–36, 144, 145, 149, 155, 160, 161, 164, 165, 169, 177, 178, 185, 187, 188, 189, 190, 194, 197, 202, 217, 240
Ben Casey 37, 97, 160, 170
Bennett, Tony 139, 151
Benny, Jack 54, 94, 169
Bensfield, Dick 136, 187, 191, 192, 193, 195, 199, 208, 217
Benson 15, 69
Bergen, Edgar 129
Berle, Milton 33
Bernard, Fred 140, 212
The Best Little Whorehouse in Texas 116
The Betty White Show 127
Betty White's Off Their Rockers 42, 102, 128
Beverly, Carl 248
The Beverly Hillbillies 53, 89, 103
Bewitched 39, 56, 69, 76, 84, 95, 112, 128, 146, 152, 163, 165
Bibleman 21
Big 84, 107, 182
The Big Bounce 160
The Big Bus 51
Big Eddie 108
Big John, Little John 47
Big Mouth 106
"The Big Mouth" 38, 82, 135, 149, 153, 196
The Big Valley 66, 98
The Bill Dana Show 66, 160
Bill Idelson's Writing Class 152

INDEX • 251

Billy Budd 66
Billy Elliott 112
Billy Jack 94
Biloxi Blues 28, 174, 180
Bilson, Bruce 4, 136–37, *137*, 185, 186, 187, 188, 193, 240
Bilson, Daniel 138
Bilson, Rachel 138
Bing, Chandler 247
The Bing Crosby Show 170
The Bionic Six 148
The Bionic Woman 116
The Birdcage 77
The Birds 98
Birnbaum, Robert 138–39, 181, 195, 196, 199, 205
Bishop, Kelly 218
Bishop, Mel 200, 205
B.J. and the Bear 113
Blair, Linda 49
Blake, Timothy 186
Blansky's Beauties 93, 153, 161
Blondie 49, 63, 93
Blossom 107
The Blue Knight 95, 104
Bob & Carol & Ted & Alice 54
The Bob Crane Show 39, 63, 140
The Bob Newhart Show 33, 39, 50, 54, 56, 59, 68, 69, 94, 106, 124, 140, 152, 167, 168, 175, 181
Bob's Burgers 248
Bochco, Stephen 109
Boles, Jim 198, 208
Bonanza 6, 26, 37, 53, 88, 90, 91, 98, 105, 112, 125
Bonino 73, 117
Bonnell, Vivian 199
Borel, Annik 192
Borge, Victor 134
Bosom Buddies 67, 230
The Boston Strangler 73, 112, 181
Boy Meets World 78
Bracken, Eddie 7, 8, *8*, 27
Bradley, Bart 28
The Brady Bunch 22, 59, 89, 127, 139, 141, 143, 152, 159, 163
The Brady Bunch Movie 58
Brando, Marlon 39
Brandt, Janet 204
Brandt, Victor 203
Braverman, Bart 15, 27–29, *215*, 216, 217, 219, 229
Braverman, Herb 28
Breaking Away 26
Bridget Loves Bernie 95, 146, 181
Brigadoon 139
Brighton Beach Memoirs 28, 124, 174, 180
Broadway Bound 22, 77, 180

Brocco, Peter 187, 189
Broderick, Matthew 22, 28, 53, 77, 110, 113, 126, 235, 239
Brooklyn Bridge 125
Brooks, Albert 29, 52, 136, 187
Brooks, Richard 114
Brooks Atkinson Theatre 28, 77, 126, 235
Brothers 95
The Brothers 159
Brother's Keeper 16, 17, 230
Bruce, Lenny 119
Bruck, Bella 29, 199, 200, 201, 203, 205, 244
Brunner, Bob 139, 197, 198, 201, 203
Bucket List 103
Buddy Buddy 88
Buffalo Bill 50, 154
Bugs Bunny 146, 163, 181
The Bugs Bunny/Road Runner Hour 163
The Bugs Bunny Show 55, 146
Bullitt 96
Bumstead, Blondie 63
Bunny Lake Is Missing 189
Buono, Victor 29–30, 45, 204, 205, 211, 229
Burnett, Carol 179
Burns, George 27, 62
Burr, Fritzi 209, 211
Burstein, Rona 25
Burton, Richard 166
Busting Loose 27, 57, 104, 108, 144, 174, 196, 218
BUtterfield 8 88
Buxton, Frank 81, 139–40, 198, 200, 204, 205, 206, 208, 210, 211, 212
Bye, Bye Birdie 96, 139
Byner, John 4, 30–32, *30*, 175, 203, 210

Cactus Flower 110, 174
Caesar, Sid 5, 153, 171, 179
Caesar's Hour 5, 179
Caged Heat 51
Cagney and Lacey 78, 95, 139
Cahn, Sammy 10, 19, 152
The Caine Mutiny 166
California Split 51
California Suite 47, 87, 180
Callan, Michael 63
Camp Runamuck 170
Candid Camera 128, 153
Cannon 54, 106, 124
A Cannon for Cordoba 61
Capitol 62
Captain Kangaroo 167
Captain Nice 46, 56, 144
Captain Video and His Video Rangers 63
Car 54, Where Are You? 56, 61, 68, 84, 108, 135, 153, 171
The Cara Williams Show 152
Carmen 67, 206

252 • INDEX

Carney, Art 7, 27, 32, 45, 84, 86, 87, 99, 102, 153, 166
The Carol Burnett Show 72, 134, 135, 153, 156, 157
Caroline in the City 143
Caron, Sandra 193
Carousel 127
The Carpenters 128
Carroll, Janice 33, 187, 192
Carrott, Ric 198
Carson, Johnny 171
Carter, Jack 4, 11, 33, 75, 111, 168, 211, 235
Carter Country 88
Casablanca 97
Cassidy, Shaun 54
Castle 28
Catch Me if You Can 88
Cavalcade of Stars 32, 33
Cavett, Dick 13, 34, 211
Chaplin, Charlie 85
Chapter Two 102, 176, 180
Charles in Charge 21
Charley the Tuna 142
Charlie Lawrence 77
Charlie Wilson's War 101
Charly 84
Chase, Chevy 175
The Cheap Detective 29
Checco, Al 102
Cheers 126
Cheng, Jennifer 202
Cheyenne 97
Chico and the Man 39, 135, 143, 147
Chiffon Margarine 197
The China Syndrome 80
Chiniquy, Gerry 140, 213
CHiPs 80, 106
A Christmas Carol 147, 188
Christopher, William 34, 48, 235
Churchill, Winston 102
Cimarron City 91
Cinderella Man 68, 84
City Slickers 150
Clark, Dick 13, 31, 35, 203
Clark, Hope 218
Clark, Roy 35–36, 127, 164, 187, 212, 229
Clayton, Bob 135
Clemente, Roberto 10
Climax 27
Clinton, Bill 126, 158, 180
Clinton, Jack R. 210
Close Encounters of the Third Kind 52, 116
Close Up 143
Clute, Sidney 200
Cohan, Martin 140, 193, 195
Colby, Barbara 120, 193
Coleman, Dabney 154
Colen, Beatrice 36, 206, 208

Collins, Jack 197, 206
Colt .45 26
Columbo 106, 124
Come Blow Your Horn 6, 11, 27, 61, 179
Comedy Minus One 29
Coming of Age 45
Company 26, 52
Constantine, Michael 36, 176, 189
Conway, Curt 36–37, 192, 200, 204, 207
Conway, Tim 82, 119
Cook, Doris 204
Cook, Elisha 209
Cookus Interruptus 140
Cooper, Hal 141, 185, 186, 190, 191, 192, 193, 194, 195, 197, 199
Copeland, Alan Weaver 37
Copland, Ronda 194, 198
Corb, Marty 206
Corby, Ellen 37–38, 190
Corsentino, Frank 164, 192
Cosby 154
The Cosby Show 158, 159, 175
Cosell, Emmy
Cosell, Howard 13, 23, 24, 34, 38, 135, 149, 164, 168, 196, 211, 241, 243, 245
Country Girl 117
The Courtship of Eddie's Father 21, 88, 141, 143, 155, 165, 170
Cox, Wally 38–39, 44, 73, 98, 196, 197
CPO Sharkey 115
Crenna, Richard 74
Cronyn, Hume 65, 100
Crosby, Bing 27, 37, 53, 66
Crosby, Joan 13, 210
Crosby, Peggy 76
Crothers, Scatman 39, 209
Crusader Rabbit 181
CSI: New York 143
Cue the Bunny on the Rainbow 167
Cunningham, Dr. Nancy 14, 67, 147, 188, 189, 190, 191, 192, 193, 222, 225
Curb Your Enthusiasm 23, 40, 45, 119
Currie, Sondra 205
Curtis, Dick 208
Cutell, Lou 4, 39–42, **40**
Cybill 25, 119

Daffy Duck 181
Dailey, Dan 27, 141, 202, 206, 235
Daitch, Barbara A. 202
Dallas 122
Dallas Cowboys 196
The Dallas Symphony 81
Damn Yankees 163
Daniel Boone 162
The Danny Kaye Show 124, 135, 146
The Danny Thomas Show 5, 160, 161, 175
Darin, Bobby 135

Darnell, Nani 212
Dastardly and Muttley 130
A Date with the Angels 127
Dave's World 78
Davey, John 201
The David Steinberg Show 119
Davis, Bette 30, 151
Davis, Jerry 83, 125, 137, 142, 145, 146, 155, 177, 240
Davis, Madelyn Pugh 145
Davis, Phyllis Elizabeth 205
Dawson, Peter 185, 193
Dawson, Richard 13, 42, 164, 212, 228
Day, Doris 98, 135, 143, 151
The Day After 159
The Days of Wine and Roses 80, 229
Dealer's Choice 64
Dean, Fabian 185
Dean, James 181
The Dean Martin Celebrity Roasts 82
The Dean Martin Show 25
DeAnda, Guillermo 193
Death Becomes Her 107, 144
Death of a Salesman 166
Death Valley Days 34, 141
DeBecque, Emile 121
Decoy 57
Dee, Sandra 135
Deegan, Homer 225
DeFarra, Louis 188
DeFazio, Frank 51
DeFazio, Laverne 83
The Defenders 36, 52, 68, 75, 160
Defending Your Life 29
Delfino, Frank 198
Delfino, Sadie 198
Delvecchio 70
Delvecchio, Al 90, 91
DePatie, David H. 10, 31, 55, 130, 140, 142, 146, 163, 237
Derns, Denise 202
Designing Women 56, 115, 119
Desk Set 88, 89
Desperate Housewives 45, 90
Detroit, Nathan 77
Deutch, Howard 17, 41, 62, 142–43
DeWolfe, Billy 93
Dexter, Alan 208
Diagnosis: Murder 105
Diamond, Don 211
Diamond, Selma 145
Diamonds Are Forever 25
Dick, Peggy Chantler 145
The Dick Cavett Show 34, 211
Dick Clark's New Year's Rockin' Eve 35
The Dick Tracy Show 181
The Dick Van Dyke Show 1, 13, 21, 26, 29, 39, 49, 66, 78, 82, 89, 95, 96, 103, 114, 120, 125, 135, 141, 148, 150, 152, 153, 154, 155, 160, 165, 166, 167, 181
Dickens, Charles 147, 188
Diff'rent Strokes 114, 136, 139, 141, 159, 165
Dillon, Matt 74
Discovery 139
The District 63
Doc 68, 154
Doc Hollywood 68
Dr. Kildare 26, 36, 37, 88, 95, 97
The Doctors 63
"Does Your Mother Know You're Out, Cecilia?" 192
Dolan, Harry 188
Don Carlos 121
Donahue, Elinor 4, 13, 30, 42–44, **43**, 195, 196, 198, 199, 200, 201, 202, 203, 204, 206, 209, 211, 221
Donald, Peter 80
The Donna Reed Show 61, 125, 167
Donohue, Jack 143, 192, 193, 194, 195, 198, 199, 204, 205, 212
Donovan, Martin 143, 209, 211
Dooley, Paul 27, 45
Doran, Ann 194
The Doris Day Show 76, 88, 106, 148, 155, 165, 176, 181
Douglas, Ronalda 15, 48, **215**, 218, 219
Doyle, Peggy 191, 207
Dragnet 39, 97, 125, 247
Dream On 45
The Drew Carey Show 50, 136
"Drift Away" 129
Duck Dodgers 55
Duckman 24
Ducktales 55
Duclon, David W. 144, 169, 187, 192, 199, 200, 210, 212
Dulo, Jane 186, 197, 202, 229
DuMont Network 32, 33
Duncan, Lee 205
Duncan, Sandy 155
Dungeons and Dragons 140
Dunn, Liam 46, 203
Durkin, Jannis 205
Dusay, Marj 190
Duteil, Jeffrrey 217, 219

Earthquake 87
East Side, West Side 152
Easy Aces 179
Eat My Dust 51
The Ed Sullivan Show 30, 160
The Ed Wynn Show 143
Edelman, Herb 10, 46–47, 90, 101, 102, 109, 124
Eight Is Enough 21, 95, 124
87th Precinct 62

254 • INDEX

Eilbacher, Cindy 193
Einfeld, Dick 76
Einstein, Albert 29
Elder, Ann 47, 115, 176, 185
The Elephant Man 112
Eli Sparkle Meets Christmas the Horse 49
Elias, Michael 203
Elliott, Peggy 144–45, *145*
Ellsworth, Allen Packard 81
Elmer Gantry 114
Emm, Colin Lionel 42
Emmich, Cliff 199, 210
Empty Nest 39, 88
Encore Encore 77
The End 33, 135
Esquire Magazine 64
Esther the whiner 56
Ethel and Albert 187
Eubanks, Bob 93
The Eugene O'Neill Theatre 8, 65, 87
European Vacation 154
Evans, Mary Jane 202
Evans, Monica 7, 13, 47, 50, 112, 185, 186, 187
Even Steven 101
Evening Shade 56, 107
An Evening with Carol Channing 153
An Evening with Nichols and May 101
Evens, Bill 180
"Evergreen" 129
Everybody Loves Raymond 14, 53, 78
The Exorcist 49, 205

F Troop 29
The Facts of Life 88, 129, 159
Family Affair 54, 82, 124
Family Feud 42
Family Guy 132
Family Man 90
Family Matters 67, 96, 107, 144, 182
Family Ties 28, 113
Fangface 28
The Fantastic Four 142, 148
Fantasy Island 80
Faraday and Company 141
Farge, Annie 29
The Farmer's Daughter 52, 66, 95
Farquhar, Ralph 217, 219
Farr, Jamie 34, 48, 235
Father Knows Best 21, 42, 97, 196
Father of the Bride 113, 179
Faulkner, Edward 204
Fay 154
Faye, Herbie 48–49, 188, 193, 195, 197, 204, 211, 229
The FBI 66, 88, 124
Feld, Fritz 211
Fell, Norman 62
Femia, John 136

Ferber, Mel 93, 192, 195, 197, 199, 203, 206, 208, 210
Ferdin, Pamelyn 49, 95, 189, 193, 195, 198
Ferguson, Craig 49–50, 235
A Few Good Men 103
Fiedler, John 50, 130, 194, 208
Field, Filip 50, 209, 210, 211
Fields, Kim 129
Fields, W.C. 120, 162
Finley, Greg 216
Firestone, Roy A. 216
First and Ten 156
The First Family 32
Fish 119, 135
Fisher, Al 207
Fisher, Eddie 223
Fitzgerald, Ella 37
Five Easy Pieces 118, 119
"The $500 Joke" 172
The Flamingo Kid 74, 161
Fleabag 15, 55, 94, 129, 130, 140, 146, 213, 214, 237, 244
The Flight of the Phoenix 176, 185
The Flintstones 94, 125
The Flip Wilson Show 35, 134
Flippen, Ruth Brooks 186
Flower Drum Song 117
Fonda, Henry 75
Fonda, Jane 9
Foofur 94
Ford, Anitra 187
Ford Television Theater 91
Forget Paris 150
The Fortune Cookie 7, 10, 34, 49, 75, 80, 86, 88
Foster, Phil 51, 57, 160, 211, 235
Fox, Mickey 51, 198, 205, 208, 211
Foxx, Redd 69, 93
Fractured Phrases 135, 153
Franciosa, Tony 117
Francis, Ivor 191
Frankie and Johnny 134, 139
Freaky Deaky 87
Fredricks, Richard 51–52, 147, 171, 192
Free Country 164
Freleng, Friz 55, 140, 142, 145–46
Fresco, David 193
Frey, Nat 7
Friedman, Ron 4, 146–48, 187, 188, 191, 192, 195, 202
Friendly Persuasion 163
Friends 10, 14, 107, 119, 230, 247, 248
The Frisco Kid 95
Fritzell, Jim 148, 151, 193
Frommer, Ben 186
The Front Page 80, 88, 113
The Fugitive 14, 26, 37, 53, 98
Full House 182

Fun in Acapulco 52
Fun with Dick and Jane 57, 135
Funny Face 155, 170
Funny Lady 95, 113
Funny Manns 95
Funny or Die Presents 248
A Funny Thing Happened on the Way to the Forum 77, 110, 111
Funt, Allen 190
Furlong, Kirby 210
Furth, George 52, 125, 138, 186, 205
Fury, Edward 192
Futurama 10

Gae, Frances 206
Gale, Paul 198
Gallant Men 115, 170
Ganz, Lowell 4, 57, 90, 92, 104, 108, 141, 148–50, 160, 169, 171, 196, 199, 200, 202, 203, 205, 206, 209, 210, 216, 217, 218
Gardner, Dee 52, 187, 190, 192, 195
Garfield and Friends 94, 147
Garland, Beverly 170
Garland, Judy 27, 158
Garner, James 120
Garr, Teri 52–53, 205
Garrett, Brad 53
Garrett, Eddie 53, 203, 206, 209, 210, 211
Garrett, Leif 28, 54, 193, 208, 212
Garroway, Dave 95
Garroway at Large 95
Gazzaniga, Don 206
G.E. College Bowl 81
Geib, Lark 202
Gelman, Larry 13, 50, 54, 101, 102, 185, 186, 187, 188, 190, 192, 194, 202, 207
General Hospital 88, 97
Gentle Ben 68
Gentlemen's Agreement 37
George of the Jungle 181
Gerber, Joan 15, 55, 213
Gerritsen, Lisa 55, 189
Get Shorty 110
Get Smart 26, 31, 46, 73, 77, 89, 90, 96, 97, 114, 136, 146, 152, 165, 175, 181
Get the Message 139, 198, 201
Getting By 67
Getting Together 154, 160
Ghost 78
The Ghost and Mr. Chicken 148, 151
The Ghost and Mrs. Muir 56, 82, 103, 111, 112, 144, 146, 159, 164, 175, 176, 181, 204
Ghostley, Alice 41, 55–56, 62, 186, 229
Ghosts of Mississippi 118
G.I. Joe 148
Gibby 152
Gibson, Virginia 139
Gidget 61, 141

Gifford, Frank 168, 169
Gifford, Gloria 218
Giles, Sandra 204
Gillespie, Dizzy 165
Gillespie, Jean 212
Gilligan's Island 159, 170
Gilmore Girls 119, 121
Gim, H.W. 195
Gimme a Break 46, 57, 67, 78, 114
Girl Happy 50
Girlfight 57
The Girl's Guide to Chaos 107
Glass, Ron 15, 28, 182–83, *183*, 215
The Glass Bottom Boat 29
Gleason, Jackie 7, 32, 33, 200, 216
Glengarry Glen Ross 80
Glimscher, Herman 152
Go On 247
Gobel, George 52, 57, 235
The Godfather 57, 110, 199
Godfrey, Arthur 39
God's Pocket 125
The Golden Girls 39, 46, 47, 118, 127, 175, 230
Goldman, Hal 208
Goldwyn, Samuel, Jr. 145, 177
Gomer Pyle, USMC 26, 33, 49, 85, 103, 135, 152, 153, 155, 164, 165, 167
The Gong Show 93
The Gong Show Movie 93
The Good Guys 47, 55, 61, 124, 125
Good Heavens 166
The Good Life 165
Good Morning, America 25
Good Morning, World 120
The Good, the Bad, and the Garlic 101
Good Times 22, 106, 116, 136, 165
The Good Wife 25, 125, 247
"Goodbye, Farewell and Amen" 170
The Goodbye Girl 27, 100, 104, 113, 180
Goodman, Benny 165
Goodwin, Doug 15, 213
Gordon, Al 208
Gottlieb, Carl 150, 210
Gough, Lloyd 187
Gould, Sid 206
The Governor and J.J. 39, 97, 141, 167, 181
Grace Under Fire 45, 154
The Graduate 56
Granger, Stewart 114
Grant, Perry 136, 208, 217
The Grapes of Wrath 65, 97
Grapey, Marc 126
The Grass Harp 86, 88
Gray, Dobie 129
Gray, Norm 151, 204, 209, 211, 212
Grease 56
The Great Impostor 73, 128
The Great Race 114

The Greatest Story Ever Told 30
Green Acres 89, 93, 97, 112
The Green Hornet 26
Green Pastures 129
Greenbaum, Everett 148, 151, 193
Greenbaum, Max 221, 243
Greene, Shecky 163
Gregory, Dick 163
Greshler, Abbey 3, 102, 198, 230
Greshler, Francine 198
Griffith, Andy 34, 48, 89, 148
Groome, Malcolm 216
Grumpier Old Men 88
Grumpy Old Men 80, 88
Guestward Ho 29, 33
Gulf Playhouse 27
Gung Ho 68, 150, 170
Gunsmoke 21, 26, 46, 54, 55, 125
Guss, Louis 57, 199, 200, 204, 210, 211
Guys and Dolls 77, 113, 114
Gwynne, Fred 110
Gypsy 75, 83

Hackensack to Hollywood 165
Hackett, Buddy 5, 73, 179
Hahn, Archie 4, 57–59, **58**, 202
Haines, Larry 10
Hal Roach Studios 162
Half-and-Half 67
Hall, Monty 59–61, **60**, 158, 164, 200, ***201***, 206, 221, 244
Hallin, Ronny 83, 161, 207
Hamlet 68, 114, 208, 224
Hangin' with Mr. Cooper 153
Hansen, Janis 14, 61, 191, 192, 194, 195, 197, 198, 202, 203, 205, 207, 230
"Happy and Peppy and Bursting with Love" 92, 93, 131, 157, 204
Happy Days 1, 12, 14, 26, 36, 73, 82, 90, 91, 94, 96, 106, 111, 113, 120, 127, 134, 135, 136, 139, 144, 150, 151, 152, 153, 158, 159, 161, 162, 163, 164, 166, 171, 172, 174, 176, 181, 188, 207, 208
The Happy Ending 114
Harlan, Heather 99
The Harlem Globetrotters Show 39
Harmon, Joy 199
Harold 50
Harper, Ron 4, 61–62
Harper Valley PTA 142
Harris, Estelle 41, 62
Harris, Phil 39
Harris Against the World 75
Harry and Tonto 33, 57, 95, 104
Harry's Law 143
Hart, Tricia 63, 202
Hartley, Ted 89
Harty, Patricia 63, 202

Hastings, Bob 63–64, 199
Have Gun, Will Travel 105
Hawaii Five-0 23, 124
Hawaiian Eye 91, 142, 170
Hawn, Goldie 144, 164, 175
Hayes, Sean 248
Head 52
Heaven Can Wait 69
Heaven for Betsy 80
Hefner, Hugh 13, 64, 168, 207
Hefti, Neal 10, 15, 19, 151–52, 240
Hell Is for Heroes 73
Hello, Larry 136
Hemingway, Ernest 117, 121
Hemsley, Sherman 64–65, 93, 235
Henderson, Cindy 193
Henderson, Wendell 161
Hennesey 29, 163
Hepburn, Katharine 88
Herbert, Tim 192
Herbie Fully Loaded 248
Herbie Rides Again 115
Herbie, the Love Bug 63
Here's Lucy 49, 88, 114, 127, 162
Herman, Woody 151
Hesseman, Howard 58, 151
Hey, Jeannie 46
Hey! Landlord 33, 36, 73, 85, 94, 103, 120, 144, 150, 153, 155, 160, 164, 177, 181, 189, 199, 230
Hickman, Darryl 65, 103, 235
The High and the Mighty 97
High Anxiety 118
Hiken, Nat 171
Hines, Shelly 210
Hingle, Pat 7, 65, 73
His Girl Friday 97
History of the World, Part One 114
Hitchcock, Alfred 98, 138, 224
Hobbs, Peter 65–66, 195, 209, 210, 211
Hoffman, Bob 199
Hoffman, Phillip Seymour 125
Hogan's Heroes 42, 85, 95, 135, 153
The Hollywood Squares 39, 47, 57
Holm, Celeste 73
Holmes and Yoyo 109
Home Alone 2: Lost in New York 27
Home Free 248
Honestly, Celeste 73
The Honeymooners 14, 32, 33, 149, 199
Hong Kong Phooey 39
Hope, Bob 13, 27, 66, 158, 162, 208
Hopkins, Kenyon 152
Hopkins, Telma 15, 66, 216, 218
Horne, Lena 218
Horne, Marilyn 13, 67, 134, 141, 157, 171, 206
Horten, Rena 190
Hot in Cleveland 100, 124, 128, 230

Hot Tub Time Machine 248
Hotchkis, Joan 67–68, 147, 188, 189, 190, 191, 192, 193
Hotel 160
Hound, Goldie 15, 55, 213
House Calls 86, 142
How Sweet It Is 83, 120, 161
How the Grinch Stole Christmas 68
How the West Was Won 54
How to Succeed in Business without Really Trying 33, 65, 102
Howard, Bob 212
Howard, Clint 33, 68, 187
Howard, Ron 138
H.R. Pufnstuf 55
Hud 37
Hudson, Kate 85
Hudson, Rock 98, 135
The Huffington Post 145
Huge 45
Hughes, Barnard 68–69
Hughes, John 142
The Hughleys 67
Hunter 113
Hunter, Blake 140
Hush...Hush Sweet Charlotte 30
The Hustler 21, 22, 33, 57, 69, 127, 152, 172, 182, 200, 216
Huston, Walter 65
Hutchins, Will 160, 175
Hutton, Betty 27, 162
Hutton, E.F. 88
Hutton, Nedenia Marjorie 88

I Dream of Jeannie 61, 95, 96, 136, 141, 167, 170, 231
I Love Lucy 28, 89, 94, 125, 145, 166, 175
I Love My Wife 174
I Love You, Alice B. Toklas 96
I Ought to Be in Pictures 87, 125
I Remember Mama 37, 123
"I Was Made for Dancing" 54
Idelson, Bill 152, 188, 191, 192, 195, 196, 208
Idol, Billy 142
Ignatowski, Jim 30
I'm Dickens, He's Fenster 24, 73
I'm Not Garbo 174
Ingels, Marty 24
Inherit the Wind 132
Inside Comedy 119
The Inspector 146
The Invaders 112
Iron Man 148
Ironside 39, 52, 53, 98, 106, 247
Irreconcilable Differences 179
Isaac, John 218
Ish, Kathryn 118, 125
Ishimoto, Dale 195

Island of Love 86
It Happened at the World's Fair 98
It's a Wonderful Life 37, 77
It's Garry Shandling's Show 136, 154, 167

The Jack Benny Program 89, 95, 96, 114, 125
The Jackie Gleason Show 32
Jackie Gleason's American Scene Magazine 84
Jacobson, Danny 248
Jake's Women 125
James, Alice 206, 208
James, Art 135
James at 16 95
Jankowitz, Walter 188
Jaress, Jill 69, 200, 216
Jarrett, Renne 138
Jarvis, Graham 210
The Jaye P. Morgan Show 92
The Jean Arthur Show 62
Jefferson, Joseph 101
The Jeffersons 64, 106, 108, 125, 144, 165, 181
The Jetsons 192
JFK 80
Joanie Loves Chachi 90, 162, 188
Joel, Billy 157
Joelson, Ben 134, 135, 152–53, 196, 206, 208
The Joey Bishop Show 5, 35, 46, 49, 73, 82, 114, 135, 154, 160
The John Forsythe Show 49, 82
The John Larroquette Show 78, 121
Johnny Bravo 24
Johnny Midnight 26
Johnson, Arch 195
Johnson, Bruce 153
Johnson, Gretchen 42
Johnson, Keg 191
Johnson, Lyndon Baines 6
Johnston, Audrey 117
Jones, Cleon 10
Jones, Davy 22
Jones, Deacon 13, 69, 159, 197
Jones, Jerry 187
Jordan, Bobbi 201
Jordan, George 206, 208
Joy, Christopher 4, 15, 69–70, **70**, **215**, 216, 219
Joyce, Elaine 180
Judd for the Defense 98
Juilliard School of Music 24, 52, 97, 121
Julian, Arthur 192
Jumpin' Jack Flash 83

Kaczynski, Ted 182
Kalcheim, Lee 202, 216
Kaprall, Bo 4, 36, 70–72, **71**, 207, 208
The Karate Kid 94
Karen 75, 77
Karras, Alex 63, 72, 174, 202, 203, 211

Karras, Endy 54
Kate and Allie 107, 231
Kazurkinsky, Tim 235
Kean, Jane 32
Keller, Sheldon 153–54
Kellin, Mike 7, 73
Kelly, Gene 27
Kelly, Gerard 235
Kennedy, Madge 194
"Kennedy Center Honors" 24, 126
Kent, Allan 186
Kent, Larry 190
Ketchum, Dave 73, 190, 192
Killers Three 35
King, Alan 163
King, Ben E. 165
King, Billie Jean 13, 74, 104, 143, 171, 204
King, Jennifer 208
King, Larry 74
King Creole 87
King Tut 30
Kino, Lloyd 207
Kirk, Mimi 202
Kiss My Face 44, 172, 200
Kissin' Cousins 52
Klane, Robert 16, 154
Klein, Dennis 154, 199, 201
Kleinschmitt, Carl 4, 154–56, *155*, 178, 186
Klugman, Adam 74, 205, 209, 210
Knievel, Evel 80
Knight Rider 121, 159, 247
Knighty Knight Bugs 146
Knots Landing 47, 122
Knotts, Don 102, 148, 151
Knute Rockne, All-American 97
Kohan, Buz 4, 134, 156–58, *157*, 203, 206, 212
Kojak 37, 39, 51, 121
Komack, James 93
Kopell, Bernie 52, 76–77, 147, 195
Kraft Music Hall 135
Kraft Playhouse 75
Kraft Theater 174
Kramden, Ralph 7, 32
Kranepool, Ed 10
Krupa, Gene 21, 165
Kruschen, Jack 11, 75, 218
Kurtzman, Harvey 101
Kutcher, Ashton 107

Ladies' Man 47
"The Lady in Red" 66
Lamarr, Hedy 91
Lamour, Dorothy 66
Lampkin, Charles 197
Lancelot Link: Secret Chimp 55
Lander, Diane 180
Landry, Clarence 205

Lane, Charles 46, 77, 201
Lane, Nathan 22, 28, 53, 77, 126, 235, 239
Lansing, Robert 62
Lansing, Stan 161
Larroquette, John 77–78, 100, 121, 235
The Larry Sanders Show 78, 107, 154
Lassie 126
Last of the Red Hot Lovers 6, 29, 80, 151, 174
The Late Show with David Letterman 53
Laughter on the 23rd Floor 27, 77
Laurel and Hardy 162
Laverne and Shirley 1, 51, 59, 71, *71*, 72, 82, 83, 108, 118, 120, 134, 136, 139, 144, 150, 151, 159, 161, 162, 163, 164, 167, 172, 174, 182, 207, 212, 231
Law and Order 62
Leach, Britt 190, 203
A League of Their Own 84, 150
Leave It to Beaver 57, 89, 96, 114, 134
Lee, Guy 195
Lee, Johnny Scott 190, 210
Lee, Virginia Ann 195
Leeds, Phil 78, 193, 194, 197, 205
Leeson, Michael 4, 158–59, 198, 204, 206
Lemmon, Chris 4, 78–79
Lemmon, Jack 3, 7, 9, 10, 32, 33, 34, 40, 48, 49, 52, 55, 62, 78, 79–80, 86, 87, 88, 121, 128, 143, 229, 236, 237, 238, 240
Lemon, Meadowlark 39
Lennon, John 45
Lennon, Thomas 248
Lenox, John Thomas 210
Lerner, Michael 206
Lesser, Robert 216, 218
Lester, Buddy 193
Let's Make a Deal 42, 44, 59, 60, 61, 126, 140, 144, 173, 187, 200, *201*, 242, 244
Letz, George Montgomery 91
Levene, Sam 17
Levy, Eugene 113, 235
Lewin, Albert E. 159, 185, 187, 189, 192, 194, 197, 198
Lewis, Buddy 204, 208
Lewis, Jerry 106, 142, 162
Lewis, Shari 171
Liars' Club 81
Lidsville 55
"Life Is Just a Bowl of Cherries" 92
The Life of Riley 89, 159
Life with Elizabeth 127
Life with Luigi 110
Lindos, Kapi 207, 209
The Lion King 28, 77
Liss, Stephen 198
Little, Marti 186
Little House on the Prairie 25
Little Miss Marker 113
Little Vic 95

Live a Little, Love a Little 127
Lloyd, Michael 54
London, Damian 187
The London Festival Orchestra 14
The Loner 98
"The Longest Walk" 92
Looney Tunes 140, 146, 163
Lorne, Marion 38
Lost in America 29, 136
Lost in Space 26
Lost in Yonkers 180
Lotsa Luck 135, 167
Love, American Style 25, 29, 39, 51, 52, 61, 69, 78, 80, 94, 96, 108, 113, 120, 127, 136, 139, 144, 147, 152, 155, 159, 160, 163, 164, 170, 171, 177, 181
The Love Boat 59, 77, 89, 129, 135, 144, 153, 155, 165, 171, 181
The Love Boat: The Next Wave 77
Love of Life 62
Love on a Rooftop 146
Love, Sidney 75, 95, 99, 139
Lover Come Back 98
Loverde, Frank 80, 189, 193, 200, 211
Lowe, Heather 209
Lu, Lisa 189
Lucas, George 131
The Lucy Show 21, 77, 94, 95, 135, 143, 160
Ludden, Allen 13, 81, 127, 164, 198
Lukas, Karl 205
Lumet, Sidney 75
Lux Video Theater 27, 108
Lymon, Frankie 23
Lyn, Dawn 54
Lynde, Janice 81, 205, 206
Lynde, Paul 49, 95, 143, 179, 181, 195, 198
Lynn, Cynthia 188

MacLeod, Gavin 77
MacRae, Sheila 32
Mad About You 39, 45, 62, 119, 157, 247
Mad as Hell in America 74
Madison, Olive 17, 91, 92, 180
The Madness of King George 145
Mahakian, Carl 159
Mahoney, Jerry 129
Maier, Anne 202
Major Bowes' Original Amateur Hour 129
Make a Face 135, 153
Make Room for Daddy 89, 125, 148
Make the Connection 27
Makin' It 90, 174
Making the Grade 126
Malcolm and Eddie 144
Mama 123
Mama Rosa 110
Mame 127, 175
"A Man and a Woman" 186

A Man Called Shenandoah 98
The Man from UNCLE 53, 98, 160, 170
The Man Is Dead 174
The Man with One Red Shoe 154
The Man with Two Brains 66
The Manchurian Candidate 159
Mandel, Alan 159-60, 189, 190
Mandel, Babaloo 148, 149, 150, 160
Manhoff, Bill 190
Mannequin 159
Mannix 46, 53, 66, 81, 98, 124, 152, 170
Many Happy Returns 42
The Many Loves of Dobie Gillis 33, 65, 89
Manza, Ralph 199
March, Alex 160, 197, 198
Marcus Welby, M.D. 22, 43, 88, 105, 196
Maren, Johnny 211
Margolin, Arnold 156
Mark Rothman's Essays 174
Marks, Guy 81–82, 209
Marlowe, Nora 188
The Marriage of Figaro 121
Marshall, Garry 11, 12, 13, 14, 15, 31, 36, 44, 51, 59, 60, 66, 70, 71, 72, 73, 74, 75, 82, 83, 85, 90, 92, 93, 94, 103, 109, 111, 118, 120, 122, 126, 132, 133, 134, 135, 138, 139, 144, 145, 147, 150, 151, 153, 155, 156, 157, 158, 160, 161, 164, 165, 169, 172, 173, 174, 175, 177, 180, 185, 186, 187, 188, 189, 190, 191, 195, 197, 202, 203, 206, 207, 208, 209, 212, 213, 229, 230, 239, 240, 241
Marshall, George 162, 195, 198
Marshall, John 122
Marshall, Marjorie 161, 162, 198, 212
Marshall, Penny 4, 14, 16, 22, 31, 44, 71, *71*, 72, 76, 82–84, 103, 154, 165, 182, 194, 195, 196, 197, 198, 199, 200, 201, 202, 203, 204, 205, 206, 207, 210, 212, 221, 230
Marshall, Tony 82, 161, 162–63, 198, 241
Martin, Barney 84, 186, 209
Martin, Dean 25, 31, 61, 82, 142, 162, 171
Marty 166
The Marvel Action Hour 148
Marx, Groucho 155
Mary 24
The Mary Tyler Moore Show 14, 39, 55, 57, 66, 83, 98, 127, 136, 140, 141, 143, 145, 158, 164, 165, 166, 167, 170, 175, 181, 186, 199
Maschiarelli, Garry Kent 160, 162
M*A*S*H 14, 23, 34, 48, 105, 109, 148, 151, 152, 154, 155, 167, 168, 170, 181, 235, 238
Mason, Marlyn 4, 84–85, **85**, 176, 188, 199, 228
Mason, Marsha 180
Masquerade Party 27, 42, 212
Mastermind 160
The Match Game 28, 42, 47, 103, 117
Matchinga, Caryn 205

Matlock 164
Matthau, Charlie 4, 85–87
Matthau, Walter 3, 6, 7, 25, 27, 34, 38, 48, 49, 51, 58, 62, 65, 75, 80, 85, 87–88, 99, 107, 121, 143, 166, 229, 236, 237, 238, 239, 240
Matty's Funnies 55
Maude 54, 56, 57, 59, 78, 95, 106, 141, 159, 164, 165, 168
Maverick 26, 80, 97
Maxwell, Marilyn 142
May, Elaine 166
Maybe This Time 127
Mayberry RFD 56, 94, 136, 141
Mays, Joe 218
Mazeroski, Bill 10, 241
McCartney, Gloria 189
McCartt, John 193
McCloud 93, 113
McDonald, Ryan 13, 28, 88, 185, 186, 187, 188, 229
McDonough, Kit 212
McGyver 116
McHale's Navy 33, 46, 52, 64, 108
McKean, Michael 120
McKimson, Robert 163, 213
The McLean Stevenson Show 135
McLendon, Serrina 193
McMillan and Wife 109
McQueen, Steve 120
McRaven, Dale 154, 155, 156, 178, 187
McVeagh, Eva 186
MDs 248
Me TV 15
Meadows, Audrey 32, 84
Medical Center 53, 81, 124
Medlinsky, Harvey 101, 102
Meet Me at the Fair 39
Meet Mr. McNutly 159
The Mentalist 28
Merlin 77
Merman, Ethel 75
Merrill, Dina 88–89, 150, 210
Mhyers, John 205
Miami Vice 159
Michael Shayne 166
Michaels, Richard 163, 188
Michaels, Shawn 196
Michenaud, Gerald 195
Midnight Caller 94
Midnight Express 73
A Midsummer Night's Dream 125
Miller, Arthur 166
Miller, Harvey 71, 163–64, 169, 176, 177, 188, 190, 191, 192, 193, 195, 196, 197, 201, 204, 206, 207, 209, 210, 241
Miller, Lynne 201
Miller, Mary Cory 217
Millhollin, James 89, 187, 196, 206

The Miracle Worker 36
Misery 103
Mishkin, Phil 164, 171, 203, 205
Miss Rona 25
Missing Links 35
Missing Persons 80
Mission: Impossible 26, 37, 52, 152
Mister Ed 33, 90, 97, 98
Mister Magoo 94
Mr. Mom 52
Mr. Peabody and Sherman 248
Mister Peepers 38, 44, 73, 86, 87, 98, 100, 111, 148, 151, 197
Mr. Rhodes 56
Mr. Saturday Night 54, 150
Mr. Sunshine 248
Mr. T. and Tina 90, 93
Mitchell, Gordon "Whitey" 164–65, 181, 186
Mitchell, Red 165
Mitchell (MitchIII), Scoey 11
Mitchell, Shirley 89–90, 205
Mittleman, Rick 165, 193, 195, 207, 208, 209
Miyagi, Mr. 94
The Mod Squad 22, 23, 98
Molinaro, Al 13, 29, 47, 59, 60, 90–91, 101, 109, 134, 156, 169, 185, 186, 187, 188, 189, 190, 191, 192, 194, 195, 197, 198, 199, 200, 201, 202, 203, 204, 205, 206, 207, 208, 209, 210, 211, 212, 221
Monday Night Football 23, 38, 149, 168, 169, 196, 211, 241
The Monkees 78, 181
Monroe, Marilyn 27
Montgomery, Elizabeth 163
Montgomery, George 91, 208
Moonjean, Hank 9
Moonstruck 57
Moore, Carroll 135
The Morey Amsterdam Show 32
Morgan, Henry 98
Morgan, Jaye P. 4, 13, 92–93, **92**, 131, 134, 157, 203, 204
Morgan, Mary Margaret 92
Morita, Pat 64, 90, 93–94, 195, 235
Mork and Mindy 73, 150, 151, 153, 159, 161, 162, 163, 165, 181
Morningstar Eveningstar 39
Mortal Storm 141
Morton, Howard 189
Morton and Hayes 164
The Most Happy Fella 121
Mostel, Zero 111, 112, 160
Mother 29, 136
The Mothers-in-Law 103, 145, 164
The Movie of the Week 124
Mozart, Wolfgang Amadeus 40, 86, 121
Mrs. Doubtfire 94
The Munsters 29, 64, 96, 110, 114, 247

The Munsters Today 110
Muppet Babies 140
The Muppet Movie 129
Murder, She Wrote 47, 165
Murphy Brown 95, 100, 161
Murrow, Edward R. 116
The Muse 29, 136
My Big Fat Greek Life 36
My Big Fat Greek Wedding 36, 176, 183
My Favorite Martian 61, 89, 95, 159, 167, 231
My Favorite Year 26, 58
"My Funny Valentine" 141
"My Girl" 6
My Happy Days in Hollywood 161
My Mother the Car 165, 193
My Mother Was Nuts: A Memoir 84
My Three Sons 5, 39, 54, 85, 89, 98, 114
My World and Welcome to It 55, 67, 112, 143
Myerson, Jessica 94, 189, 191, 201

NAB Broadcasting Hall of Fame 131
The Naked and the Dead 166
Naked City 37, 57, 160
Name That Tune 84
The Nanny 57
Nanny and the Professor 29, 54, 88, 159
National Actors Theatre 17, 99, 122, 212
National Lampoon's Vacation 27
National Radio Hall of Fame 131
NBC Television Opera Theater 114
Near, Timothy 187
Needles and Pins 76
Nelson, Craig T. 63
Nelson, Frank 4, 15, 94, 130, 142, 213, 237
The New Andy Griffith Show 151
The New Dick Van Dyke Show 42, 123, 154, 166
A New Kind of Family 67
The New Odd Couple 1, 4, 10, 15, 16, 27, 28, 48, 56, 66, 67, 69, 70, 79, 95, 96, 105, 106, 108, 109, 110, 120, 129, 135, 136, 149, 151, 153, 161, 172, 174, 182, *183*, 191, 194, 199, 200, 203, 215–19, *215*, *218*, 228, 229, 241
The New Phil Silvers Show 48
The New Temperature's Rising 56
New York City Ballet Company 125, 202
The New York Daily News 139, 236
The New York Herald 97, 210, 221, 226
Newhart 14, 39, 88, 98, 107
Newman, Paul 62, 200, 216
Nice Dreams 51
Nichols, Mike 7, 45, 65, 87, 101, 121, 165–66, 239
Night at the Museum: Battle of the Smithsonian 248
Night Court 24, 59, 62, 78, 118, 168, 170
Nightline 23

90 Bristol Court 75
No Time for Sergeants 34, 48, 89
The Noose Hangs High 125
Norma Rae 65
North and South 115
Norton, Cliff 94–95, 202, 208
Norton, Ed 7, 32
Nothing in Common 161
Nudell, Sam 95, 193, 205, 206
Nutcracker 125
NYPD 160

Oatman, Doney 49, 95, 195, 198, 209, 212
Obama, Barack 74
The Object Is 35
O'Brien, Barry 219
Occasional Wife 63
O'Connell, William 209
Odd Couple: Together Again 4, 16, 25, 76, 83, 84, 99, 107, 123, 126, 151, 154, 156, 164, 226, 229, 237, 245, 247
Odd Couple II 4, 17, 24, 25, 39, 40, 55, 56, 61, 62, 63, 68, 79, 80, 86, 87, 88, 110, 114, 115, 118, 120, 143, 151, 226, 238
The Oddball Couple 4, 10, 15, 55, 94, 129, 130, 140, 142, 146, 151, 163, 213–14, 237, 244
Oh, God 139
O'Hanlon, George 192
Olam, Beth 69
Old Dogs 54
"An Old-Fashioned Love Song" 128, 209
Olivier, Sir Laurence 47
Omnibus 174
On the Town 46
On the Waterfront 65
Once and Again 45
Once More, with Feeling 87
One Day at a Time 57, 136, 167
One Flew over the Cuckoo's Nest 39, 100
One Life to Live 81, 104, 110
One Man's Family 98, 152
One of the Boys 77
O'Neal, Ryan 160
O'Neill, Eugene 8, 65, 87
Operation: Petticoat 24
Oregon Trail 76
O'Reilly, Erin 205
Orenstein, Bernie 104
Orlando, Tony 67
Osmond, Cliff 188
The Other Sister 73, 161
Our Gang Comedies 27
The Out-of-Towners 80, 180
Out to Sea 88
The Outer Limits 26, 37
Overboard 134, 139
Owens, Gary 167

Paar, Jack 34, 127
Pace, Judy 216
Pajama Party 52
The Palm Springs Walk of Stars 25, 165
Palm Tree in a Rose Garden 62
Pandemonium 106
The Paper Chase 160
Paper Lion 160
The Parent Trap 179
Parenthood 68, 150
Paris, Jerry 1, 44, 83, 138, 144, 150, 155, 166, 177, 185, 187, 189, 190, 191, 193, 196, 197, 199, 200, 201, 202, 204, 207, 211
Parker, Jim 156
Parks, Michael 83
The Partners 123
The Partridge Family 35, 46, 59, 135, 136, 146, 153, 154, 158, 160, 165, 167, 170, 181
Password 42, 61, 81, 82, 127, 140, 144, 160, 194, 198, 227
The Patty Duke Show 34, 78, 84, 136, 167
The Paul Lynde Show 49, 95, 143, 181, 195, 198
Paul Sand in Friends and Lovers 72, 83, 103, 207
Paulsen, Albert 212
Payne, Carolyn 191
Payton, Jo Marie 95, 217
Peaker, E.J. 96, 189
Peanuts 49, 111, 147
Peck, Ed 96, 197, 205, 211
Pedi, Tom 212
Pee Wee's Playhouse 40, 139
Pelish, Thelma 192
Peppard, George 61
Perfect Strangers 160, 182, 231
Perkins, Anthony 27
Perkins, Jack 193
Perry Mason 26, 36, 66, 96, 125, 170
Peschkowsky, Michael Igor 165
Pete and Gladys 33, 95
Pete 'n' Tillie 51
Peter Gunn 26
Peters, Jocelyn 205
Peterson, Maggie 205, 210
Peterson, Norm 126
Petticoat Junction 5, 49, 89
Peyton Place 37, 163
Phantom of the Paradise 129
The Phil Silvers Show 26, 46, 48, 63, 68, 84, 108, 171, 173, 179
Philco Playhouse 73, 117
Phyllis 55, 57, 120, 158
The Phyllis Diller Show 24, 77, 120
Picture This 135, 153
Piglet 50, 130
Pillow Talk 98
The Pink Panther 142, 146, 163

Pink Phink 146
Pinky and the Brain 24
Pinza, Ezio 73, 117
Pitlik, Noam 208
The Planet of the Apes 62
Platt, Ed 96–97, 190
Playboy 13, 61, 64, 101, 168, 169, 207, 222, 223, 225, 230, 245
Playboy After Dark 168
Playhouse 90 117
Plaza Suite 6, 87, 166, 237
Please Don't Eat the Daisies 176
Plowright, Joan 47
Polic, Henry, II 217
Police Academy 26, 58, 107, 116, 167
Police Academy 5: Assignment Miami Beach 58
Police Academy 6: City under Siege 26
Police Woman 106, 113
Porky Pig 146
Portlandia 127
Post, Marjorie 88
Powers, Ben 216
The Practice 45
Pratt, Deborah 217
Presley, Elvis 46, 50, 85, 87, 98, 127, 152
Preston, J.A. 217
Pretty in Pink 142
Pretty Woman 161
Prince, Michael 216
The Princess Bride 103
The Prisoner on Second Avenue 6, 96, 118, 166, 174
Private Benjamin 164, 179
The Producers 22, 28, 77, 84, 111, 113
Protocol 58, 164
Pryor's Place 156
Pryor, Ensign 80
The Public Life of Cliff Norton 95
Pulver, Ensign 80

Qualen, John 97, 189, 191, 199
The Queen and I 93
Quincy, M.E. 51, 53, 75, 81, 89, 113, 122, 126, 147, 160, 203, 209
Quinn, Bill 97–98, 186, 188, 199
Quiz Show 112

Radio's Golden Age 140
Rafkin, Alan 167, 177, 189, 190
Ragaway, Martin A. 211
"The Rainbow Connection" 129
"Rainy Days and Mondays" 128
Raising Helen 85
Rappaport, John 4, 167–70, **168**, 207, 211
Rapport, Michael 216
Ray, Marguerite 208
The Real McCoys 85, 89, 148, 151
Reasoner, Harry 116

The Red Skelton Show 37, 143, 165
Redfield, William 100, 206
Reddy, Helen 128
Reds 139
Reed, Tracy 11, 197, 219
Reeves, Keanu 124
Regalbuto, Joe 78, 100, 235
Regan, Patty 202
Reicheg, Richard 100–102
Reid, Elliott 196
Reilly, Charles Nelson 65, 102–103, 117, 235
Reiner, Carl 103, 166, 173
Reiner, Estelle 103
Reiner, Rob 82, 83, 103–104, 161, 164, 165, 207, 230
The Reivers 120
The Reluctant Astronaut 148, 151
Reno 911 248
Report Cards 174
Resnick, Sidney 212, 213
Rewrites 180
Reynolds, Debbie 120, 223
Reynolds, Frank 116
Rhine, Larry 212, 213
Rhoades, Barbara 104, 199, 209
Rhyme and Reason 93
Rhythm and Blues 56
Rich, Buddy 165
Rich Man, Poor Man 88
Riggs, Bobby 13, 45, 74, 104, 143, 164, 171, 204, 225, 244, 245
Robert Montgomery Presents 117
The Robert Q. Lewis Show 153
Roberts, Pernell 37, 105, 175, 208, 209, 245
Robin Hood: Men in Tights 123
Robinson, Bartlett 212
The Rockford Files 23, 92, 95, 124
Rocky 108
Rocky and His Friends 181
Rodgers, Bob 170, 186, 194
Rodgers and Hammerstein 117, 141, 186
Rogers, Eric 15, 213
Rogers, Ginger 91, 175
Rolle, Esther 105–106, 216
Rondeau, Charles R. 170, 186, 188
The Rookies 70, 106
Room for One More 142
Rooney, Mickey 9, 11, 99
Roosevelt, Franklin D. 102
Rose, Mickey 170, 191, 204, 205, 206, 207
Roseanne 78
Rosenberg, Leonard 98
Ross, Jerry 216
Ross, Leonard 186
Ross, Marion 151
Rothman, Abe 171
Rothman, Mark 1, 4, 27, 57, 63, 90, 92, 103, 104, 108, 120, 129, 139, 141, 148, 169, 171–74, *172*, 196, 199, 200, 202, 203, 205, 206, 209, 210, 211, 216, 217, 218
Rounding Third 176
Roustabout 46
Rowan and Martin's Laugh-In 42, 47, 115, 168
Rowe, Vern 106, 206, 208
The Royal Danish Ballet 125
Rubin, Andy 106, 198, 199
Rubinowitz, Barry 149
Rugged Path 108
Rumors 125
"Runaround Sue" 54
The Runaway Bride 161
Rupp, Debra Jo 107
Russell, Leon 187
Russell, Mark 192
Russell, Nipsey 11
The Russians Are Coming, the Russians Are Coming 95
Rydell, Tracy 198

Sabella, Ernie 218
St. Elsewhere 47
Saint-Subber, Arnold 6
Saks, Gene 9, 174–75, 236, 237, 240
Sally Hemings: An American Scandal 22
Same Time Next Year 176
Sampras, Pete 182
Samson, Ken 191
Sandrich, Jay 4, 72, 175–76, 192, 202, 207, 208, 210
Sands, Billy 108, 193, 196, 206, 209, 219
The Sands of Iwo Jima 181
Sanford and Son 15, 22, 56, 93, 109, 129, 148, 151, 164, 165, 181, 182
Santoni, Reni 188
Sajak, Pat 107–108, 235
The Saturday Night Beechnut Show 35
Saturday Night Live 72, 113, 128
Save the Tiger 80
Scattergories 35
Scharlach, Ed 4, 144, 145, 176–77, *176*, 185, 189, 190, 194, 199
Schiller, Norbert 192
Schmidt, Georgia 211, 212
Schoenfeld, Gerald 6
Schuck, John 4, 15, 47, 108–110, *108*, *215*, 216, 217, 218, 219
Schull, Rebecca 110
Schwimmer, David 248
Scott, Tom 200
Scotti, Vito 110, 193
Scotto, Renatta 52
Sea Hunt 163
Sean Saves the World 248
Search 52, 80
Search for Tomorrow 63
Second Chance 248

Second City 45, 113, 126, 166
The Second Hundred Years 143, 146
The Secret Storm 66
See the Jaguar 181
Seems Like Old Times 175
Seinfeld 22, 40, 41, 63, 84, 114, 119
Seinfeld, Jerry 84
Send Me No Flowers 98, 135
Serling, Rod 49
Serpico 120
17 Again 248
77 Sunset Strip 105, 142
The Shaggy D. A. 106
The Shakiest Gun in the West 104, 151
Shalhoub, Tony 248
Shandling, Garry 136, 154, 167
Shane 33, 37, 112
Shaw, Reta 111, 204, 229
Shea, Christopher 111–12, 189, 190
Sheiner, David 10
Sheldon, Les 63
Sheldon, Sidney 155
Shelley, Carole 7, 13, 15, 47, 50, 112, 185, 186, 187
Shelley, Joshua 112, 199, 211
Shelly, Norman 199
She's the Sheriff 171, 174
The Shining 39
Shore, Dinah 91, 153
Shorr, Sidney 99
Short, Martin 22, 113, 235
A Shot in the Dark 174
The Shubert Brothers 6
Shyer, Charles 4, 159, 160, 177–79, 189, 190, 211
The Sign in Sidney Brustein's Window 56
Silk Stalkings 32
Silver, Johnny 113, 114, 174, 187, 190, 195, 211
Silver, Stu 218
Silver Spoons 57, 141, 144
Silver Streak 39
Silver, the Wonder Dog 25, 208, 242, 243, 245
Silverman, Jonathan 17, 113, 114
Silverman, Treva 145
Simmons, Jean 114–15, 196
Simon, Arlene 5
Simon, Danny 5, 6, 75, 102
Simon, Neil 3, 5, 6, 7, 8, 9, 11, 13, 17, 19, 22, 25, 26, 27, 28, 29, 41, 47, 48, 49, 56, 58, 61, 76, 77, 83, 86, 87, 92, 93, 96, 99, 100, 101, 102, 110, 112, 113, 118, 121, 122, 124, 127, 145, 151, 155, 161, 166, 167, 169, 171, 174, 179–80, 185, 210, 211, 221, 236, 237, 238, 239, 240
The Simpsons Movie 29
Sinatra, Frank 10, 37, 143, 151, 153, 158
Sinclair, Arlene 204

Singapore 37
Siracusa, Joe 15, 213
Sirota's Court 36, 51, 154, 164, 176, 177
Six Feet Under 81
The Six Million Dollar Man 91, 105
Skelton, Judy 51, 198, 243
Skelton, Red 37, 143, 165
Skolnick, Harvey 163, 164, 177, 190, 192, 195
Skyward 151
Slattery, John 125
Slattery, Richard X. 47, 115, 185
Sledge Hammer 139
Sleeper 66
A Small Part of History 145
Smart, Jean 115
Smiff, Knucklehead 129
Smith, Bubba 13, 115–16, 201
Smith, Hal 116, 193, 198
Smith, Howard K. 13, 116, 209
Smith, Queenie 199
Smith, Snuffy 134
Smokey and the Bandit 129, 135, 179
Soap 31, 104, 118, 175
"Some Kind of Wonderful" 143
Some Like It Hot 80
Somers, Brett 14, 28, 74, 75, 76, 93, 103, 117, 122, 124, 147, 165, 193, 195, 197, 203, 229
Sometimes a Great Notion 199
The Songwriter's Hall of Fame 129
Soo, Jack 117, 195
The Sopranos 125
South Pacific 121, 174
Southstreet, Benny 113
Soylent Green 46
Space 130
Spaceballs 114
Spartacus 114
Spelling, Aaron 153
Spenser for Hire 107
Spider Woman 122
Spiderman 140
Spiffy 15, 55, 73, 94, 130, 140, 142, 146, 213, 214, 237, 244
Splash 68, 150
Splendor in the Grass 62
Spy Kids 35
Stahl, Richard 118, 125, 186, 189, 192, 193, 197, 203, 205, 208, 210, 228
Stalag 17 33
Stamos, John 76
Stand by Me 103
"Stand by Me" 165
Stanley 5, 73, 179
Stanley, Florence 118
Stanley, Kim 37
A Star Is Born 120, 129
A Star Is Bought 29
Star-Spangled Girl 6, 7, 27

Star Trek 14, 21, 22, 45, 50, 68, 96, 110, 126, 127
Star Trek: Deep Space Nine 45, 68
Star Trek V: The Final Frontier 98
Star Walk: A Guide to Palm Springs' Walk of Stars 165
Starman 95
Starsky and Hutch 23, 39, 106
Steinberg, David 13, 119, 192
Stellar, Carolyn 190
Stepping Out 112
Stern, Leonard 73, 109, 124
Steve Canyon 166
Stevens, Connie 62
Stevens, Inger 143
Stewart, Tom 193
Still the Beaver 134
The Sting 25
Stivic, Gloria 119
Stivic, Mike 103, 104
Stone, Cynthia 78, 80
Stone, Ezra 138
Stop the Music 92
Storch, Larry 93
The Story of Vic and Sade 152
Strasberg, Lee 62, 67, 166
The Streets of San Francisco 80, 97, 113
Strike Force 47
Studio One 73, 91
Studio 60 on the Sunset Strip 247
Stumpers 81
Suddenly Susan 26, 167
Sugarfoot 105
Sullivan, Dan 13, 210, 237
The Sun Also Rises 117
The Sunset Six 156
Sunshine, Madelyn 109, 218, 219
Sunshine, Steven 218, 219
The Sunshine Boys 17, 27, 58, 87, 180
The Super 164
The Super Six 142, 163
Suppose They Gave a War and Nobody Came 95
"Surfin' USA" 54
Surfside 6 96, 142
Sutton, Grady 119–20, 205
Swan Lake 126, 202, 243
Sweet Bird of Youth 62
Sweet Charity 7, 127, 180
Swenson, Karl 199
Swiss Family Robinson 21
Swofford, Ken 187
Sydney 248
Sylvester 146
Szysznyk 25

Tabitha 144, 170
Take the Money and Run 170

Talbot, Ogden 120, 188, 191, 195, 199, 202
Tannenbaum, Eric 248
Tannenbaum, Kim 248
Tarzan 162
"A Taste of Honey" 190
Taxi 30, 57, 69, 116, 158, 159
Taylor, Dub 188
Taylor, Kurt 217
Taylor, Wally 205, 216
Tchin Tchin 75
Teahouse of the August Moon 66
The Ted Knight Show 108, 141, 144, 174
Teen Angel 56
Tell Them Willie Boy Is Here 127, 181
Temple, Shirley 143
The Temptations 6
The $10,000 Pyramid 35
The Tender Trap 139
Texaco Star Theater 33
Thank God It's Friday 154
That Funny Feeling 135
That Girl 34, 60, 76, 83, 89, 95, 96, 112, 120, 141, 143, 144, 145, 152, 155, 164, 165, 176, 181
That 70s Show 107
That Wonderful Guy 80
"That's All I Want from You" 92
That's My Mama 147
Then Came Bronson 11, 83
They Shoot Horses, Don't They? 188
They're Playing Our Song 180
This Is Spinal Tap 58, 103
This Is Tom Jones 35
This Is Your Life 116, 198
Thompson, Elizabeth 211
Thompson, Hilarie 191
Thompson, Lea 143
Thompson, Marshall 29
Thompson, Victoria 187
The Thorn Birds 115
Thorson, Russell 190, 199
Those Whiting Girls 166
Three Dog Night 128
Three for the Road 54
The Three Musketeers 97
Thurber, James 67
The Thurber Carnival 61
Tigger 50, 130
'Til Death 53
Timberman, Sarah 248
"Tiny Bubbles" 185
To Kill a Mockingbird 56
Tobin, Dan 191
Tom, Dick and Mary 75
The Tom Ewell Show 56
The Tonight Show Starring Johnny Carson 24, 35
Tony and Me: A Story of Friendship 76, 99

266 • INDEX

The Tony Randall Show 25, 59, 75, 84, 95, 99, 101, 186, 208
Too Close for Comfort 171
Too Many Girls 27
Tootsie 52
Torme, Mel 151
Torres, Liz 109, 120–21, **215**, 217
Towers, Edmund 200
Toys in the Attic 88
Tozzi, Georgio 52, 121, 171, 209
Tracey Takes On 154
Tracy, John 217
Tracy, Marlene 186
Tracy, Spencer 88, 108
Transformers 140, 148
Trapper John, M. D. 105
The Trouble with Girls 85
Turnabout 109, 118
Turner, Kathalynn 198, 211
Turner, Lloyd 165, 181, 186, 189
Turturro, John 125
The Tuxedo 159
TV Guide's 100 Greatest Episodes of All Time 81
Tweety 146
12 Angry Men 50, 75, 152, 186
12 O'Clock High 88, 159
Twenty Good Years 232
20/20 23
The Twilight Zone 21, 26, 32, 36, 37, 49, 50, 75, 126, 128
The Twilight Zone—The Movie 98
227 56, 136, 171
Tyne, George 181, 187, 194, 195
Tyrell, David 87

The Ugly Family 29, 91
Ugly Betty 121, 233
Uncle Kracker 129
Under the Influence 124
Underdog 39
Unfaithfully Yours 154
Unhappily Ever After 125
The United States of Tara 84
The Untouchables 36, 80, 96, 160, 166
Upton, Albert William 21
Urich, Robert 28

Valentine's Day 117, 162
Van, Bobby 180
Van Ark, Joan 4, 27, 121–23, **121**, 195
Vandis, Titos 201
Van Dyke, Dick 1, 13, 21, 26, 29, 39, 42, 49, 66, 78, 82, 89, 95, 96, 103, 105, 114, 120, 123, 125, 135, 141, 148, 150, 152, 153, 154, 155, 160, 165, 166, 167, 181
Van Dyke, Jerry 135
Van Dyke and Company 165
Van Meter, Sherry Alberoni 143

Van Patten, Dick 4, 16, 123–24
Van Patten, Jimmy 195
Van Patten, Joyce 4, 124–25, 138, 186
Van Pelt, Linus 111, 189
Van Pelt, Lucy 49
Van Zandt, Billy 217
Vegas 28
Verdi 121, 243
Veronica's Closet 167
The View 132
Vigran, Herb 125, 189
Villella, Edward 13, 45, 125–26, 141, 147, 175, 202, 224
Virgo, Peter, Sr. 186
Viva Las Vegas 52
Von Linden, Liv 190

The Wackiest Ship in the Army 73, 80, 162
Walberg, Garry 4, 16, 76, 101, 126, 154, 160, 185, 186, 187, 188, 190, 192, 194, 200, 202, 210
Waldo, Janet 117
Walker, Nancy 93
Walking Tall 115
The Waltons 38, 95
The War of the Roses 89, 159
Ward, Jay 181
Warden, Jack 38
Watanabe, Hiroko 195
The Wearing of the Greens 63, 174
Weaver, Charley 57
Weaver, Dennis 68
Webster 72, 108, 153
Weekend at Bernies 114, 154
Weekend at Bernies II 154
Weller, Carolyn 202
Welles, Orson 47
Wendt, George 126–27, 235
Wendy and Me 62
Weskitt, Harvey 87
West Side Story 24, 91, 92
"We've Only Just Begun" 128
What Do You Say to a Naked Lady? 177, 190
What Planet Are You From? 159
Whatever Happened to Baby Jane? 30
What's Going On? 95
What's Up, Tiger Lily? 140, 170
Wheeler, John 127, 192, 200, 206, 212, 229
When Harry Met Sally 103
When Things Were Rotten 56, 76, 123
"Where or When" 141
Where the Action Is 35
Where the Heart Is 62
Whipple, Randy 192, 193
The Whirlybirds 105
White, Betty 13, 42, 81, 100, 102, 127–28, **127**, 164, 198
White, David 128, 204

The White Gorilla 80
Who Wants Fame? 174
The Whole Ten Yards 143
Who's the Boss? 141, 160
Why Do Fools Fall in Love? 23
Wicked 112
Wild in the Country 152
The Wild Wild West 39, 98
Williams, Anson 91, 151
Williams, Mentor 129
Williams, Paul 13, 53, 95, 128, 164, 209, 242
Wills, Maury 10
Wilson, Demond 4, 15, 28, 56, 70, 109, 129, 182, *183*, *215*
Wilson, Flip 35, 134
Wilson, Joyce Vincent 66
Wilson, Mark 212
Win with the Stars 81
Winchell, Paul 4, 50, 94, 129, 142, 237
Winchell-Mahoney Time 129
Windom, William 55, 67, 143
Wings 110
Winkler, Harry 188
Winnie-the-Pooh 50, 116, 130
Winter, Jack 181–82, 190, 196, 201, 202, 211, 240
Winters, Jonathan 134
WKRP in Cincinnati 118
Wolfe, Ian 217
Wolfman Jack 13, 45, 93, *130*, 131, 203, 204
Wonder Woman 36, 69, 147, 247
"The Wonderful Thing About Tiggers" 130
Woodson, William 3, 12, 131–32, *131*, 189, 202

WPIX-TV 14
Wyler, Gretchen 217
Wyner, George 190

Yashimas, Momo 204
Yates, Jack 218
Yemana, Sergeant Nick 117, 195
Yepremian, Garo 207
Yes, Dear 144
"Yesterday, When I Was Young" 35–36
York, Francine 188
Yosemite Sam 146
You Again? 53, 74, 76, 82, 104, 167
"You and Me Against the World" 128, 209
"You Belong to Me" 194
Young, Robert 43, 196
Young, Sean 120
The Young and the Restless 81, 88
Young Doctors in Love 73, 120
Young Frankenstein 40, 46, 52
Youngman, Henny 25, 202
Your Show of Shows 5, 179
Your Three Minutes Are Up 95

Zacharias, Steve 198
Zacherle, John 82
Zane Grey Theater 105
Ziegfeld Follies 100, 143
Zimmerman, Crazy Rhoda 208, 222, 242
Zorich, Louis 45
Zorro 148
Zwick, Joel 4, 79, 109, 182–83, *183*, 216, 217, 218, 219

www.ingramcontent.com/pod-product-compliance
Lightning Source LLC
Chambersburg PA
CBHW051213300426
44116CB00006B/561